D1551054

SAMS Teach Yourself

PHP

in 24 Hours

THIRD EDITION

Matt Zandstra

SAMS   800 East 96th Sreet, Indianapolis, Indiana 46240

Sams Teach Yourself PHP in 24 Hours, Third Edition

Copyright © 2004 by Sams Publishing

All rights reserved. No part of this book shall be reproduced, stored in a retrieval system, or transmitted by any means, electronic, mechanical, photocopying, recording, or otherwise, without written permission from the publisher. No patent liability is assumed with respect to the use of the information contained herein. Although every precaution has been taken in the preparation of this book, the publisher and author assume no responsibility for errors or omissions. Nor is any liability assumed for damages resulting from the use of the information contained herein.

International Standard Book Number: 0-672-32619-1

Library of Congress Catalog Card Number: 2003109402

Printed in the United States of America

First Printing: December 2003

09 08 07   5 6 7 8 9

Trademarks

All terms mentioned in this book that are known to be trademarks or service marks have been appropriately capitalized. Sams Publishing cannot attest to the accuracy of this information. Use of a term in this book should not be regarded as affecting the validity of any trademark or service mark.

Warning and Disclaimer

Every effort has been made to make this book as complete and as accurate as possible, but no warranty or fitness is implied. The information provided is on an "as is" basis. The author and the publisher shall have neither liability nor responsibility to any person or entity with respect to any loss or damages arising from the information contained in this book or from the use of the programs accompanying it.

Bulk Sales

Sams Publishing offers excellent discounts on this book when ordered in quantity for bulk purchases or special sales. For more information, please contact:

U.S. Corporate and Government Sales
1-800-382-3419
corpsales@pearsontechgroup.com

For sales outside of the U.S., please contact:

International Sales
+1-317-581-3793
international@pearsontechgroup.com

Acquisitions Editor
Shelley Johnston

Development Editor
Scott D. Meyers

Managing Editor
Charlotte Clapp

Project Editor
George Nedeff

Production Editor
Megan Wade

Indexer
Heather McNeill

Proofreader
Juli Cook

Technical Editors
Steph Fox
Brian France
Sara Goleman
Chris Newman

Team Coordinator
Vanessa Evans

Designer
Gary Adair

Page Layout
Stacey Richwine-DeRome

Contents at a Glance

Part IV: Extending PHP

Table of Contents

Part IV: Extending PHP

About the Author

Matt Zandstra is a writer and consultant specializing in server programming. With his business partner, Max Guglielmino, he runs Corrosive (http://www.corrosive.co.uk), a technical agency that plans, designs, and builds Internet applications. Matt is interested in all aspects of object-oriented programming and is currently exploring enterprise design patterns for PHP 5. When he is not reading, writing, or thinking about coding in PHP and Java, Matt shoots alien invaders in the park with his four-year-old daughter Holly. He lives by the sea in Brighton, Great Britain, with his partner Louise McDougall and their children Holly and Jake.

Acknowledgments

As always, my greatest thanks go to Louise for knowing when to make me stop working. Our daughter Holly was born during the writing of the first edition of this book, and our son Jake was born this time round. The three of you make up my world.

Thanks to all at Sams who worked so hard to knock my code, prose, and time management into shape. Particular thanks to Shelley Johnston, George Nedeff, and Steph Fox. Thanks and apologies must also go to Megan Wade, who imposed order and coherence upon my writing. It could not have been fun.

Writing often takes me away from other duties. I am fortunate in having such supportive friends and colleagues at Corrosive. Max Guglielmino and Tolan Blundell weathered my prolonged absence from the front line and filled the breach magnificently.

Dedication

For my father. Who would have approved.

Tell Us What You Think!

As the reader of this book, *you* are our most important critic and commentator. We value your opinion and want to know what we're doing right, what we could do better, what areas you'd like to see us publish in, and any other words of wisdom you're willing to pass our way.

You can email or write me directly to let me know what you did or didn't like about this book—as well as what we can do to make our books stronger.

Please note that I cannot help you with technical problems related to the topic of this book, and that due to the high volume of mail I receive, I might not be able to reply to every message.

When you write, please be sure to include this book's title and author as well as your name and phone or fax number. I will carefully review your comments and share them with the author and editors who worked on the book.

Email: webdev@samspublishing.com

Mail: Mark Taber
Associate Publisher
Sams Publishing
800 East 96th Street
Indianapolis, IN 46240 USA

Introduction

This is a book about PHP, arguably the most popular Web scripting language in the world. It is also a book about programming. In the space available, it is neither possible to create a complete guide to programming in PHP nor to cover every function and technique PHP offers. Nevertheless, whether you are an experienced programmer considering a move to PHP or a newcomer to scripting, the steps in this book should provide enough information to get your journey off to a good start.

Who Should Read This Book?

This book will take you from the first principles through to a good working knowledge of the PHP programming language. No prior experience of programming is assumed, although if you have worked with a language such as C or Perl in the past, you will find the going much easier.

PHP is a Web programming language. To get the most from this book, you should have some understanding of the World Wide Web and of HTML in particular. If you are just starting out, you will still be able to use this book, although you should consider acquiring an HTML tutorial. If you are comfortable creating basic documents and can build a basic HTML table, you will be fine.

PHP is designed to integrate well with databases. Some of the examples in this book are written to work with SQL databases. We include a short introduction to SQL, but if you intend to use PHP to work with databases, you might want to spend some time reading up on the subject. Numerous introductory SQL tutorials are available online. If you intend to work with a database other than MySQL, many of the examples in this book will be relatively easy to reproduce with the equivalent PHP functions designed to query your database.

How This Book Is Organized

This book is divided into four parts:

- ▶ Part I, "Getting Started," is an introduction to PHP.
- ▶ Part II, "The Language," covers the basic features of the language. Pay particular attention to this section if you are new to programming.

▶ Part III, "Working with PHP," covers PHP in more detail, looking at the functions and techniques you will need to become a proficient PHP programmer.

▶ Part IV, "Extending PHP," examines library code, both code that you can create yourself and PEAR, a repository of library code you can include in your own projects.

Part I contains Hours 1–3 and handles the information you will need to get your first script up and running:

▶ Hour 1, "PHP: From Home Page to Web Enterprise," describes the history and capabilities of PHP and looks at some of the compelling reasons for deciding to learn this scripting language.

▶ Hour 2, "Installing PHP," explains how to install PHP on a Unix system and discusses some of the configuration options you might want to choose when compiling PHP. In this hour, we also examine ways of configuring PHP after it is installed.

▶ Hour 3, "A First Script," covers the different ways in which you can embed a PHP script in a document and create a script that writes text to the user's browser.

Part II comprises Hours 4–9. In this part, you will learn the basic components of the PHP language:

▶ Hour 4, "The Building Blocks," covers the basics of PHP. You will learn about variables, data types, operators, and expressions.

▶ Hour 5, "Going with the Flow," covers the syntax for controlling program flow in your scripts. In addition to if and switch constructs, you will learn about loops using for and while statements.

▶ Hour 6, "Functions," explores the use of functions to organize your code.

▶ Hour 7, "Arrays," discusses the array data type that can be used to hold list information. We will also look at some of the functions PHP provides to manipulate arrays.

▶ Hour 8, "Working with Strings," covers the functions you can use to manipulate strings.

▶ Hour 9, "Objects," introduces PHP's support for classes and objects. Throughout the course of the hour, we will develop a working example.

Part III consists of Hours 10–22. In this part, you will come to grips with the features and techniques of the language:

▶ Hour 10, "Working with Forms," introduces the dimension of user input through the mechanism of the HTML form. You will learn how to gather data submitted via a form.

▶ Hour 11, "Working with Files," shows you how to work with files and directories on the local machine.

▶ Hour 12, "Working with the DBA Functions," demonstrates PHP's support for DBM-style database systems, versions of which are available on most systems.

▶ Hour 13, "Database Integration—SQL," provides a brief introduction to SQL syntax and introduces functions and classes for working with the MySQL database, the SQLite library, and the PEAR::DB package.

▶ Hour 14, "Beyond the Box," covers some of the details of HTTP requests and looks at PHP network functions.

▶ Hour 15, "Images On-the-Fly," explores PHP's image functions. With these, you can create PNG files dynamically.

▶ Hour 16, "Working with Dates and Times," covers the functions and techniques you can use for date arithmetic. We create a calendar example.

▶ Hour 17, "Advanced Objects," examines PHP's new extended support for objects and object-oriented techniques.

▶ Hour 18, "Working with Regular Expressions," introduces regular expression functions. You can use these to find and replace complex patterns in strings.

▶ Hour 19, "Saving State with Cookies and Query Strings," shows you some techniques for passing information across scripts and requests.

▶ Hour 20, "Saving State with Session Functions," extends the techniques explored in Hour 19, using PHP's built-in session functions.

▶ Hour 21, "Working with the Server Environment," shows you how to call external programs from your scripts and incorporate their output into your own.

▶ Hour 22, "XML," looks at PHP's support for the Extensible Markup Language (XML). We examine the XML Parser functions as well as more advanced topics such as DOM and XSLT.

Part IV consists of Hours 23 and 24. In these, we move beyond the core language to examine the ways in which libraries can be used to extend PHP's functionality:

▶ Hour 23, "PEAR: Reusable Components to Extend the Power of PHP," introduces the PHP Extension and Application Repository. You learn how to install packages and work with some examples.

▶ Hour 24, "Towards a Framework for Larger Projects," builds up a code library of your own. We explore some techniques that might be used in deploying a Front Controller enterprise pattern. This example utilizes some of PHP's most advanced object-oriented features.

Finally, we include a glossary that defines some of the more technical terms you might encounter as you work through the book.

PART I

Getting Started

PHP: From Home Page to Web Enterprise

What You'll Learn In This Hour:

▶ What PHP is

▶ About PHP's history

▶ What improvements can be found in PHP 5

▶ Some options that add features to your PHP binary

▶ Some reasons you should choose to work with PHP

Welcome to PHP! Throughout this book you will look at almost every element of the PHP language. But first, you will explore PHP as a product—its history, features, and future.

What Is PHP?

PHP is a language that has outgrown its name. It was originally conceived as a set of macros to help coders maintain personal home pages, and its name grew from its purpose. Since then, PHP's capabilities have been extended, taking it beyond a set of utilities to a full-featured programming language, capable of managing huge database-driven online environments.

As PHP's capabilities have grown, so too has its popularity. According to NetCraft (http://www.netcraft.com), PHP was running on more than 1 million hosts in November 1999. As of September 2001, that figure had already risen to over 6 million hosts, and by October 2003 PHP was reportedly installed on almost 14 million hosts. According to SecuritySpace.com, PHP is the most popular Apache module available, beating mod_ssl, Perl, and FrontPage.

PHP is officially known as PHP: Hypertext Preprocessor. It is a server-side scripting language often written in an HTML context. Unlike an ordinary HTML page, a PHP script is not sent directly to a client by the server; instead, it is parsed by the PHP engine. HTML elements in the script are left alone, but PHP code is interpreted and executed. PHP code in a script can query databases, create images, read and write files, talk to remote servers—the possibilities are endless. The output from PHP code is combined with the HTML in the script and the result sent to the user.

PHP is also installed as a command-line application, making it an excellent tool for scripting on a server. Many system administrators now use PHP for the sort of automation that has been traditionally handled by Perl or shell scripting.

What Need Does PHP Fulfill?

There have been scripting solutions for as long as there has been a World Wide Web. As the need to create sites with dynamic content has grown in recent years, so has the pressure to create robust environments quickly and efficiently. Although C can be a great solution for creating fast server tools, it is also hard to work with and can easily produce security holes if not carefully deployed. Perl, a language originally developed for text processing naturally met the demand for dynamic Web environments. Much easier to deploy safely than C, its slower performance has always been more than balanced by the comparatively fast development cycle it offers. Even more useful has been the increasing availability of a large number of stable code libraries for Perl.

So where does PHP fit in? PHP was written especially for the Web. Many of the issues and problems faced by Web programmers are addressed within the language itself. Whereas a Perl programmer must use an external library or write code to acquire data submitted by the user of a Web page, PHP makes this data automatically available. Whereas a Perl programmer must install modules to enable her to write database-driven environments, PHP bundles a powerful SQL database library and provides built-in support for a whole range of third-party databases. In short, because PHP has been created for Web programmers, it has a set of functions for almost any typical problem you might encounter, from managing user sessions to handling XML documents.

So, do we have to pay for this ease of use with even slower performance? Not at all. PHP is designed to run as a module with many server applications, which means that there are none of the start-up overheads associated with CGI scripts. The fact that many typical tasks are handled by PHP means that developers are freed from reliance on utility libraries that can slow things down.

It is not the case that PHP does not provide libraries, though. Perl has the Comprehensive Perl Archive Network (CPAN), and PHP has the PHP Extension and Application Repository (PEAR)—its own repository of powerful packages that extend PHP's power.

What's New in PHP 5

PHP 5 introduces numerous new features that will make the programmer's life more interesting. Let's take a quick look at some of them. If they don't make sense to you now, don't worry, we cover all these features in detail in this book:

- ► PHP has new integrated for support for XML. The various functions and classes provided to handle XML in different ways all now use the same underlying library (libxml2). This should make XML features more stable and interoperable.

- ► The SQLite SQL library is now bundled with PHP, together with all the functions you need to work with it.

- ► PHP now supports private and protected methods and properties in classes.

- ► PHP supports class constants.

- ► Objects passed to functions and methods are now passed by reference. That is, a reference to an object is passed around your script rather than copies of objects. This significantly reduces the likelihood of bugs in object-oriented code.

- ► PHP supports static methods and properties, making more advanced object-oriented designs possible.

- ► Methods can now be declared to require particular object types.

- ► The comparison operator (===) now checks that two references point to the same object. Previously, it was hard to test objects in this way.

- ► PHP now supports abstract classes and interfaces.

Many of these improvements are due to some fundamental changes under the hood.

The Zend Engine

When PHP 3 was written, an entirely new parser was created from the ground up. The introduction of PHP 4 represented a similar revolution in the code base. Zend is a scripting engine that sits below the PHP-specific modules. It was optimized to ensure massively improved performance and extensibility.

PHP 5 brings new fundamental improvements with the introduction of the Zend Engine 2. We have already touched on the great change ushered in by ZE2. The engine provides significantly enhanced support for object-oriented programming. For the first time, objects and object-oriented design lie at the heart of PHP, making it an even more suitable platform for large enterprise applications.

Why Choose PHP?

There are some compelling reasons to work with PHP. For many projects, you will find that the production process is significantly faster than you might expect if you are used to working with other scripting languages. At Corrosive we work with both PHP and Java. We choose PHP when we want to see results quickly without sacrificing stability. As an open-source product, PHP is well supported by a talented production team and a committed user community. Furthermore, PHP can be run on all the major operating systems and with most servers.

Speed of Development

Because PHP allows you to separate HTML code from scripted elements, you will notice a significant decrease in development time on many projects. In many instances, you will be able to separate the coding stage of a project from the design and build stages. Not only can this make life easier for you as a programmer, but it also can remove obstacles that stand in the way of effective and flexible design.

PHP Is Open Source

To many people, *open source* simply means free, which is, of course, a benefit in itself.

Well-maintained open-source projects offer users additional benefits, though. You benefit from an accessible and committed community that offers a wealth of experience in the subject. Chances are that any problem you encounter in your coding can be answered swiftly and easily with a little research. If that fails, a question sent to a mailing list can yield an intelligent, authoritative response.

You also can be sure that bugs will be addressed as they are found, and that new features will be made available as the need is defined. You will not have to wait for the next commercial release before taking advantage of improvements.

There is no vested interest in a particular server product or operating system. You are free to make choices that suit your needs or those of your clients, secure that your code will run whatever you decide.

Performance

Because of the powerful Zend engine, PHP shows solid performance compared with other server scripting languages, such as ASP, Perl, and Java Servlets, in benchmark tests. To further improve performance, you can acquire a caching tool (Zend Accelerator) from `http://www.zend.com/`; it stores compiled code in memory, eliminating the overhead of parsing and interpreting source files for every request.

Portability

PHP is designed to run on many operating systems and to cooperate with many servers and databases. You can build for a Unix environment and shift your work to NT without a problem. You can test a project with Personal Web Server and install it on a Unix system running on PHP as an Apache module.

What's New in This Edition

Since the first edition of this book, PHP has consolidated its position as one of the best options for Web development. PHP, in common with any popular open-source project, is a fast-moving target. In this edition we have extensively checked and updated the examples and tutorials. Where new features have appeared, we have extended our coverage. We have significantly revised our coverage of objects, XML, and SQL to take account of changes in PHP 5.

In addition to reviewing and extending existing material, we have added coverage for PEAR, an entirely new chapter on advanced objects, and a set of libraries for managing larger projects.

Summary

In this hour, we introduced PHP. You learned the history of PHP from a simple set of macros to the powerful scripting environment it has become. You found out about PHP and the Zend scripting engine, and how they incorporate new features and more efficiency. Finally, you discovered some of the features that make PHP a compelling choice as a Web programming language.

I hope that you've been convinced by this chapter that PHP is the language for you. In the next hour, we dive straight in and install the PHP engine.

Q&A

Q *Is PHP an easy language to learn?*

A In short, yes. You really can learn the basics of PHP in 24 hours. PHP provides an enormous wealth of functions that allow you to do things for which you would have to write custom code in other languages.

Understanding the syntax and structures of a programming language is only the beginning of the journey. You will only really learn by building your own projects and by making mistakes. You should see this book as a starting point.

Workshop

Quiz

1. True or false: PHP was originally developed for use in the banking industry.

2. How much does PHP cost?

3. What is the name of the scripting engine that powers PHP?

4. Name a new feature introduced with PHP 5.

Answers

1. False. PHP was originally developed for Web publishing.

2. PHP costs nothing at all.

3. Sitting below PHP is a scripting engine called the Zend Engine 2.

4. PHP 5 introduces (among other things) SQLite support, improved XML support, and a significantly improved object model.

Exercise

1. Jot down the reasons you have for deciding to learn PHP. How will the features covered in this chapter help you with your projects? Define two or three projects that you would like to be able to complete after you have finished this book. As you read the book, keep a note of language features and techniques that will help you in the development of these projects.

HOUR 2

Installing PHP

What You'll Learn in This Hour:

▶ Which platforms, servers, and databases are supported by PHP

▶ Where to find PHP and other useful open-source software

▶ One way of installing PHP on Linux

▶ Some options that add features to your PHP binary

▶ Some configuration directives

▶ How to find help when things go wrong

Before getting started with the PHP language, you must first acquire, install, and configure the PHP engine. PHP is available for a wide range of platforms and works in conjunction with many servers.

Platforms, Servers, Databases, and PHP

PHP is truly cross-platform. It runs on the Windows operating system; most versions of Unix, including Linux; and Macintosh OS X. Support is provided for a range of Web servers including Apache (itself open-source and cross-platform), Microsoft Internet Information Server, WebSite Pro, the iPlanet Web Server, and Microsoft's Personal Web Server. The latter is useful if you want to test your scripts offline on a Windows machine, although Apache can also be run on Windows.

On most servers PHP can be installed as a server module. In other words, it runs as part of the server process rather than as a separate application. PHP is also installed as a standalone command-line application.

In this book, we will concentrate on building Web applications, but do not underestimate the power of PHP as a general scripting tool comparable to Perl. The fact that

PHP runs as a command-line application means that any server that supports CGI scripts should be able to work with it. Configuration, though, will vary from server to server.

PHP is designed to integrate easily with databases. This feature is one of the factors that makes the language such a good choice for building sophisticated Web applications. PHP supports almost every database currently available, either directly or via Open Database Connectivity (ODBC).

Throughout this book, we will use a combination of Linux, Apache, and MySQL. We will also introduce SQLite, a lightweight but powerful SQL library that is newly bundled with PHP 5. All these are free to download and use and can be installed relatively easily on a PC.

Where to Find PHP and More

You can find PHP at http://www.php.net/. PHP is open-source software, which means you won't need your credit card when you download it.

The PHP Web site is an excellent resource for PHP coders. The entire manual can be read online at http://www.php.net/manual/, complete with helpful annotations from other PHP coders. You can also download the manual in several formats.

You can find out more about getting Linux for your computer at http://www. linux.org/help/beginner/distributions.html. If you want to run Linux on a Power PC, you can find information about Yellow Dog Linux at http://www. yellowdoglinux.com/. Mac OS X, Apple's latest operating system, is based on Unix BSD and can run PHP with no problems. If you are running OS X, you can find installation information at http://www.php.net/manual/en/install.macosx.php.

If you want to run PHP with Windows, you can find complete installation instructions at http://www.php.net/manual/en/install.windows.php.

MySQL, one of the two databases we will use in this book, can be downloaded from http://www.mysql.com. Versions are available for many operating systems, including Unix, Windows, and OS/2.

Installing PHP for Linux and Apache

In this section, we will look at one way of installing PHP with Apache on Linux. The process is more or less the same for any Unix operating system. You might be able to find prebuilt versions of PHP for your system, which are simple to install.

Compiling PHP, though, gives you greater control over the features built in to your binary.

Before you install, you should ensure that you are logged in to your system as the root user. If you are not allowed access to your system's root account, you might need to ask your system administrator to install PHP for you.

There are two ways of compiling an Apache PHP module. You can either recompile Apache, statically linking PHP into it, or you can compile PHP as a dynamic shared object (DSO). If your version of Apache was compiled with DSO support, it is capable of supporting new modules without the need for recompiling the server. This method is the easiest way to get PHP up and running, and it is the one we cover in this section.

To test that Apache supports DSOs, you should launch the Apache binary (httpd) with the -l argument, like so:

```
/usr/local/apache/bin/httpd -l
```

By the Way

Where Is Apache?

httpd, the Apache application, can be installed in different places on a system. One standard location is /usr/local/apache/bin/httpd, but you may find that it is somewhere else on your server. If it has been placed in your path, you may not even have to use the full path in order to invoke the application. You would then be able call apache like this:

```
httpd -l
```

You should see a list of modules. If you see

```
mod_so.c
```

among them, you should be able to proceed; otherwise, you might need to recompile Apache. The Apache distribution contains full instructions for this.

By the Way

Compile Apache with DSO Support

If you do install Apache, remember to ensure that you compile DSO support in. You can do this by passing --enable-module=so to the configure script, like this:

```
./configure --enable-module=so
```

If you have not already done so, you need to download the latest distribution of PHP (PHP 5.0.0b1 at the time of writing). Your distribution will be archived as a tar file and compressed with gzip, so you will need to unpack it:

```
tar -xvzf php-5.0.0b1.tar.gz
```

After your distribution is unpacked, you should move to the PHP distribution directory:

```
cd php-5.0.0b1
```

Within your distribution directory you will find a script called `configure`. This accepts additional information that should be provided when the `configure` script is run from the command line. These command-line arguments control the features that PHP supports. For this example, we will include some useful command-line arguments, although you might want to specify arguments of your own. We will discuss some of the `configure` options available to you later in the hour:

```
./configure \
  --prefix=/home/usr/local/php5/ \
  --with-mysql \
  --with-apxs=/usr/local/apache/bin/apxs \
  --with-xsl \
  --with-gdbm \
  --with-gd \
  --with-freetype=/usr/include/freetype/ \
  --with-zlib-dir=/usr/include \
  --with-ttf \
  --with-jpeg-dir=/usr/lib
```

By the Way

Installing PHP with Apache 2

It is currently recommended that you run PHP with Apache 1.3 rather than Apache 2. However, you can find full instructions for installing PHP with Apache 2 at `http://www.php.net/manual/en/install.apache2.php`. The main installation difference lies in a flag to the configure script. You should use `--with-apxs2` rather than `--with-apxs`.

The directives chosen in this example are designed to support the features discussed in this book. Most of them require that your system has certain libraries installed before you can compile PHP. The configure script will complain if the relevant libraries cannot be located.

Of these configure options, the one that is absolutely essential is `--with-apxs` because it associates PHP with your server. The argument you use depends on the location of Apache on your server. If you are running Linux and are not sure where to find Apache, try running the `locate` command at the command line, like so:

```
locate apxs
```

It lists all the paths on your system that contain the string apxs.

After the `configure` script has run, you can run the make program. You need a C compiler on your system to run this command successfully:

```
make
make install
```

These commands should end the process of PHP compilation and installation. You should now be able to configure and run Apache.

Some `configure` **Options**

When we ran the `configure` script, we included some command-line arguments that determined the features the PHP engine will include. The `configure` script itself gives you a list of available options. From the PHP distribution directory, type the following:

```
./configure --help
```

The list produced is long, so you might want to add it to a file for reading at leisure:

```
./configure --help > configoptions.txt
```

Although the output from this command is very descriptive, we will look at a few useful options—especially those that might be needed to follow this book.

`--with-gdbm`

The `--with-gdbm` option includes support for the Gnu Database Manager. This or another DBM-type library needs to be supported for you to work with the DBA functions discussed in Hour 11, "Working with Files." If you are running Linux, this library is probably present, but see Hour 12, "Working with the DBA Functions," for alternatives. If your DBM library is in a nonstandard location, you might need to specify a path, as shown here:

```
--with-gdbm=/path/to/dir
```

`--with-gd`

`--with-gd` enables support for the GD library, which, if installed on your system, allows you to create dynamic GIF or PNG images from your scripts. You can read more about creating dynamic images in Hour 15, "Images On-the-Fly." You can optionally specify a path to your GD library's install directory:

```
--with-gd=/path/to/dir
```

If your compile fails, you should try explicitly setting the path when using this option.

Successful option combinations for compiling with GD support are subject to occasional change, so you should check the manual at http://www.php.net/gd for the latest information.

At the time of writing, it is also necessary to specify a path to the zlib compression library (http://www.gzip.org/zlib/) to install GD successfully. We specified the path for the standard location like so:

```
--with-zlib-dir=/usr/include
```

We also want to use the GD library to work with JPEG files, so we have compiled in support for this as well:

```
--with-jpeg-dir=/usr/lib
```

This path points to the standard install directory for the jpeg-6b library that can be downloaded from ftp://ftp.uu.net/graphics/jpeg/.

--with-freetype

--with-freetype provides support for the FreeType 1 library that enables you to include fonts in any dynamic image you create. To enable this option, you must have the FreeType 1 library installed. You can find out more about FreeType at http://www.freetype.org. As with many other directives, if you run into problems you should try specifying a path:

```
--with-freetype=/path/to/dir
```

--with-mysql

--with-mysql enables support for the MySQL database:

```
--with-mysql=/path/to/dir
```

MySQL is no longer bundled with PHP 5, so you should include this option if you intend to work with MySQL. As you know, PHP provides support for other databases. Table 2.1 lists some of them and the configure options you will need to use them.

TABLE 2.1 Some Database `configure` Options

Database	`configure` Option
DBA	`--with-dba`
DBM	`--with-dbm`
GDBM	`--with-gdbm`
Adabas D	`--with-adabas`
FilePro	`--with-filepro`
msql	`--with-msql`
informix	`--with-informix`
iODBC	`--with-iodbc`
OpenLink ODBC	`--with-openlink`
Oracle	`--with-oracle`
PostgreSQL	`--with-pgsql`
Solid	`--with-solid`
Sybase	`--with-sybase`
Sybase-CT	`--with-sybase-ct`
Velocis	`--with-velocis`
LDAP	`--with-ldap`

`--with-xslt`

This book explores a number of XML features in Hour 22, "XML." All PHP functions now use the same library—libxml2, which is available from `http://www.xmlsoft.org/`. At the time of writing, of the standard sets of XML functions, only XSLT needs to be explicitly referenced when you run the configure script. Include this option to ensure that you can run all the examples in Hour 22.

Configuring Apache

After you have compiled PHP and Apache, you should check Apache's configuration file, `httpd.conf`, which you will find in a directory called `conf` in the Apache install directory. Add the following lines to this file:

```
AddType application/x-httpd-php .php
```

This ensures that the PHP engine will parse files that end with the `.php` extension.

If you want to offer to your users PHP pages with extensions more familiar to them, you can choose any extension you want. You can even ensure that files with the .html extension are treated as PHP files with the following:

```
AddType application/x-httpd-php .html
```

Note that treating files with the .html extension as PHP scripts could slow down your site because every page with this extension will be parsed by the PHP engine before it is served to the user.

If PHP has been preinstalled and you have no access to the Apache configuration files, you might be able to change the extensions that determine which files are treated as PHP executables by including an AddType directive in a file called .htaccess. After you have created this file, the directive affects the enclosing directory, as well as any subdirectories. This technique works only if the AllowOverride directive for the enclosing directory is set to either FileInfo or All.

Although the filename .htaccess is the default for an access control file, it might have been changed. Check the AccessFileName directive in httpd.conf to find out. Even if you don't have root access, you might be able to read the Apache configuration files.

An .htaccess file can be an excellent way of customizing your server space if you do not have access to the root account. The principal way of configuring the behavior of PHP, however, is the php.ini file.

php.ini

After you have compiled or installed PHP, you can still change its behavior with a file called php.ini. On Unix systems, the default location for this file is /usr/local/lib; on a Windows system, the default location is the Windows directory. You should find a sample php.ini file in your distribution directory, which contains factory settings. Factory settings are used if no php.ini file is used. Directives in the php.ini file come in two forms: values and flags. **Value** directives take the form of a directive name and a value separated by an equals sign. Possible values vary from directive to directive. **Flag** directives take the form of directive name and a positive or negative term separated by an equals sign. Positive terms can be 1, On, Yes, and True; negative terms can be 0, Off, No, and False. White space is ignored.

If PHP has been preinstalled on your system, you might want to check some of the settings in php.ini.

You can change your `php.ini` settings at any time; however, if you are running PHP as an Apache module, you should restart the server for the changes to take effect.

short_open_tag

The `short_open_tag` directive determines whether you can begin a block of PHP code with the symbol <? and close it with ?>. If this has been disabled, you will see one of the following:

```
short_open_tag = Off
short_open_tag = False
short_open_tag = No
```

To enable the directive, you can use one of the following:

```
short_open_tag = On
short_open_tag = True
short_open_tag = Yes
```

You can read more about PHP open and close tags in Hour 3, "A First Script."

Error Reporting Directives

To diagnose bugs in your code, you should enable the directive that allows error messages to be written to the browser. This is on by default:

```
display_errors = On
```

You should turn this off for production code—that is, code that is displayed to the general public. The reason for this is that error messages displayed on the browser can give away weaknesses in your code to potential attackers. For production code, you should log errors instead, like so:

```
log_errors = On
```

You can also set the level of error reporting. For the examples you'll be working through in this book, you should set this to the following:

```
error_reporting = E_ALL & ~E_NOTICE
```

This will report all errors, apart from notices. This setting is the default and gives you a good sense of what is happening in your scripts.

Variable Directives

PHP makes certain variables available to you as a result of a GET request, POST request, or cookie. You can influence this in the php.ini file.

The register_globals directive determines whether values resulting from an HTTP request should be made available as global variables. This is now officially deprecated, and register_globals is set to off by default:

```
register_globals = Off
```

None of the scripts in this edition of *Sams Teach Yourself PHP in 24 Hours* rely on this directive, and you should keep it disabled.

Changing php.ini Directives Locally

If you are running Apache with the module version of PHP and your configuration allows the use of the .htaccess file, you can enable and disable php.ini directives on a per-directory basis.

Within the .htaccess file you can use the php_flag directive to set a php.ini flag (a directive that requires 'On' or 'Off') and the php_value directive to set a php.ini value (a directive that requires a string or number):

```
php_flag  short_open_tag  On
php_value include_path ".:/home/corrdev"
```

If you are not running Apache, all is not lost. As of PHP 4.0.5, the function ini_set() was introduced. It enables you to set some php.ini directives from within your code. ini_set() requires two strings—the directive name, and the value to set:

```
ini_set( "include_path", ".:/home/corrdev" );
```

You can read more about functions in Hour 6, "Functions."

Help!

Help is always at hand on the Internet, particularly for problems concerning open-source software. Wait a moment before you hit the Send button, however. No matter how intractable your installation, configuration, or programming problem might seem, chances are you are not alone. Someone will have already answered your question.

When you hit a brick wall, your first recourse should be to the official PHP site at `http://www.php.net/`, particularly the annotated manual at `http://www.php.net/manual`.

If you still can't find your answer, don't forget that the PHP site is searchable. The advice you are seeking might be lurking in a press release or a frequently asked questions file. Another excellent and searchable resource is the PHP Builder site at `http://www.phpbuilder.com`.

Still no luck? You can search the mailing list archives at `http://www.php.net/search.php`. These archives represent a huge information resource with contributions from many of the great and the good in the PHP community. Spend some time trying out a few keyword combinations.

If you are still convinced that your problem has not been addressed, you may well be doing the PHP community a service by exposing it.

You can join the PHP mailing lists at `http://www.php.net/mailing-lists.php`. Although these lists are often high volume, you can learn a lot from them. If you are serious about PHP scripting, you should certainly subscribe at least to a digest list. Once subscribed to the list that matches your concerns, you might consider posting your problem.

When you post a question, you should include as much information as possible (without writing a novel). The following items often are pertinent:

▶ Your operating system

▶ The version of PHP you are running or installing

▶ The `configure` options you chose

▶ Any output from the `configure` or `make` commands that preceded an installation failure

▶ A reasonably complete example of the code that is causing problems

Why all these cautions about posting a question to a mailing list? First, developing research skills will stand you in good stead. A good researcher can generally solve a problem quickly and efficiently. Asking a naive question on a technical list often involves a wait rewarded only by a message or two referring you to the archives where you should have begun your search for answers.

Second, remember that a mailing list does not offer technical support as a right. No one is paid to answer your questions. Despite this, you have access to an impressive resource of talent and knowledge, including that of some of the creators of PHP itself. A good question and its answer will be archived to help other coders. Asking a question that has been answered several times just adds more noise.

Having said this, don't be afraid to post a problem to the list. PHP developers are a civilized and helpful breed, and by bringing a problem to the attention of the community, you might be helping others solve the same problem.

Summary

PHP is open-source software. It is also open in the sense that it does not demand that you use a particular server, operating system, or database.

In this hour, you learned where to locate PHP and other open-source software that can help you host and serve Web sites. You learned how to compile PHP as an Apache module on Linux. If you download a PHP binary for another platform, your distribution contains step-by-step instructions. You learned some of the `configure` options that can change the features your binary supports. You also learned about `php.ini` and some of the directive it contains. Finally, you learned about sources of support. You should now be ready to come to grips with the language itself.

In the next hour, we will write and run our first script. You will encounter some of the special syntax you will need to use to distinguish HTML from PHP code.

Q&A

Q *You have covered an installation for Linux and Apache. Does that mean that this book will not apply to my server and operating system?*

A No; one of PHP's great strengths is that it runs on multiple platforms. If you are having trouble installing PHP to work on your operating system or with your server, don't forget to read the files that came with your PHP distribution. You should find comprehensive, step-by-step instructions for installation. If you are still having problems, review the "Help!" section earlier in this hour. The online resources mentioned there will almost certainly contain the answers you need.

Workshop

Quiz

1. Where can you find the PHP online manual?

2. From a Unix operating system, how would you get help on configuration options (the options you pass to the `configure` script in your PHP distribution)?

3. What is Apache's configuration file typically called?

4. Which line should you add to the Apache configuration file to ensure that the `.php` extension is recognized?

5. What is PHP's configuration file called?

Answers

1. The manual for PHP is available at `http://www.php.net/manual/`.

2. You can get help on configuration options by calling the `configure` script in the PHP distribution folder and passing it the `--help` argument:

   ```
   ./configure -help
   ```

3. The Apache configuration file is called `httpd.conf`.

4. The line is

   ```
   AddType application/x-httpd-php .php
   ```

   It ensures that Apache treats files ending with the `.php` extension as PHP scripts.

5. PHP's configuration file is called `php.ini`.

Exercise

1. Install PHP on your system. If it is already in place, review your `php.ini` file and check your configuration.

A First Script

What You'll Learn in This Hour:

▶ How to create, upload, and run a PHP script

▶ How to incorporate HTML and PHP in the same document

▶ How to make your code clearer with comments

You installed and configured PHP in the last hour. It is now time to put it to the test. In this hour, you will create your first script and spend a little time analyzing its syntax. By the end of the hour, you should be ready to create documents that include both HTML and PHP.

Our First Script

Let's jump right in with a PHP script. To begin, open your favorite text editor. Like HTML documents, PHP files are made up of plain text, so you can create them with any text editor, such as Notepad and HomeSite on Windows, Simple Text and BBEdit on Mac OS, or VI and Emacs on Unix operating systems. Most popular HTML editors provide at least some support for PHP.

> Keith Edmunds maintains a handy list of PHP-friendly editors at
> `http://phpeditors.linuxbackup.co.uk`.

Did you Know?

Type in the example in Listing 3.1 and save the file. We'll name our file `listing3.1.php`.

LISTING 3.1 A First PHP Script

```
1: <?php
2: phpinfo();
3: ?>
```

The code in Listing 3.1 causes information about our PHP installation to be output to the browser. The phpinfo() function is very useful for debugging scripts because of the contextual information it provides.

The extension to the PHP document is important because it tells the server to treat the file as PHP code and invoke the PHP engine. The default PHP extension for a PHP document is .php. This can be changed, however, by altering the server's configuration. You saw how to do this in Hour 2, "Installing PHP." System administrators occasionally configure servers to work with non-default extensions, so some server setups might expect extensions such as .phtml or .php5. As you saw in the last hour, for example, Apache uses the AddType directive to determine how a file should be treated. AddType is usually found in Apache's configuration file, httpd.conf:

```
AddType application/x-httpd-php .php
```

If you are not working directly on the machine that will be serving your PHP script, you will probably need to use an FTP client, such as WS_FTP for Windows or RBrowser Lite for MacOS, to upload your saved document to the server.

Watch Out!

> For historical reasons, different operating systems use different character combinations to denote the end of a line of text. You should save your PHP documents with the correct line breaks for the operating system that runs your server. A document with the wrong line breaks for the operating system might be read as a single very long line of text by the PHP engine. This usually causes no problems, but the occasional bug can result. Most good text editors allow you to nominate your target operating system.

After the document is in place, you should be able to access it via your browser. If all has gone well, you should see the script's output. Figure 3.1 shows the output from the listing3.1.php script.

If PHP is not installed on your server or your file's extension is not recognized, you might not see the output shown in Figure 3.1. In these cases, you might see the source code created in Listing 3.1, or you might be prompted to download the file! The effect of a misconfiguration depends your platform, server and browser. Figure 3.2 shows what happens to Internet Explorer when an unknown extension is encountered by Apache running PHP as a module on Linux.

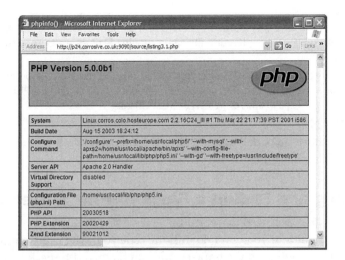

FIGURE 3.1
Success: The output from Listing 3.1.

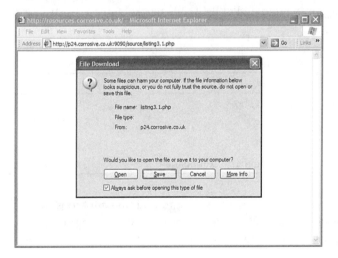

FIGURE 3.2
Failure: The extension is not recognized.

If this happens, or you see the script's source code in the browser window, first check the extension with which you saved your PHP script. If you are used to working with HTML files, for example, check that you have not saved your script with a `.html` extension. If the file extension is as it should be, you might need to check that PHP has been installed properly and that your server is configured to work with the extension you have used for your script. You can read more about installing and configuring PHP in Hour 2. To produce the output shown in Figure 3.2, we removed the `AddType` directive from Apache's configuration file.

By the
Way

> Configuration problems vary between servers and platforms. Omitting the `Action` directive from Apache's `httpd.conf` file when running PHP as a CGI results in errors, for example.
>
> If you encounter unexpected behavior, you should refer to the installation instructions for your server. You can find complete instructions for setting up PHP with most servers at `http://www.php.net/installation`.

Now that you have uploaded and tested your script, you can take a look at the code in a little more detail.

Beginning and Ending a Block of PHP Statements

When writing PHP, you need to inform the PHP engine that you want it to execute your commands. If you don't do this, the code you write will be mistaken for HTML and will be output to the browser. You can do this with special tags that mark the beginning and end of PHP code blocks. Table 3.1 lists four such PHP delimiter tags.

TABLE 3.1   PHP Start and End Tags

Tag Style	Start Tag	End Tag
Standard tags	`<?php`	`?>`
Short tags	`<?`	`?>`
ASP tags	`<%`	`%>`
Script tags	`<script language="php">`	`</script>`

Of the tags in Table 3.1, only the standard and the script tags can be guaranteed to work on any configuration. The short and ASP style tags must be explicitly enabled in your `php.ini`, which you examined in Hour 2.

To activate recognition for short tags, you must make sure that the `short_open_tag` switch is set to "On" in `php.ini`, like so:

```
short_open_tag = On;
```

Short tags are enabled by default, so you need to edit `php.ini` only if you want to disable these.

To activate recognition for the ASP tags, you must enable the `asp_tags` setting, like so:

```
asp_tags = On;
```

After you have edited `php.ini`, you should be able to choose from any of the four styles for use in your scripts. Having said this, it is not advisable to use anything but the standard `<?php ?>` tags. It is the officially supported syntax, it works well with XML, and it works in any PHP context. Furthermore, there is no guarantee that short tags will be supported forever.

The character sequence `<?` tells an XML parser to expect a processing instruction:

```
<?xml version="1.0" encoding="UTF-8"?>
```

This syntax clashes with the PHP short tag. Used as part of an XML or XHTML document, PHP short tags could confuse an XML validator, the PHP engine, or both. Disable short tags if you intend to use PHP in an XML context.

Watch Out!

You should also avoid short or ASP tags if you want your script to be portable. Third-party servers might not be configured to support these tags.

Let's run through some of the ways in which you can legally write the code in Listing 3.1. You could use any of the four PHP start and end tags that you have seen:

```
<?
phpinfo();
?>

<?php
phpinfo();
?>

<%
phpinfo();
%>

<script language="php">
phpinfo();
</script>
```

Single lines of code in PHP also can be presented on the same line as the PHP start and end tags, like so:

```
<?php phpinfo(); ?>
```

Now that we have proved to ourselves that PHP is working, let's move on and write some more code.

The `print()` Function

In Listing 3.1 we used the `phpinfo()` function. In Listing 3.2 we change our script so that we print something to the browser for ourselves.

LISTING 3.2   Printing a Message

```
1: <?php
2: print "hello world";
3: ?>
```

`print()` is a language construct that outputs data. Although it is not a function, it behaves like one: It accepts a collection of characters, known as a *string*. Strings must be enclosed by quotation marks, either single or double. The string passed to `print()` is then output, usually to the browser or command line.

By the Way

> Similar to the `print()` statement is `echo()`, which behaves in the same way (except that it does not return a value). For most examples in this book, you could replace all uses of `print()` with `echo()` without any noticeable effect.

By the Way

> Function calls generally require parentheses after their names, regardless of whether they demand arguments. `print()` is, strictly speaking, a language construct rather than a function and does not demand the use of parentheses. As parentheses are omitted by convention, we will usually omit them in our examples.

We ended our only line of code in Listing 3.2 with a semicolon. The semicolon informs the PHP engine that we have completed a statement.

A **statement** represents an instruction to the PHP engine. Broadly, it is to PHP what a sentence is to written or spoken English. A sentence should end with a period; a statement should usually end with a semicolon. Exceptions to this include statements that enclose other statements and statements that end a block of code. In most cases, however, failure to end a statement with a semicolon confuses the PHP engine and results in an error being reported at the following line in the script.

Because the statement in Listing 3.3 is the final one in that block of code, the semicolon is optional.

Combining HTML and PHP

The code in Listing 3.1 and Listing 3.2 is pure PHP. You can incorporate this into an HTML document simply by adding HTML outside the PHP start and end tags, as shown in Listing 3.3.

LISTING 3.3 A PHP Script Including HTML

```
1: <!DOCTYPE html PUBLIC
2:   "-//W3C//DTD XHTML 1.0 Strict//EN"
3: "http://www.w3.org/TR/xhtml1/DTD/xhtml1-strict.dtd">
4: <html>
5: <head>
6: <title>Listing 3.2 A PHP Script Including HTML</title>
7: </head>
8: <body>
9: <div><b>
10: <?php
11: print "hello world";
12: ?>
13: </b></div>
14: </body>
15: </html>
```

By the Way

As new devices access the Web running new browsers on ever more platforms, standards are becoming increasingly important. Where possible, the output from code examples in this book now conform to Extensible Hypertext Markup Language (XHTML) standards. XHTML is an XML-based version of HTML that can be parsed and validated. Because of this, it is more accessible to lightweight browsers running on small memory devices. XHTML also helps to promote genuinely cross-browser mark-up. You can read more about XHTML at http://www.w3.org/TR/xhtml1/.

Notice that Listing 3.3 starts with a complex-looking element. This is known as the DOCTYPE declaration, and it declares the XHTML version to which the document conforms.

As you can see, incorporating HTML into a PHP document is simply a matter of typing in the code. The PHP engine ignores everything outside PHP open and close tags. If you were to view Listing 3.3 with a browser, as shown in Figure 3.3, you would see the string hello world in bold. If you were to view the document source, as shown in Figure 3.4, the listing would look like a normal HTML document.

FIGURE 3.3
The output of
Listing 3.2 as
viewed in a
browser.

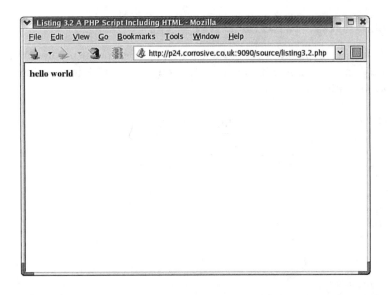

FIGURE 3.4
The output of
Listing 3.2 as
HTML source code.

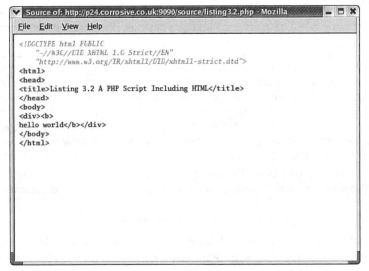

You can include as many blocks of PHP code as you need in a single document, interspersing them with HTML as required. Although you can have multiple blocks of code in a single document, they combine to form a single script. Any variables defined in the first block usually are available to subsequent blocks.

Adding Comments to PHP Code

Code that seems clear at the time of writing can resemble a hopeless tangle when you try to amend it six months later. Adding comments to your code as you write can save you time later and help other programmers more easily work with your code.

A **comment** is text in a script that is ignored by the PHP engine. Comments can be used to make code more readable or to annotate a script.

Single-line comments begin with two forward slashes (//) or a single hash sign (#). All text from either of these marks until either the end of the line or the PHP close tag is ignored. Here's an example:

```
// this is a comment
# this is another comment
```

Multiline comments begin with a forward slash followed by an asterisk (/*) and end with an asterisk followed by a forward slash (*/), as in the following:

```
/*
this is a comment
none of this will
be parsed by the
PHP engine
*/
```

The PHP Extension and Application Repository (PEAR) provides a growing collection of libraries and scripts for extending PHP's functionality. It includes a package called phpDocumentor, which can convert your inline comments into hyperlinked documentation. This is extremely useful for maintaining large projects. You can read more about PHPDocumentor at `http://phpdocu.sourceforge.net`. We cover PEAR and phpDocumentor in more detail in Hour 23, "PEAR: Reusable Components to Extend the Power of PHP."

Did you Know?

Summary

You should now have the tools at your disposal to run a simple PHP script on a properly configured server.

In this hour, you created your first PHP script. You also learned how to use a text editor to create and name a PHP document. You examined four sets of tags that you can use to begin and end blocks of PHP code, and you learned how to use `print()` to send data to the browser. Then you brought HTML and PHP together into the same script. Finally, you learned about comments and how to add them to PHP documents.

In the next hour, you will use these skills to test some of the fundamental building blocks of the PHP language, including variables, data types, and operators.

Q&A

Q *Which are the best start and end tags to use?*

A It is largely a matter of preference. For the sake of portability, the standard tags (`<?php` and `?>`) are probably the safest choice. Short tags are enabled by default and have the virtue of brevity, but to promote portability, it might be safest to avoid them.

Q *Which editors should I avoid when creating PHP code?*

A Do not use word processors that format text for printing (such as Word or OpenOffice). Even if you save files created using this type of editor in plain text format, hidden characters can creep into your code.

Q *When should I comment my code?*

A This is a matter of preference once again. Some short scripts will be self-explanatory to you, even after a long interval. For scripts of any length or complexity, you should comment your code. This will save you time and frustration in the long run.

Workshop

Quiz

1. Can a user read the source code of PHP script you have successfully installed?

2. What do the standard PHP delimiter tags look like?

3. What do the ASP PHP delimiter tags look like?

4. What do the script PHP delimiter tags look like?

5. What syntax would you use to output a string to the browser?

Answers

1. No, the user sees only the output of your script.

2.
```
....<?php
....// your code here
....?>.
```

3.
```
....<%
....// your code here
....%>.
```

4.
```
....<script language="php">
....// your code here
....</script>.
```

5. We would usually use `print()` to write to the browser, although we could use `echo()` with the same results.

Exercise

1. Familiarize yourself with the process of creating, uploading, and running PHP scripts. In particular, create your own "hello world" script. Add HTML code to it and additional blocks of PHP. Experiment with the various PHP delimiter tags. Which ones are enabled in your configuration? Take a look at your `php.ini` file to confirm your findings, and don't forget to add some comments to your code.

PART II

The Language

HOUR 4

The Building Blocks

What You'll Learn in This Hour:

▶ About variables—what they are, why you need to use them, and how to use them

▶ How to define and access variables

▶ About data types

▶ About some of the more commonly used operators

▶ How to use operators to create expressions

▶ How to define and use constants

In this hour, you will get your hands dirty with some of the nuts and bolts of the language.

There's a lot of ground to cover, and if you are new to programming, you might feel bombarded with information. Don't worry—you can always refer to this chapter later. Concentrate on understanding rather than memorizing the features covered.

If you're already an experienced programmer, you should at least skim this hour's lesson. It covers a few PHP-specific features.

Variables

A **variable** is a special container you can define to hold a value. Variables are fundamental to programming. Without them, you'd be forced to hard-code all the values in your scripts. In adding two numbers together and printing the result, we have achieved something useful:

```
print (2 + 4);
```

This script is useful only for people who want to know the sum of 2 and 4, however. To get around this, we could write a script for finding the sum of another set of numbers, say 3 and 5. This approach to programming is clearly absurd. Variables enable you to create templates for operations (adding two numbers, for example) without worrying about what values the variables contain. The variables are given values when the script is run, possibly through user input or a database query.

You should use a variable whenever the data that is being subjected to an operation in your script is liable to change from one script execution to another, or even within the lifetime of the script itself.

A variable consists of a name that you can choose, preceded by a dollar ($) sign. The variable name can include letters, numbers, and the underscore character (_). Variable names cannot include spaces or characters that are not alphanumeric, and they should begin with a letter or an underscore. The following code defines some legal variables:

```
$a;
$a_longish_variable_name;
$_2453;
$sleepyZZZZ;
```

Remember that a semicolon (;) is used to end a PHP statement. The semicolons in the previous fragment of code are not part of the variable names.

A **variable** is a holder for a type of data. It can hold numbers, strings of characters, objects, arrays, or booleans. The contents of a variable can be changed at any time.

As you can see, you have plenty of choices about naming. To declare a variable, you need only to include it in your script. You usually declare a variable and assign a value to it in the same statement, like so:

```
$num1 = 8;
$num2 = 23;
```

The preceding lines declare two variables, using the assignment operator (=) to give them values. You will learn about assignment in more detail in the section "Operators and Expressions," later in the hour. After you give your variables values, you can treat them exactly as if they were the values themselves. In other words

```
print $num1;
```

is equivalent to

```
print 8;
```

as long as $num1 contains 8.

Data Types

Different types of data take up different amounts of memory and can be treated differently when they are manipulated in a script. Some programming languages therefore demand that the programmer declare in advance which type of data a variable will contain. By contrast, PHP is **loosely typed**, which means it calculates data types as data is assigned to each variable. This is a mixed blessing. On the one hand, it means that variables can be used flexibly, holding a string at one point and an integer at another. On the other hand, this can lead to problems in larger scripts if you expect a variable to hold one data type when, in fact, it holds something completely different. You might have created code designed to work with an array variable, for example. If the variable in question contains a number value instead, errors might occur when the code attempts to perform array-specific operations on the variable.

Table 4.1 shows the six standard data types available in PHP.

TABLE 4.1   Standard Data Types

Type	Example	Description
Integer	5	A whole number
Double	3.234	A floating-point number
String	"hello"	A collection of characters
Boolean	true	One of the special values true or false
Object		See Hour 9, "Objects"
Array		See Hour 7, "Arrays"

Of PHP's six standard data types, we will leave arrays and objects for Hours 7 and 9.

PHP also provides two special data types, which are listed in Table 4.2.

TABLE 4.2   Special Data Types

Type	Description
Resource	Reference to a third-party resource (a database, for example)
NULL	An uninitialized variable

Resource types are often returned by functions that deal with external applications or files. You will see examples of resource types throughout the book. The type NULL is reserved for variables that have not been initialized (that is, they have not yet had a value assigned to them).

You can use PHP's built-in function gettype() to acquire the type of any variable. If you place a variable between the parentheses of the function call, gettype() returns a string representing the relevant type. Listing 4.1 assigns five different data types to a single variable, testing it with gettype()each time.

By the Way

You can read more about calling functions in Hour 6, "Functions."

LISTING 4.1   Displaying the Type of a Variable

```
 1: <!DOCTYPE html PUBLIC
 2:    "-//W3C//DTD XHTML 1.0 Strict//EN"
 3:    "http://www.w3.org/TR/xhtml1/DTD/xhtml1-strict.dtd">
 4: <html>
 5: <head>
 6: <title>Listing 4.1 Testing the type of a variable</title>
 7: </head>
 8: <body>
 9: <div>
10: <?php
11: $testing; // declare without assigning
12: print gettype( $testing ); // NULL
13: print "<br />";
14: $testing = 5;
15: print gettype( $testing ); // integer
16: print "<br />";
17: $testing = "five";
18: print gettype( $testing ); // string
19: print "<br />";
20: $testing = 5.0;
21: print gettype( $testing ); // double
22: print "<br />";
23: $testing = true;
24: print gettype( $testing ); // boolean
25: print "<br />";
26: ?>
27: </div>
28: </body>
```

This script produces the following:

```
NULL
integer
string
double
boolean
```

When we declare our $testing variable in line 11, we do not assign a value to it. So, when we first use the gettype() function to test the variable in line 12, we get the string NULL. After this, we assign values to $testing by using = before passing it to gettype(). An *integer* (5), assigned to the $testing variable in line 14, is a whole or real number. In simple terms, it can be said to be a number without a decimal point. A *string* ("five"), assigned to the $testing variable in line 17, is a collection of characters. When you work with strings in your scripts, they should always be surrounded by double quotation marks (") or single quotation marks ('). A *double* (5.0), assigned to the $testing variable in line 20, is a floating-point number. That is, it's a number that includes a decimal point. A *boolean* (true), assigned to the $testing variable in line 23, can be one of two special values: true or false.

There is a difference between double quotation marks and single quotation marks when used with strings. Double quotation marks allow the parsing of variables. If you include a variable within double quotation marks the PHP engine substitutes the variable's value, like so:

```
$name = "john";
print "hello, $name"; // hello, john
```

If you use single quotation marks to enclose the same string, the variable is not substituted:

```
print 'hello, $name'; // hello, $name
```

Double-quoted strings are also parsed for escape characters. Escape characters take on or lose special meaning when preceded by a backslash (\) character. Notable among these are \n for a newline character, \t for a tab, \" to print a double-quoted character within a double-quoted string, \\ to print a backslash, and \$ to print a dollar sign (so that it is not mistaken for the start of a variable).

As a rule of thumb, if you want a string to be output exactly as you typed it, you can use single quotation marks. This can help your code to run more quickly because the interpreter does not have to parse the string. If you want to take advantage of escape characters such as \n and use variable substitution, you should use double quotation marks.

By the Way

Prior to PHP 4, there was no boolean type. Although true was used, it was actually a constant (a special kind of variable that we will cover later in this chapter) with the integer value of 1.

Both NULL and Resource types were added with PHP 4.

By the Way

Displaying Type Information with var_dump()

gettype() is a specialized tool. It does what it promises and returns a variable's type. var_dump() tells you a variable's type and its contents. More than that, for complex types such as arrays and objects, var_dump() provides information about all the types contained within the variable, as well as about the variable itself.

So, by altering line 11 of Listing 4.1, we can put var_dump() to the test:

```
$testing = 5;
var_dump( $testing );
```

This fragment gives us the following result:

```
int(5)
```

This tells us that the variable $testing contains an integer and that the value of that integer is 5. Notice that we did not need to print the result of var_dump(); this is because the function prints its findings directly to the browser or command line.

Testing for a Specific Data Type

gettype() is useful for debugging because it tells you exactly what type any variable is. Often, though, you will want to check only whether a variable contains a specific type. PHP provides a special function corresponding to each data type. These functions accept a variable or value and return a boolean. Table 4.3 lists these functions.

TABLE 4.3 Functions to Test Data Types

Function	Description
is_array()	Returns true if the argument is an array
is_bool()	Returns true if the argument is boolean
is_double()	Returns true if the argument is a double
is_int()	Returns true if the argument is an integer
is_object()	Returns true if the argument is an object
is_string()	Returns true if the argument is a string
is_null()	Returns true if the argument is null
is_resource()	Returns true if the argument is a resource

In Hour 5, "Going with the Flow," we examine the if statement, which enables you to alter the behavior of a script according to the results of a test. These type testing functions are frequently used in conjunction with if statements to enforce the type of a variable passed to a function or object method.

Changing Type with settype()

PHP provides the function settype() to change the type of a variable. To use settype(), you must place the variable to change (and the type to change it to) between the parentheses and separate them by commas. Listing 4.2 converts the value 3.14 (a double) to the four types we are covering in this hour.

LISTING 4.2   Changing the Type of a Variable with settype()

```
 1: <!DOCTYPE html PUBLIC
 2:   "-//W3C//DTD XHTML 1.0 Strict//EN"
 3:   "http://www.w3.org/TR/xhtml1/DTD/xhtml1-strict.dtd">
 4: <html>
 5: <head>
 6: <title>Listing 4.2 Changing the Type of a Variable with settype()</title>
 7: </head>
 8: <body>
 9: <div>
10: <?php
11: $undecided = 3.14;
12: print gettype( $undecided ); // double
13: print " -- $undecided<br />"; // 3.14
14: settype( $undecided, string );
15: print gettype( $undecided ); // string
16: print " -- $undecided<br />"; // 3.14
17: settype( $undecided, int );
18: print gettype( $undecided ); // integer
19: print " -- $undecided<br />"; // 3
20: settype( $undecided, double );
21: print gettype( $undecided ); // double
22: print " -- $undecided<br />"; // 3.0
23: settype( $undecided, bool );
24: print gettype( $undecided ); // boolean
25: print " -- $undecided<br />"; // 1
26: ?>
27: </div>
28: </body>
29: </html>
```

In each case, we use gettype() to confirm that the type change worked and then print the value of the variable $undecided to the browser. When we convert the string 3.14 to an integer in line 17, any information beyond the decimal point is lost forever. That's why $undecided still contains 3 after we have changed it back to a double in line 20. Finally, in line 23, we convert $undecided to a boolean.

Any number other than 0 becomes true when converted to a boolean. When printing a boolean in PHP, true is represented as 1 and false as an empty string, so in line 21, $undecided is printed as 1.

Changing Type by Casting

By placing the name of a data type in parentheses in front of a variable, you create a copy of that variable's value converted to the data type specified.

The principle difference between settype() and a cast is the fact that casting produces a copy, leaving the original variable untouched. Listing 4.3 illustrates this.

LISTING 4.3   Casting a Variable

```
 1: <!DOCTYPE html PUBLIC
 2:    "-//W3C//DTD XHTML 1.0 Strict//EN"
 3:    "http://www.w3.org/TR/xhtml1/DTD/xhtml1-strict.dtd">
 4: <html>
 5: <head>
 6: <title>Listing 4.3 Casting a Variable</title>
 7: </head>
 8: <body>
 9: <div>
10: <?php
11: $undecided = 3.14;
12: $holder = ( double ) $undecided;
13: print gettype( $holder ) ; // double
14: print " -- $holder<br />";   // 3.14
15: $holder = ( string ) $undecided;
16: print gettype( $holder ); // string
17: print " -- $holder<br />";   // 3.14
18: $holder = ( integer ) $undecided;
19: print gettype( $holder ); // integer
20: print " -- $holder<br />";   // 3
21: $holder = ( double ) $undecided;
22: print gettype( $holder ); // double
23: print " -- $holder<br />";   // 3.14
24: $holder = ( boolean ) $undecided;
25: print gettype( $holder ); // boolean
26: print " -- $holder<br />";   // 1
27: ?>
28: </div>
29: </body>
30: </html>
```

We never actually change the type of $undecided, which remains a double throughout. We illustrate this on line 25 by using the gettype() function to output the type of $undecided.

In fact, by casting $undecided, we create a copy that is then converted to the type we specify. This new value is then stored in the variable $holder, first in line 12 and then also in lines 15, 18, 21, and 24. Because we are working with a copy of $undecided, we never discard any information from it as we did in lines 17 and 23 of Listing 4.2.

Now that we can change the contents of a variable from one type to another, either using settype() or a cast, we should consider why this might be useful. It is certainly not a procedure you will use often because PHP automatically casts for you when the context requires. However, an automatic cast is temporary, and you might want to make a variable persistently hold a particular data type.

Numbers typed in to an HTML form by a user are made available to your script as a string. If you try to add two strings containing numbers, PHP helpfully converts the strings into numbers while the addition is taking place. So

```
"30cm" + "40cm"
```

produces the integer 70. In casting the strings, PHP ignores the non-numeric characters. However, you might want to clean up your user input yourself. Imagine that a user has been asked to submit a number. We can simulate this by declaring a variable and assigning to it, like so:

```
$test = "30cm";
```

As you can see, the user has mistakenly added units to the number. We can ensure that the user input is clean by casting it to an integer, as shown here:

```
$test = (integer)$test;
print "Your imaginary box has a width of $test centimeters";
```

More Ways of Changing Type

You have already seen two ways of converting data types: You can cast a value or use the settype() function. In addition to these techniques, PHP provides functions to convert values into integers, doubles, and strings. These functions accept values of any type apart from array or object and return a converted value. Table 4.4 lists these functions.

TABLE 4.4   Functions to Convert Data Types

Function	Description
doubleval()	Accepts a value and returns double equivalent
intval()	Accepts a value and returns integer equivalent
strval()	Accepts a value and returns string equivalent

Why Test Type?

Why might it be useful to know the type of a variable? Many circumstances occur in programming in which data is passed to you from another source. In Hour 6, for example, you learn how to create functions in your scripts. Functions can accept information from calling code in the form of arguments. For the function to work with the data it is given, you often need to first check that it has been given values of the correct data type. A function that is expecting a resource, for example, will not work well when passed a string.

Operators and Expressions

You can now assign data to variables, and you can even investigate and change the data type of a variable. A programming language isn't very useful, though, unless you can manipulate the data you can store. **Operators** are symbols that enable you to use one or more values to produce a new value. A value that is operated on by an operator is referred to as an **operand**.

An **operator** is a symbol or series of symbols that, when used in conjunction with values, performs an action and usually produces a new value.

An **operand** is a value used in conjunction with an operator. There are usually two operands to one operator.

Let's combine two operands with an operator to produce a new value:

```
4 + 5
```

4 and 5 are operands and are operated on by the addition operator (+) to produce 9. Operators almost always sit between two operands, although you will see a few exceptions later in this hour.

The combination of operands with an operator to manufacture a result is called an **expression**. Although most operators form the basis of expressions, an expression need not contain an operator. In fact, in PHP, an *expression* is defined as anything that can be used as a value. This includes integer constants such as 654, variables such as $user, and function calls such as gettype(). (4 + 5) therefore is an expression that consists of two further expressions and an operator. When an expression produces a value, it is often said to *resolve to* that value. That is, when all subexpressions are taken into account, the expression can be treated as if it were a code for the value itself.

An **expression** is any combination of functions, values, and operators that resolves to a value. As a rule of thumb, if you can use it as if it were a value, it is an expression.

Now that we have the principles out of the way, it's time to take a tour of PHP's more common operators.

The Assignment Operator

You have seen the assignment operator each time we have initialized a variable. It consists of the single character =. The assignment operator takes the value of its right operand and assigns it to its left operand, like so:

```
$name = "matt";
```

The variable $name now contains the string "matt". Interestingly, this construct is an expression. At first glance, it might seem like the assignment operator simply changes the variable $name without producing a value, but in fact, a statement that uses the assignment operator always resolves to a copy of the value of the right operand. Thus

```
print ( $name = "matt" );
```

prints the string "matt" to the browser in addition to assigning "matt" to $name.

Arithmetic Operators

The arithmetic operators do exactly what you would expect. Table 4.5 lists these operators. The addition operator adds the right operand to the left operand, whereas the subtraction operator subtracts the right operand from the left. The division operator divides the left operand by the right, and the multiplication operator multiplies the left operand by the right. The modulus operator returns the remainder of the left operand divided by the right.

TABLE 4.5 Arithmetic Operators

Operator	Name	Example	Example Result
+	Addition	10+3	13
-	Subtraction	10-3	7
/	Division	10/3	3.3333333333333
*	Multiplication	10*3	30
%	Modulus	10%3	1

The Concatenation Operator

The concatenation operator is a single period (.). Treating both operands as strings, it appends the right operand to the left. So

```
"hello"." world"
```

is equivalent to

```
"hello world"
```

Regardless of the data types of the operands, they are treated as strings and the result is always a string. You will encounter concatenation frequently throughout this book when we need to combine the results of an expression of some kind with a string. Here's an example:

```
$centimeters = 212;
print "the width is ".($centimeters/100)." meters";
```

Combined Assignment Operators

Although there is really only one assignment operator, PHP provides a number of combination operators that transform the left operand as well as return a result. As a rule, operators use their operands without changing their values; however, assignment operators break this rule. A combined assignment operator consists of a standard operator symbol followed by an equals sign. Combination assignment operators save you the trouble of using two operators yourself. For example

```
$x = 4;
$x = $x + 4; // $x now equals 8
```

can instead be written as

```
$x = 4;
$x += 4; // $x now equals 8
```

There is an assignment operator for each of the arithmetic operators and one for the concatenation operator. Table 4.6 lists some of the most common ones.

TABLE 4.6   **Some Combined Assignment Operators**

Operator	Example	Equivalent to
+=	$x += 5	$x = $x + 5
-=	$x -= 5	$x = $x - 5
/=	$x /= 5	$x = $x / 5

TABLE 4.6 Continued

Operator	Example	Equivalent to
*=	`$x *= 5`	`$x = $x * 5`
%=	`$x %= 5`	`$x = $x % 5`
.=	`$x .= " test"`	`$x = $x." test"`

Each of the examples in Table 4.6 transforms the value of $x using the value of the right operand.

Comparison Operators

Comparison operators perform tests on their operands. They return the boolean value `true` if the test is successful and return `false` otherwise. This type of expression is useful in control structures, such as `if` and `while` statements. You will meet these in Hour 5.

To test whether the value contained in $x is smaller than 5, for example, you would use the less than operator:

```
$x < 5
```

If $x contained 3, this expression would be equivalent to the value `true`. If $x contained 7, the expression would resolve to `false`.

Table 4.7 lists the comparison operators.

TABLE 4.7 Comparison Operators

Operator	Name	Returns True if	Example ($x is 4)	Result
==	Equivalence	Left is equivalent to right	`$x == 5`	false
!=	Non-equivalence	Left is not equivalent to right	`$x != 5`	true
===	Identical	Left is equivalent to right and they are the same type	`$x === 5`	false
>	Greater than	Left is greater than right	`$x > 4`	false
>=	Greater than or equal to	Left is greater than or equal to right	`$x >= 4`	true
<	Less than	Left is less than right	`$x < 4`	false
<=	Less than or equal to	Left is less than or equal to right	`$x <= 4`	true

These operators are most commonly used with integers or doubles, although the equivalence operator is also used to compare strings.

> With the advent of PHP 5, === can be used to test whether two variables hold the same object. PHP 4 implements === in a different way, comparing the properties of two objects and returning true if all properties match and both objects are instances of the same class. This behavior is quite different in the two versions of PHP, in that two different objects of the same type can have the same properties. In PHP 4, such objects would be held to be equivalent, whereas in PHP 5 the objects would not match.
>
> We cover objects in detail in Hour 9, "Objects," and Hour 17, "Advanced Objects."

Creating More Complex Test Expressions with the Logical Operators

The logical operators test combinations of booleans. The or operator—which is indicated by two pipe characters (¦¦) or simply the characters or—returns true if either the left or the right operand is true. So

```
true ¦¦ false
```

returns true.

The and operator, which is indicated by either two ampersand characters (&&) or the characters and, returns true only if both the left and right operands are true. So

```
true && false
```

returns false. It's unlikely that you would use a logical operator to test boolean constants, however. It would make more sense to test two or more expressions that resolve to a boolean. For example

```
( $x > 2 ) && ( $x < 15 )
```

would return true if $x contained a value greater than 2 and smaller than 15. We include the parentheses to make the code easier to read. Table 4.8 lists the logical operators.

TABLE 4.8 Logical Operators

Operator	Name	Returns True if...	Example	Result
¦¦	Or	Left or right is true	true ¦¦ false	true
or	Or	Left or right is true	true ¦¦ false	true
xor	Xor	Left or right is true but not both	true xor true	false

TABLE 4.8   Continued

Operator	Name	Returns True if...	Example	Result
&&	And	Left and right are true	`true && false`	`false`
and	And	Left and right are true	`true && false`	`false`
!	Not	The single operand is not true	`! true`	`false`

Why are there two versions of both the or and the and operators? The answer lies in operator precedence, which we will look at later in this section.

Automatically Incrementing and Decrementing an Integer Variable

When coding in PHP, you will often need to increment or decrement an integer variable. You usually need to do this when you are counting the iterations of a loop. You have already learned two ways of doing this. We could increment the integer contained by $x with the addition operator, like so:

```
$x = $x + 1; // $x is incremented
```

Or we could use a combined assignment operator, as shown here:

```
$x += 1; // $x is incremented
```

In both cases, the resultant integer is assigned to $x. Because expressions of this type are so common, PHP provides some special operators that enable you to add or subtract the integer constant 1 from an integer variable and assign the result to the variable itself. These are known as the post-increment and post-decrement operators. The post-increment operator consists of two plus symbols appended to a variable name, as shown in this example:

```
$x++; // $x is incremented
```

This increments the variable $x by one. Using two minus symbols in the same way, we can decrements the variable:

```
$x--; // $x is decremented
```

If you use the post-increment or post-decrement operator in conjunction with a conditional operator, the operand is modified only after the test has been completed:

```
$x = 3;
$x++ < 4; // true
```

In the previous example, $x contains 3 when it is tested against 4 with the less than operator, so the test expression returns true. After this test is complete, $x is incremented.

In some circumstances, you might want to increment or decrement a variable in a test expression before the test is performed. PHP provides the pre-increment and pre-decrement operators for this purpose. On their own, these operators behave in exactly the same way as the post-increment and post-decrement operators. They are written with the plus or minus symbols preceding the variable:

```
++$x; // $x is incremented
--$x; // $x is decremented
```

If these operators are used as part of a test expression, the incrementation occurs before the test is carried out, like so:

```
$x = 3;
++$x < 4; // false
```

In the previous fragment, $x is incremented before it is tested against 4. The test expression returns false because 4 is not smaller than 4.

Operator Precedence

When you use an operator, the PHP engine usually reads your expression from left to right. For complex expressions that use more than one operator, though, the waters can become a little murky. First, consider a simple case:

```
4 + 5
```

There's no room for confusion, here. PHP simply adds 4 to 5. What about the next fragment?

```
4 + 5 * 2
```

This presents a problem. Does it mean the sum of 4 and 5, which should then be multiplied by 2, giving a result of 18? Or, does it mean 4 plus the result of 5 multiplied by 2, resolving to 14? If you were to read simply from left to right, the former would be true. In fact, PHP attaches different precedence to operators. Because the multiplication operator has higher precedence than the addition operator does, the second solution to the problem is the correct one.

You can force PHP to execute the addition expression before the multiplication expression with parentheses:

```
( 4 + 5 ) * 2
```

Whatever the precedence of the operators in a complex expression, you should use parentheses to make your code clearer and save you from obscure bugs. Table 4.9 lists the operators covered in this hour in precedence order (highest first) .

TABLE 4.9   Order of Precedence for Selected Operators

Operators

```
++  --  (cast)
/  *  %
+  -
<  <=  =>  >
==  ===  !=
&&
||
=  +=  -=  /=  *=  %=  .=
and
xor
or
```

As you can see, or has a lower precedence than || and and has a lower precedence than &&, so you could use the lower-precedence logical operators to change the way a complex test expression is read. This is not necessarily a good idea, however. The following two expressions are equivalent, but the second is much easier to read:

```
$x and $y || $z
$x && ( $y || $z ) )
```

The order of precedence is the only reason that both && and and are present in PHP. The same is true of || and or. In most, if not all circumstances, however, use of parentheses makes for clearer code and fewer bugs than code that takes advantage of the difference in precedence of these operators. Throughout this book, we will use the more common || and && operators.

Constants

Variables offer a flexible way of storing data because you can change their values and the type of data they store at any time. If, however, you want to work with a value that you do not want to alter throughout your script's execution, you can define a constant. You must use PHP's built-in function `define()` to create a constant. After you have done this, the constant cannot be changed. To use the `define()` function, you must place the name of the constant and the value you want to give it within the call's parentheses. These values must be separated by a comma, like so:

```
define( "CONSTANT_NAME", 42 );
```

The value you want to set can only be a number or a string. By convention, the name of the constant should be in uppercase letters. Constants are accessed with the constant name only; no dollar symbol is required. Listing 4.4 defines and accesses a constant.

LISTING 4.4   Defining a Constant

```
 1: <!DOCTYPE html PUBLIC
 2:   "-//W3C//DTD XHTML 1.0 Strict//EN"
 3:   "http://www.w3.org/TR/xhtml1/DTD/xhtml1-strict.dtd">
 4: <html>
 5: <head>
 6: <title>Listing 4.4 Defining a constant</title>
 7: </head>
 8: <body>
 9: <div>
10: <?php
11: define ( "USER", "Gerald" );
12: print "Welcome ".USER;
13: ?>
14: </div>
15: </body>
16: </html>
```

Notice that in line 11 we used the concatenation operator to append the value held by our constant to the string `"Welcome"`. This is because the PHP engine has no way of distinguishing between a constant and a string within quotation marks.

`define()` optionally accepts a third boolean argument that determines whether the constant name should be case insensitive. By default, constants are case sensitive, but by passing `true` to the `define()` function you can change this behavior. So, if we were to set up our USER constant in this way

```
Define( "USER", "Gerald", true );
```

we could access its value without worrying about case. So

```
print User;
print usEr;
print USER;
```

would all be equivalent. This feature can make scripts a little friendlier for programmers who work with your code, in that they will not need to consider case when accessing a constant you have defined. On the other hand, the fact that other constants are case sensitive could make for more rather than less confusion as programmers forget which constants to treat in which way. Unless you have a compelling reason to act otherwise, the safest course is to keep your constants case sensitive and define them using uppercase characters, which is an easily remembered convention.

Predefined Constants

PHP automatically provides some built-in constants for you. __FILE__, for example, returns the name of the file currently being read by the PHP engine, and __LINE__ returns the line number of the file. These constants are useful for generating error messages. You can also find out which version of PHP is interpreting the script with PHP_VERSION. This can be useful if you want to limit a script to run on a particular PHP release.

Summary

This hour covered some of the basic features of the PHP language. You learned about variables and how to assign to them using the assignment operator. You were introduced to operators and learned how to combine some of the most common of these into expressions. Finally, you learned how to define and access constants.

Now that you have mastered some of the fundamentals of PHP, the next hour will really put you in the driver's seat. You will learn how to make scripts that can make decisions and repeat tasks, with help of course from variables, expressions, and operators.

Q&A

Q *Why can it be useful to know the type of data a variable holds?*

A Often the data type of a variable constrains what you can do with it. You might want to ensure that a variable contains an integer or a double before using it in a mathematical calculation, for example.

Q *Should I obey any conventions when naming variables?*

A Your goal should always be to make your code easy to both read and understand. A variable such as $ab123245 tells you nothing about its role in your script and invites typos. Keep your variable names short and descriptive.

A variable named $f is unlikely to mean much to you when you return to your code after a month or so. A variable named $filename, on the other hand, should make more sense.

Q *Should I learn the operator precedence table?*

A There is no reason why you shouldn't, but I would save the effort for more useful tasks. By using parentheses in your expressions, you can make your code easy to read at the same time as defining your own order of precedence.

Workshop

Quiz

1. Which of the following variable names is not valid?

```
$a_value_submitted_by_a_user
$666666xyz
$xyz666666
$____counter____
$the first
$file-name
```

2. What will the following code fragment output?

```
$num = 33;
(boolean) $num;
print $num;
```

3. What will the following statement output?

```
print gettype("4");
```

4. What will be the output from the following code fragment?

```
$test_val = 5.4566;
settype( $test_val, "integer" );
print $test_val;
```

5. Which of the following statements does not contain an expression?

```
4;
gettype(44);
5/12;
```

6. Which of the statements in question 5 contains an operator?

7. What value will the following expression return, and what data type will the returned value be?

```
5 < 2
```

Answers

1. The variable name $666666xyz is not valid because it does not begin with a letter or an underscore character. The variable name $the first is not valid because it contains a space. $file-name is also invalid because it contains a nonalphanumeric character.

2. The fragment will print the integer 33. The cast to boolean produced a converted copy of the value stored in $num. It did not alter the value actually stored there.

3. The statement will output the string "string".

4. The code will output the value 5. When a double is converted to an integer, any information beyond the decimal point is lost.

5. They are all expressions because they all resolve to values.

6. The statement 5/12; contains a division operator.

7. The expression will resolve to false, which is a boolean value.

Exercises

1. Create a script that contains at least five different variables. Populate them with values of different data types and use the gettype() function to print each type to the browser.

2. Assign values to two variables. Use comparison operators to test whether the first value is

- ▶ The same as the second
- ▶ Less than the second
- ▶ Greater than the second
- ▶ Less than or equal to the second

Print the result of each test to the browser.

Change the values assigned to your test variables and run the script again.

HOUR 5

Going with the Flow

What You'll Learn in This Hour:

▶ How to use the `if` statement to execute code only when a condition is met

▶ How to execute alternative blocks of code when the condition of an `if` statement is not met

▶ How to use the `switch` statement to execute code based on the value returned by a test expression

▶ How to repeat execution of code using a `while` statement

▶ How to use `for` statements to make neater loops

▶ How to break out of loops

▶ How to nest one loop within another

▶ How to use PHP's start and end tags within control structures

The scripts created in the last hour flow only in a single direction. The same statements are executed in the same order every time a script is run. This does not leave much room for flexibility. We now will look at some structures that enable your scripts to adapt to circumstances.

Switching Flow

Most scripts evaluate conditions and change their behavior accordingly. This facility to make decisions makes your PHP pages dynamic, capable of changing their output according to circumstances. In common with most programming languages, PHP enables you to do this with an `if` statement.

if **Statement**

An if statement is a way of controlling the execution of a statement that follows it (that is, a single statement or a block of code inside braces). The if statement evaluates an expression between parentheses. If this expression results in a true value, the statement is executed. Otherwise, the statement is skipped entirely. This enables scripts to make decisions based on any number of factors.

In the following fragment, we show the structure of an if statement. The test expression is represented by the string 'expression':

```
if ( expression ) {
  // code to execute if the expression evaluates to true
}
```

Listing 5.1 executes a block of code only if a variable contains the string "very".

LISTING 5.1 An if **Statement**

```
 1: <!DOCTYPE html PUBLIC
 2:   "-//W3C//DTD XHTML 1.0 Strict//EN"
 3:   "http://www.w3.org/TR/xhtml1/DTD/xhtml1-strict.dtd">
 4: <html>
 5: <head>
 6: <title>Listing 5.1 An if Statement</title>
 7: </head>
 8: <body>
 9: <div>
10: <?php
11: $satisfied = "very";
12: if ( $satisfied == "very" ) {
13:   print "We are pleased that you are happy with our service";
14:   // register customer satisfaction in some way
15: }
16: ?>
17: </div>
18: </body>
19: </html>
```

You use the comparison operator (==) to compare the variable $satisfied with the string "very". If they match, the expression evaluates to true and the code block below the if statement is executed. Although the code block is wrapped in braces in the example, this is only necessary if the block contains more than one line. The following fragment, therefore, would be acceptable:

```
if ( $satisfied == "very" )
  print "We are pleased that you are happy with our service";
```

> Style guides often discourage the omission of braces from single-line code blocks. Using braces, it is argued, promotes readability and guards against errors that might occur when adding new lines to previously single-line code blocks.

By the Way

If you change the value of $satisfied to "no" and run the script, the expression in the if statement evaluates to false and the code block is skipped. The script remains sulkily silent.

Using the else Clause with the if Statement

When working with the if statement, you will often want to define an alternative block of code that should be executed if the expression you are testing evaluates to false. You can do this by adding else to the if statement followed by a further block of code, like so:

```
if ( expression ) {
  // code to execute if the expression evaluates to true
} else {
  // code to execute in all other cases
}
```

Listing 5.2 amends the example in Listing 5.1 so that a default block of code is executed if $satisfied is not equivalent to "very".

LISTING 5.2 An if Statement That Uses else

```
1: <!DOCTYPE html PUBLIC
2:   "-//W3C//DTD XHTML 1.0 Strict//EN"
3:   "http://www.w3.org/TR/xhtml1/DTD/xhtml1-strict.dtd">
4: <html>
5: <head>
6: <title>Listing 5.2 An if Statement That Uses else</title>
7: </head>
8: <body>
9: <div>
10: <?php
11: // $satisfied = "very";
12: if ( $satisfied == "very" ) {
13:   print "We are pleased that you are happy with our service";
14:   // register customer satisfaction in some way
15: } else {
16:   print "Please take a moment to rate our service";
17:   // present pulldown
18: }
19: ?>
20: </div>
21: </body>
22: </html>
```

Notice that the assignment to the $satisfied variable on line 11 has been commented out, so the expression in the if statement in line 12 evaluates to false. This means the first block of code (line 13) is skipped. The block of code after else, therefore, is executed and the message "Please take a moment to rate our service" is printed to the browser.

Using the else clause with the if statement enables scripts to make sophisticated decisions, but you currently are limited to an either-or branch. PHP allows you to evaluate multiple expressions one after the other.

Using the else if Clause with the if Statement

You can use an if/else else/if construct to test multiple expressions before offering a default block of code:

```
if ( expression ) {
  // code to execute if the expression evaluates to true
} else if ( another expression ) {
  // code to execute if the previous expression failed
  // and this one evaluates to true
} else {
  // code to execute in all other cases
}
```

If the first expression does not evaluate to true, the first block of code is ignored. The else if clause then causes another expression to be evaluated. Once again, if this expression evaluates to true, the second block of code is executed. Otherwise, the block of code associated with the else clause is executed. You can include as many else if clauses as you want, and if you don't need a default action, you can omit the else clause.

By the Way

> The else if clause can also be written as a single word: elseif. The syntax you employ is a matter of taste.

Listing 5.3 adds an else if clause to the previous example.

LISTING 5.3   An if statement That Uses else and else if

```
1: <!DOCTYPE html PUBLIC
2:   "-//W3C//DTD XHTML 1.0 Strict//EN"
3:   "http://www.w3.org/TR/xhtml1/DTD/xhtml1-strict.dtd">
4: <html>
5: <head>
6: <title>Listing 5.3 An if statement That Uses else and else if</title>
7: </head>
8: <body>
9: <div>
```

LISTING 5.3   Continued

```
10: <?php
11: $satisfied = "no";
12: if ( $satisfied == "very" ) {
13:   print "We are pleased that you are happy with our service";
14:   // register customer satisfaction in some way
15: } else if ( $satisfied == "no" ) {
16:   print "We are sorry that we have not met your expectations";
17:   // request further feedback
18: } else {
19:   print "Please take a moment to rate our service";
20:   // present pulldown
21: }
22: ?>
23: </div>
24: </body>
25: </html>
```

Once again, $satisfied holds a string ("no") in line 11. This is not equivalent to "very", so the first block in line 13 is ignored. The else if clause in line 15 tests for equivalence between the contents of $satisfied and "no", which evaluates to true. This block of code is therefore executed. From line 18, we provide default behavior. If none of the test conditions have been fulfilled, we simply print a message requesting input.

The switch Statement

The switch statement is an alternative way of changing program flow according to the evaluation of an expression. Some key differences exist between the switch and if statements. Using the if statement in conjunction with else if, you can evaluate multiple expressions. switch evaluates only one expression, executing different code according to the result of that expression, as long as the expression evaluates to a simple type (a number, string, or Boolean). The result of an expression evaluated as part of an if statement is read as either true or false, whereas the expression of a switch statement yields a result that is tested against any number of values, as shown here:

```
switch ( expression ) {
    case result1:
      // execute this if expression results in result1
      break;
    case result2:
      // execute this if expression results in result2
      break;
    default:
      // execute this if no break statement
      // has been encountered hitherto
}
```

The switch statement's expression is often simply a variable. Within the switch statement's block of code, you find a number of case statements. Each of these tests a value against the result of the switch statement's expression. If these are equivalent, the code after the case statement is executed. The break statement ends execution of the switch statement altogether. If this is omitted, the next case statement's expression is evaluated. If the optional default statement is reached, its code is executed.

Watch Out!

In most circumstances, don't forget to include a break statement at the end of any code that will be executed as part of a case statement. Without break, the program flow continues to the next case statement and ultimately to the default statement. In most cases, this is not the behavior you expect.

Having said that, this feature can also be used to your advantage. In particular, you might want to omit a break for a case statement so that multiple tests can result in a single action. In the following fragment, we group case conditions together in this way:

```
switch ( $satisfied ) {
    case "very":
    case "quite":
    case "almost":
        print "We are pleased...";
        break;

    case "disatisfied":
    case "no":
    case "unhappy":
        print "We are sorry...";
        break;
    // ...
}
```

Be aware of your breaks!

Listing 5.4 re-creates the functionality of the if statement example, using the switch statement.

LISTING 5.4   A switch **Statement**

```
1: <!DOCTYPE html PUBLIC
2:   "-//W3C//DTD XHTML 1.0 Strict//EN"
3:   "http://www.w3.org/TR/xhtml1/DTD/xhtml1-strict.dtd">
4: <html>
5: <head>
6: <title>Listing 5.4 A switch Statement</title>
7: </head>
8: <body>
9: <div>
10: <?php
11: $satisfied = "no";
12: switch ( $satisfied ) {
```

LISTING 5.4   Continued

```
13:    case "very":
14:        print "We are pleased that you are happy with our service";
15:        break;
16:    case "no":
17:        print "We are sorry that we have not met your expectations";
18:        break;
19:    default:
20:        print "Please take a moment to rate our service";
21: }
22: ?>
23: </div>
24: </body>
25: </html>
```

In line 11 the $satisfied variable is initialized to "no", and the switch statement in line 12 uses this variable as its expression. The first case statement in line 13 tests for equivalence between "very" and the value of $satisfied. There is no match, so script execution moves on to the second case statement in line 16. The string "no" is equivalent to the value of $satisfied, so this block of code is executed. The break statement in line 18 ends the process.

Using the ? Operator

The ?, or **ternary**, operator is similar to the if statement but returns a value derived from one of two expressions separated by a colon. Which expression is used to generate the value returned depends on the result of a test expression:

```
( expression )?returned_if_expression_is_true:returned_if_expression_is_false;
```

If the test expression evaluates to true, the result of the second expression is returned; otherwise, the value of the third expression is returned. Listing 5.5 uses the ternary operator to set the value of a variable according to the value of $satisfied.

LISTING 5.5   Using the ? Operator

```
 1: <!DOCTYPE html PUBLIC
 2:    "-//W3C//DTD XHTML 1.0 Strict//EN"
 3:    "http://www.w3.org/TR/xhtml1/DTD/xhtml1-strict.dtd">
 4: <html>
 5: <head>
 6: <title>Listing 5.5 Using the ? Operator</title>
 7: </head>
 8: <body>
 9: <div>
10: <?php
11: $satisfied = "no";
12:
```

LISTING 5.5   Continued

```
13: $pleased = "We are pleased that you are happy with our service";
14: $sorry = "We are sorry that we have not met your expectations";
15:
16: $text = ( $satisfied=="very" )?$pleased:$sorry;
17: print "$text";
18: ?>
19: </div>
20: </body>
21: </html>
```

In line 11, $satisfied is set to "no". Then, in line 16, $satisfied is tested for equivalence to the string "very". Because this test returns false, the result of the third of the three expressions is returned. Note that variables are used on lines 13 and 14 to store the alternative output strings. This makes the code more readable than it would be with the strings embedded in the ternary statement.

The ternary operator can be difficult to read but is useful if you are dealing with only two alternatives and like to write compact code.

Loops

So far we've looked at decisions a script can make about which code to execute. Scripts can also decide how many times to execute a block of code. **Loop** statements enable you to achieve repetitive tasks. Almost without exception, a loop continues to operate until either a condition is achieved or you explicitly choose to exit the loop.

The while Statement

The while statement looks similar in structure to a basic if statement:

```
while ( expression ) {
    // do something
}
```

As long as a while statement's expression evaluates to true, the code block is executed repeatedly. Each execution of the code block in a loop is often called an **iteration**. Within the block, you usually change something that affects the while statement's expression; otherwise, your loop continues indefinitely. Listing 5.6 creates a while loop that calculates and prints multiples of 2 up to 24.

LISTING 5.6 A while Statement

```
 1: <!DOCTYPE html PUBLIC
 2:    "-//W3C//DTD XHTML 1.0 Strict//EN"
 3:    "http://www.w3.org/TR/xhtml1/DTD/xhtml1-strict.dtd">
 4: <html>
 5: <head>
 6: <title>Listing 5.6 A while Statement</title>
 7: </head>
 8: <body>
 9: <div>
10: <?php
11: $counter = 1;
12: while ( $counter <= 12 ) {
13:    print "$counter times 2 is ".($counter*2)."<br />";
14:    $counter++;
15: }
16: ?>
17: </div>
18: </body>
19: </html>
```

In this example, we initialize a variable called $counter in line 11. The while statement in line 12 tests the $counter variable. As long as the integer contained by $counter is smaller than or equal to 12, the loop continues to run. Within the while statement's code block, the value contained by $counter is multiplied by 2, and the result is printed to the browser. $counter is incremented in line 14. This last stage is extremely important: If you were to forget to change $counter, the while expression would never resolve to false and the loop would never end.

The do...while **Statement**

A do...while statement looks a little like a while statement turned on its head. The essential difference between the two is that the code block is executed before the truth test and not after it, like so:

```
do  {
   // code to be executed
} while ( expression );
```

> The test expression of a do...while statement should always end with a semi-colon.
>
> **By the Way**

This statement might be useful if you want the code block to be executed at least once even if the while expression evaluates to false. Listing 5.7 creates a do...while statement in which the code block is executed a minimum of one time.

LISTING 5.7   The do...while **Statement**

```
1: <!DOCTYPE html PUBLIC
2:    "-//W3C//DTD XHTML 1.0 Strict//EN"
3:    "http://www.w3.org/TR/xhtml1/DTD/xhtml1-strict.dtd">
4: <html>
5: <head>
6: <title>Listing 5.7 The do...while Statement</title>
7: </head>
8: <body>
9: <div>
10: <?php
11: $num = 1;
12: do {
13:   print "Execution number: $num<br />\n";
14:   $num++;
15: } while ( $num > 200 && $num < 400 );
16: ?>
17: </div>
18: </body>
19: </html>
```

The do...while statement tests whether the variable $num contains a value that is greater than 200 and smaller than 400. In line 11, we have initialized $num to 1 so this expression returns false. Nonetheless, the code block is executed before the expression is evaluated, so the statement prints a single line to the browser.

The for **Statement**

You cannot achieve anything with a for statement that you could not also manage with a while statement. On the other hand, the for statement is often a neater and safer way of achieving the same effect. Earlier, Listing 5.6 initialized a variable outside the while statement. The while statement then tested the variable in its expression, and the variable was incremented within the code block. The for statement enables you to achieve this on a single line, making your code more compact and making it less likely that you'll forget to increment a counter variable, thereby creating an infinite loop. Here's its syntax:

```
for ( initialization expression; test expression; modification expression ) {
  // code to be executed
}
```

Each expression within the parentheses of the for statement is separated by a semicolon. Usually, the first expression initializes a counter variable, the second expression is the test condition for the loop, and the third expression increments the counter. Listing 5.8 shows a for statement that re-creates the example in Listing 5.6, which multiplies 12 numbers by 2.

LISTING 5.8 Using the for Statement

```
 1: <!DOCTYPE html PUBLIC
 2:   "-//W3C//DTD XHTML 1.0 Strict//EN"
 3:   "http://www.w3.org/TR/xhtml1/DTD/xhtml1-strict.dtd">
 4: <html>
 5: <head>
 6: <title>Listing 5.8 Using the for Statement</title>
 7: </head>
 8: <body>
 9: <div>
10: <?php
11: for ( $counter=1; $counter<=12; $counter++ ) {
12:   print "$counter times 2 is ".($counter*2)."<br />";
13: }
14: ?>
15: </div>
16: </body>
17: </html>
```

The results of Listings 5.6 and 5.8 are exactly the same. The for statement, though, makes the code more compact. Because $counter is initialized and incremented at the top of the statement, the logic of the loop is clear at a glance. In line 11, within the for statement's parentheses, the first expression initializes the $counter variable and sets it to 1. The test expression checks that $counter contains a value that is less than or equal to 12; then the final expression increments the $counter variable.

When program flow reaches the for loop, the $counter variable is initialized and the test expression is evaluated. If the expression evaluates to true, the code block is executed. The $counter variable is then incremented and the test expression evaluated again. This process continues until the test expression evaluates to false.

Breaking Out of Loops with the break **Statement**

Both while and for statements incorporate a built-in test expression with which you can end a loop. The break statement, though, enables you to break out of a loop according to additional tests. This can provide a safeguard against error. Listing 5.9 creates a simple for statement that divides a large number by a variable that is incremented, printing the result to the screen.

LISTING 5.9 A for Loop That Divides 4000 by Ten Incremental Numbers

```
 1: <!DOCTYPE html PUBLIC
 2:   "-//W3C//DTD XHTML 1.0 Strict//EN"
 3:   "http://www.w3.org/TR/xhtml1/DTD/xhtml1-strict.dtd">
 4: <html>
 5: <head>
 6: <title>Listing 5.9 A for Loop That Divides Ten Numbers</title>
 7: </head>
```

LISTING 5.9   Continued

```
 8: <body>
 9: <div>
10: <?php
11: for ( $counter=1; $counter <= 10; $counter++ ) {
12:    $temp = 4000/$counter;
13:    print "4000 divided by $counter is.. $temp<br />";
14: }
15: ?>
16: </div>
17: </body>
18: </html>
```

In line 11, this example initializes the variable $counter to 1. The for statement's test expression checks that $counter is smaller than or equal to 10. Within the code block, 4000 is divided by $counter, printing the result to the browser.

This seems straightforward enough. But what if the value you place in $counter comes from user input? The value could be a minus number or even a string. Let's take the first instance. Changing the initial value of $counter from 1 to –4 causes 4000 to be divided by 0 as the code block is executed for the fifth time, which is not advisable. Listing 5.10 guards against this by breaking out of the loop if the $counter variable contains 0.

LISTING 5.10   Using the break Statement

```
 1: <!DOCTYPE html PUBLIC
 2:    "-//W3C//DTD XHTML 1.0 Strict//EN"
 3:    "http://www.w3.org/TR/xhtml1/DTD/xhtml1-strict.dtd">
 4: <html>
 5: <head>
 6: <title>Listing 5.10 Using the break Statement</title>
 7: </head>
 8: <body>
 9: <div>
10: <?php
11: $counter = -4;
12: for ( ; $counter <= 10; $counter++ ) {
13:    if ( $counter == 0 ) {
14:       break;
15:    }
16:    $temp = 4000/$counter;
17:    print "4000 divided by $counter is.. $temp<br />";
18: }
19: ?>
20: </div>
21: </body>
22: </html>
```

> Dividing a number by zero does not cause a fatal error in PHP. Instead, a warning is generated and execution continues.

By the Way

We use an if statement, shown in line 13, to test the value of $counter. If it is equivalent to zero, the break statement immediately halts execution of the code block and program flow continues after the for statement.

Notice that we initialized the $counter variable in line 11, outside the for statement's parentheses, to simulate a situation in which the value of $counter is set according to form input or a database lookup.

> You can omit any of the expressions of a for statement, but you must remember to retain the semicolons.

Did you Know?

Skipping an Iteration with the continue Statement

The continue statement ends execution of the current iteration but doesn't cause the loop as a whole to end. Instead, the next iteration is immediately begun. Using the break statement in Listing 5.10 is a little drastic. With the continue statement in Listing 5.11, you can avoid a divide-by-zero error without ending the loop completely.

LISTING 5.11   Using the continue Statement

```
 1: <!DOCTYPE html PUBLIC
 2:   "-//W3C//DTD XHTML 1.0 Strict//EN"
 3:   "http://www.w3.org/TR/xhtml1/DTD/xhtml1-strict.dtd">
 4: <html>
 5: <head>
 6: <title>Listing 5.11 Using the continue Statement</title>
 7: </head>
 8: <body>
 9: <div>
10: <?php
11: $counter = -4;
12: for ( ; $counter <= 10; $counter++ ) {
13:   if ( $counter == 0 ) {
14:     continue;
15:   }
16:   $temp = 4000/$counter;
17:   print "4000 divided by $counter is.. $temp<br />";
18: }
19: ?>
20: </div>
21: </body>
22: </html>
```

In line 14, we have swapped the break statement for a continue statement. If the $counter variable is equivalent to zero, the iteration is skipped and the next one immediately is started.

> The break and continue statements can make code more difficult to read. Because they often add layers of complexity to the logic of the loop statements that contain them, they are best used with care.

Nesting Loops

Loop statements can contain other loop statements. This combination is particularly useful when working with dynamically created HTML tables. Listing 5.12 uses two for statements to print a multiplication table to the browser.

LISTING 5.12   Nesting Two for Loops

```
 1: <!DOCTYPE html PUBLIC
 2:   "-//W3C//DTD XHTML 1.0 Strict//EN"
 3:   "http://www.w3.org/TR/xhtml1/DTD/xhtml1-strict.dtd">
 4: <html>
 5: <head>
 6: <title>Listing 5.12 Nesting Two for Loops</title>
 7: </head>
 8: <body>
 9: <div>
10: <?php
11: print "<table border=\"1\">\n";
12: for ( $y=1; $y<=12; $y++ ) {
13:    print "<tr>\n";
14:    for ( $x=1; $x<=12; $x++ ) {
15:       print "\t<td>";
16:       print ($x*$y);
17:       print "</td>\n";
18:    }
19:    print "</tr>\n";
20: }
21: print "</table>";
22: ?>
23: </div>
24: </body>
25: </html>
```

Before we examine the for loops, let's take a closer look at line 11 in Listing 5.12:

```
print "<table border=\"1\">\n";
```

Notice that we have used the backslash character (\) before each of the quotation marks within the string. This is necessary to tell the PHP engine we want to quote the quotation character, rather than interpret it as the beginning or end of a string. If we did not do this, the statement would not make sense to the engine, consisting as it would of a string followed by a number followed by another string. This would generate an error. You will encounter this backslash technique, known as *escaping*, again in Hour 7, "Arrays."

The outer for statement (line 12) initializes a variable called $y, setting its starting value to 1. It defines an expression that tests whether $y is smaller or equal to 12 and defines the increment for $y. For each iteration, the code block prints a TR (table row) HTML element (line 13) and defines another for statement (line 14). This inner loop initializes a variable called $x and defines expressions along the same lines as for the outer loop. For each iteration, the inner loop prints a TD (table cell) element to the browser (line 15), as well as the result of $x multiplied by $y (line 16). In line 17, we close the table cell. After the inner loop has completed, we fall back through to the outer loop where we close the table row on line 19, ready for the process to begin again. When the outer loop has finished, the result is a neatly formatted multiplication table. We wrap things up by closing the table on line 21.

Code Blocks and Browser Output

In Hour 3, "A First Script," we established that you can slip in and out of HTML mode at will, using the PHP start and end tags. In this chapter you have discovered that you can present distinct output to the user according to a decision-making process you can control with if and switch statements. In this section, we will combine these two techniques.

Imagine a script that outputs a table of values only when a variable is set to the Boolean value true. Listing 5.13 shows a simplified HTML table constructed with the code block of an if statement.

LISTING 5.13   A Code Block Containing Multiple print() Statements

```
1: <!DOCTYPE html PUBLIC
2:   "-//W3C//DTD XHTML 1.0 Strict//EN"
3:   "http://www.w3.org/TR/xhtml1/DTD/xhtml1-strict.dtd">
4: <html>
5: <head>
6: <title>Listing 5.13 A Code Block Containing Multiple print()
statements</title>
7: </head>
8: <body>
9: <div>
10: <?php
11: $display_prices = true;
12:
```

LISTING 5.13   Continued

```
13: if ( $display_prices ) {
14:    print "<table border=\"1\">";
15:    print "<tr><td colspan=\"3\">";
16:    print "todays prices in dollars";
17:    print "</td></tr><tr>";
18:    print "<td>14</td><td>32</td><td>71</td>";
19:    print "</tr></table>";
20: }
21:
22: ?>
23: </div>
24: </body>
25: </html>
```

If $display_prices is set to true in line 11, the table is printed. For the sake of
readability, we split the output into multiple print() statements, and once again
we escape any quotation marks. There's nothing wrong with that, but we can
save ourselves some typing by simply slipping back into HTML mode within the
code block. In Listing 5.14, we do just that.

LISTING 5.14   Returning to HTML Mode Within a Code Block

```
 1: <!DOCTYPE html PUBLIC
 2:    "-//W3C//DTD XHTML 1.0 Strict//EN"
 3:    "http://www.w3.org/TR/xhtml1/DTD/xhtml1-strict.dtd">
 4: <html>
 5: <head>
 6: <title>Listing 5.14 Returning to HTML Mode Within a Code Block</title>
 7: </head>
 8: <body>
 9: <div>
10: <?php
11: $display_prices = true;
12:
13: if ( $display_prices ) {
14: ?>
15:    <table border="1">
16:    <tr><td colspan="3">todays prices in dollars</td></tr><tr>
17:    <td>14</td><td>32</td><td>71</td>
18:    </tr></table>
19: <?php
20: }
21:
22: ?>
23: </div>
24: </body>
25: </html>
```

The important thing to note here is that the shift to HTML mode on line 14 occurs only if the condition of the if statement is fulfilled. This can save you the bother of escaping quotation marks and wrapping your output in print() statements. It might, however, affect the readability of your code in the long run, especially as your script begins to grow.

Summary

In this hour, you learned about control structures and the ways in which they can help make your scripts flexible and dynamic. Most of these structures will reappear regularly throughout the rest of the book.

You learned how to define an if statement and how to provide for alternative actions with the else if and else clauses. You learned how to use the switch statement to change flow according to multiple equivalence tests on the result of an expression. You also learned about loops—in particular, the while and for statements—and learned how to use break and continue to prematurely end the execution of a loop or skip an iteration. You learned how to nest one loop within another and saw a typical use for this structure. Finally, you looked at a technique for using PHP start and end tags in conjunction with conditional code blocks.

You should now have enough information to write scripts of your own. Your scripts can now make decisions and perform repetitive tasks. In the next hour, we will examine a way of adding even more power to your applications. Functions will enable you to organize your code, preventing duplication and improving reusability.

Q&A

Q *Must a control structure's test expression result in a Boolean value?*

A Ultimately, yes. However, in the context of a test expression, zero, an undefined variable, or an empty string is converted to false for the purposes of the test. All other values evaluate to true.

Q *Must I always surround a code block in a control statement with brackets?*

A If the code you want executed as part of a control structure consists of only a single line, you can omit the brackets. The code examples in this book retain brackets to promote readability. Retaining the brackets for single-line control statements can also help guard against bugs as new lines are added to the block over time.

Q *Does this hour cover every kind of loop there is?*

A No. In Hour 7, you'll encounter the `foreach` statement, which enables you to loop through every element in an array.

Workshop

Quiz

1. How would you use an `if` statement to print the string `"Youth message"` to the browser if an integer variable, $age, is between 18 and 35? If $age contains any other value, the string `"Generic message"` should be printed to the browser.

2. How would you extend your code in question 1 to print the string `"Child message"` if the $age variable is between 1 and 17?

3. How would you create a `while` statement that prints every odd number between 1 and 49?

4. How would you convert the `while` statement you created in question 3 into a `for` statement?

Answers

1. ```
$age = 22;

if ($age >= 18 && $age <= 35) {
  print "Youth message
\n";
} else {
  print "Generic message
\n";
}
```

2. ```
$age = 12;

if ( $age >= 18 && $age <= 35 ) {
  print "Youth message<br />\n";
} else if ( $age >= 1 && $age <= 17 ) {
  print "Child message<br />\n";
} else {
  print "Generic message<br />\n";
}
```

3.
```
$num = 1;
while ( $num <= 49 ) {
  print "$num<br />\n";
  $num += 2;
}
```

4.
```
for ( $num = 1; $num <= 49; $num += 2 ) {
  print "$num<br />\n";
}
```

Exercises

1. Review the syntax for control structures. Think about how these techniques will help you in your scripting. Perhaps some of the script ideas you are developing will be capable of behaving in different ways according to user input or will loop to display an HTML table. Start to build the control structures you will be using. Use temporary variables to mimic user input or database queries for the time being.

2. Review the section on the ternary operator. What distinguishes it from the control structures covered in the rest of the chapter? Why might it be useful?

HOUR 6

Functions

What You'll Learn in This Hour:

▶ How to define and call functions
▶ How to pass values to functions and receive values in return
▶ How to call a function dynamically using a string stored in a variable
▶ How to access global variables from within a function
▶ How to give a function a "memory"
▶ How to pass data to functions by reference
▶ How to create anonymous functions
▶ How to check that a function exists before calling it

Functions are the heart of a well-organized script, making code easy to read and reuse. No large project would be manageable without them.

Throughout this hour, we will investigate functions and demonstrate some of the ways in which they can save you from repetitive work.

What Is a Function?

You can think of a function as a machine. A machine takes the raw materials you feed it and works with them to achieve a purpose or produce a product. A function accepts values from you, processes them, and then performs an action (printing to the browser, for example) or returns a new value, possibly both.

If you needed to bake a single cake, you would probably do it yourself. If you needed to bake thousands of cakes, you would probably build or acquire a cake-baking machine. Similarly, when deciding whether to create a function, the most important factor to consider is the extent to which it can save you from repetition.

A **function**, then, is a self-contained block of code that can be called by your scripts. When called, the function's code is executed. You can pass values to functions, which they then work with. When finished, a function can pass a value back to the calling code.

Calling Functions

Functions come in two flavors—those built in to the language and those you define yourself. PHP has hundreds of built-in functions. One of the earliest scripts in this book used the gettype() function:

```
gettype( $testing );
```

We called gettype() and passed it the $testing variable. The function then went about the business of testing the variable. A function call consists of the function name—gettype in this case—followed by parentheses. If you want to pass information to the function, you place it between these parentheses. A piece of information passed to a function in this way is called an **argument**. Some functions require that more than one argument be passed to them. Arguments in these cases must be separated by commas, like so:

```
some_function( $an_argument, $another_argument );
```

gettype() is typical in that it returns a value. Most functions give you some information back when they've completed their task, if only to tell you whether their mission was successful. gettype() reports on its testing by returning a string that contains the type of the argument it was passed.

abs() is another example of a built-in function. It requires a signed numeric value and returns the absolute value of that number. Let's try it in Listing 6.1.

LISTING 6.1   Calling the Built-in abs() Function

```
 1: <!DOCTYPE html PUBLIC
 2:    "-//W3C//DTD XHTML 1.0 Strict//EN"
 3:    "http://www.w3.org/TR/xhtml1/DTD/xhtml1-strict.dtd">
 4: <html>
 5: <head>
 6: <title>Listing 6.1 Calling the Built-in abs() function</title>
 7: </head>
 8: <body>
 9: <div>
10: <?php
11: $num = -321;
12: $newnum = abs( $num );
13: print $newnum;
14: // prints "321"
```

LISTING 6.1 Continued

```
15: ?>
16: </div>
17: </body>
18: </html>
```

In this example, we assign the value -321 to a variable $num. We then pass that variable to the abs() function, which makes the necessary calculation and returns a new value. We assign this to the variable $newnum and print the result. In fact, we could have dispensed with temporary variables altogether, passing our number straight to abs(), and directly printing the result:

```
print( abs( -321 ) );
```

We used the temporary variables $num and $newnum, though, to make each step of the process as clear as possible. Sometimes your code can be made more readable by breaking it up into a greater number of simple expressions.

You can call user-defined functions in exactly the same way we have been calling built-in functions.

Defining a Function

You can define a function using the function statement:

```
function some_function( $argument1, $argument2 ) {
    // function code here
}
```

The name of the function follows the function statement and precedes a set of parentheses. If your function is to require arguments, you must place comma-separated variable names within the parentheses. These variables are filled by the values passed to your function. If your function requires no arguments, you must nevertheless supply the parentheses.

Listing 6.2 declares a function.

LISTING 6.2 Declaring a Function

```
1: <!DOCTYPE html PUBLIC
2:   "-//W3C//DTD XHTML 1.0 Strict//EN"
3:   "http://www.w3.org/TR/xhtml1/DTD/xhtml1-strict.dtd">
4: <html>
5: <head>
6: <title>Listing 6.2 Declaring a Function</title>
7: </head>
8: <body>
```

LISTING 6.2 Continued

```
 9: <div>
10: <?php
11: function bighello() {
12:    print "<h1>HELLO!</h1>";
13: }
14: bighello();
15: ?>
16: </div>
17: </body>
18: </html>
```

The script in Listing 6.2 simply outputs the string "HELLO" wrapped in an HTML
<h1> element. We declare a function, bighello(), that requires no arguments.
Because of this, we leave the parentheses empty. bighello() is a working function but is not terribly useful. Listing 6.3 creates a function that requires an argument and actually does something helpful with it.

LISTING 6.3 Declaring a Function That Requires Arguments

```
 1: <!DOCTYPE html PUBLIC
 2:    "-//W3C//DTD XHTML 1.0 Strict//EN"
 3:    "http://www.w3.org/TR/xhtml1/DTD/xhtml1-strict.dtd">
 4: <html>
 5: <head>
 6: <title>Listing 6.3 Declaring a Function That Requires Arguments</title>
 7: </head>
 8: <body>
 9: <div>
10: <?php
11: function printBR( $txt ) {
12:    print ("$txt<br />\n");
13: }
14: printBR("This is a line");
15: printBR("This is a new line");
16: printBR("This is yet another line");
17: ?>
18: </div>
19: </body>
20: </html>
```

You can see the output from the script in Listing 6.3 in Figure 6.1. In line 11, the
printBR() function expects a string, so we place the variable name $txt between
the parentheses when we declare the function. Whatever is passed to printBR() is
stored in $txt. Within the body of the function, in line 12, we print the $txt variable and append a <br /> element and a newline character to it.

Now when we want to write a line to the browser, such as in line 14, 15, or 16, we
can call printBR() instead of the built-in print(), saving us the bother of typing
the <br /> element.

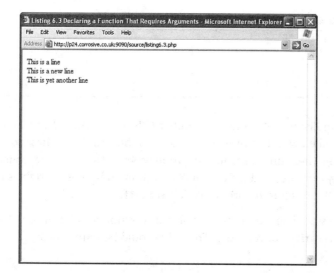

FIGURE 6.1
A function that
prints a string
with an appended

 tag.

Returning Values from User-Defined Functions

In our previous example, we output an amended string to the browser within the printBR() function. Sometimes, however, you will want a function to provide a value you can work with yourself. If your function has transformed a string you have provided, you might want to get the amended string back so you can pass it to other functions. A function can return a value using the return statement in conjunction with a value. return stops the execution of the function and sends the value back to the calling code.

Listing 6.4 creates a function that returns the sum of two numbers.

LISTING 6.4   A Function That Returns a Value

```
1: <!DOCTYPE html PUBLIC
2:    "-//W3C//DTD XHTML 1.0 Strict//EN"
3:    "http://www.w3.org/TR/xhtml1/DTD/xhtml1-strict.dtd">
4: <html>
5: <head>
6: <title>Listing 6.4 A Function That Returns a Value</title>
7: </head>
8: <body>
9: <div>
10: <?php
11: function addNums( $firstnum, $secondnum ) {
12:    $result = $firstnum + $secondnum;
13:    return $result;
14: }
15: print addNums(3,5);
```

LISTING 6.4   Continued

```
16: // will print "8"
17: ?>
18: </div>
19: </body>
20: </html>
```

The script in Listing 6.4 prints the number 8. Notice in line 11 that addNums() should be called with two numeric arguments (line 15 shows those to be 3 and 5 in this case). These are stored in the variables $firstnum and $secondnum. Predictably, addNums() adds the numbers contained in these variables together and stores the result in a variable called $result.

The return statement can return a value or nothing at all. How a value passed by return is arrived at can vary. The value could be hard-coded:

```
return 4;
```

It could also be the result of an expression:

```
return ( $a/$b );
```

Finally, it could be the value returned by yet another function call:

```
return ( another_function( $an_argument ) );
```

Dynamic Function Calls

You can assign function names as strings to variables and then treat these variables exactly as you would the function name itself. Listing 6.5 creates a simple example of this.

LISTING 6.5   Calling a Function Dynamically

```
1: <!DOCTYPE html PUBLIC
2:    "-//W3C//DTD XHTML 1.0 Strict//EN"
3:    "http://www.w3.org/TR/xhtml1/DTD/xhtml1-strict.dtd">
4: <html>
5: <head>
6: <title>Listing 6.5 Calling a Function Dynamically</title>
7: </head>
8: <body>
9: <div>
10: <?php
11: function sayHello() {
12:    print "hello<br />";
13: }
14: $function_holder = "sayHello";
```

LISTING 6.5 Continued

```
15: $function_holder();
16: ?>
17: </div>
18: </body>
19: </html>
```

A string identical to the name of the sayHello() function is assigned to the $function_holder variable on line 14. After this is done, we can use this variable in conjunction with parentheses to call the sayHello() function. We do this on line 15.

Why would we want to do this? In the example, we simply made more work for ourselves by assigning the string "sayHello" to $function_holder. Dynamic function calls are useful when you want to alter program flow according to changing circumstances. We might want our script to behave differently according to a parameter set in a URL's query string, for example. We could extract the value of this parameter and use it to call one of a number of functions.

PHP's built-in functions also use this feature. The array_walk() function, for example, uses a string to call a function for every element in an array. You can see an example of array walk() in action in Hour 7, "Arrays."

Variable Scope

A variable declared within a function remains local to that function. In other words, it will not be available outside the function or within other functions. In larger projects, this can save you from accidentally overwriting the contents of a variable when you declare two variables of the same name in separate functions.

Listing 6.6 creates a variable within a function and then attempts to print it outside the function.

LISTING 6.6 Variable Scope: A Variable Declared Within a Function Is Unavailable Outside the Function

```
1: <!DOCTYPE html PUBLIC
2:    "-//W3C//DTD XHTML 1.0 Strict//EN"
3:    "http://www.w3.org/TR/xhtml1/DTD/xhtml1-strict.dtd">
4: <html>
5: <head>
6: <title>Listing 6.6 Local Variable Unavailable Outside a Function</title>
7: </head>
8: <body>
9: <div>
10: <?php
11: function test() {
```

LISTING 6.6   Continued

```
12:   $testvariable = "this is a test variable";
13: }
14: print "test variable: $testvariable<br/>";
15: ?>
16: </div>
17: </body>
18: </html>
```

You can see the output of the script in Listing 6.6 in Figure 6.2. The value of the variable $testvariable is not printed because no such variable exists outside the test() function. Note that the attempt in line 14 to access a nonexistent variable does not cause an error.

By the Way

Attempting to access an undefined variable causes a NOTICE to be generated. A NOTICE is an error message associated with nonfatal error conditions. By default, NOTICE messages are not displayed. This behavior is dependent on the php.ini error_reporting directive, however. If error_reporting is set to include the E_NOTICE flag, such messages are displayed.

You can enable all error messages apart from NOTICE messages by altering the error_reporting flag in your php.ini file as follows:

```
error_reporting = E_ALL & ~E_NOTICE
```

FIGURE 6.2
Attempting to reference a variable defined within a function.

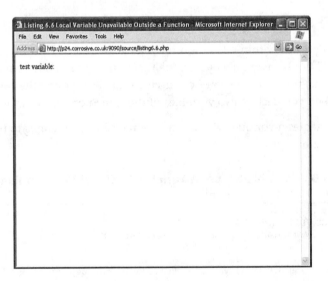

Similarly, a variable declared outside a function is not automatically available within it.

Accessing Variables with the `global` **Statement**

From within a function, by default you can't access a variable that has been defined elsewhere. If you attempt to use a variable of the same name, you will set or access a local variable only. Let's put this to the test in Listing 6.7.

LISTING 6.7 Variables Defined Outside Functions Are Inaccessible from Within a Function by Default

```
1: <!DOCTYPE html PUBLIC
 2:   "-//W3C//DTD XHTML 1.0 Strict//EN"
 3:   "http://www.w3.org/TR/xhtml1/DTD/xhtml1-strict.dtd">
 4: <html>
 5: <head>
 6: <title>Listing 6.7 No Default Access to Globals in Functions</title>
 7: </head>
 8: <body>
 9: <div>
10: <?php
11: $life = 42;
12: function meaningOfLife() {
13:   print "The meaning of life is $life<br />";
14: }
15: meaningOfLife();
16: ?>
17: </div>
18: </body>
19: </html>
```

You can see the output from the script in Listing 6.7 in Figure 6.3. As you might expect, the `meaningOfLife()` function has no access to the `$life` variable from line 11; `$life` is empty when the function attempts to print it. On the whole, this is a good thing. We're saved from potential clashes between identically named variables, and a function can always demand an argument if it needs information about the outside world. Occasionally, however, you might want to access an important global variable from within a function without passing it in as an argument. This is where the `global` statement comes into its own. Listing 6.8 uses `global` to restore order to the universe.

LISTING 6.8 Accessing Global Variables with the `global` **Statement**

```
1: <!DOCTYPE html PUBLIC
 2:   "-//W3C//DTD XHTML 1.0 Strict//EN"
 3:   "http://www.w3.org/TR/xhtml1/DTD/xhtml1-strict.dtd">
 4: <html>
 5: <head>
 6: <title>Listing 6.8 The global Statement</title>
 7: </head>
 8: <body>
 9: <div>
10: <?php
11: $life=42;
```

LISTING 6.8   Continued

```
12:
13: function meaningOfLife() {
14:   global $life;
15:   print "The meaning of life is $life<br />";
16: }
17: meaningOfLife();
18: ?>
19: </div>
20: </body>
21: </html>
```

FIGURE 6.3
Attempting to print a global variable from within a function.

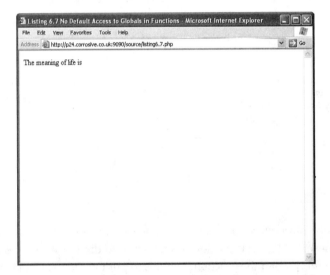

You can see the output from the script in Listing 6.8 in Figure 6.4. By placing global in front of the $life variable when we declare it in the meaning_of_life() function (line 14), we make it refer to the global $life variable declared outside the function (line 11).

You need to use the global statement for every function that wants to access a particular global variable.

Be careful, though. If you manipulate the contents of the variable within the function, $life is changed for the script as a whole.

You can declare more than one variable at a time with the global statement; you simply separate each of the variables you wish to access with commas:

```
global $var1, $var2, $var3;
```

In Hour 10, "Working with Forms," you will encounter the $GLOBALS superglobal array, which is a way of accessing global variables from anywhere in your script.

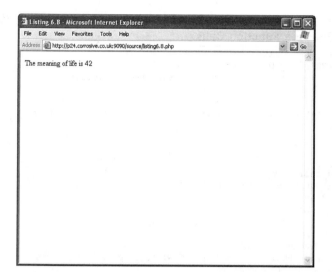

FIGURE 6.4
Successfully
accessing a global
variable from within
a function using the
`global` keyword.

> Usually, an argument is a copy of whatever value is passed by the calling code; changing it in a function has no effect beyond the function block. Changing a global variable within a function, on the other hand, changes the original and not a copy. Use the `global` statement sparingly.

Watch Out!

Saving State Between Function Calls with the `static` Statement

Variables within functions have a short but happy life on the whole. They come into being when the function is called and die when execution is finished. This is as it should be. It is usually best to build a script as a series of self-contained blocks, each with as little knowledge of others as possible. Occasionally, however, you might want to give a function a rudimentary memory.

Let's assume we want a function to keep track of the number of times it has been called. Why? In our examples, the function is designed to create numbered headings in a script that dynamically builds online documentation.

We could, of course, use our newfound knowledge of the `global` statement to do this. We have a crack at this in Listing 6.9.

LISTING 6.9   Using the `global` Statement to Remember the Value of a Variable Between Function Calls

```
 1: <!DOCTYPE html PUBLIC
 2:   "-//W3C//DTD XHTML 1.0 Strict//EN"
 3:   "http://www.w3.org/TR/xhtml1/DTD/xhtml1-strict.dtd">
 4: <html>
 5: <head>
 6: <title>Listing 6.9 Tracking with the global Statement</title>
 7: </head>
 8: <body>
 9: <div>
10: <?php
11: $num_of_calls = 0;
12: function numberedHeading( $txt ) {
13:   global $num_of_calls;
14:   $num_of_calls++;
15:   print "<h1>$num_of_calls. $txt</h1>";
16: }
17: numberedHeading("Widgets");
18: print "<p>We build a fine range of widgets</p>";
19: numberedHeading("Doodads");
20: print "<p>Finest in the world</p>";
21: ?>
22: </div>
23: </body>
24: </html>
```

This does the job. We declare a variable, $num_of_calls, on line 11, outside the function numberedHeading(). We make this variable available to the function with the global statement on line 13. You can see the output of Listing 6.9 in Figure 6.5.

FIGURE 6.5
Using the global statement to keep track of the number of times a function has been called.

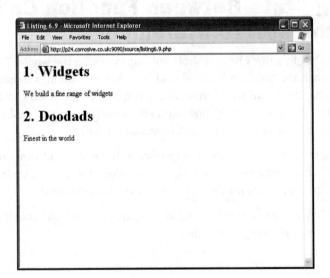

Every time `numberedHeading()` is called, `$num_of_calls` is incremented (line 14). We can then print a heading complete with a heading number.

This is not the most elegant solution, however. Functions that use the `global` statement cannot be read as standalone blocks of code. In reading or reusing them, you need to look out for the global variables they manipulate.

This is where the `static` statement can be useful. If you declare a variable within a function in conjunction with the `static` statement, the variable remains local to the function. On the other hand, the function "remembers" the value of the variable from execution to execution. Listing 6.10 adapts the code from Listing 6.9 to use the `static` statement.

LISTING 6.10   Using the `static` **Statement to Remember the Value of a Variable Between Function Calls**

```
 1: <!DOCTYPE html PUBLIC
 2:   "-//W3C//DTD XHTML 1.0 Strict//EN"
 3:   "http://www.w3.org/TR/xhtml1/DTD/xhtml1-strict.dtd">
 4: <html>
 5: <head>
 6: <title>Listing 6.10 Using the static Statement</title>
 7: </head>
 8: <body>
 9: <div>
10: <?php
11: function numberedHeading( $txt ) {
12:    static $num_of_calls = 0;
13:    $num_of_calls++;
14:    print "<h1>$num_of_calls. $txt</h1>";
15: }
16: ?>
17: numberedHeading("Widgets");
18: print "<p>We build a fine range of widgets</p>";
19: numberedHeading("Doodads");
20: print "<p>Finest in the world</p>";
21: </div>
22: </body>
23: </html>
```

`numberedHeading()` has become entirely self-contained. When we declare the `$num_of_calls` variable on line 12, we assign an initial value to it. This assignment is made when the function is first called on line 17. This initial assignment is ignored when the function is called a second time on line 19. Instead, the previous value of `$num_of_calls` is remembered. We can now paste the `numberedHeading()` function into other scripts without worrying about global variables. Although the output of Listing 6.10 is exactly the same as that for Listing 6.9, we have made the code more elegant.

More About Arguments

You've already seen how to pass arguments to functions, but there's more to cover yet. In this section, you'll look at a technique for giving your arguments default values and explore a method of passing variables by reference rather than by value. This means that the function is given an alias to the original value rather than a copy of it.

Setting Default Values for Arguments

PHP gives you a nifty feature to help build flexible functions. Until now, we've said that some functions demand one or more arguments. By making some arguments optional, you can render your functions a little less autocratic.

Listing 6.11 creates a useful little function that wraps a string in an HTML heading element. We want to give the user of the function the chance to change the heading element's size, so we demand a $size argument in addition to the string (line 10). If the client code provides a $size argument of 1, the string provided in $txt is wrapped in an h1 element and printed. If $size is 2, the string is wrapped in an h2 element, and so on.

LISTING 6.11   A Function Requiring Two Arguments

```
 1: <!DOCTYPE html PUBLIC
 2:   "-//W3C//DTD XHTML 1.0 Strict//EN"
 3:   "http://www.w3.org/TR/xhtml1/DTD/xhtml1-strict.dtd">
 4: <html>
 5: <head>
 6: <title>Listing 6.11</title>
 7: </head>
 8: <body>
 9: <?php
10: function headingWrap( $txt, $size ) {
11:     print "<h$size>$txt</h$size>";
12: }
13: headingWrap("Book title", 1);
14: headingWrap("Chapter title",2);
15: headingWrap("Section heading",3);
16: ?>
17: </body>
18: </html>
```

You can see the output from the script in Listing 6.11 in Figure 6.6. Useful though this function is, we really only need to change the heading size occasionally. Most of the time we would like to default to outputting an h3 element. By assigning a value to an argument variable within the function definition's parentheses, we can make the $size argument optional. If the function call doesn't define an argument for this, the value we have assigned to the argument is used instead. Listing 6.12 uses this technique to make the $size argument optional.

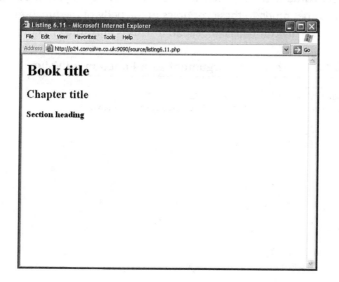

FIGURE 6.6
A function that formats and outputs strings.

LISTING 6.12   **A Function with an Optional Argument**

```
 1: <!DOCTYPE html PUBLIC
 2:    "-//W3C//DTD XHTML 1.0 Strict//EN"
 3:    "http://www.w3.org/TR/xhtml1/DTD/xhtml1-strict.dtd">
 4: <html>
 5: <head>
 6: <title>Listing 6.11</title>
 7: </head>
 8: <body>
 9: <?php
10: function headingWrap( $txt, $size=3 ) {
11:   print "<h$size>$txt</h$size>";
12: }
13: headingWrap("Book title", 1);
14: headingWrap("Chapter title",2);
15: headingWrap("Section heading");
16: headingWrap("Another Section heading");
17: ?>
18: </body>
19: </html>
```

When the headingWrap() function is called with a second argument, as in line 13, this value is used to generate the heading element. When we omit this argument, as in lines 15 and 16, the default value of 3 is used instead. You can create as many optional arguments as you want, but when you've given an argument a default value, all subsequent arguments should also be given defaults.

Passing References to Variables to Functions

When you pass arguments to functions, they are stored as copies in parameter variables. Any changes made to these variables in the body of the function are local to that function and are not reflected beyond it. This is illustrated in Listing 6.13.

LISTING 6.13   Passing an Argument to a Function by Value

```
1: <!DOCTYPE html PUBLIC
2:    "-//W3C//DTD XHTML 1.0 Strict//EN"
3:    "http://www.w3.org/TR/xhtml1/DTD/xhtml1-strict.dtd">
4: <html>
5: <head>
6: <title>Listing 6.13</title>
7: </head>
8: <body>
9: <div>
10: <?php
11: function addFive( $num ) {
12:    $num += 5;
13: }
14: $orignum = 10;
15: addFive( $orignum );
16: print( $orignum );
17: ?>
18: </div>
19: </body>
20: </html>
```

The addFive() function accepts a single numeric value and adds 5 to it. It returns nothing. We assign a value to a variable $orignum in line 14 and then pass this variable to addFive() in line 15. A copy of the contents of $orignum is stored in the variable $num. Although we increment $num by 5, this has no effect on the value of $orignum. When we print $orignum, we find that its value is still 10. By default, variables passed to functions are passed by value—in other words, local copies of the values of the variables are made.

We can change this behavior by creating a reference to our original variable. You can think of a **reference** as a signpost that points to a variable. In working with the reference, you are manipulating the value to which it points.

Listing 6.14 shows this technique in action. When you pass an argument to a function by reference, as in line 15, the contents of the variable you pass ($orignum) are accessed by the argument variable and manipulated within the function, rather than just a copy of the variable's value (10). Any changes made to an argument in these cases change the value of the original variable. You can pass an argument by reference by adding an ampersand to the argument name in the function definition, as shown in line 11.

LISTING 6.14 Using a Function Definition to Pass an Argument to a Function by Reference

```
1: <!DOCTYPE html PUBLIC
2:   "-//W3C//DTD XHTML 1.0 Strict//EN"
3:   "http://www.w3.org/TR/xhtml1/DTD/xhtml1-strict.dtd">
4: <html>
5: <head>
6: <title>Listing 6.14</title>
7: </head>
8: <body>
9: <div>
10: <?php
11: function addFive( &$num ) {
12:    $num += 5;
13: }
14: $orignum = 10;
15: addFive( $orignum );
16: print( $orignum );
17: ?>
18: </div>
19: </body>
20: </html>
```

Until recently, it was also usual to set up pass by reference from within the calling code rather than at the function declaration. This technique is referred to as **call-time pass-by-reference** and involves prepending an ampersand to the variable in the function call rather than in the function declaration. This technique has been deprecated and so should not be used.

If you are using library code that falls foul of this deprecation, you can temporarily suppress PHP's warning messages by setting the `allow_call_time_pass_reference` directive to on in your `php.ini` file.

Watch Out!

Returning References from Functions

Functions return by value. So, if you pass a variable to a function by reference and then return that variable to the calling code, you return a copy of the variable's value. You do not, by default, return a variable reference. You can change this behavior by prepending an ampersand to the name of your function, like so:

```
function &addFive( &$num ) {
  $num+=5;
  return $num;
}
```

$num is now both passed to addFive() and returned from it by reference. We can illustrate this by calling addFive():

```
$orignum = 10;
$retnum = & addFive( $orignum );
$orignum += 10;
print( $retnum ); // prints 25
```

In this fragment we assign the result of calling addFive() to another variable, $retnum. Notice that we place an ampersand before the function call to enforce assignment by reference. Now when we add 10 to $orignum, the change is reflected in $retnum. Both $orignum and $retnum now alias one another.

Creating Anonymous Functions

You can create functions on-the-fly during script execution. Because such functions are not themselves given a name but are stored in variables or passed to other functions, they are known as **anonymous** functions. PHP provides the create_function() function for creating anonymous functions; it requires two string arguments. The first argument should contain a comma-delimited list of argument variables, exactly the same as the argument variables you would include in a standard function declaration. The second argument should contain our function body.

In Listing 6.15, we create a simple anonymous function to add two numbers together.

LISTING 6.15   A Simple Anonymous Function

```
 1: <!DOCTYPE html PUBLIC
 2:   "-//W3C//DTD XHTML 1.0 Strict//EN"
 3:   "http://www.w3.org/TR/xhtml1/DTD/xhtml1-strict.dtd">
 4: <html>
 5: <head>
 6: <title>Listing 6.15</title>
 7: </head>
 8: <body>
 9: <div>
10: <?php
11: $my_anon = create_function( '$a, $b', 'return $a+$b;' );
12: print $my_anon( 3, 9 );
13:
14: // prints 12
15: ?>
16: </div>
17: </body>
18: </html>
```

Note that we used single quotation marks when passing arguments to create_function(). That saved us from having to escape the variable names within the arguments. We could have used double quotation marks, but the function call would have been a little more involved:

```
$my_anon = create_function( "\$a, \$b", "return \$a+\$b;" );
```

So, what use are anonymous functions? In practical terms you will probably use them only when built-in functions need to be passed callback functions. A **callback** function is generally written by the user and designed to be invoked (usually repeatedly) by the function to which it is passed. You will see examples of this in Hour 16, "Working with Dates and Times."

The second argument to create_function() is the function body. Don't forget to end the last statement in this string with a semicolon. The interpreter will complain and your anonymous function will not be executed if you omit it.

Watch Out!

Testing for Function Existence

You have seen that you do not always know that a function exists before you try to invoke it. If your code were to work with a function name stored in a variable, for example, it would be useful for you to be able to test whether the function exists before you attempted to call it. Furthermore, different builds of the PHP engine can include different functionality. If you are writing a script that might be run on multiple servers, you might want to check that key features are available. You might write code that will use MySQL if mysql functions are available but simply log data to a text file otherwise.

You can use function_exists() to check for the availability of a function. function_exists() requires a string representing a function name. It returns true if the function can be located and false otherwise.

Listing 6.16 shows function_exists() in action and illustrates some of the other topics covered in this chapter.

LISTING 6.16   Testing for a Function's Existence

```
1: <!DOCTYPE html PUBLIC
2:    "-//W3C//DTD XHTML 1.0 Strict//EN"
3:    "http://www.w3.org/TR/xhtml1/DTD/xhtml1-strict.dtd">
4: <html>
5: <head>
6: <title>Listing 6.16</title>
```

LISTING 6.16   Continued

```
 7: </head>
 8: <body>
 9: <div>
10: <?php
11:
12: function tagWrap( $tag, $txt, $func="" ) {
13:    if ( function_exists( $func ) )
14:      $txt = $func( $txt );
15:    return "<$tag>$txt</$tag>\n";
16: }
17:
18: function subscript( $txt ) {
19:    return "<sub>$txt</sub>";
20: }
21:
22: print tagWrap('b', 'make me bold');
23: // <b>make me bold</b>
24:
25: print tagWrap('i', 'shrink me too', "subscript");
26: // <i><sub>shrink me too</sub></i>
27:
28: print tagWrap('i', 'make me italic and quote me',
29:    create_function('$txt', 'return ""$txt"";'));
30: // <i>"make me italic and quote me"</i>
31:
32: ?>
33: </div>
34: </body>
35: </html>
```

We define two functions, tagWrap() (line 12) and subscript() (line 18). TagWrap() accepts three strings, a tag, the text to be formatted, and an optional function name. It returns a formatted string. subscript() requires a single argument, the text to be formatted, and returns the text wrapped in <sub> tags.

When we first call tagWrap() on line 22, we pass it the character b and the string make me bold. Because we haven't passed a value for the function argument, the default value (an empty string) is used. On line 13, we check whether the $func variable contains characters and, if it is not empty, we call function_exists() to check for a function by that name. Of course, the $func variable is empty, so we wrap the $txt variable in <b> tags on line 15 and return the result.

We next call tagWrap() on line 25 with the string i, some text, and a third argument: subscript. function_exists() does find a function called subscript() (line 13), so this is called and passed the $txt argument variable before any further formatting is done. The result is an italicized string rendered as subscript.

Finally, we call tagWrap() on line 28 with an anonymous function (which wraps text in quotation entities). Of course, it would be quicker to simply add the entities to the text to be transformed ourselves, but this does illustrate the point that function_exists() works as well on anonymous functions as it does on strings representing function names.

Summary

In this hour, you learned about functions and how to deploy them. You learned how to define and pass arguments to a function. You learned how to use the global and static statements. You learned how to pass references to functions and how to create default values for function arguments. Finally, you learned how to create anonymous functions and test for function existence.

Q&A

Q *Apart from the* global *keyword, is there any way that a function can access and change global variables?*

A You can also access global variables anywhere in your scripts with a built-in associative array called $GLOBALS. To access a global variable called $test within a function, you could reference it as $GLOBALS['test']. You can learn more about associative arrays in the next hour.

You can also change global variables from within a function if it has been passed in by reference.

Q *Can you include a function call within a string, as you can with a variable?*

A No. You must call functions outside quotation marks.

Workshop

Quiz

1. True or False: If a function doesn't require an argument, you can omit the parentheses in the function call.

2. How do you return a value from a function?

3. What would the following code fragment print to the browser?

```
$number = 50;

function tenTimes() {
   $number = $number * 10;
}

tenTimes();
print $number;
```

4. What would the following code fragment print to the browser?

```
$number = 50;

function tenTimes() {
   global $number;
   $number = $number * 10;
}

tenTimes();
print $number;
```

5. What would the following code fragment print to the browser?

```
$number = 50;

function tenTimes( $n ) {
   $n = $n * 10;
}

tenTimes( $number );
print $number;
```

6. What would the following code fragment print to the browser?

```
$number = 50;

function tenTimes( &$n ) {
   $n = $n * 10;
}

tenTimes( $number );
print $number;
```

Answers

1. The statement is false. You must always include the parentheses in your function calls, whether or not you are passing arguments to the function.

2. You must use the `return` keyword.

3. It would print 50. The `tenTimes()` function has no access to the global `$number` variable. When it is called, it manipulates its own local `$number` variable.

4. It would print 500. We have used the global statement, which gives the `tenTimes()` function access to the `$number` variable.

5. It would print 50. When we pass an argument to the `tenTimes()` function, it is passed by value. In other words, a copy is placed in the parameter variable `$n`. Any changes we make to `$n` have no effect on the `$number` variable.

6. It would print 500. By adding the ampersand to the parameter variable `$n`, we ensure that this argument is passed by reference. `$n` and `$number` point to the same value, so any changes to `$n` are reflected when you access `$number`.

Exercise

1. Create a function that accepts four string variables and returns a string that contains an HTML table element, enclosing each of the variables in its own cell.

HOUR 7

Arrays

Arrays, and the tools to manipulate them, greatly enhance the scope and flexibility of PHP scripts. After you've mastered arrays, you will be able to store and organize complex data structures.

This hour introduces arrays and some of the functions that help you work with them.

What You'll Learn in This Hour:

▶ What arrays are and how to create them
▶ How to access data from and about arrays
▶ How to access and sort the data contained in arrays
▶ How to create more flexible functions using arrays

What Is an Array?

You already know that a variable is a "bucket" in which you can temporarily store a value. By using variables, you can create a script that stores, processes, and outputs different information every time it is run. Unfortunately, you can store only one value at a time in a variable. **Arrays** are special variables that enable you to overcome this limitation. An array enables you to store as many values as you want in the same variable. Each value is indexed within the array by a number or string. If a variable is a bucket, you can think of an array as a filing cabinet—a single container that can store many discrete items.

Of course, if you have five values to store, you could always define five variables. So, why use an array rather than a variable? First, an array is flexible. It can store two values or two hundred values without the need to define further variables. Second, an array enables you to work easily with all its items. You can loop through each item or pull one out at random. You can sort items numerically, alphabetically, or even according to a system of your own.

Each item in an array is commonly referred to as an **element**. Each element can be accessed directly via its index. An index to an array element can be either a number or string.

By default, array elements are indexed by numbers, starting at 0. It's important to remember, therefore, that the index of the last element of a sequential numerically indexed array is always one less than the number of elements the array contains.

For example, Table 7.1 shows the elements in an array called users. Notice that the third element has an index of 2.

TABLE 7.1   The Elements in the users Array

Index Number	Value	Which Element?
0	Bert	First
1	Sharon	Second
2	Betty	Third
3	Harry	Fourth

Indexing arrays by string can be useful in cases where you need to store both names and values.

PHP provides tools to access and manipulate arrays indexed by both name and number.

Creating Arrays

By default, arrays are lists of values indexed by number. Values can be assigned to an array in two ways: with the array() construct or directly using empty square brackets ([ ]). You'll meet both of these in the next two sections.

Defining Arrays with the array() Construct

The array() construct is useful when you want to assign multiple values to an array at one time. Let's define an array called $users and assign four strings to it:

```
$users = array("Bert", "Sharon", "Betty", "Harry" );
```

You can now access the third element in the $user array by using the index 2:

```
print $users[2];
```

This would return the string Betty. The index of an array element is placed between square brackets directly after the array name. You can use this notation to either set or retrieve a value.

Remember that arrays are indexed from zero by default, so the index of any element in a sequentially indexed array always is one less than the element's place in the list.

Defining or Adding to Arrays with the Array Identifier

You can create a new array (or add to an existing one) by using the array identifier in conjunction with the array name. The array identifier is a set of square brackets with no index number or name inside it.

Let's re-create our $users array in this way:

```
$users[] = " Bert";
$users[] = " Sharon";
$users[] = " Betty";
$users[] = " Harry";
```

Notice that we didn't need to place any numbers between the square brackets. PHP automatically takes care of the index number, which saves you from having to work out which is the next available slot.

We could have added numbers if we wanted, and the result would have been exactly the same. It's not advisable to do this, though. Take a look at the following code:

```
$users[0] = " Bert";
$users[200] = "Sharon";
```

The array has only two elements, but the index of the final element is 200. PHP will not initialize the intervening elements, which could lead to confusion when attempting to access elements in the array. On the other hand, in some circumstances you will want to use arbitrary index numbers in your array.

In addition to creating arrays, you can use the array identifier to add new values onto the end of an existing array. In the following code, we define an array with the array() construct and use the array identifier to add a new element:

```
$users = array ("Bert", " Sharon", "Betty", "Harry" );
$users[] = "Sally";
```

Populating an Array with `array_fill()`

If you want to pad an array with default values, you can use the `array()` function, like so:

```
$membertypes = array( "regular", "regular", "regular", $regular" );
```

You could also use the empty brackets approach:

```
$membertypes[] = "regular";
$membertypes[] = "regular";
$membertypes[] = "regular";
$membertypes[] = "regular";
```

PHP provides a flexible function to automate this task. `array_fill()` requires three arguments: a number representing the index from which to start filling, another integer representing the number of elements to populate, and the value to add to the array. Using `array_fill()`, we can rewrite the previous fragments:

```
$membertypes = array_fill( 0, 4, "regular" );
```

Associative Arrays

Numerically indexed arrays are useful for storing values in the order they were added or according to a sort pattern. Sometimes, though, you need to access elements in an array by name. An associative array is indexed with strings between the square brackets rather than numbers. Imagine an address book. Which would be easier, indexing the name field as 4 or as name?

Again, you can define an associative array using either `array()` or the array operator `[ ]`.

> The division between an associative array and a numerically indexed array is not absolute in PHP. They are not separate types as arrays and hashes are in Perl are. Nevertheless, you should treat them separately because each demands different strategies for access and manipulation.

Defining Associative Arrays with the `array()` Construct

To define an associative array with the `array()` construct, you must define both the key and value for each element. The following code creates an associative array called `$character` with four elements:

```
$character = array (
    "name" => "bob",
```

```
"occupation" => "superhero",
"age" => 30,
"special power" => "x-ray vision"
);
```

We can now access any of the fields of $character:

```
print $character['age'];
```

The keys in an associative array are strings, but in its default error reporting state the engine won't complain if array keys aren't quoted.

Omitting quotation marks for array keys is poor practice, however. If you use unquoted strings as keys and your error reporting is set to a higher-than-standard level, the engine will complain every time such an element is met. Even worse, if an unquoted array key coincides with a constant, the value of the constant will be substituted for the key as typed.

> You should enclose an associative array key with quotation marks when the key in question is a string literal:
>
> ```
> print $character[age]; // wrong
> print $character["age"]; // right
> ```
>
> If the key is stored in a variable, you do not need to use quotation marks:
>
> ```
> $agekey = "age";
> print $character[$agekey]; // right
> ```

Directly Defining or Adding to an Associative Array

You can create or add a name/value pair to an associative array simply by assigning a value to a named element. In the following, we re-create our $character array by directly assigning a value to each key:

```
$character["name"] = "bob";
$character["occupation"] = "superhero";
$character["age"] = 30;
$character["special power"] = "x-ray vision";
```

Multidimensional Arrays

Until now, we've simply said that elements of arrays are values. In our $character array, three of the elements held strings and one held an integer. The reality is a little more complex, however. In fact, an element of an array could be a value, an object, or even another array. A **multidimensional** array is an array of arrays. Imagine an array that stores an array in each of its elements. To access the third element of the second element, we would have to use two indices:

```
$array[1][2]
```

The fact that an array element can itself be an array enables you to create sophisticated data structures relatively easily. Listing 7.1 defines an array that has an associative array as each of its elements.

LISTING 7.1   Defining a Multidimensional Array

```
 1: <!DOCTYPE html PUBLIC
 2:    "-//W3C//DTD XHTML 1.0 Strict//EN"
 3:    "http://www.w3.org/TR/xhtml1/DTD/xhtml1-strict.dtd">
 4: <html>
 5: <head>
 6: <title>Listing 7.1 Defining a Multidimensional Array</title>
 7: </head>
 8: <body>
 9: <div>
10: <?php
11:
12: $characters = array (
13:        array (
14:          "name"=> "bob",
15:          "occupation" => "superhero",
16:          "age" => 30,
17:          "specialty" =>"x-ray vision"
18:        ),
19:        array (
20:          "name" => "sally",
21:          "occupation" => "superhero",
22:          "age" => 24,
23:          "specialty" => "superhuman strength"
24:        ),
25:        array (
26:          "name" => "mary",
27:          "occupation" => "arch villain",
28:          "age" => 63,
29:          "specialty" =>"nanotechnology"
30:        )
31:     );
32:
33: print $characters[0][occupation];
34: // prints "superhero"
35: ?>
36: </div>
37: </body>
38: </html>
```

Notice that we have nested array construct calls within an array construct call. At the first level, we define an array. For each of its elements, we define an associative array.

Accessing $characters[2], therefore, gives us access to the third associative array (beginning on line 25) in the top-level array (beginning on line 12). We can then access any of the associative array's fields. $characters[2]['name'] will be mary, and $characters[2]['age'] will be 63.

When this concept is clear, you will be able to easily create complex combinations of associative and numerically indexed arrays.

Accessing Arrays

So far, you've seen the ways in which you can create and add to arrays. In this section, you will examine some of the tools PHP provides to allow you to acquire information about arrays and access their elements.

Getting the Size of an Array

You can access an element of an array by using its index:

```
print $user[4]
```

Because of the flexibility of arrays, however, you won't always know how many elements a particular array contains. That's where the count() function comes into play. count() returns the number of elements in an array. In the following code, we define a numerically indexed array and use count() to access its last element:

```
$users = array ("Bert", " Sharon", "Betty", "Harry" );
print $users[count($users)-1];
```

Notice that we subtract one from the value returned by count(). This is because count() returns the number of elements in an array, not the index of the last element.

Although arrays are indexed from zero by default, you can change this. For the sake of clarity and consistency, however, this is not usually advisable.

Although count() gives you the size of an array, you can use it to access the last element in the array only if you are sure that array elements have been added consecutively. For example, say we had initialized the $user array with values at arbitrary indices:

```
$users[66] = "Bert";
$users[100] = "Sharon";
$users[556] = "Betty";
$users[703] = "Harry";
```

count() would not be of any use in finding the final element. The array still contains only four elements, but there is no element indexed by 3. If you are not certain that your array is consecutively indexed, you can use the end() function to retrieve the final element in the array. end() requires an array as its only argument and returns the given array's last element. The following statement prints the final element in the $users array no matter how it was initialized:

```
print end($users);
```

Looping Through an Array

PHP's powerful foreach statement is the best way of looping through each element of an array. In the context of numerically indexed arrays, you would use a foreach statement like this:

```
foreach( $array as $temp ) {
    //...
}
```

In this statement $array is the array you want to loop through and $temp is a variable in which you will temporarily store each element.

In the following code, we define a numerically indexed array and use foreach to access each of its elements in turn:

```
$users = array ("Bert", "Sharon", "Betty", "Harry" );
foreach ( $users as $val ) {
  print "$val<br />";
  }
```

You can see the output from this code fragment in Figure 7.1.

FIGURE 7.1
Looping through an array.

The value of each element is temporarily placed in the variable $val, which we then print to the browser. If you are moving to PHP from Perl, be aware of a significant difference in the behavior of foreach: Changing the value of the temporary variable in a Perl foreach loop changes the corresponding element in the array. Changing the temporary variable in the preceding example would have no effect on the $users array.

Looping Through an Associative Array

To access both the keys and values of an associative array, you need to alter the use of foreach slightly.

In the context of associative arrays, you would use a foreach statement like this:

```
foreach( $array as $key=>$value ) {
    //...
}
```

In this statement $array is the array we are looping through, $key is a variable that temporarily holds each key, and $value is a variable that temporarily holds each value.

Listing 7.2 creates an associative array and accesses each key and value in turn.

LISTING 7.2   Looping Through an Associative Array with foreach

```
 1: <!DOCTYPE html PUBLIC
 2:    "-//W3C//DTD XHTML 1.0 Strict//EN"
 3:    "http://www.w3.org/TR/xhtml1/DTD/xhtml1-strict.dtd">
 4: <html>
 5: <head>
 6: <title>Listing 7.2 Using foreach</title>
 7: </head>
 8: <body>
 9: <div>
10: <?php
11: $character = array (
12:        "name" => "bob",
13:        "occupation" => "superhero",
14:        "age" => 30,
15:        "special power" => "x-ray vision"
16:        );
17: foreach ( $character as $key=>$val ) {
18:    print "$key = $val<br />";
19: }
20:
21: ?>
22: </div>
23: </body>
24: </html>
```

The array is created on line 11, and we use the `foreach` statement on line 17 to loop through the character array. Each key is placed in a variable called $key, and each value is placed in a variable called $val. They are printed on line 18. You can see the output from Listing 7.2 in Figure 7.2.

FIGURE 7.2
Looping through an associative array.

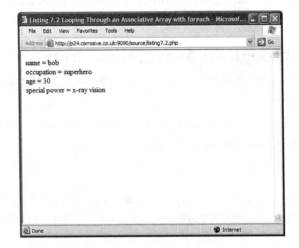

Outputting a Multidimensional Array

You can now combine these techniques to output the multidimensional array created in Listing 7.1. Listing 7.3 defines a similar array and uses `foreach` to loop through each of its elements.

LISTING 7.3   Looping Through a Multidimensional Array

```
 1: <!DOCTYPE html PUBLIC
 2:    "-//W3C//DTD XHTML 1.0 Strict//EN"
 3:    "http://www.w3.org/TR/xhtml1/DTD/xhtml1-strict.dtd">
 4: <html>
 5: <head>
 6: <title>Listing 7.3 Looping Through a Multidimensional Array</title>
 7: </head>
 8: <body>
 9: <div>
10: <?php
11: $characters = array (
12:      array (
13:         "name"=> "bob",
14:         "occupation" => "superhero",
15:         "age" => 30,
16:         "specialty" =>"x-ray vision"
17:      ),
18:      array (
19:         "name" => "sally",
20:         "occupation" => "superhero",
```

LISTING 7.3   Continued

```
21:           "age" => 24,
22:           "specialty" => "superhuman strength"
23:        ),
24:        array (
25:           "name" => "mary",
26:           "occupation" => "arch villain",
27:           "age" => 63,
28:           "specialty" =>"nanotechnology"
29:        )
30:     );
31:
32: foreach ( $characters as $val ) {
33:   print "<p>";
34:   foreach ( $val as $key=>$final_val ) {
35:     print "$key: $final_val<br />";
36:   }
37:   print "</p>";
38: }
39:
40: ?>
41: </div>
42: </body>
43: </html>
```

You can see the output from Listing 7.3 in Figure 7.3. We create two foreach loops (lines 32 and 34). The outer loop on line 32 accesses each element in the numerically indexed array $characters, placing each one in $val. Because $val itself then contains an associative array, we can loop through this on line 34, outputting each of its elements (temporarily stored in $key and $final_val) to the browser.

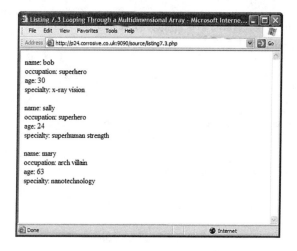

FIGURE 7.3
Looping through a multidimensional array.

For this technique to work as expected, we need to ensure in advance that $val will always contain an array. To make this code a little more robust, we could use the function is_array() to test $val. is_array() accepts a variable, returning true if the variable is an array or false otherwise. Alternatively, we could cast the $val variable created on line 29 to an array, thereby ensuring that it is always an array, whatever type it started out as. Here's how:

```
$val = (array) $val;
```

Examining Arrays with print_r()

Listing 7.3 demonstrates a way of using foreach loops to access elements in an array. This is fine for working with an array or presenting data neatly. But if you only want a quick peek at an array's contents to debug a script, it seems like a lot of work. The print_r() function accepts any variable and outputs information about the argument's contents and structure. If you pass an array to print_r(), you get a listing of the array's elements. print_r() reports in full on each element and explores all structures (such as objects or arrays) it finds. If you develop scripts of any size or complexity, you will probably become a great friend of the print_r() function.

In Listing 7.4 we test this by passing a cut-down version of the $characters array to print_r().

LISTING 7.4   Examining an Array with print_r()

```
1: <!DOCTYPE html PUBLIC
 2:    "-//W3C//DTD XHTML 1.0 Strict//EN"
 3:    "http://www.w3.org/TR/xhtml1/DTD/xhtml1-strict.dtd">
 4: <html>
 5: <head>
 6: <title>Listing 7.4 Testing the print_r() Function</title>
 7: </head>
 8: <body>
 9: <div>
10: <?php
11: $characters = array (
12:        array (
13:          "name"=> "bob",
14:          "occupation" => "superhero",
15:        ),
16:        array (
17:          "name" => "sally",
18:          "occupation" => "superhero",
19:        )
20:     );
21:
22: print_r( $characters );
23:
24: /*
25: prints:
```

LISTING 7.4   Continued

```
26: Array
27: (
28:    [0] => Array
29:       (
30:          [name] => bob
31:          [occupation] => superhero
32:       )
33:
34:    [1] => Array
35:       (
36:          [name] => sally
37:          [occupation] => superhero
38:       )
39:
40: )
41: */
42:
43: ?>
44: </div>
45: </body>
46: </html>
```

We create a cut-down version of the $characters array on line 11 and pass it to the print_r() function on line 22. That effectively ends our script, but we include comments between lines 24 and 43 to show the script's output. Note that you will not see the formatting if you view this script's output in a browser because the line breaks and spacing will be ignored. You can restore the formatting by wrapping your call to print_r() in <pre> tags, like so:

```
print "<pre>";
print_r( $characters );
print "</pre>";
```

As of PHP 4.3, you can capture the output from print_r() in a variable rather than printing directly to the browser. print_r() optionally accepts Boolean as a second argument. If this is set to true, print_r() returns its output as a string:

```
$str = print_r( $characters, true );
```

Manipulating Arrays

You can now populate arrays and access their elements, but PHP has functions to help you do much more than that with arrays. If you're used to Perl, you'll find some of these eerily familiar!

Joining Two Arrays with `array_merge()`

`array_merge()` accepts two or more arrays and returns a merged array combining all their elements. In the following example, we create two arrays, joining the second to the first, and loop through the resultant third array:

```
$first = array("a", "b", "c");
$second = array(1,2,3);
$third = array_merge( $first, $second );

foreach ( $third as $val ) {
  print "$val<br />";
}
```

The `$third` array contains copies of all the elements of both the `$first` and `$second` arrays. The `foreach` statement prints this combined array (`'a'`, `'b'`, `'c'`, 1, 2, 3) to the browser with a `<br />` tag between each element. Remember that the arrays passed to `array_merge()` are not themselves transformed. If two arrays passed to `array_merge()` have elements with the same string index, those of the first array are overwritten by their namesakes in the second.

Adding Multiple Variables to an Array

`array_push()` accepts an array and any number of further parameters, each of which is added to the array. Note that the `array_push()` function is unlike `array_merge()` in that the array passed in as the first argument is transformed. `array_push()` returns the total number of elements in the array. Let's create an array and add some more values to it:

```
$first = array("a", "b", "c");
$total = array_push( $first, 1, 2, 3 );

print "There are $total elements in \$first<p>";
foreach ( $first as $val ) {
  print "$val<br/>";
}
print "</p>";
```

Because `array_push()` returns the total number of elements in the array it transforms, we can store this value (6) in a variable and print it to the browser. The `$first` array now contains its original elements as well the three integers we passed to the `array_push()` function. All of these are printed to the browser within the `foreach` statement.

Notice that we used a backslash character when we printed the string `"\$first"`. If you use a dollar sign followed by numbers and letters within a string, PHP attempts to insert the value of a variable by that name. In the previous example, we wanted to print the string '$first' rather than the value of the $first variable. To print the special character $, therefore, we must precede it with a backslash. PHP will now print the character instead of interpreting it. This process is often referred to as *escaping* a character.

> Perl users beware! If you're used to working with Perl's push(), you should note that, if you pass a second array variable to array_push(), it will be added as a single element, creating a multidimensional array. If you want to combine two arrays, use array_merge().

Watch Out!

If you need to add new elements to the beginning of an array, you can use the array_unshift() function, which accepts an array and any number of additional values. It will add the value arguments to the start of the given array. The following amends our previous fragment to use array_unshift():

```
$first = array("a", "b", "c");
$total = array_unshift( $first, 1, 2, 3 );
```

$first now contains the following:

```
1, 2, 3, "a", "b", "c"
```

array_unshift() returns the new size of the array it transforms.

Removing the First Element of an Array with array_shift()

array_shift() removes and returns the first element of an array passed to it as an argument. In the following example, we use array_shift() in conjunction with a while loop. We test the value returned from count() to check whether the array still contains elements:

```php
<?php
$an_array = array("a", "b", "c");

while ( count( $an_array ) ) {
  $val = array_shift( $an_array );
  print "$val<br />";
  print "there are ".count( $an_array )." elements in \$an_array <br />";
}
?>
```

You can see the output from this fragment of code in Figure 7.4.

array_shift() is useful when you need to create a queue and act on it until the queue is empty.

FIGURE 7.4
Using `array_shift()` to remove and print every element in an array.

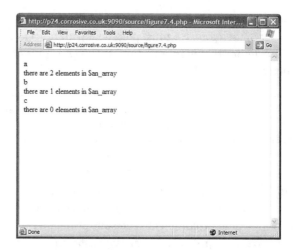

```
a
there are 2 elements in $an_array
b
there are 1 elements in $an_array
c
there are 0 elements in $an_array
```

Slicing Arrays with `array_slice()`

`array_slice()` enables you to extract a chunk of an array. It accepts an array as an argument, a starting position (offset), and a length (optional). If the length is omitted, `array_slice()` generously assumes that you want all elements from the starting position onward returned. `array_slice()` does not alter the array you pass to it; it returns a new array containing the elements you have requested.

In the following example, we create an array and extract a new three-element array from it:

```
$first = array("a", "b", "c", "d", "e", "f");
$second = array_slice($first, 2, 3);

foreach ( $second as $var ) {
  print "$var<br />";
}
```

This prints the elements `'c'`, `'d'`, and `'e'`, separating each by a `<br />` tag. Notice that the offset is inclusive if we think of it as the index number of the first element we are requesting. In other words, the first element of the `$second` array is equivalent to `$first[2]`.

If we pass `array_slice()` an offset argument that is less than zero, the returned slice begins that number of elements from the end of the given array.

If we pass `array_slice()` a length argument that is less than zero, the returned slice contains all elements from the offset position to that number of elements from the end of the given array.

Sorting Arrays

Sorting is perhaps the greatest magic you can perform on an array. Thanks to the functions PHP offers to achieve just this, you can truly bring order from chaos. This section introduces some functions that allow you to sort both numerically indexed and associative arrays.

Sorting Numerically Indexed Arrays with `sort()`

`sort()` accepts an array as its argument and sorts it either alphabetically if any strings are present or numerically if all elements are numbers. The function doesn't return any data, transforming the array you pass it. Note that it differs from Perl's `sort()` function in this respect. The following fragment of code initializes an array of single character strings, sorts it, and outputs the transformed array:

```
$an_array = array("x","a","f","c");
sort( $an_array );

foreach ( $an_array as $var ) {
  print "$var<br />";
}
```

> Don't pass an associative array to `sort()`. You will find that the values are sorted as expected but that your keys have been lost—replaced by numerical indices that follow the sort order.

Watch Out!

You can reverse sort a numerically indexed array by using `rsort()` in exactly the same way as `sort()`.

Sorting an Associative Array by Value with `asort()`

`asort()` accepts an associative array and sorts its values just as `sort()` does. However, it preserves the array's keys:

```
$first = array("first"=>5,"second"=>2,"third"=>1);
asort( $first );

foreach ( $first as $key => $val ) {
  print "$key = $val<br />";
}
```

You can see the output from this fragment of code in Figure 7.5.

You can reverse sort an associative array by value with `arsort()`.

FIGURE 7.5
Sorting an associative array by its values with `asort()`.

FIGURE 7.5
Sorting an associative array by its values with `asort()`.

Sorting an Associative Array by Key with `ksort()`

`ksort()` accepts an associative array and sorts its keys. Once again, the array you pass it is transformed and nothing is returned:

```
$first = array("x"=>5,"a"=>2,"f"=>1);
ksort( $first );

foreach ( $first as $key => $val ) {
  print "$key = $val<br />";
}
```

You can see the output from this fragment of code in Figure 7.6.

FIGURE 7.6
Sorting an associative array by its keys with `ksort()`.

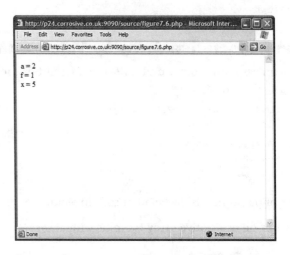

You can reverse sort an associative array by key with `krsort()`.

Functions Revisited

Now that we have covered arrays, we can examine some built-in functions that could help you make your own functions more flexible. If you have programmed in Perl before, you will know that you can easily create subroutines that accept a variable number of arguments. PHP provides functions that make it just as easy.

Imagine that you have created a function that accepts three string arguments and returns a single string containing each of the provided arguments wrapped in an HTML table, which includes the sum of the numbers in its final row:

```
function addNums( $num1, $num2 ) {
    $result = $num1 + $num2;
    $ret = "<table border=\"1\">";
    $ret .= "<tr><td>number 1: </td><td>$num1 </td></tr>";
    $ret .= "<tr><td>number 2: </td><td>$num2 </td></tr>";
    $ret .= "<tr><td>result:   </td><td>$result</td></tr>";
    $ret .= "</table>";
    return $ret;
}

print addNums( 49, 60 );
```

This very simple function does its job well enough, but it is not very flexible. Imagine now that you are asked to amend the function to handle four arguments, or six, or, well, pretty much any number of integers. The simplest solution would be to ask that the calling code provide a single array containing all the numbers rather than two individual integers. This would mean that a lot of code would have to be changed in the project as a whole as well as in the function. It would be better, then, to change the function to accept any number of integers.

The tools for this job are func_num_args() and func_get_arg(). func_num_args() returns the number of arguments that have been passed to the function; it does not itself require an argument. func_get_arg() requires an integer representing the index of the argument required and returns its value. As with arrays, arguments are indexed from zero, so to get the first argument passed to a function you would use

```
func_get_arg(0);
```

It is your responsibility to check that the index you pass to func_get_arg() is within the number of arguments that were passed to the function you are testing. If the index is out of range, func_get_arg() returns false and an error is generated. Now we can rewrite our addNums() function:

```
function addNums() {
    $ret = "<table border=\"1\">";
    for ( $x=0; $x<func_num_args(); $x++ ) {
```

```
        $arg = func_get_arg( $x );
        $result += $arg;
        $ret .= "<tr><td>number ".($x+1).": </td><td>$arg</td></tr>";
    }
    $ret .= "<tr><td>result: </td><td>$result</td></tr>";
    $ret .= "</table>";
    return $ret;
}

print addNums( 49, 60, 44, 22, 55 );
```

Notice that we do not provide any argument variables at all in the function declaration. Instead, we use a for loop to access each of the arguments in turn. The
loop executes just the right number of times because our upper limit is set by
func_num_args().

So, given that we haven't actually used an array in this example, why is this section in a chapter on arrays? First, the way in which arguments to functions are
indexed makes them somewhat array-like. Mainly, though, we have yet to cover
another function: func_get_args(). func_get_args() returns an array containing
all the arguments passed to our function. This means we can rewrite our example
to work with a familiar foreach loop:

```
function addNums() {
    $args = func_get_args();
    $ret = "<table border=\"1\">";
    foreach( $args as $key => $val ) {
        $result += $val;
        $ret .= "<tr><td>number ".($key+1).": </td><td>$val</td></tr>";
    }
    $ret .= "<tr><td>result: </td><td>$result</td></tr>";
    $ret .= "</table>";
    return $ret;
}

print addNums( 49, 60, 44, 22, 55 );
```

Rather than access our arguments one at a time, we simply decant the lot into an
array variable called $args. Then it's simply a matter of looping through the array.

Summary

In this hour, you learned about arrays and some of the many tools PHP provides
to work with them. You should now be able to create both numerically indexed
and associative arrays and output data from them using a foreach loop.

You should be able to combine arrays to create multidimensional arrays and loop
through the information they contain. You learned how to manipulate arrays by

adding or removing multiple elements and examined some of the techniques PHP makes available to sort arrays. Finally, you learned about functions that use array-like indexing to help make your own functions more flexible.

In Hour 8, "Working with Strings," we complete our tour of PHP fundamentals by taking a look at PHP's support for objects. PHP developers are increasingly creating libraries using classes and objects, so this is an area well worth studying.

Q&A

Q *Are there any functions for manipulating arrays that we have not covered here?*

A PHP supports many array functions. You can find all these in the official PHP manual at http://www.php.net/manual/ref.array.php.

Q *I can discover the number of elements in an array, so should I use a* for *statement to loop through an array?*

A You should be cautious of this technique. If you are not absolutely sure that the array you are reading is indexed by consecutively numbered keys, you might get unexpected results.

Workshop

Quiz

1. Which construct can you use to define an array?

2. What is the index number of the last element of the array defined here?

   ```
   $users = array("Harry", "Bob", "Sandy");
   ```

3. Without using a function, what would be the easiest way of adding the element "Susan" to the $users array defined previously?

4. Which function could you use to add the string "Susan" to the $users array?

5. How would you find out the number of elements in an array?

6. How would you loop through an array?

7. Which function would you use to merge two arrays?

8. How would you sort an associative array by its keys?

Answers

1. You can create an array with the array() construct.

2. The last element is $users[2]. Remember that arrays are indexed from zero by default.

3. You should use $users[] = "Susan";.

4. You should use array_push($users, "Susan");.

5. You can count the number of elements in an array with the count() function.

6. You can loop through an array using the foreach statement.

7. You can merge arrays with the array_merge() function.

8. You can sort an associative array by its keys with the ksort() function.

Exercises

1. Create a multidimensional array of movies organized by genre. This should take the form of an associative array with genres as keys ("SF", "Action", "Romance", and so on). Each of this associative array's elements should be an array containing movie names ("2001", "Alien", "Terminator", and so on).

2. Loop through the array you created in exercise 1, outputting each genre and its associated movies to the browser.

HOUR 8

Working with Strings

What You'll Learn in This Hour:

- ▶ How to format strings
- ▶ How to determine the length of a string
- ▶ How to find a substring within a string
- ▶ How to break down a string into component parts
- ▶ How to remove white space from the beginning or end of a string
- ▶ How to replace substrings
- ▶ How to change the case of a string

The World Wide Web is very much a plain-text environment. No matter how rich Web content becomes, HTML lies behind it all. It is no accident, then, that PHP provides many functions with which you can format, investigate, and manipulate strings.

Formatting Strings

Until now, we have simply printed any strings we want to display directly to the browser. PHP provides two functions that allow you first to apply formatting, whether to round doubles to a given number of decimal places, define alignment within a field, or display data according to different number systems. In this section, you learn a few of the formatting options provided by printf() and sprintf().

Working with printf()

If you have any experience with C, you will be familiar with the printf() function. The PHP version is similar but not identical. printf() requires a string argument, known as a **format control string**. It also accepts additional arguments of different types. The format control string contains instructions as to how to display these additional arguments. The following fragment, for example, uses printf() to output an integer as a decimal:

```
printf("This is my number: %d", 55 );
// prints "This is my number: 55"
```

Within the format control string (the first argument), we have included a special code, known as a **conversion specification**.

A **conversion specification** begins with a percent (%) symbol and defines how to treat the corresponding argument to printf(). You can include as many conversion specifications as you want within the format control string, as long as you send an equivalent number of arguments to printf().

The following fragment outputs two numbers using printf():

```
printf("First number: %d<br/>\nSecond number: %d<br/>\n", 55, 66 );
// Output:
// First number: 55
// Second number: 66
```

The first conversion specification corresponds to the first of the additional arguments to printf(), which is 55. The second conversion specification corresponds to 66. The d following the percent symbol requires that the data be treated as a decimal integer. This part of a conversion specification is called a **type specifier**.

printf() **and Type Specifiers**

You have already come across one type specifier, d, which displays data in decimal format. Table 8.1 lists the other available type specifiers.

TABLE 8.1   Type Specifiers

Specifier	Description
d	Displays an argument as a decimal number
b	Displays an integer as a binary number
c	Displays an integer as its ASCII equivalent
f	Displays an integer as a floating-point number (double)
o	Displays an integer as an octal number (base 8)
s	Displays an argument as a string
x	Display an integer as a lowercase hexadecimal number (base 16)
X	Displays an integer as an uppercase hexadecimal number (base 16)

Listing 8.1 uses `printf()` to display a single number according to some of the type specifiers listed in Table 8.1.

Notice that we do not only add conversion specifications to the format control string. Any additional text we include will be printed.

LISTING 8.1 Demonstrating Some Type Specifiers

```
 1: <!DOCTYPE html PUBLIC
 2:   "-//W3C//DTD XHTML 1.0 Strict//EN"
 3:   "http://www.w3.org/TR/xhtml1/DTD/xhtml1-strict.dtd">
 4: <html>
 5: <head>
 6: <title>Listing 8.1 Demonstrating Some Type Specifiers</title>
 7: </head>
 8: <body>
 9: <div>
10: <?php
11: $number = 543;
12: printf("Decimal: %d<br/>", $number );
13: printf("Binary: %b<br/>", $number );
14: printf("Double: %f<br/>", $number );
15: printf("Octal: %o<br/>", $number );
16: printf("String: %s<br/>", $number );
17: printf("Hex (lower): %x<br/>", $number );
18: printf("Hex (upper): %X<br/>", $number );
19: ?>
20: </div>
21: </body>
22: </html>
```

Figure 8.1 shows the output for Listing 8.1. As you can see, `printf()` is a quick way of converting data from one number system to another and outputting the result.

When you specify a color in HTML, you combine three hexadecimal numbers between 00 and FF, representing the values for red, green, and blue. You can use `printf()` to convert three decimal numbers between 0 and 255 to their hexadecimal equivalents, like so:

```
$red = 204;
$green = 204;
$blue = 204;
printf( "#%X%X%X", $red, $green, $blue );
// prints "#CCCCCC"
```

Although you can use the type specifier to convert from decimal to hexadecimal numbers, you can't use it to determine how many characters the output for each argument should occupy. Within an HTML color code, each hexadecimal number should be padded to two characters, which would become a problem if we changed our $red, $green, and $blue variables in the previous fragment to contain 1, for example. We would end up with the output "#111". You can force the output of leading zeroes by using a padding specifier.

FIGURE 8.1
Demonstrating con-
version specifiers.

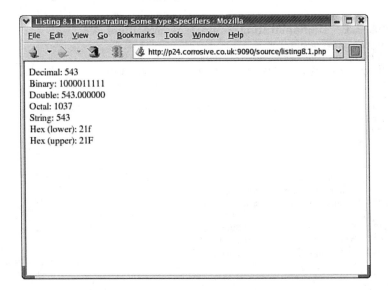

Padding Output with the Padding Specifier

You can require that output be padded by leading characters. The padding specifier should directly follow the percent sign that begins a conversion specifi-cation. To pad output with leading zeroes, the padding specifier should consist of a zero followed by the number of characters you want the output to take up. If the output occupies fewer characters than this total, the difference is filled with zeroes:

```
printf( "%04d", 36 );
// prints "0036"
```

To pad output with leading spaces, the padding specifier should consist of a space character followed by the number of characters the output should occupy:

```
printf( "% 4d", 36 );
// prints "  36"
```

A browser does not display multiple spaces in an HTML document. However, you can force the display of spaces and newlines by placing `<pre>` tags around your output:

By the Way

```
<pre>
<?php
print "The     spaces     will be visible";
?>
</pre>
```

If you want to format an entire document as text, you can use the `header()` function to change the Content-Type header, as shown here:

```
header("Content-Type: Text/Plain");
```

Remember that your script must not have sent any output to the browser for the `header()` function to work as desired.

You can specify any character other than a space or zero in your padding specifier with a single quotation mark followed by the character you want to use:

```
printf ( "%'x4d", 36 );
// prints "xx36"
```

We now have the tools we need to complete our HTML code example. Until now, we could convert three numbers, but we could not pad them with leading zeroes:

```
$red = 1;
$green = 1;
$blue = 1;
printf( "#%02X%02X%02X", $red, $green, $blue );
// prints "#010101"
```

Each variable is output as a hexadecimal number. If the output occupies fewer than two spaces, leading zeroes are added.

Specifying a Field Width

You can specify the number of spaces within which your output should sit. The field width specifier is an integer that should be placed after the percent sign that begins a conversion specification (assuming no padding specifier is defined). The following fragment outputs a list of four items, all of which sit within a field of 20 spaces. To make the spaces visible on the browser, we place all our output within a PRE element:

```
print "<pre>";
printf("%20s\n", "Books");
printf("%20s\n", "CDs");
printf("%20s\n", "Games");
printf("%20s\n", "Magazines");
print "</pre>";
```

Figure 8.2 shows the output of this fragment.

FIGURE 8.2
Aligning with field
width specifiers.

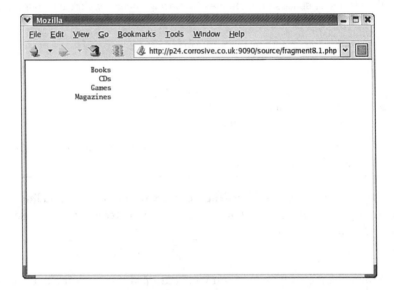

By default, output is right-aligned within the field you specify. You can make it left-aligned by prepending a minus symbol (-) to the field width specifier:

```
printf("%-20s\n", "Left aligned");
```

Note that alignment applies to the decimal portion of any number you output. In other words, only the portion before the decimal point of a double sits flush to the end of the field width when right aligned.

Specifying Precision

If you want to output data in floating-point format, you can specify the precision to which you want to round your data. This is particularly useful when dealing with currency. The precision identifier should be placed directly before the type specifier. It consists of a dot followed by the number of decimal places to which you want to round. This specifier has an effect only on data that is output with the f type specifier:

```
printf( "%.2f", 5.333333 );
// prints "5.33"
```

In the C language, you can use a precision specifier with printf() to specify padding for decimal output. The precision specifier has no effect on decimal output in PHP. Use the padding specifier to add leading zeroes to integers.

Conversion Specifications: A Recap

Table 8.2 lists the specifiers that can make up a conversion specification in the order in which they would be included. Using both a padding specifier and a field width specifier is difficult—you should choose to use one or the other, but not both.

TABLE 8.2 Components of Conversion Specification

Name	Description	Example
Padding specifier	Determines the number of characters the output should occupy and the characters to add otherwise	' 4'
Field width specifier	Determines the space within which output should be formatted	'20'
Precision specifier	Determines the number of decimal places to which a double should be rounded	'.4'
Type specifier	Determines the data type that should be output	'd'

Listing 8.2 uses `printf()` to output a list of products and prices.

LISTING 8.2 Using `printf()` to Format a List of Product Prices

```
 1: <!DOCTYPE html PUBLIC
 2:   "-//W3C//DTD XHTML 1.0 Strict//EN"
 3:   "http://www.w3.org/TR/xhtml1/DTD/xhtml1-strict.dtd">
 4: <html>
 5: <head>
 6: <title>Listing 8.2 Using printf() to Format a List of Product Prices</title>
 7: </head>
 8: <body>
 9: <?php
10: $products = array(
11:     "Green armchair"=>222.4,
12:     "Candlestick"=>4,
13:     "Coffee table"=>80.6
14:     );
15: print "<pre>";
16: printf("%-20s%23s\n", "Name", "Price");
17: printf("%'-43s\n", "");
18: foreach ( $products as $key=>$val ) {
19:   printf( "%-20s%20.2f\n", $key, $val );
20: }
21: print "</pre>";
22: ?>
23: </body>
24: </html>
```

We first define an associative array containing product names and prices on line 8. We print a PRE element so the browser will recognize our spaces and newlines. Our first printf() call on line 12 defines the following format control string:

```
"%-20s%23s\n"
```

The first conversion specification ("%-20s") uses a field width specifier of 20 characters, with the output left-justified. We use a string type specifier, and the second conversion specification ("%23s") sets up a right-aligned field width. The printf() call then outputs our field headers.

Our second printf() function call on line 13 draws a line of - characters across a field of 43 characters. We achieve this with a padding specifier, which adds padding to an empty string.

The final printf() call on line 15 is part of a foreach statement that loops through our product array. We use two conversion specifications. The first ("%-20s") prints the product name as a string left-justified within a 20-character field. The second conversion specification ("%20.2f") uses a field width specifier to ensure that output will be right-aligned within a 20-character field, and it also uses a precision specifier to ensure that the double we output is rounded to two decimal places.

Figure 8.3 shows the output of Listing 8.2.

FIGURE 8.3
Products and prices formatted with printf().

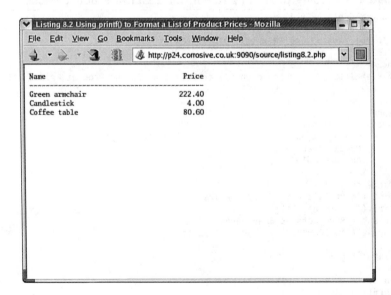

Argument Swapping

As of PHP 4.0.6, you can use the format control string to change the order in which the provided arguments are incorporated into output.

Imagine, for example, that we are printing dates to the browser. We have the dates in a multidimensional array and are using `printf()` to format the output:

```php
<?php
$dates = array(
      array( 'mon'=> 12, 'mday'=>25, 'year'=>2001 ),
      array( 'mon'=> 5, 'mday'=>23, 'year'=>2000 ),
      array( 'mon'=> 10, 'mday'=>29, 'year'=>2001 )
      );

$format = include( "local_format.php" );
foreach( $dates as $date ) {
  printf( "$format", $date['mon'], $date['mday'], $date['year'] );
}
?>
```

We are getting our format control string from an include file called `local_format.php`. Assume that this file contains only the following:

```php
<?php
return "%02d/%02d/%d<br/>";
?>
```

Our output is therefore in the format mm/dd/yyyy:

```
12/25/2001
05/23/2000
10/29/2001
```

Imagine now that we are installing our script for a British site. In the United Kingdom, dates are commonly presented with days before months (dd/mm/yyyy). The core code cannot be changed, but configuration files such as `local_format.php` can. Luckily, we can now alter the order in which the arguments are presented from within the format control code:

```php
return "%2\$02d/%1\$02d/%3\$d<br/>";
```

We can insert the argument number we are interested in after the initial percentage character that marks each conversion specification, followed by an escaped dollar character ($). So, in the previous fragment we are demanding that the second argument be presented, followed by the first, followed by the third. The result is a list of dates in British format:

```
25/12/2001
23/05/2000
29/10/2001
```

Storing a Formatted String

printf() outputs data to the browser, which means that the results are not available to your scripts. You can, however, use the function sprintf(), which works in exactly the same way as printf() except that it returns a string you can then store in a variable for later use. The following fragment uses sprintf() to round a double to two decimal places, storing the result in $dosh:

```
$dosh = sprintf("%.2f", 2.334454);
print "You have $dosh dollars to spend";
```

A particular use of sprintf() is to write a formatted data to a file. You can call sprintf() and assign its return value to a variable that can then be printed to a file with file_put_contents().

Investigating Strings

You do not always know everything about the data with which you are working. Strings can arrive from many sources, including user input, databases, files, and Web pages. Before you begin to work with data from an external source, you often need to find out more about it. PHP provides many functions that enable you to acquire information about strings.

A Note About Indexing Strings

We will frequently use the word **index** in relation to strings. You will have come across the word more frequently in the context of arrays. In fact, strings and arrays are not as different as you might imagine. You can think of a string as an array of characters. So, you can access individual characters of a string as if they were elements of an array:

```
$test = "scallywag";
print $test[0]; // prints "s"
print $test[2]; // prints "a"
```

It is important to remember, therefore, that when we talk about the position or index of a character within a string, characters—like array elements—are indexed from 0.

Finding the Length of a String with strlen()

You can use strlen() to determine the length of a string. strlen() requires a string and returns an integer representing the number of characters in the variable you have passed it. `strlen()` is typically used to check the length of user input. The following fragment tests a membership code to ensure that it is four digits long:

```
if ( strlen( $membership ) == 4 ) {
  print "Thank you!";
} else {
  print "Your membership number must have 4 digits";
}
```

The user is thanked for his input only if the global variable $membership contains four characters; otherwise, an error message is generated.

Finding a Substring Within a String with `strstr()`

You can use `strstr()` to test whether a string exists embedded within another string. `strstr()` requires two arguments: a source string and the substring you want to find within it. The function returns `false` if the substring is absent; otherwise, it returns the portion of the source string beginning with the substring. For the following example, imagine that we want to treat membership codes that contain the string AB differently from those that do not:

```
$membership = "pAB7";
if ( strstr( $membership, "AB" ) ) {
  print "Thank you. Don't forget that your membership expires soon!";
} else {
  print "Thank you!";
}
```

Because our test variable, $membership, does contain the string AB, `strstr()` returns the string AB7. This resolves to `true` when tested, so we print a special message. What happens if our user enters "pab7"? `strstr()` is case sensitive, so AB is not found. The `if` statement's test fails, and the default message is printed to the browser. If we want to search for either AB or ab within the string, we must use `stristr()`, which works in exactly the same way but is not case sensitive.

Finding the Position of a Substring with `strpos()`

`strpos()` tells you both whether a string exists within a larger string and where it is to be found. `strpos()` requires two arguments: the source string and the substring you are seeking. The function also accepts an optional third argument, an integer representing the index from which you want to start searching. If the substring does not exist, `strpos()` returns `false`; otherwise, it returns the index at which the substring begins. The following fragment uses `strpos()` to ensure that a string begins with the string mz:

```
$membership = "mz00xyz";
if ( strpos($membership, "mz") === 0 ) {
  print "hello mz";
}
```

Notice the trick we had to play to get the expected results. strpos() finds mz in our string, but it finds it at the first element of the string. Therefore, it returns zero, which resolves to false in our test. To work around this, we use PHP's equivalence operator (===), which returns true if the left and right operands are equivalent and of the same type.

Extracting Part of a String with substr()

substr() returns a portion of a string based on the start index and length of the portion for which you are looking. strstr() demands two arguments—a source string and the starting index. It returns all the characters from the starting index to the end of the string you are searching. substr() optionally accepts a third argument, which should be an integer representing the length of the string you want returned. If this argument is present, substr() returns only the number of characters specified from the start index onward:

```
$test = "scallywag";
print substr($test,6); // prints "wag"
print substr($test,6,2); // prints "wa"
```

If you pass substr() a negative number as its second (starting index) argument, it counts from the end rather than the beginning of the string. The following fragment writes a specific message to people who have submitted an email address ending in .uk:

```
$test = "matt@corrosive.co.uk";
if ( $test = substr( $test, -3 ) == ".uk" ) {
  print "Don't forget our special offers for British customers";
} else {
  print "Welcome to our shop!";
}
```

Tokenizing a String with strtok()

You can parse a string word by word using strtok(). strtok() initially requires two arguments, the string to be tokenized and the delimiters by which to split the string. The delimiter string can include as many characters as you want. strtok() returns the first token found, and after strtok() has been called for the first time, the source string is cached. For subsequent calls, you should pass only strtok() the delimiter string. The function returns the next found token every time it is called, returning false when the end of the string is reached. strtok() usually is called repeatedly within a loop. Listing 8.3 uses strtok() to tokenize a URL, splitting the host and path from the query string and further dividing the name/value pairs of the query string. Figure 8.4 shows the output from Listing 8.3.

LISTING 8.3   Dividing a String into Tokens with `strtok()`

```
1: <!DOCTYPE html PUBLIC
2:   "-//W3C//DTD XHTML 1.0 Strict//EN"
3:   "http://www.w3.org/TR/xhtml1/DTD/xhtml1-strict.dtd">
4: <html>
5: <head>
6: <title>Listing 8.3 Dividing a string into
7:      tokens with strtok()</title>
8: </head>
9: <body>
10: <div>
11: <?php
12: $test = "http://p24.corrosive.co.uk/tk.php";
13: $test .= "?id=353&sec=44&user=harry&context=php";
14:
15: $delims = "?&";
16: $word = strtok( $test, $delims );
17: while ( is_string( $word ) ) {
18:   if ( $word ) {
19:     print "$word<br/>";
20:   }
21:   $word = strtok( $delims );
22: }
23: ?>
24: </div>
25: </body>
26: </html>
```

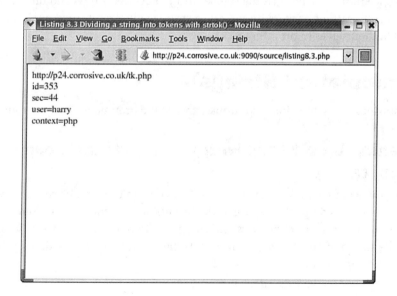

FIGURE 8.4
Tokenizing a string.

strtok( ) is something of a blunt instrument, and a few tricks are required to work with it. We first store the delimiters we want to work with in a variable, $delims on line 15. We call strtok( ) on line 16, passing it the URL we want to tokenize and the $delims string. We store the first result in $word. Within the conditional expression of the while loop on line 17, we test that $word is a string. If it isn't, we know that the end of the string has been reached and no further action is required.

We are testing the return type because a string containing two delimiters in a row would cause strtok( ) to return an empty string when it reaches the first of these delimiters. So, a more conventional test such as

```
while ( $word ) {
    $word = strtok( $delims );
}
```

would fail if $word were an empty string, even if the end of the source string had not yet been reached.

Having established that $word contains a string, we can work with it. If $word does not contain an empty string, we print it to the browser on line 19. We must then call strtok( ) again on line 21 to repopulate the $word variable for the next test. Notice that we don't pass the source string to strtok( ) a second time. If we were to do this, the first word of the source string would be returned again and we would find ourselves in an infinite loop.

Manipulating Strings

PHP provides many functions that transform a string argument, subtly or radically.

Cleaning Up a String with trim( ), ltrim( ), and strip_tags( )

When you acquire text from the user or a file, you can't always be sure that you haven't also picked up white space at the beginning and end of your data. trim( ) shaves any white space characters, including newlines, tabs, and spaces, from both the start and end of a string. It accepts the string to be modified, returning the cleaned-up version:

```
$text = "\t\t\tlots of room to breathe    ";
$text = trim( $text );
print $text;
// prints "lots of room to breathe";
```

Of course, this might be more work than you require. You might want to keep white space at the beginning of a string but remove it from the end. You can use PHP's rtrim() function exactly the same as you would trim(). Only white space at the end of the string argument is removed, however:

```
$text = "\t\t\tlots of room to breathe    ";
$text = rtrim( $text );
print $text;
// prints "        lots of room to breathe";
```

PHP provides the ltrim() function to strip white space only from the beginning of a string. Once again, this is called with the string you want to transform and returns a new string, shorn of tabs, newlines, and spaces:

```
$text = "\t\t\tlots of room to breathe    ";
$text = ltrim( $text );
print "<pre>$text</pre>";
// prints "lots of room to breathe    ";
```

Notice that we wrapped the $text variable in a <pre> element. Remember that the <pre> element preserves space and newlines, so we can use it to check on the performance of the ltrim() function.

PHP by its nature tends to work with markup text. It is not unusual to have to remove tags from a block to present it without formatting. PHP provides the strip_tags() function, which accepts two arguments, for this purpose. The first argument it accepts is the text to transform. The second argument is optional and should be a list of HTML tags that strip_tags() can leave in place. Tags in the exception list should not be separated by any characters, like so:

```
$string = "<p>I <i>simply</i> will not have it,";
$string .= "<br/>said Mr Dean</p><b>The end</b>";
print strip_tags( $string, "<br/>" );
```

In the previous code fragment, we create an HTML-formatted string. When we call strip_tags(), we pass it the $string variable and a list of exceptions. The result is that the <p> and <br/> elements are left in place and all other tags are stripped out.

Replacing a Portion of a String Using substr_replace()

substr_replace() works similarly to substr() except it enables you to replace the portion of the string you extract. The function requires three arguments: the string you are transforming, the text you want to add to it, and the starting

index. It also accepts an optional length argument. `substr_replace()` finds
the portion of a string specified by the starting index and length arguments,
replacing this portion with the string provided in the replace string argument and
returning the entire transformed string.

In the following code fragment, to renew a user's membership code, we must
change its second two characters:

```
<?
$membership = "mz99xyz";
$membership = substr_replace( $membership, "00", 2, 2 );
print "New membership number: $membership<br/>";
// prints "New membership number: mz00xyz"
?>
```

Replacing Substrings Using `str_replace()`

`str_replace()` replaces all instances of a string within another string. It requires
three arguments: a search string, the replacement string, and the string on which
this transformation is to be effected. The function returns the transformed string.
The following example uses `str_replace()` to change all instances of 2000 to
2001 within a string:

```
$string = "Site contents copyright 2003. ";
$string .= "The 2003 Guide to All Things Good in Europe";
print str_replace("2003","2004",$string);
```

As of PHP 4.05, `str_replace()` has been enhanced to accept arrays as well as
strings for all its arguments. This enables you to perform multiple search and
replace operations on a subject string, and even on more than one subject string:

```
<?php
$source = array(
"The package which is at version 4.2 was released in 2000",
  "The year 2000 was an excellent period for PointyThing4.2" );
$search = array( "4.2", "2000" );
$replace = array( "5.0", "2001" );
$source = str_replace( $search, $replace, $source );
foreach( $source as $str )
  print "$str<br>";

// prints:
// The package which is at version 5.0 was released in 2001
// The year 2001 was an excellent period for PointyThing5.0
?>
```

When `str_replace()` is passed an array of strings for its first and second arguments, it attempts to switch each search string with its corresponding replace

string in the text to be transformed. When the third argument is an array, the `str_replace()` returns an array of strings. The search and replace operations are executed upon each string in the array.

Converting Case

PHP provides several functions that enable you to convert the case of a string. When you write user-submitted data to a file or database, you might want to convert it all to upper- or lowercase text first, to let you more easily compare it later. To get an uppercase version of a string, use the function `strtoupper()`. This function requires only the string you want to convert and returns the converted string:

```
$membership = "mz00xyz";
$membership = strtoupper( $membership );
print "$membership<P>"; // prints "MZ00XYZ"
```

To convert a string to lowercase characters, use the function `strtolower()`. Again, this requires the string you want to convert and returns a converted version:

```
$home_url = "WWW.CORROSIVE.CO.UK";
$home_url = strtolower( $home_url );
if ( ! ( strpos ( $home_url, "http://" ) === 0 ) )
  $home_url = "http://$home_url";
print $home_url; // prints "http://www.corrosive.co.uk"
```

PHP also provides a case function that has a useful cosmetic purpose. `ucwords()` makes the first letter of every word in a string uppercase. The following fragment makes the first letter of every word in a user-submitted string uppercase:

```
$full_name = "violet elizabeth bott";
$full_name = ucwords( $full_name );
print $full_name; // prints "Violet Elizabeth Bott"
```

Although this function makes the first letter of each word uppercase, it does not touch any other letters. So, if the user had had problems with her Shift key in the previous example and submitted VIolEt eLIZaBeTH bOTt, our approach would not have done much to fix the string. We would have ended up with VIolEt ELIZaBeTH BOTt, which isn't much of an improvement. We can deal with this by making the submitted string lowercase with `strtolower()` before invoking `ucwords()`:

```
$full_name = "VIolEt eLIZaBeTH bOTt";
$full_name = ucwords( strtolower($full_name) );
print $full_name; // prints "Violet Elizabeth Bott"
```

Wrapping Text with wordwrap() and nl2br()

When you present plain text within a Web page, you are often faced with the problems that newlines are not displayed and your text runs together into a featureless blob. nl2br() is a convenient method that converts every newline into an HTML break. So

```
$string = "one line\n";
$string .= "another line\n";
$string .= "a third for luck\n";
print nl2br( $string );
```

prints the following:

```
one line<br />
another line<br />
a third for luck<br />
```

Notice that the <br> tags are output in XHTML-compliant form. This was introduced in PHP 4.0.5.

nl2br() is great for honoring newlines that are already in the text you are converting. Occasionally, though, you might want to add arbitrary line breaks to format a column of text. The wordwrap() function is perfect for this; it requires one argument, the string to be transformed. By default, wordwrap() wraps lines every 75 characters and uses \n as its line-break character. So, the code fragment

```
$string = "Given a long line, wordwrap() is useful as a means of ";
$string .= "breaking it into a column and thereby making it easier to read";
print wordwrap($string);
```

would output

```
Given a long line, wordwrap() is useful as a means of breaking it into a
column and thereby making it easier to read
```

Because the lines are broken with the character \n, the formatting does not show up in HTML mode. wordwrap() has two more optional arguments: a number representing the maximum number of characters per line and a string representing the end of the line string you want to use. Applying the function call

```
print wordwrap( $string, 24, "<br/>\n" );
```

to our $string variable, our output would be

```
Given a long line,<br/>
wordwrap() is useful as<br/>
a means of breaking it<br/>
into a column and<br/>
thereby making it easier<br/>
to read
```

`wordwrap()` doesn't automatically break at your line limit if a word has more characters than the limit. You can, however, use an optional fourth argument to enforce this. The argument should be a positive integer. Using `wordwrap()` in conjunction with the fourth argument, we can now wrap a string, even where it contains words that extend beyond the limit we are setting. This fragment

```
$string = "As usual you will find me at http://www.witteringonaboutit.com/";
$string .= "chat/eating_green_cheese/forum.php. Hope to see you there!";
print wordwrap( $string, 24, "<br/>\n", 1 );
```

outputs the following:

```
As usual you will find<br/>
me at<br/>
http://www.witteringonab<br/>
outit.com/chat/eating_gr<br/>
een_cheese/forum.php.<br/>
Hope to see you there!
```

Breaking Strings into Arrays with `explode()`

The delightfully named `explode()` function is similar in some ways to `strtok()`. `explode()`, though, breaks up a string into an array, which you can then store, sort, or examine as you want. `explode()` requires two arguments: the delimiter string you want to use to break up the source string and the source string itself. `explode()` optionally accepts a third argument that determines the maximum number of pieces the string can be broken into. The delimiter string can include more than one character, all of which form a single delimiter (unlike multiple delimiter characters passed to `strtok()`, each of which is a delimiter in its own right). The following fragment breaks up a date and stores the result in an array:

```
$start_date = "2000-01-12";
$date_array = explode("-", $start_date);
// $date[0] == "2000"
// $date[1] == "01"
// $date[2] == "12"
```

Formatting Numbers As Text

We have already looked at `printf()` and `sprintf()`, which are powerful functions for formatting numbers of all types in a string context. `printf()` is not, however, an ideal tool for adding commas to larger numbers. For that, we can turn to `number_format()`.

At a minimum, `number_format()` accepts a number to be transformed. It returns a string representation of the number with commas inserted after every three digits, as shown here:

```
print number_format(100000.56 );
// 100,001
```

In the previous fragment, we pass `100000.56` to `number_format()`, and it returns `100,001`. It has removed the decimal part and rounded the number up and has also inserted a comma. We might want to keep the full number, so `number_format()` enables us to determine the precision we require using a second argument: an integer. Here's how:

```
print number_format(100000.56, 2 );
// 100,001.56
print number_format(100000.56, 4 );
// 100,001.5600
```

We can even alter the characters used to represent the decimal point and the thousands separator. To do this, we should pass two further strings to `number_format()`—the first representing the thousands separator and the second representing the decimal point:

```
print number_format(100000.56, 2, "-", " ");
// 100 000-56
```

Formatting Currency with `money_format()`

By the Way

The `money_format()` function is not available on Windows platforms.

Although the `printf()` function is a useful way of presenting currency data, as of PHP 4.3, a more specialized tool has become available. `money_format()` is similar to `printf()` and `sprintf()` in that it works with a format specification to transform its data.

`money_format()` requires two arguments: a string containing a format specification and a double. It returns a formatted string. In contrast to `printf()`, you cannot pass the function additional arguments, so you should use it to format one number at a time.

The format specification should begin with a percent symbol and can be followed by optional flags, a field width specifier, left and right precision specifiers, and a conversion character. Of these, only the percent character and the conversion character are required.

The output of this function is affected by the locale of your system. This determines the symbol used for currency, the decimal point character, and other attributes that change from region to region. For our examples, we will use a function called setLocale() to set the context to U.S. English explicitly:

```
setLocale(LC_ALL, 'en_US');
```

Having done this, we can set up some test values and store them in an array:

```
$cash_array = array( 235.31, 5, 2000000.45 );
```

Let's take a look at the most basic format specification possible:

```
foreach ( $cash_array as $cash ) {
  print money_format("%n\n", $cash);
}
/*
$235.31
$5.00
$2,000,000.45
*/
```

We pass a string and a floating-point number, stored in the $cash variable, to money_format(). The format specification is made up of the % character and a conversion character (n), which stands for "national." This conversion character causes the number to be formatted according to national conventions for money. In this case, it signifies the use of the dollar character, as well as commas inserted to break up the thousands in larger numbers. The alternative conversion specifier is i, which causes an international format to be applied. Replacing the n specifier with an i specifier in the previous fragment would yield the following:

```
USD 235.31
USD 5.00
USD 2,000,000.45
```

A field width specifier can optionally follow the percent character (or follow the flags described next if they are set). This provides padding to ensure that the output matches at least the given number of characters:

```
foreach ( $cash_array as $cash ) {
  print money_format("%40n\n", $cash);
}
/*
                  $235.31
                    $5.00
            $2,000,000.45
*/
```

In the previous fragment, we set the field width to 40 simply by adding 40 to the format specification after the percent sign. Notice that the numbers are right-aligned by default.

We can also define padding for the left side of the decimal point in a number using a left precision specifier. This follows the field width specifier and consists of a hash character (#) followed by a number representing the number of characters to pad:

```
foreach ( $cash_array as $cash ) {
  print money_format("%#10n\n", $cash);
}
/*
$     235.31
$       5.00
$  2,000,000.45
*/
```

In the example, we used #10 to pad the left side of the decimal place. Notice that the gap between the dollar character and the decimal place is greater than 10 characters—this allows room for the grouping characters (that is, the commas that separate the thousands in numbers to aid readability). So, to combine a field width of 40 with a left precision of 10, we would use %40#10n. This would give us the following output:

```
$     235.31
$       5.00
$  2,000,000.45
```

We can also control the number of decimal places to display using the right precision specifier. This follows the left precision specifier and consists of a decimal point and the number of decimal places to display. To show five decimal places, we might extend the previous format specification: %40#10.5n. This would give the following output:

```
$     235.31000
$       5.00000
$  2,000,000.45000
```

Finally, you can use optional flags directly after the percent character to change the way in which formatting occurs. Table 8.3 lists the available flags and shows their effects on output when applied to a format specifier of %#10n. Let's take a look at the effect of this format specifier without a flag:

```
print money_format("%#10n", -2000000.45);
/*
-$  2,000,000.45
*/
```

TABLE 8.3   Format Specifier Flags

Flag	Description	Example Format	Example Output
!	Suppress currency character	%!#10n	- 2,000,000.45
^	Suppress number grouping	%^#10n	-$ 2000000.45
+	Include +/- symbol	%+#10n	-$ 2,000,000.45
(	Use brackets to distinguish minus numbers	%(#10n	($ 2,000,000.45)
-	Left-justify (default is right-justify)	%-#10n	-$2,000,000.45
=n	Use n character to fill left padding	%=.#10n	-$....2,000,000.45

Summary

Strings are PHP's principal means of communication with the outside world and of storing information for later use. This hour has covered some of the functions that enable you to take control of the strings in your scripts.

You learned how to format strings with printf() and sprint(). You should be able to use these functions both to create strings that transform data and to lay it out. You learned about functions that investigate strings. You should now be able to discover the length of a string with strlen(), determine the presence of a sub-string with strpos(), and extract a substring with substr(). You should also be able to tokenize a string with strtok().

Finally, you learned about functions that transform strings. You can now remove white space from the beginning or end of a string with trim(), ltrim(), and rtrim(). You can change case with strtoupper(), strtolower(), and ucwords(), and you can replace all instances of a string with str_replace().

Finally, you learned about two functions for formatting numbers: number_format() and money_format().

Believe it or not, you are not finished with strings yet. PHP supports regular expressions, which are an even more powerful means of working with strings than the functions already examined. We will look at these in detail in Hour 18, "Working with Regular Expressions."

Q&A

Q *Are there any other string functions that might be useful to me?*

A Yes. PHP has about 60 string functions! You can read about them all in the PHP online manual at `http://www.php.net/manual/ref.strings.php`.

Q *In the example that demonstrated `printf()`, you showed the formatting by wrapping your output in `<pre>` tags. Is this the best way of showing format- ted plain text on a browser?*

A `<pre>` tags can be useful if you want to preserve plain-text formatting in an HTML context. If you want to output an entire text document to the brows- er, however, it is neater to tell the browser to format the entire output as plain text. You can do this with the `header()` function:

```
Header("Content-Type: Text/Plain");
```

Workshop

Quiz

1. Which conversion specifier would you use with `printf()` to format an integer as a double? Write down the full syntax required to convert the integer 33.

2. How would you pad the conversion you effected in question 1 with zeroes so that the part before the decimal point is four characters long?

3. How would you specify a precision of two decimal places for the floating-point number you have been formatting in the previous questions?

4. Which function would you use to determine the length of a string?

5. Which function would you use to acquire the starting index of a substring within a string?

6. Which function would you use to extract a substring from a string?

7. How might you remove white space from the beginning of a string?

8. How would you convert a string to uppercase characters?

9. How would you break up a delimited string into an array of substrings?

Answers

1. The conversion specifier f is used to format an integer as a double:

```
printf("%f", 33 );
```

2. You can pad the output from printf() with the padding specifier—that is, a space or a zero followed by a number representing the number of characters by which you want to pad:

```
printf("%04f", 33 );
```

3. The precision specifier consists of a dot (.) followed by a number representing the precision you want to apply. It should be placed before the conversion specifier:

```
printf("%04.2f", 33 );
```

4. The strlen() function returns the length of a string.

5. The strstr() function returns the starting index of a substring.

6. The substr() function extracts and returns a substring.

7. The ltrim() function removes white space from the start of a string.

8. The strtoupper() function converts a string to uppercase characters.

9. The explode() function splits up a string into an array.

Exercises

1. Create a function that works with two arguments. The first argument should be a username, and the second should be an email address. Use case conversion functions to capitalize the first letter of the username. Convert the email address to lowercase characters and check that it contains the @ sign. If you can't find the @ character, return false; otherwise, return an array containing the converted arguments. Test the function.

2. Create an array of doubles and integers. Loop through the array converting each element to a floating-point number with a precision of 2. Right-align the output within a field of 20 characters.

HOUR 9

Objects

What You'll Learn in This Hour:

▶ What objects and classes are

▶ How to create classes and instantiate objects

▶ How to create and access properties and methods

▶ How to manage access to properties and methods

▶ How to create classes that inherit functionality from others

▶ How to find out about objects in your code

▶ How to save objects to a string that can be stored in a file or database

Object-oriented programming is dangerous. It can change the way you think about coding, and once the concepts have a hold on you, they don't let go. PHP, like Perl before it, has progressively incorporated more object-oriented aspects into its syntax and structure. PHP 4 made it possible to use object-oriented code at the heart of a project. PHP 5 has extended PHP's object-oriented features still further.

Throughout this hour, you'll take a tour of PHP's object-oriented features and apply them to some real-world code.

What Is an Object?

An **object** is an enclosed bundle of variables and functions forged from a special template called a class. Objects hide a lot of their inner workings away from the code that uses them, providing instead easy interfaces through which you can send them orders and they can return information. These interfaces are special functions called methods. All the methods of an object have access to special variables called properties.

By defining a class, you lay down a set of characteristics. By creating objects of that type, you create entities that share these characteristics but might initialize them as different values. You might create an automobile class, for example. This class would have a color characteristic. All automobile objects would share the characteristic of color, but some would initialize it to "blue," others to "green," and so on.

Perhaps the greatest benefit of object-oriented code is its reusability. Because the classes used to create objects are self-enclosed, they can be easily pulled from one project and used in another. Additionally, it is possible to create child classes that inherit and override the characteristics of their parents. This technique can allow you to create progressively more complex and specialized objects that can draw on base functionality while adding more of their own.

Perhaps the best way to explain object-oriented programming is to do it.

Creating an Object

To create an object, you must first design the template from which it can be instantiated. This template is known as a **class**, and in PHP, you must declare it with the class keyword:

```
class Item {
    // a very minimal class
}
```

The Item class is the basis from which you can instantiate any number of Item objects. To create an instance of an object, you must use the new statement:

```
$obj1 = new Item();
$obj2 = new Item();
print "\$obj1 is an ".gettype($obj1)."<br />";
print "\$obj2 is an ".gettype($obj2)."<br />";
```

You can test that $obj1 and $obj2 contain objects with PHP's gettype() function. gettype() accepts any variable and returns a string that should tell you what you are dealing with. In a loosely typed language like PHP, gettype() is useful when checking arguments sent to functions. In the previous code fragment, gettype() returns the string "object", which is then written to the browser.

So you have confirmed that you have created two objects. Of course, they're not very useful yet, but they help to make an important point. You can think of a class as a mold with which you can press as many objects as you want. Let's add some more features to the class to make your objects a little more interesting.

Object Properties

Objects have access to special variables called properties. You can declare them anywhere within the body of your class, but for the sake of clarity, you should define them at the top. A property can be a value, an array, or even another object:

```
class Item {
  var $name = "item";
}
```

Notice that we declared our variable with the var keyword. In PHP 4, this was the only way to declare a property. We will look at some additional approaches that PHP 5 makes available later in the hour. If you are writing code that needs to be compatible with PHP 4, then you should use var.

Now any Item object that is created contains a property called $name with the value of "item". You can access this property from outside the object and even change it:

```
class Item {
    var $name = "item";
}

$obj1 = new Item();
$obj2 = new Item();
$obj1->name = "widget 5442";
print "$obj1->name<br />";
print "$obj2->name<br />";

// prints:
// widget 5442
// item
```

The -> operator allows you to access or change the properties of an object. Although $obj1 and $obj2 were born with the name of "item", we have given $obj2 an individual identity by assigning the string "widget 5442" to its $name property, before using the -> operator once again to print each object's name property to the screen.

You can use objects to store information, but that makes them only a little more interesting than associative arrays. In the next section, we will look at object methods, and your objects can get a little more active.

Object Methods

A **method** is a function defined within a class. Every object instantiated from the class has the method's functionality. Listing 9.1 adds a method to the Item class (line 5).

LISTING 9.1   A Class with a Method

```
 1: <?php
 2: class Item {
 3:   var $name = "item";
 4:
 5:   function getName() {
 6:     return "item";
 7:   }
 8: }
 9:
10: $item = new Item();
11: print $item->getName();
12: // outputs "item"
13: ?>
```

As you can see, a method looks and behaves much like a normal function. A method is always defined within a class, however. You can call an object method using the -> operator. Importantly, methods have access to the class's member variables. In Listing 9.2, we return the string "item" when asked for the Item object's name. Clearly, this isn't good practice: the method's return value should be a copy of the $name property and not a string literal. You've already seen how to access a property from outside an object, but how does an object refer to itself? Find out in Listing 9.2.

LISTING 9.2   Accessing a Property from Within a Method

```
 1: <?php
 2: class Item {
 3:   var $name = "item";
 4:
 5:   function getName() {
 6:     return $this->name;
 7:   }
 8: }
 9:
10: $item = new Item();
11: $item->name = "widget 5442";
12: print $item->getName();
13: // outputs "widget 5442"
14: ?>
```

A class uses the special variable $this to refer to the currently instantiated object
(line 6). You can think of it as a personal pronoun. Although you refer to an
object by the handle you have assigned it to ($item, for example), an object must
refer to itself by means of the $this variable. Combining the $this pseudo-
variable and ->, you can access any property or method in a class from within
the class itself.

Imagine that you want to allow some objects to have different $name property val-
ues than others. You could do this by manually resetting the $name property as
you did earlier, or you could create a method to do it for you, as shown in Listing
9.3 on line 10.

LISTING 9.3   Changing the Value of a Property from Within a Method

```
 1: <?php
 2: class Item {
 3:    var $name = "item";
 4:
 5:    function setName( $n ) {
 6:       $this->name = $n;
 7:    }
 8:
 9:    function getName() {
10:       return $this->name;
11:    }
12: }
13:
14: $item = new Item();
15: $item->setName("widget 5442");
16: print $item->getName();
17: // outputs "widget 5442"
18: ?>
```

The name property of the object begins as "item" (line 3), but after the object's
setName() method is called on line 15, it is changed to "widget 5442". Notice
how the object is capable of adjusting its own property. Notice also that you can
pass arguments to the method in exactly the same way as you would to a normal
function.

Object Constructors

In our previous example, we used a method, setName(), to amend the $name
property. The initial value for the name property was hard-coded into the class:

```
var $name = "item";
```

If we expect the $name property to hold a different value for every instance of the Item class, we would do better to offer the client coder the chance to set the $name property when the object is initialized. We can use a special function called a **constructor** to set properties and perform any other preparatory work we require. A constructor is automatically called when the object is instantiated using the new keyword.

You can create constructors in two ways. Prior to PHP 5, the constructor was always a function that took the same name as the class that contained it. Listing 9.4 adds a traditional constructor to the Item class. This code remains valid in PHP 5.

LISTING 9.4   A Class with a Constructor

```
 1: <?php
 2: class Item {
 3:   var $name;
 4:
 5:   function Item( $name="item" ) {
 6:     $this->name = $name;
 7:   }
 8:
 9:   function setName( $n ) {
10:     $this->name = $n;
11:   }
12:
13:   function getName() {
14:     return $this->name;
15:   }
16: }
17:
18: $item = new Item("widget 5442");
19: print $item->getName();
20: // outputs "widget 5442"
21: ?>
```

The Item() constructor method on line 5 is automatically called when we instantiate an Item object. We set up a default so that the string "item" is assigned to the parameter if we don't include an argument when we create our object.

PHP 5 introduces a new syntax for constructor methods. Instead of using the name of the class, you can use the special syntax __construct(). So we could convert line 5 of Listing 9.4 to use the new syntax by replacing Item() with __construct():

```
function __construct( $name="listing" ) {
  // ..
}
```

This is not change for its own sake. We will encounter a good reason for using the new constructor syntax later in the chapter.

The __construct() **Method Works with PHP 5 Only**

The __construct() method was introduced with PHP 5. The method name does not have special significance in PHP 4, and the method is not called automatically.

Watch Out!

Limiting Access to Object Properties

PHP 4 provided no protection for object properties. Client code could get or set object properties at will. So what's wrong with that? Often, there is no problem having publicly accessible properties, although it is generally good practice to narrow access to your objects as much as possible. In Listing 9.5, we can see a condition in which we would definitely want to limit access to the $name property in our Item class.

LISTING 9.5   A Class with Public Properties

```php
 1: <?php
 2: class Item {
 3:   var $name;
 4:   var $code;
 5:   var $productString;
 6:
 7:   function Item( $name="item", $code=0 ) {
 8:     $this->name = $name;
 9:     $this->code = $code;
10:     $this->setName( $name );
11:   }
12:
13:   function getProductString() {
14:     return $this->productString;
15:   }
16:
17:   function setName( $n ) {
18:     $this->name - $n;
19:     $this->productString = $this->name." ".$this->code;
20:   }
21:
22:   function getName() {
23:     return $this->name;
24:   }
25: }
26:
27: $item = new Item("widget", 5442);
28: print $item->getProductString();
29: // outputs "widget 5442"
30:
31: print "<br />";
32:
33: $item->name = "widget-upgrade";
34: print $item->getProductString();
35: // outputs "widget 5442", not "widget-upgrade 5442"
36: ?>
```

We have made some changes to the Item class in Listing 9.5. The constructor now expects two arguments on line 7, $name and $code. In our example, then, a product has a human-readable name (such as widget) and a product code (such as 5442) used by a database. We have a new property, $productString, which is a combination of the item's $name and $code properties. Whenever client code uses setName() to change the name property on line 17, the method also updates $productString. So when we bypass the setName() method on line 33 and set the $name property manually, we break the object. The $productString property is no longer correct.

PHP 5 gives us a different way to declare our properties. In place of the var keyword, we could use one of three new keywords. They will be familiar to anyone moving from Java to PHP. We list PHP 5's new property declaration keywords in Table 9.1.

TABLE 9.1 PHP 5 Property Declaration Keywords

Privacy Level	Description
public	Accessible to all. Equivalent to var.
private	Available only to the containing class.
protected	Available only to the containing class and subclasses.

We can amend our properties in Listing 9.5 to make them private:

```
private $name;
private $code;
private $productString;
```

Now, our attempt to change the $name property of the Item object on line 34 would result in the following error message:

```
Fatal error: Cannot access private property Item::$name
➥in /home/mz/htdocs/listing9.5.php on line 33
```

Client coders are now forced to use the setName() method to change the $name property.

The private keyword is the most extreme mechanism for ensuring privacy. You might often want child classes to have access to a property. In these cases, you would use the protected keyword, which allows no access from client code but does allow access by classes derived from the current class. We will look at inheritance and privacy in the section "Inheritance."

Limiting Access to Object Methods

A principle of object-oriented code is that you should only expose as much of a class as you absolutely have to. Objects should have clearly defined responsibilities and clear public interfaces. You might want to create all sorts of utility methods for a function. Unless they are useful to client code, and part of the class's core responsibility, you should hide them from the wider world. Let's say, for example, that we would like to delegate the creation of the $productString property in Listing 9.5 to a method.

Currently, all work takes place in the setName() method:

```
function setName( $n ) {
    $this->name = $n;
    $this->productString = $this->name." ".$this->code;
}
```

Because the mechanism for creating product strings might become more complex, and because other methods might want to reset the string themselves for various reasons, we extract the line that assigns to the $productString property, replacing it with a call to a new method:

```
function setName( $n ) {
    $this->name = $n;
    $this->makeProductString( $n, $this->code );
}

function makeProductString( $string, $code) {
    return $this->productString = "$string $code";
}
```

Of course, we've now made trouble for ourselves because client code can access the makeProductString() method and mess with our data. We want the object and only the object to construct this property. In PHP 5, we can apply privacy to methods just as we can to properties:

```
private function makeProductString( $string, $code) {
    // ...
```

The makeProductString() function is now accessible only by methods in the Item class. You can apply three possible privacy keywords to method declarations. public is the default and is implicit. A method declared with the public keyword (or with no privacy keyword at all) is accessible from any context. Methods declared private are accessible only to other methods in the enclosing class. Methods declared with the protected keyword are available only to the enclosing class and any child classes that extend the closing class. Once again, we will cover child classes in the section "Inheritance," later in this chapter.

> ### public, protected, and private **Work with PHP 5 Only**
> The keywords public, protected, and private were introduced with PHP 5. Using them with methods or properties in PHP 4 will cause your script to fail.

Constraining Arguments to Methods with Hints

In PHP 4, and most of the time in PHP 5, you have to rely on type-checking code and naming conventions to signal the argument types your methods expect. This generally suffices but can lead to error-prone code when the wrong data type is passed to the wrong argument variable.

Let's create a method that collects Item objects to illustrate some of the dangers that a relaxed attitude toward type can bring:

```
class ItemLister {
  private $items = array();

  function addItem( $item ) {
    array_push( $this->items, $item );
  }

  function splurgeItems() {
    foreach( $this->items as $item ) {
      print $item->getProductString();
      print "<br />";
    }
  }
}
```

The ItemLister class is very simple indeed. It uses the addItem() method to collect Item objects. The splurgeItems() method simply loops through all stored Item objects, calling the getProductString() method on each of them. Here's how we might work with the ItemLister class:

```
$lister = new ItemLister();
$lister->addItem( new Item("widget", 5442) );
$lister->addItem( new Item("spogget", 676) );
$lister->addItem( new Item("kapotchnak", 88) );
$lister->addItem( new Item("floobit", 21) );
$lister->splurgeItems();
```

As long as you are in charge of working with `ItemLister`, all should be well. What happens, though, if a coder joins your project without a good understanding of `Item` and `ItemLister` objects and passes an `ItemLister` the wrong kind of object?

```
class WrongClass { }
$lister = new ItemLister();
$lister->addItem( new WrongClass() );
$lister->splurgeItems();
```

This code generates an error, but only when the `splurgeItems()` method of the `ItemLister` object attempts to invoke `WrongClass::getProductString()`:

```
Fatal error: Call to undefined method wrongclass::getProductString()
➥ in /home/mz/htdocs/wrongargs.php on line 11
```

In other words, the `ItemLister` class has stored the wrong kind of object in its `$items` property, and we only find out about it some time later. This kind of separation between the cause of an error and its effect can be hard to debug. Ideally, we want to catch the error when `addItem()` is called and not at some indeterminate future point.

We can do so in PHP 4 by adding type-checking code to `addItem()`. This is a time-consuming chore, however, and in practice usually omitted. We will cover techniques for testing object types in the section "Testing Classes and Objects."

PHP 5 gives us a neat way of constraining the type of object arguments. We can use hints. A **hint** is simply the name of an object type placed before the argument variable in a method declaration:

```
function addItem( Item $item ) {
  array_push( $this->items, $item );
}
```

If anything other than an `Item` object is passed to `addItem()` in this fragment, a fatal error is generated:

```
Fatal error: Argument 1 must be an instance of Item
```

Unfortunately, this kind of checking only works with objects. You still must manually test primitive types such as integers and floats.

Inheritance

To create a class that inherits functionality from a parent class, we need to alter our class declaration slightly. Listing 9.6 simplifies the Item class and creates an inheriting class called PriceItem.

LISTING 9.6   Creating a Class That Inherits from Another

```
 1: <?php
 2: class Item {
 3:   var $name;
 4:
 5:   function Item( $name="item", $code=0 ) {
 6:       $this->name = $name;
 7:       $this->code = $code;
 8:   }
 9:
10:   function getName() {
11:       return $this->name;
12:   }
13: }
14:
15: class PriceItem extends Item {
16:
17: }
18:
19: $item = new PriceItem( "widget", 5442 );
20: print $item->getName();
21: // outputs "widget"
22:
23: ?>
```

In addition to the simple Item class defined on line 2, we have created an even more basic PriceItem class on line 15. Notice the extends clause in the class declaration. This means that a PriceItem object inherits all the functionality laid down in the Item class. Any PriceItem object will have access to a getName() method and a name property just as any Item object would (depending upon privacy settings).

If that's not enough, there's even more magic in Listing 9.6. Notice that we didn't define a constructor method for the PriceItem class. So how was the $name property changed from the default, "item", to the value ("widget") passed to the PriceItem class? Because we didn't provide a constructor in PriceItem, the Item class's constructor was automatically called.

By the Way

If a class extending another doesn't contain a constructor method, the parent class's constructor method will be called automatically when a child object is created. This feature was introduced in PHP 4.

Overriding the Method of a Parent Class

The PriceItem class currently creates objects that behave in exactly the same way as Item objects. In object-oriented code, child classes can override the methods of their parents, allowing objects instantiated from them to behave differently, while otherwise retaining much of the same functionality. Listing 9.7 gives the PriceItem class its own getName() method.

LISTING 9.7   The Method of a Child Class Overriding That of Its Parent (PHP 4 Syntax)

```
 1: <?php
 2: class Item {
 3:    var $name;
 4:
 5:    function Item( $name="item", $code=0 ) {
 6:       $this->name = $name;
 7:       $this->code = $code;
 8:    }
 9:
10:    function getName() {
11:       return $this->name;
12:    }
13: }
14:
15: class PriceItem extends Item {
16:    function getName() {
17:       return "(price) ".$this->name;
18:    }
19: }
20:
21: $item = new PriceItem( "widget", 5442 );
22: print $item->getName();
23: // outputs "(price) widget"
24:
25: ?>
```

The getName() method in the PriceItem class (line 16) is called in preference to that in the parent class. At this point, we can pause for a moment and consider the effect of making the $name property in the Item class private:

```
class Item {
  private $name;
  // ...
```

Making this change to Listing 9.7 would cause the output to change from the following:

```
(price) widget
```

The new output is

```
(price)
```

The `PriceItem` class does not have access to the `$name` property. If your child classes need to access methods or properties of their ancestor classes, then you should use the `protected` keyword in preference to `private`.

Calling an Overridden Method

Occasionally, you want the functionality of a parent class's method as well as the benefit of your own additions. Object-oriented programming allows you to have your cake and eat it, too. You can refer to a parent class using the `parent` keyword. In Listing 9.8, the `PriceItem`'s `getName()` method calls the method in the `Item` class that it has overridden.

LISTING 9.8 Calling an Overridden Method (PHP 5 Syntax)

```
 1: <?php
 2: class Item {
 3:    private $name;
 4:
 5:    function __construct( $name="item", $code=0 ) {
 6:        $this->name = $name;
 7:        $this->code = $code;
 8:    }
 9:
10:    function getName() {
11:        return $this->name;
12:    }
13: }
14:
15: class PriceItem extends Item {
16:    function getName() {
17:        return "(price) ".parent::getName();
18:    }
19: }
20:
21: $item = new PriceItem( "widget", 5442 );
22: print $item->getName();
23: // outputs "(price) widget"
24:
25: ?>
```

By using the following syntax, we can call any method that we have overridden:

```
parent::methodname()
```

We do so in the `PriceItem` class's `getName()` method on line 17. Because the `PriceItem` class no longer works directly with the `Item` class's `$name` property, we could at this point declare the `$name` property `private`, with no effect on output. If you are working exclusively with PHP 5, it is good practice to lock down your methods and properties as far as you can.

Working with Constructors

We have seen that a parent class's constructor is automatically called if the child class does not define its own constructor method. If the child class does define a constructor, it becomes responsible for calling the constructor of its parent. In Listing 9.9, we add a constructor to our `PriceItem` class.

LISTING 9.9 Adding a Constructor to `PriceItem`

```php
1: <?php
2: class Item {
3:    private $name;
4:
5:    function __construct( $name="item", $code=0 ) {
6:       $this->name = $name;
7:       $this->code = $code;
8:    }
9:
10:    function getName() {
11:       return $this->name;
12:    }
13: }
14:
15: class PriceItem extends Item {
16:    private $price;
17:
18:    function __construct( $name, $code, $price ) {
19:      parent::__construct( $name, $code );
20:      $this->price = $price;
21:    }
22:
23:    function getName() {
24:       return "(price) ".parent::getName();
25:    }
26: }
27:
28: $item = new PriceItem( "widget", 5442, 5.20 );
29: print $item->getName();
30: // outputs "(price) widget"
31:
32: ?>
```

We create a constructor method on line 18, accepting arguments for name and code and adding a new one for price. We use the `parent` keyword to invoke the `Item` class's constructor (line 19) before setting the `$price` property ourselves. It is here that we can see one reason for PHP 5's new syntax for constructors. The following line is nicely generic:

```php
parent::__construct( $name, $code );
```

If we insert a new class into the inheritance hierarchy between Item and PriceItem, the constructor of the new class would be invoked according to the altered extends clause of PriceItem. Prior to PHP 5, however, it was necessary to refer to a parent class's constructor, which was the name of the parent class itself:

```
parent:Item( $name, $code );
```

It was a common bug in object-oriented code that a class's extends clause would be modified to point to an intermediate parent class, and the constructor call would be forgotten, causing unexpected and hard-to-analyze errors. The new syntax addresses this bug to some extent.

We will return to the Item and PriceItem classes in Hour 17, "Advanced Objects."

Testing Classes and Objects

We have already seen how we can use functions like gettype(), is_int(), and so on to test data types. This process is very useful in ensuring that functions are supplied with the right arguments.

By the Way

The Reflection API

If you want to examine your script's objects, methods, and properties in fine detail at runtime, you should look at another feature new to PHP 5. Discussing the Reflection API is beyond the scope of this book, but by the time you read this, documentation for it should be available in the manual at http://www.php.net/manual.

The Reflection API is a set of built-in classes with methods for discovering everything you might need to know about an object's class given an instance of the object. Typical uses for this tool include automatic documentation and dynamic mechanisms for querying objects and saving their data to relational databases.

All objects belong to the "object" data type, but we sometimes need more information than that.

Finding the Class of an Object

We have already seen that we can use hints with PHP 5 to ensure that we are working with an object belonging to a particular type. Sometimes, you might still want to confirm the type of an object. You can query the type of any object with the get_class() function. get_class() accepts an object and returns the name of its class (in lowercase letters). So given an array of objects, you might want to test each one before working with it:

```
foreach ( $objectArray as $obj ) {
  if ( get_class( $obj ) == "priceitem" ) {
    print "doing a pricey thing\n";
  } else {
    die( "not designed to handle ".get_class( $obj ) );
  }
}
```

`get_class()` will only tell us that an object belongs to a certain class. This information is of limited use. We generally need to know the type of an object rather than its class. In the preceding fragment, a subclass of `PriceItem` would fail the `get_class()` test. This is probably not what we want because objects from `PriceItem` subclasses are guaranteed to support the same interface as those instantiated from `PriceItem` itself.

Finding the Family of an Object

In PHP 4, the `is_a()` function provides us with the best tool for determining type. `is_a()` accepts an object and the name of the class from which the object should be derived. If the object's class is the same as, or a subclass of, the class argument provided, the function returns `true`; otherwise, it returns `false`.

So if you are not running PHP 5, or if you have written PHP 4 compatible code, you can test a method to an argument using `is_a()`:

```
function addItem( $item ) {
  if ( ! is_a( $item, "item" ) ) {
    die( "required a item object" );
  }
  array_push( $this->items, $item );
}
```

When testing object types in PHP 5, you should use the new `instanceof` keyword. `instanceof` provides the same information as the `is_a()` function, but it uses operator rather than function syntax. You can see it in action in the following fragment:

```
if ( ! $item instanceof item ) {
  //...
}
```

The object to be tested is the left operand, and the class name to test the object against is the right operand. The entire expression reads like a sentence: "`$item` is an instance of `item`."

Checking for Class and Method Existence

As libraries grow, classes become increasingly interdependent. With this inter-dependence comes the possibility that a class might attempt to invoke another that is not available to the script. PHP provides you with functions for testing both class and method existence.

class_exists() requires a string representing a class name. If the user-defined class is found, the function returns true. Otherwise, it returns false. class_exists() is especially useful when using class names stored in strings:

```php
if ( class_exists( $class_name ) ) {
  $obj = new $class_name( );
}
```

method_exists() requires two arguments, an object and a string containing the name of the method you are checking for:

```php
if ( method_exists( $filter_object, "filter" ) ) {
  print $filter_object->filter( "hello you<br />" );
}
```

Automatically Loading Include Files with __autoload()

In a large project, code files tend to fill up with calls to include_once(). Very often, you will find that you are loading many files unnecessarily as you copy around amended source files. By the same token, you waste time adding include_once() calls to class files, only to run the script and discover that more files need including. PHP 5 provides the built-in __autoload() function, which is automatically called whenever you try to instantiate an nonexistent class. __autoload() is passed a string variable representing the class name that was not found. You can then use this string to include a source file:

```php
<?php
function __autoload( $class ) {
  $file = "$class.inc.php";
  include_once( $file );
}

$test = new Artichoke();
?>
```

In this fragment, we attempt to instantiate an object from a nonexistent Artichoke class. __autoload() is automatically called. As long as a file called artichoke.inc.php exists and contains the Artichoke class, the file will be included and the object instantiated. Remember, however, that __autoload was introduced with PHP 5.

Storing and Retrieving Objects

Usually, you separate your objects from data storage. In other words, you use saved data to construct objects, and then when you are done, you store the data again. Occasionally, however, you want your object and data to persist intact. PHP provides two functions to help you.

To "freeze-dry" an object, you should pass it to the serialize() function. serialize() produces a string that you can then store in a file or a database or transmit to another script:

```
class apple {
  var $flavor="sweet";
}
$app = new apple();
$stored = serialize( $app );
print $stored;
// prints "O:5:"apple":1:{s:6:"flavor";s:5:"sweet";}"
```

You can convert the string produced by serialize() back into an object with the unserialize() function. If the original class is present at the time unserialize() is called, an exact copy of the original object is produced:

```
$new_app = unserialize( $stored );
print $new_app->flavor;
// prints "sweet"
```

In some circumstances, you need your objects to clean up a little before storage. This cleanup is particularly important if an object has a database connection open or is working with a file. By the same token, you might want your object to perform some sort of initialization when it is woken up. You can handle these needs by including two special methods in any object that might need to be serialized.

The __sleep() method is automatically called by serialize() before it packs up the object. This process allows you to perform any cleanup operations you might need. For the serialization to work, your __sleep() method must return an array of the property names that you want to be saved in the serialized string:

```
class apple {
  var $flavor="sweet";
  var $frozen = 0;
```

```
function __sleep() {
  $this->frozen++;
  // any clean up stuff goes here
  return array_keys( get_object_vars( $this ) );
}
}
$app = new apple();
$stored = serialize( $app );
print $stored;
// prints "O:5:"apple":2:{s:6:"flavor";s:5:"sweet";s:6:"frozen";i:1;}"
```

Notice the trick we used at the end of the __sleep() method to list the names of
all the properties in the object. We used the built-in function get_object_vars().
This function requires an object and returns an associative array of all the properties belonging to it. We pass the result of our call to get_object_vars() to the
array_keys() function. array_keys() accepts an array (usually an associative
array) and returns an array of its keys.

PHP also supports a special method called __wakeup(). If it is defined, it is automatically called by unserialize(). This process enables you to resume database
connections or to provide any other initialization the object might need. We
might add the following method to our apple class:

```
function __wakeup() {
  print "This apple has been frozen ".$this->frozen." time(s)";
  // any initialization stuff goes here
}
```

Now that we have added __wakeup(), we can call unserialize():

```
$new_app = unserialize( $stored );
// prints "This apple has been frozen 1 time(s)"
```

Summary

We have only scratched the surface of PHP's support for objects in this hour. We
will cover more in Hour 17.

The extent to which you use objects and classes in your projects is a matter of
choice. It is likely that heavily object-oriented projects will be somewhat more
resource-intensive at runtime than more traditional code. However, effective
deployment of object-oriented techniques can significantly improve the flexibility
and organization of your code.

Throughout this hour, you learned how to create classes and instantiate objects
from them. You learned how to create and access properties and methods. You

learned how to build new classes that inherit and override the features of other classes.

Finally, you learned how to determine the class of an object and whether an object's class is a subclass of another.

Now that we have covered the core of the PHP language, we are ready to move on and begin to explore some of its wider features. In the next hour, we look at PHP's support for handling HTML forms.

Q&A

Q *This hour introduced some unfamiliar concepts. Do I really need to understand object-oriented programming to become a good PHP programmer?*

A The short answer is no. Most PHP scripts use little or no object-oriented code at all. The object-oriented approach won't help you do things that you couldn't otherwise achieve. The benefits of object-oriented programming lie in the organization of your scripts, their reusability, and their extensibility. The benefits of object-oriented design can be enormous, however, which is one reason why PHP 5 provides extended support for objects.

Even if you decide not to produce object-oriented code, you might need to decipher third-party programs that contain classes. This hour should help you understand such code.

Q *I'm confused by the special variable* $this.

A Within a class, you sometimes need to call the class's methods or access its properties. By combining the $this variable and the -> operator, you can do both. The $this variable is the handle a class is automatically given to refer to itself and to its components.

Workshop

Quiz

1. How would you declare a class called emptyClass() that has no methods or properties?

2. Given a class called emptyClass(), how would you create an object that is an instance of it?

3. How can you declare a property within a class?

4. How would you choose a name for a constructor method?

5. How would you prevent a method from being accessed except from within the current class and child classes?

6. How would you create a private method in PHP 4?

7. How can you access and set properties or methods from within a class?

8. How would you access an object's properties and methods from outside the object's class?

9. What should you add to a class definition if you want to make it inherit functionality from another class?

Answers

1. You can declare a class with the `class` keyword:

```
class emptyClass {

}
```

2. You should use the `new` operator to instantiate an object:

```
$obj = new emptyClass();
```

3. In PHP 4, you can declare a property using the `var` keyword:

```
class Point {
  // properties
  var $x = 0;
  var $y = 0;
}
```

Using PHP 5, you can also use the `private`, `protected`, or `public` keywords.

4. A constructor must either take the name of the class that contains it (for PHP 4 compatibility) or it should be named __construct().

5. You can limit the availability of a method to the current class and child classes by using the `protected` keyword:

```
protected function dontTouchMe( ) {
  // no access outside current class and children
}
```

6. There is no way of enforcing privacy in PHP 4. There is, however, a convention that functions beginning with an underscore character should be treated as private:

```
function _pleaseDontTouchMe() {
// not enforceable
}
```

7. Within a class, you can access a property or method by combining the $this variable and the -> operator:

```
class Point {
  // properties
  public $x = 0;
  public $y = 0;

  // constructor
  function __construct( $x, $y ) {
    // calling a method
    $this->moveTo( $x, $y );
  }

  // method
  public function moveTo( $x, $y ) {
    // setting properties
    $this->x = $x;
    $this->y = $y;
  }
}
```

8. You can call an object's methods and access its properties using a reference to the object (usually stored in a variable) in conjunction with the -> operator:

```
// instantiating an object
$p = new Point( 40, 60 );

// calling an object's method
$p->moveTo( 20, 200 );

// accessing an object's property
print $p->x;
```

9. For a class to inherit from another, it must be declared with the extends keyword and the name of the class from which you want to inherit:

```
class funkyPoint extends Point {
}
```

Exercises

1. Create a class called baseCalc() that stores two numbers as properties. Give it a calculate() method that prints the numbers to the browser.

2. Create a class called addCalc() that inherits its functionality from baseCalc(). Override the calculate() method so that the sum of the properties is printed to the browser.

3. Repeat activity 2 for a class called minusCalc(). Give minusCalc() a calculate method that subtracts the first property from the second, outputting the result to the browser.

PART III

Working with PHP

HOUR 10

Working with Forms

What You'll Learn in This Hour:

- ▶ How to get and use server variables
- ▶ How to access information from form fields
- ▶ How to work with form elements that allow multiple selections
- ▶ How to create a single document that contains both an HTML form and the PHP code that handles its submission
- ▶ How to save state with hidden fields
- ▶ How to redirect the user to a new page
- ▶ How to build HTML forms that upload files and how to write the PHP code to handle them

Until now, all the examples in this book have been missing a crucial dimension. You can set variables and arrays, create and call functions, and work with objects. All this work is meaningless if users can't reach into a language's environment to offer it information. In this hour, you will look at strategies for acquiring and working with user input.

On the World Wide Web, HTML forms are the principle means by which substantial amounts of information can pass from the user to the server. PHP is designed to acquire and work with information submitted via HTML forms.

Superglobal Variables

Before you actually build a form and use it to acquire data, we need to make a small detour and look at superglobal variables. We first met global variables in Hour 6, "Functions." A **global variable** is any variable declared at the "top level" of a script—that is, declared outside a function. **Superglobal variables** are arrays built in to PHP. They are populated for you automatically with useful elements, and they are available in any scope. You can access a superglobal array within a function or method without using the `global` keyword. We will encounter superglobal variables throughout the rest of this book. Table 10.1 provides a summary.

TABLE 10.1   PHP Superglobal Arrays

Array	Description
$_COOKIE	Contains keys and values set as browser cookies
$_ENV	Contains keys and values set by the script's shell context
$_FILES	Contains information about uploaded files
$_GET	Contains keys and values submitted to the script using the HTTP get method
$_POST	Contains keys and values submitted to the script using the HTTP post method
$_REQUEST	A combined array containing values from the $_GET, $_POST, and $_COOKIES superglobal arrays
$_SERVER	Variables made available by the server
$GLOBALS	Contains all global variables associated with the current script

The $_SERVER Array

The $_SERVER array contains elements set by your script's context, usually the server. There is no guarantee that any or all of the common elements will be set in it. If you are running PHP as a server module, however, it is likely that you will find at least the elements summarized in Table 10.2. They can be very useful in providing additional information about the context of a user request.

In Listing 10.1, we loop through the $_SERVER array, printing the results to the browser.

LISTING 10.1   Looping Through the $_SERVER Array

```
1: <!DOCTYPE html PUBLIC
2:     "-//W3C//DTD XHTML 1.0 Strict//EN"
3:     "http://www.w3.org/TR/xhtml1/DTD/xhtml1-strict.dtd">
4: <html>
5: <head>
6: <title>Listing 10.1 Looping through the $_SERVER array</title>
7: </head>
8: <body>
```

LISTING 10.1   Continued

```
 9: <div>
10: <?php
11: foreach ( $_SERVER as $key=>$value ) {
12:    print "\$_SERVER[\"$key\"] == $value<br/>";
13: }
14: ?>
15: </div>
16: </body>
17: </html>
```

We use a foreach loop to access the keys and values in $_SERVER, printing to the browser on line 12. If PHP is running as a server module, you should find the elements listed in Table 10.2 in the output.

TABLE 10.2   Some Common $_SERVER Elements

Variable	Contains	Example
$_SERVER['PHP_SELF']	The current script. Suitable for use in links and form element action arguments.	/phpbook/source/ listing10.1.php
$_SERVER['HTTP_USER_AGENT']	The name and version of the client.	Mozilla/4.6 -(X11; I;Linux2.2. 6-15apmac ppc)
$_SERVER['REMOTE_ADDR']	The IP address of the client.	158.152.55.35
$_SERVER['REQUEST_METHOD']	Whether the request was GET or POST.	POST
$_SERVER['QUERY_STRING']	For GET requests, the encoded data sent appended to the URL.	name=matt&address =unknown
$_SERVER['REQUEST_URI']	The full address of the request, including query string.	/phpbook/source/ listing10.1.php? name=matt
$_SERVER['HTTP_REFERER']	The address of the page from which the request was made.	http://p24. corrosive. co.uk/ref.html

Note the PHP_SELF element in particular. We use it to point forms and links back at their enclosing scripts in examples throughout this book.

A Script to Acquire User Input

For now, we'll keep our HTML separate from our PHP code. Listing 10.2 builds a simple HTML form.

LISTING 10.2   A Simple HTML Form

```
 1: <!DOCTYPE html PUBLIC
 2:     "-//W3C//DTD XHTML 1.0 Strict//EN"
 3:     "http://www.w3.org/TR/xhtml1/DTD/xhtml1-strict.dtd">
 4: <html>
 5: <head>
 6: <title>Listing 10.2 A Simple HTML Form</title>
 7: </head>
 8: <body>
 9: <div>
10: <form action="listing10.3.php" method="get">
11: <p><input type="text" name="user"/></p>
12: <p>
13: <textarea name="address" rows="5" cols="40">
14: </textarea>
15: </p>
16: <p><input type="submit" value="hit it!" /></p>
17: </form>
18: </div>
19: </body>
20: </html>>
```

We define a form that contains a text field with the name "user" on line 11, a text area with the name "address" on line 13, and a submit button on line 16. It is beyond the remit of this book to cover HTML in detail. If you find the HTML in these examples hard going, take a look at *Sams Teach Yourself HTML in 24 Hours* or one of the numerous online HTML tutorials. The form element's action argument points to a file called listing10.3.php, which processes the form information. Because we haven't added anything more than a filename to the action argument, the file listing10.3.php should be in the same directory on the server as the document that contains our HTML.

Listing 10.3 creates the code that receives our users' input.

LISTING 10.3   Reading Input from the Form in Listing 10.2

```
 1: <!DOCTYPE html PUBLIC
 2:     "-//W3C//DTD XHTML 1.0 Strict//EN"
 3:     "http://www.w3.org/TR/xhtml1/DTD/xhtml1-strict.dtd">
 4: <html>
 5: <head>
 6: <title>Listing 10.3 Reading Input from the Form in Listing 10.2</title>
 7: </head>
 8: <body>
```

LISTING 10.3   Continued

```
 9: <div>
10: <?php
11: print "Welcome <b>".$_GET['user']."</b><br/>\n\n";
12: print "Your address is: <br/><b>".$_GET['address']."</b>";
13: ?>
14: </div>
15: </body>
16: </html>
```

This script is the first script in this book that is not designed to be called by hitting a link or typing directly into the browser's location field. We include the code from Listing 10.3 in a file called listing10.3.php. This file is called when a user submits the form defined in Listing 10.2.

In the code, we have accessed two elements of the superglobal $_GET array, user and address. It should come as no surprise that these variables contain the values that the user added to the text field named "user" and the text area named "address". We use the $_GET array because the form uses the HTTP get method to submit its data. Had we used the HTTP post method, we would have accessed elements of the $_POST array:

```
<form action="listing10.3.php" method="post">
```

We do not have to know or test the submission method used, however. PHP provides us with the $_REQUEST array. It will contain the merged contents of $_POST, $_GET, and $_COOKIE. We could therefore rewrite the code to output our elements in Listing 10.3 so that the script would work with both post and get methods.

```
print "Welcome <b>".$_REQUEST['user']."</b><br/>\n\n";
print "Your address is: <br/><b>".$_REQUEST['address']."</b>";mmnmnnnn ,, nn 1 ln
,
```

> **The register_globals php.ini Directive Is Disabled**
>
> Versions of PHP prior to 4.2 shipped with the php.ini register_globals directive set to 'Yes' by default. This caused submitted parameters ('user' and 'address' in Listing 10.2) to be generated as global variables ($user, $address). This functionality is now disabled by default, and register_globals is set to 'No'. You can reverse this setting yourself by setting register_globals back to 'Yes' in the php.ini file, but use of automatic globals is now actively discouraged because of the potential security risks involved.
>
> The superglobal variables $_GET, $_SET, and $_REQUEST are unaffected by the register_globals directive.

Watch Out!

Importing User Input into Global Scope

It is possible, but not recommended, to import fields from a form submission into global variables. This behavior was once the default for PHP. Although it was useful for quick scripts, it represented a security risk, with the prospect of user-submitted values overwriting script variables. You can change the new default by altering the php.ini file. You can also import user input explicitly with the import_request_variables() function. This function requires a string representing the types to import and another optional but advisable string that adds a prefix to all imported variable names. The types argument can be any combination of g, p and c, standing for get, post, and cookies, respectively. If you only use one or two of these letters, then only the corresponding parameters are imported. The order is important in that earlier types are overwritten by later ones. That is, with the string gp, get variables are overwritten by post variables of the same name. Suppose an input element called username is submitted via the get method:

```
<input type="text" name="username" />
```

We could call import_request_variables() in the following way:

```
import_request_variables( "g", "import_" );
```

This line would create a global variable called $import_username, containing the user-submitted value for the username field. All other fields submitted would be similarly imported.

Accessing Form Input with User-Defined Arrays

The examples so far enable us to gather information from HTML elements that submit a single value per element name. This leaves us with a problem when working with select elements. These elements make it possible for the user to choose multiple items. Suppose we name the select element with a plain name:

```
<select name="products" multiple="multiple">
```

The script that receives this data will only have access to a single value corresponding to this name in $_REQUEST['products']. We can change this behavior by renaming any elements of this kind so that its name ends with an empty set of square brackets. We do so in Listing 10.4.

LISTING 10.4 An HTML Form with a `select` Element

```
 1: <!DOCTYPE html PUBLIC
 2:    "-//W3C//DTD XHTML 1.0 Strict//EN"
 3:    "http://www.w3.org/TR/xhtml1/DTD/xhtml1-strict.dtd">
 4: <html>
 5: <head>
 6: <title>Listing 10.4 An HTML Form with a 'select' Element</title>
 7: </head>
 8: <body>
 9: <div>
10: <form action="listing10.5.php" method="post">
11: <p><input type="text" name="user" /></p>
12: <p>
13: <textarea name="address" rows="5" cols="40">
14: </textarea>
15: </p>
16: <p>
17: <select name="products[]" multiple="multiple">
18: <option>Sonic Screwdriver</option>
19: <option>Tricorder</option>
20: <option>ORAC AI</option>
21: <option>HAL 2000</option>
22: </select>
23: </p>
24: <p><input type="submit" value="hit it!" /></p>
25: </form>
26: </div>
27: </body>
28: </html>
```

In the script that processes the form input, we now find that input from the "products[]" form element created on line 17 will be available as an array indexed by the name products in either $_POST or $_REQUEST. products[] is a select element, and we offer the user multiple choices using the option elements on lines 18 to 21. We demonstrate that the user's choices are made available in an array in Listing 10.5.

LISTING 10.5 Reading Input from the Form in Listing 10.4

```
 1: <!DOCTYPE html PUBLIC
 2:    "-//W3C//DTD XHTML 1.0 Strict//EN"
 3:    "http://www.w3.org/TR/xhtml1/DTD/xhtml1-strict.dtd">
 4: <html>
 5: <head>
 6: <title>Listing 10.5 Reading Input from the Form in Listing 10.4</title>
 7: </head>
 8: <body>
 9: <div>
10: <?php
11: print "Welcome <b>".$_POST['user']."</b><br/>\n";
12: print "Your address is:<br/><b>".$_POST['address']."</b><br/>\n";
13:
```

LISTING 10.5   Continued

```
14: if ( is_array( $_POST['products'] ) ) {
15: print "<p>Your product choices are:</p>\n";
16: print "<ul>\n";
17:     foreach ( $_POST['products'] as $value ) {
18:         print "<li>$value</li>\n";
19:     }
20: print "</ul>\n";
21: }
22: ?>
23: </div>
24: </body>
25: </html>
```

On line 11, we access the $_POST['user'] element, which is derived from the user form element. On line 14, we test the $_POST['products'] element. If the element is an array as we expect, we loop through it on line 17, outputting each choice to the browser on line 18.

Although this technique is particularly useful with the select element, in fact it works with any form element at all. By giving a number of check boxes the same name, for example, you can allow a user to choose many values within a single field name. As long as the name you choose ends with empty square brackets, PHP compiles the user input for this field into an array. We can replace the select element from lines 12–17 in Listing 10.4 with a series of check boxes to achieve exactly the same effect:

```
<input type="checkbox" name="products[]"
➥value="Sonic Screwdriver" />Sonic Screwdriver<br/>
<input type="checkbox" name="products[]" value="Tricorder" />Tricorder<br/>
<input type="checkbox" name="products[]" value="ORAC AI" />ORAC AI<br/>
<input type="checkbox" name="products[]" value="HAL 2000" />HAL 2000<br/>
```

Combining HTML and PHP Code on a Single Page

For some smaller scripts, you might want to include form-parsing code on the same page as a hard-coded HTML form. Such a combination can be useful if you need to present the same form to the user more than once. You would have more flexibility if you were to write the entire page dynamically, of course, but you would miss out on one of the great strengths of PHP. The more standard HTML you can leave in your pages, the easier they will be for designers and page builders to amend without reference to you. You should avoid scattering substantial chunks of PHP code throughout your documents, however. This practice makes them hard to read and maintain. Where possible, you should create functions that can be called from within your HTML code and can be reused in other projects.

For the following examples, imagine that we are creating a site that teaches basic math to preschool children and have been asked to create a script that takes a number from form input and tells the user whether it is larger or smaller than a target integer.

Listing 10.6 creates the HTML. For this example, we need only a single text field and some PHP to display the user input.

LISTING 10.6   An HTML Form That Calls Itself

```
 1: <!DOCTYPE html PUBLIC
 2:     "-//W3C//DTD XHTML 1.0 Strict//EN"
 3:     "http://www.w3.org/TR/xhtml1/DTD/xhtml1-strict.dtd">
 4: <html>
 5: <head>
 6: <title>Listing 10.6 An HTML Form that Calls Itself</title>
 7: </head>
 8: <body>
 9: <div>
10: <?php
11: if ( ! empty( $_POST['guess'] ) ) {
12:     print "last guess: ".$_POST['guess'];
13: }
14: ?>
15: <form method="post" action="<?php print $_SERVER['PHP_SELF']?>">
16: <p>
17: Type your guess here: <input type="text" name="guess" />
18: </p>
19: </form>
20: </div>
21: </body>
22: </html>
```

We open our form element on line 15. Notice that we use $_SERVER['PHP_SELF'] to point the form back at its enclosing script. We could leave the action element out altogether, and most browsers would resubmit the form by default. That would break our conformance to XHTML, however. On line 11, we test the $_POST array for the existence of a 'guess' element and print it to the browser if we find it.

In Listing 10.7, we begin to build up the PHP logic of the page. First, we need to define the number that the user will guess. In a fully working version, we would probably randomly generate it, but for now we keep it simple. We assign 42 to the $num_to_guess variable on line 2. Next, we need to decide whether the form has been submitted so that we do not attempt to assess arguments that have not yet been made available. We test that the 'guess' element has been set in the $_POST array on line 4. If a user has submitted the form, this element is set, even if he has submitted an empty string or 0. So if the 'guess' element is absent, we can safely assume that the user has arrived at the page without submitting a form. If the element *is* present, we can go ahead and test the value it contains.

LISTING 10.7   A PHP Number-Guessing Script

```
 1: <?php
 2: $num_to_guess = 42;
 3: $message = "";
 4: if ( ! isset( $_POST['guess'] ) ) {
 5:    $message = "Welcome to the guessing machine!";
 6: } else if ( $_POST['guess'] > $num_to_guess ) {
 7:    $message = $_POST['guess']." is too big! Try a smaller number";
 8: } else if ( $_POST['guess'] < $num_to_guess ) {
 9:    $message = $_POST['guess']." is too small! Try a larger number";
10: } else { // must be equivalent
11:    $message = "Well done!";
12: }
13:
14: ?>
15: <!DOCTYPE html PUBLIC
16:    "-//W3C//DTD XHTML 1.0 Strict//EN"
17:    "http://www.w3.org/TR/xhtml1/DTD/xhtml1-strict.dtd">
18: <html>
19: <head>
20: <title>Listing 10.7 A PHP Number Guessing Script</title>
21: </head>
22: <body>
23: <h1>
24: <?php print $message ?>
25: </h1>
26: <form method="post" action="<?php print $_SERVER['PHP_SELF']?>">
27: <p>
28: Type your guess here: <input type="text" name="guess" />
29: <input type="submit" value="submit" />
30: </p>
31: </form>
32: </body>
33: </html>
```

The logic of this script consists of an if statement that determines which string to assign to the variable $message. If the $_POST['guess'] element has not been set, we assume that the user has arrived for the first time and assign a welcome string to the $message variable on line 5.

Otherwise, we test the 'guess' element against the number we have stored in $num_to_guess and assign advice to $message accordingly. We test whether 'guess' is larger than $num_to_guess on line 6 and whether it is smaller than

$num_to_guess on line 8. If 'guess' is neither larger nor smaller than $num_to_guess, we can assume that it is equivalent and assign a congratulations message to the variable (line 11). Now all we need to do is print the $message variable within the body of the HTML.

There are a few more additions yet, but you can probably see how easy it would be to hand this page over to a designer. He can make it beautiful without having to disturb the programming in any way.

Using Hidden Fields to Save State

The script in Listing 10.7 has no way of knowing how many guesses a user has made. We can use a hidden field to keep track of this. The mark-up for a hidden field is similar to that of a text field. From the user's perspective, however, it has no output. A user cannot see a hidden field, unless he views the HTML source of the document that contains it. Listing 10.8 adds a hidden field to the number-guessing script and some PHP to work with it.

LISTING 10.8   Saving State with a Hidden Field

```
 1: <?php
 2: $num_to_guess = 42;
 3: $message = "";
 4: if ( ! isset( $_POST['guess'] ) ) {
 5:    $message = "Welcome to the guessing machine!";
 6: } else if ( $_POST['guess'] > $num_to_guess ) {
 7:    $message = $_POST['guess']." is too big! Try a smaller number";
 8: } else if ( $_POST['guess'] < $num_to_guess ) {
 9:    $message = $_POST['guess']." is too small! Try a larger number";
10: } else { // must be equivalent
11:    $message = "Well done!";
12: }
13: $guess = (int) $_POST['guess'];
14: $num_tries = (int) $_POST['num_tries'];
15: $num_tries++;
16: ?>
17: <!DOCTYPE html PUBLIC
18:     "-//W3C//DTD XHTML 1.0 Strict//EN"
19:     "http://www.w3.org/TR/xhtml1/DTD/xhtml1-strict.dtd">
20: <html>
21: <head>
22: <title>Listing 10.8 A PHP Number Guessing Script</title>
23: </head>
24: <body>
25: <div>
26: <h1>
27: <?php print $message ?>
28: </h1>
29: Guess number: <?php print $num_tries?><br/>
30:
```

LISTING 10.8   Continued

```
31: <form method="post" action="<?php print $_SERVER['PHP_SELF']?>">
32: <p>
33: <input type="hidden" name="num_tries" value="<?php print $num_tries?>" />
34: Type your guess here: <input type="text" name="guess"
35:                           value="<?php print $guess?>"/>
36: </p>
37: </form>
38: </div>
39: </body>
40: </html>
```

The hidden field on line 33 is given the name "num_tries". We also use PHP to write its value. While we're at it, we do the same for the "guess" field on line 27 so that the user can always see his last guess. This technique is useful for scripts that parse user input. If we were to reject a form submission for some reason, we can at least allow our user to edit his previous query.

> ## You Can Automate print() with Short Opening Tags
>
> When you need to output the value of an expression to the browser, you can of course use print() or echo(). When you are entering PHP mode explicitly to output such a value, you can also take advantage of a special extension to PHP's short opening tags. If you add an equals (=) sign to the short PHP opening tag, the value contained will be printed to the browser. Note the following line:
>
>   <? print $test;?>
>
> It is equivalent to
>
>   <?=$test?>
>
> Remember, though, that the short open tag might be disabled on some sites and interfere with XML.

The variables $guess and $num_tries were extracted from the $_POST array on lines 13 and 14. We cast the values to integers and add one to $num_tries. The $num_tries variable is written to the value of the hidden field named 'num_tries' on line 33. Every time the user submits the form, the $_POST['num_tries'] element will have been incremented.

Watch Out!

> ## Be Careful with Client Stored Data
>
> Don't entirely trust hidden fields. You don't know where their values have been! This isn't to say that you shouldn't use them; just be aware that your users are capable of viewing and amending source code should they want to cheat your scripts.

Redirecting the User

Our simple script still has one major drawback. The form is rewritten whether or not the user guesses correctly. The fact that the HTML is hard-coded makes it difficult to avoid writing the entire page. We can, however, redirect the user to a congratulations page, thereby sidestepping the issue altogether.

When a server script communicates with a client, it must first send some headers that provide information about the document to follow. PHP usually handles this task for you automatically, but you can choose to send your own header lines with PHP's header() function.

To call the header() function, you must be sure that no output has been sent to the browser. The first time that content is sent to the browser, PHP sends out headers and it is too late for you to send your own. Any output from your document, even a line break or a space outside of your script tags, causes headers to be sent. If you intend to use the header() function in a script, you must make certain that nothing precedes the PHP code that contains the function call. You should also check any libraries that you might be using.

Listing 10.9 shows a request (lines 1 and 2) followed by typical response headers sent to the browser by PHP.

LISTING 10.9 A Request Prompts Response Headers from a PHP Script

```
1: HEAD /phpbook/source/listing10.8.php HTTP/1.0
2: Host:matt.corrosive.co.uk
3:
4: HTTP/1.1 200 OK
5: Date: Wed, 03 Sep 2003 13:52:09 GMT
6: Server: Apache/2.0.47 (Unix) PHP/5.0.0b1
7: X-Powered-By: PHP/5.0.0b1
8: Connection: close
9: Content-Type: text/html; charset=ISO-8859-1
```

You Can Browse the Web with Telnet

Did you Know?

You can see headers sent in response to a request by using a Telnet client. Connect to a Web host at port 80 and then type

```
HEAD /path/to/file.html HTTP/1.0
Host:www.example.com
```

followed by two returns. The headers should appear on your client.

By sending a "Location" header instead of PHP's default, you can cause the browser to be redirected to a new page:

```
header( "Location: http://www.corrosive.co.uk" );
```

Assuming that we have created a suitably upbeat page called congrats.html, we can amend our number-guessing script to redirect the user if she guesses correctly, as shown in Listing 10.10.

LISTING 10.10   Using header() to Send Raw Headers

```
 1: <?php
 2: $num_to_guess = 42;
 3: $message = "";
 4: if ( ! isset( $_POST['guess'] ) ) {
 5:    $message = "Welcome to the guessing machine!";
 6: } else if ( $_POST['guess'] > $num_to_guess ) {
 7:    $message = $_POST['guess']." is too big! Try a smaller number";
 8: } else if ( $_POST['guess'] < $num_to_guess ) {
 9:    $message = $_POST['guess']." is too small! Try a larger number";
10: } else { // must be equivalent
11:    header("Location:congrats.html");
12:    exit;
13: }
14: $guess = (int) $_POST['guess'];
15: $num_tries = (int) $_POST['num_tries'];
16: $num_tries++;
17: ?>
18: <!DOCTYPE html PUBLIC
19:    "-//W3C//DTD XHTML 1.0 Strict//EN"
20:    "http://www.w3.org/TR/xhtml1/DTD/xhtml1-strict.dtd">
21: <html>
22: <head>
23: <title>Listing 10.10 A PHP Number Guessing Script</title>
24: </head>
25: <body>
26: <div>
27: <h1>
28: <?php print $message ?>
29: </h1>
30: Guess number: <?php print $num_tries?><br/>
31:
32: <form method="post" action="<?php print $_SERVER['PHP_SELF']?>">
33: <p>
34: <input type="hidden" name="num_tries" value="<?php print $num_tries?>" />
35: Type your guess here: <input type="text" name="guess"
36:                        value="<?php print $guess?>"/>
37: </p>
38: </form>
39: </div>
40: </body>
41: </html>
```

The `else` clause of our `if` statement on line 10 now causes the browser to request `congrats.html`. We ensure that all output from the current page is aborted with the `exit` statement on line 12, which immediately ends execution and output, whether HTML or PHP.

Remember that sending content to the browser causes HTTP headers to be sent. If you then call the `header()` function, you cause an error. You code defensively by checking that headers have not been sent before calling `header()`:

```
if ( ! headers_sent() ) {
    header( "Location: http://www.example.com" );
    exit;
}
```

If headers have been sent, the `headers_sent()` function returns `true`. `headers_sent()` also optionally accepts two empty variables, into which it places the filename and line number, defining the point at which headers were sent. This function can be very useful for debugging:

```
if ( headers_sent( $file, $num ) ) {
    print "headers were sent in file: $file on line: $line";
}
```

File Upload Forms and Scripts

So far we've looked at simple form input. Browsers Netscape 2 or better and Internet Explorer 4 or better all support file uploads, and so, of course, does PHP. In this section, you will examine the features that PHP makes available to deal with this kind of input.

First, we need to create the HTML. HTML forms that include file upload fields must include an `ENCTYPE` argument:

```
ENCTYPE="multipart/form-data"
```

PHP also works with an optional hidden field that you can insert before the file upload field. It should be called `MAX_FILE_SIZE` and should have a value representing the maximum size in bytes of the file that you are willing to accept. This size cannot override the maximum size set in the `upload_max_filesize` field in your `php.ini` file that defaults to 2MB. The `MAX_FILE_SIZE` field is obeyed at the browser's discretion, so you should rely upon the `php.ini` setting to cap unreasonable uploads. After the `MAX_FILE_SIZE` field is entered, you are ready to add the upload field itself. It is simply an `input` element with a type argument of `"file"`. You can give it any name you want. Listing 10.11 brings all this work together into an HTML upload form.

LISTING 10.11 A Simple File Upload Form

```
1: <!DOCTYPE html PUBLIC
2:     "-//W3C//DTD XHTML 1.0 Strict//EN"
3:     "http://www.w3.org/TR/xhtml1/DTD/xhtml1-strict.dtd">
4: <html>
5: <head>
6: <title>Listing 10.11 A Simple File Upload Form</title>
7: </head>
8: <body>
9: <form enctype="multipart/form-data"
10:     action="<?print $_SERVER['PHP_SELF']?>" method="post">
11: <p>
12: <input type="hidden" name="MAX_FILE_SIZE" value="102400" />
13: <input type="file" name="fupload" /><br/>
14: <input type="submit" value="upload!" />
15: </p>
16: </form>
17: </body>
18: </html>
```

Notice that once again, this form calls the page that contains it. We are going to
add some PHP code to handle the uploaded file. We limited file uploads to 100KB
on line 12 and named our upload field "fupload" on line 13. As you might
expect, this name will soon become important.

When a file is successfully uploaded, it is given a unique name and stored in a
temporary directory. On Unix systems, the default temporary directory is /tmp,
but you can set it with the upload_tmp_dir directive in php.ini.

Information about the uploaded file will become available to you in the superglobal $_FILES array, which will be indexed by the names of each upload field in
the form. The corresponding value for each of these keys is itself an associative
array. These fields are described in Table 10.2.

TABLE 10.2 $_FILE Elements

Element	Contains	Example
$ FILES['fupload']['name']	Name of uploaded file	test.gif
$_FILES['fupload']['tmp_name']	Path to temporary file	/tmp/phprDfZvN
$_FILES['fupload']['size']	Size (in bytes) of uploaded file	6835
$_FILES['fupload']['error']	An error code corresponding to a PHP constant	UPLOAD_ERR_ FORM_SIZE
$_FILES['fupload']['type']	MIME type of uploaded file (where given by client)	image/gif

You can use the error element of an element in $_FILES to diagnose the reason for a failed upload. Assuming a file upload named 'fupload', we would find the error code in

```
$_FILES['fupload']['error]
```

Table 10.3 lists the possible error codes.

TABLE 10.3 $_FILE Error Constants

Constant Name	Value	Explanation
UPLOAD_ERR_OK	0	No problem
UPLOAD_ERR_INI_SIZE	1	File size exceeds php.ini limit set in upload_max_filesize
UPLOAD_ERR_FORM_SIZE	2	File size exceeds limit set in hidden element named MAX_FILE_SIZE
UPLOAD_ERR_PARTIAL	3	File only partially uploaded
UPLOAD_ERR_NO_FILE	4	File was not uploaded

Armed with this information, we can write a quick and dirty script that displays information about uploaded files (see Listing 10.12). If the uploaded file is in GIF format, the script will even attempt to display it.

LISTING 10.12 A File Upload Script

```
 1: <!DOCTYPE html PUBLIC
 2:     "-//W3C//DTD XHTML 1.0 Strict//EN"
 3:     "http://www.w3.org/TR/xhtml1/DTD/xhtml1-strict.dtd">
 4: <html>
 5: <head>
 6: <title>Listing 10.12 A File Upload Script</title>
 7: </head>
 8: <body>
 9: <div>
10: <?php
11: if ( isset( $_FILES['fupload'] ) ) {
12:
13:     print "name: ".     $_FILES['fupload']['name']      ."<br />";
14:     print "size: ".     $_FILES['fupload']['size'] ." bytes<br />";
15:     print "temp name: ".$_FILES['fupload']['tmp_name']   ."<br />";
16:     print "type: ".     $_FILES['fupload']['type']       ."<br />";
17:     print "error: ".    $_FILES['fupload']['error']      ."<br />";
18:
19:     if ( $_FILES['fupload']['type'] == "image/gif" ) {
20:
21:         $source = $_FILES['fupload']['tmp_name'];
22:         $target = "upload/".$_FILES['fupload']['name'];
23:         move_uploaded_file( $source, $target );// or die ("Couldn't copy");
```

LISTING 10.12 Continued

```
24:          $size = getImageSize( $target );
25:
26:          $imgstr  = "<p><img width=\"$size[0]\" height=\"$size[1]\" ";
27:          $imgstr .= "src=\"$target\" alt=\"uploaded image\" /></p>";
28:
29:          print $imgstr;
30:      }
31: }
32: ?>
33: </div>
34: <form enctype="multipart/form-data"
35:      action="<?php print $_SERVER['PHP_SELF']?>" method="post">
36: <p>
37: <input type="hidden" name="MAX_FILE_SIZE" value="102400" />
38: <input type="file" name="fupload" /><br/>
39: <input type="submit" value="upload!" />
40: </p>
41: </form>
42: </body>
43: </html>
```

In Listing 10.12, we first check that the $_FILES['fupload'] element exists. If so, we can assume that the user has at least attempted to upload a file. We output each of the elements of the $_FILES['fupload'] array on lines 13 to 17. We then test the $_FILES['fupload']['type'] element. If we are dealing with a GIF image file, we can go ahead and print an img element. To do so, we need to move the uploaded file away from its temporary location (stored in $_FILES['fupload'] ['tmp_name']) and to a directory in our Web space. We use a new function, move_uploaded_file(), to achieve this goal on line 23. move_uploaded_file() requires two arguments, a source and a destination, and moves one to the other. It is the safest way of working with uploaded files because it confirms that the source file referenced is an uploaded file and not a server file that should not be exposed to the world at large. Having moved the file to our Web space, we call another new function, getImageSize(). getImageSize() requires a path to an image and returns an array. The first two elements of the return array are the width and height of the image. We now have enough information to write out an img element, which we do on line 27.

Do Not Expect Sensible Filenames!

Beware of the names of uploaded files. Operating systems such as Mac OS and Windows are pretty relaxed when it comes to file naming, so expect uploaded files to come complete with spaces, quotation marks, and all manner of other unexpected characters. It is therefore a good idea to filter filenames. You can learn more about techniques for testing and checking strings in Hour 8, "Working with Strings," and Hour 18, "Working with Regular Expressions."

Summary

If you've kept up so far, things should be getting exciting now. You have the tools to create truly sophisticated and interactive environments. There are still a few things missing, of course. Now that you can get information from the user, it would be nice to be able to do something with it—write it to a file, perhaps. That is the subject of the next hour.

Throughout this hour, you have learned how to work with the $_SERVER, $_POST, $_GET, $_REQUEST, and $_FILE superglobal arrays to acquire predefined variables, form input, and uploaded file information. You have also learned how to send raw headers to the client to redirect a browser. You have learned how to acquire list information from form submissions and how to pass information from script call to script call using hidden fields.

Q&A

Q *Can I create arrays for values entered into elements other than select and check box fields?*

A Yes, in fact any element name ending with empty square brackets in a form resolves to an array element when the form is submitted. You can use this fact to group values submitted from multiple fields of any type into an array.

Q *The* header() *function seems powerful. Will we look at HTTP headers in more detail?*

A We cover HTTP (Hypertext Transfer Protocol) in more detail in Hour 14, "Beyond the Box."

Workshop

Quiz

1. Which $_SERVER array element could you use to determine the IP address of a user?

2. Which predefined variable could you use to find out about the browser that called your script?

3. What should you name your form fields if you want to find an array in the element $_REQUEST['form_array']?

4. Which superglobal associative array contains all values submitted as part of a GET request?

5. Which superglobal associative array contains all values submitted as part of a POST request?

6. What function would you use to redirect the browser to a new page? What string would you pass it?

7. How can you limit the size of a file that a user can submit via a particular upload form?

8. How can you set a limit on the size of upload files for all forms and scripts?

Answers

1. The $_SERVER['REMOTE_ADDR'] element should store the user's IP address.

2. Browser type and version, as well as the user's operating system, are usually stored in an element called 'HTTP_USER_AGENT' in the $_SERVER array.

3. Creating multiple fields with the name form_array[] creates a populated array in $_REQUEST['form_array'] when the form is submitted.

4. The superglobal array $_GET contains all values submitted as part of a GET request.

5. The superglobal array $_POST contains all values submitted as part of a POST request.

6. You can redirect a user by calling the header() function. You should pass it a Location header:

```
header("Location: anotherpage.html");
```

7. When creating upload forms in PHP, you can include a hidden field called MAX_FILE_SIZE:

```
<input type="hidden" name="MAX_FILE_SIZE" value="51200" />
```

8. The php.ini option upload_max_filesize determines the maximum size of an upload file that any script will accept. It is set to 2MB by default.

Exercises

1. Create a calculator script that allows the user to submit two numbers and choose an operation to perform on them (addition, multiplication, division, subtraction).

2. Use hidden fields with the script you created in exercise 1 to store and display the number of requests that the user has submitted.

HOUR 11

Working with Files

What You'll Learn in This Hour:

▶ How to include files in your documents
▶ How to test files and directories
▶ How to open a file before working with it
▶ How to read data from files
▶ How to write or append to a file
▶ How to lock a file
▶ How to work with directories

Testing, reading, and writing to files are staple activities for any full-featured programming language. PHP is no exception, providing you with functions that make the process straightforward.

Including Files with `include()`

The `include()` statement enables you to incorporate files into your PHP documents. PHP code in these files can be executed as if it were part of the main document. This can be useful for including library code in multiple pages.

Having created a killer function, your only option without `include()` would be to paste it into every document that needs to use it. Of course, if you discover a bug or want to add a feature, you must find every page that uses the function to make the change. The `include()` statement can save you from this chore. You can add the function to a single document and, at runtime, read this into any page that needs it. The `include()` statement requires a single argument—a relative path to the file to be included. Listing 11.1 creates a simple PHP script that uses `include()` to incorporate and output the contents of a file.

By the Way

PHP also provides the require() statement, which is identical to include() in almost every respect. The key difference is that require() halts script execution if the file it seeks to include cannot be found. The include() statement generates a warning if a file cannot be found but does not stop execution.

LISTING 11.1   Using include()

```
 1: <!DOCTYPE html PUBLIC
 2:    "-//W3C//DTD XHTML 1.0 Strict//EN"
 3:    "http://www.w3.org/TR/xhtml1/DTD/xhtml1-strict.dtd">
 4: <html>
 5: <head>
 6: <title>Listing 11.1 Using include()</title>
 7: </head>
 8: <body>
 9: <div>
10: <?php
11: include("listing11.2.php");
12: ?>
13: </div>
14: </body>
15: </html>
```

The include() statement in Listing 11.1 incorporates the document listing11.2.php, the contents of which you can see in Listing 11.2. When run, Listing 11.1 outputs the string "I have been included!!", which might seem strange, given that we have included plain text within a block of PHP code. Shouldn't this cause an error? In fact, the contents of an included file are displayed as HTML by default. If you want to execute PHP code in an included file, you must enclose it in PHP start and end tags. In Listings 11.3 and 11.4, we amend the previous example so that code is executed in the included file.

LISTING 11.2   The File Included in Listing 11.1

```
1: I have been included!!
```

LISTING 11.3   Using the include() Statement to Execute PHP in Another File

```
 1: <!DOCTYPE html PUBLIC
 2:    "-//W3C//DTD XHTML 1.0 Strict//EN"
 3:    "http://www.w3.org/TR/xhtml1/DTD/xhtml1-strict.dtd">
 4: <html>
 5: <head>
 6: <title>Listing 11.3 Using include() to Execute PHP in Another File</title>
 7: </head>
 8: <body>
 9: <div>
```

LISTING 11.3   Continued

```
10: <?php
11: include("listing11.4.php");
12: ?>
13: </div>
14: </body>
15: </html>
```

LISTING 11.4   An Include File Containing PHP Code

```
1: <?php
2: print "I have been included!!<BR>";
3: print "But now I can add up.. 4 + 4 = ".(4 + 4);
4: ?>
```

Returning a Value from an Included Document

Included files in PHP can return a value in the same way as functions do. As in a function, using the `return` statement ends the execution of code within the included file. Additionally, no further HTML is included. In Listings 11.5 and 11.6, we include a file and assign its return value to a variable.

LISTING 11.5   Using `include()` to Execute PHP and Assign the Return Value

```
1: <!DOCTYPE html PUBLIC
2:   "-//W3C//DTD XHTML 1.0 Strict//EN"
3:   "http://www.w3.org/TR/xhtml1/DTD/xhtml1-strict.dtd">
4: <html>
5: <head>
6: <title>Listing 11.5 Acquiring a Return Value with include()</title>
7: </head>
8: <body>
9: <div>
10: <?php
11: $addResult = include("listing11.6.php");
12: print "The include file returned $addResult";
13: ?>
14: </div>
15: </body>
16: </html>
```

LISTING 11.6   An Include File That Returns a Value

```
1: <?php
2: $retval = ( 4 + 4 );
3: return $retval;
4: ?>
5: This HTML should never be displayed because it comes after a return statement!
```

By the Way Returning values from included files would work in PHP 3 only if the `return` statement was contained in a function. The code in Listing 11.6 would cause an error.

Using `include()` **Within Control Structures**

You can use an `include()` statement in a conditional statement, and the referenced file is read only if the condition is met. The `include()` statement in the following fragment is never called, for example:

```
$test = false;
if ( $test ) {
  include( "a_file.txt" ); // won't be included
}
```

If you use an `include()` statement within a loop, it is replaced with the contents of the referenced file each time the `include()` statement is called. This content is executed for every call. Listing 11.7 illustrates this by using an `include()` statement in a for loop. The `include()` statement references a different file for each iteration.

LISTING 11.7 Using `include()` **Within a Loop**

```
 1: <!DOCTYPE html PUBLIC
 2:   "-//W3C//DTD XHTML 1.0 Strict//EN"
 3:   "http://www.w3.org/TR/xhtml1/DTD/xhtml1-strict.dtd">
 4: <html>
 5: <head>
 6: <title>Listing 11.7 Using include() Within a Loop</title>
 7: </head>
 8: <body>
 9: <div>
10: <?php
11: for ( $x=1; $x<=3; $x++ ) {
12:   $incfile = "incfile".$x.".txt";
13:   print "<p>";
14:   print "Attempting include $incfile<br/>";
15:   include( "$incfile" );
16:   print "</p>";
17: }
18: ?>
19: </div>
20: </body>
21: </html>
```

When Listing 11.7 is run, it includes the content of three files: incfile1.txt, incfile2.txt, and incfile3.txt. Assuming that each of these files simply contains a confirmation of its own name, the output should look something like this:

```
Attempting include incfile1.txt
This is incfile1.txt
```

```
Attempting include incfile2.txt
This is incfile2.txt

Attempting include incfile3.txt
This is incfile3.txt
```

include_once()

One of the problems caused by using multiple libraries within your code is the danger of calling `include()` twice on the same file. This can occur in larger projects when different library files call `include()` on a common file. Including the same file twice often results in the repeated declaration of functions and classes, thereby causing the PHP engine great unhappiness.

The situation is saved by the `include_once()` statement, which requires the path to an include file and behaves in the same way as `include()` the first time it is called. If `include_once()` is called again for the same file during script execution, however, the file is *not* included again.

This makes `include_once()` an excellent tool for the creation of reusable code libraries.

> PHP also provides the `require_once()` statement, which behaves in the same way as `include_once()` with a single exception. If the target file is not encountered when you use `require_once()`, script execution is halted with a fatal error. If the target file is not encountered when you use `include_once()`, a warning is generated but script execution continues.
>
> **By the Way**

Using `include_once()` **and** `include_path` **to Manage Larger Projects**

As your projects grow larger in scope and you find yourself including more and more files, keeping track of your work can be difficult. You can recover control by organizing code into libraries and organizing your libraries into packages.

As you work on a project, you should look for opportunities to create libraries that might also be useful for other projects. Try to create code that is as independent of your wider application as possible. The most reusable classes or functions will require data and perform tasks without relying on global variables. As you add to your stock of code, you can organize it using the file system itself. Let's imagine a programmer named Mary Jones. Mary has created the following range of useful classes in files:

```
DatabaseLayer.php
XmlHelper.php
Logger.php
```

Mary might use directories to organize these libraries, like so:

```
maryjones/db/DatabaseLayer.php
maryjones/xml/XmlHelper.php
maryjones/util/Logger.php
```

When it comes to accessing her libraries, Mary faces a problem. She can use a relative path to reference a library, like so:

```
include_once( "../lib/maryjones/db/DatabaseLayer.php" );
```

Or she could use an absolute path, like so:

```
include_once( "/home/mary/htdocs/lib/maryjones/db/DatabaseLayer.php" );
```

Both these approaches have their problems. The absolute path ties Mary's project to the current server, so she will not be able to deploy the project on another server without changing the absolute paths throughout. The relative path approach is better, but it forces Mary to include the maryjones packages within the calling project. It would be more effective to make the libraries globally available. Furthermore, even relative paths reduce flexibility to some extent. Mary cannot move the maryjones directory without updating all files that include it.

Mary can deal with this shortcoming using the include_path configuration option in the php.ini file. You can use include_path to define a list of directories that will be searched when include() type functions specify relative paths. Directories should be separated by colons (semicolons on Windows platforms), as shown here:

```
include_path=".:/home/mary/php_lib:/usr/local/lib/php"
```

In the previous fragment, Mary has added a path to a php_lib directory. She stores her maryjones directory there. Now any PHP file can include a maryjones package library:

```
include_once("maryjones/db/DatabaseLayer.php");
include_once("maryjones/xml/XmlHelper.php");
include_once("maryjones/util/Logger.php");
```

As long as the include_path is set, Mary's code runs on another server without any changes.

If Mary has no access to the `php.ini` file on her server, she still has other options. If she is running Apache, she can set the `include_path` option in an `.htaccess` file:

```
php_value include_path /home/mary/php_lib
```

She could also use the `ini_set()` function to set the option at runtime:

```
ini_set("include_path", "/home/mary/php_lib");
```

As of PHP 4.3, she can use the `set_include_path()`function to achieve the same effect, like so:

```
set_include_path( "/home/mary/php_lib" );
```

Testing Files

Before you work with a file or directory, you should learn more about it. PHP provides many functions that help you discover information about files on your system. This section briefly covers some of the most useful ones.

Checking for Existence with `file_exists()`

You can test for the existence of a file with the `file_exists()` function, which requires a string representing an absolute or a relative path to a file that might or might not be there. If the file is found, it returns `true`; otherwise, it returns `false`:

```
if ( file_exists("test.txt") ) {
  print "The file exists!";
}
```

A File or a Directory?

You can confirm that the entity you are testing is a file, as opposed to a directory, with the `is_file()` function. `is_file()` requires the file path and returns a Boolean value:

```
if ( is_file( "test.txt" ) ) {
  print "test.txt is a file!";
}
```

Conversely, you might want to check that the entity you are testing is a directory. You can do this with the `is_dir()` function. `is_dir()` requires the path to the directory and returns a Boolean value:

```
if ( is_dir( "/tmp" ) ) {
  print "/tmp is a directory";
}
```

Checking the Status of a File

When you know that a file exists, and it is what you expect it to be, you can then find out some things you can do with it. Typically, you might want to read, write to, or execute a file. PHP can help you with all these.

`is_readable()` tells you whether you can read a file. On Unix systems, you might be able to see a file but still be barred from reading its contents. `is_readable()` accepts the file path as a string and returns a Boolean value:

```
if ( is_readable( "test.txt" ) ) {
  print "test.txt is readable";
}
```

`is_writable()` tells you whether you can write to a file. Once again, it requires the file path and returns a Boolean value:

```
if ( is_writable( "test.txt" ) ) {
  print "test.txt is writable";
}
```

`is_executable()` tells you whether you can run a file, relying on either the file's permissions or its extension depending on your platform. It accepts the file path and returns a Boolean value:

```
if ( is_executable( "test.txt" ) {
  print "test.txt is executable";
}
```

Determining File Size with `filesize()`

Given the path to a file, `filesize()` attempts to determine and return its size in bytes. It returns `false` if it encounters problems:

```
print "The size of test.txt is. ";
print filesize( "test.txt" );
```

Getting Date Information About a File

Sometimes you will need to know when a file was last written to or accessed. PHP provides several functions that can provide this information.

You can find out when a file was last accessed with `fileatime()`. This function requires the file path and returns the date on which the file was last accessed. To access a file means either to read or write to it. Dates are returned from all these functions in Unix epoch format—that is, the number of seconds since January 1, 1970. In our examples, we use the `date()`function to translate this into human readable form. You'll learn more about date functions in Hour 16, "Working with Dates and Times."

> `fileatime()` does not work as advertised for operating systems that use a FAT filesytem (such as Windows 95 and Windows 98).

By the Way

```
$atime = fileatime( "test.txt" );
print "test.txt was last accessed on ";
print date("D d M Y g:i A", $atime);
// Sample output: Tue 19 Aug 2003 4:26 PM
```

You can discover the modification date of a file with the function `filemtime()`, which requires the file path and returns the date in Unix epoch format. To modify a file means to change its contents in some way, like so:

```
$mtime = filemtime( "test.txt" );
print "test.txt was last modified on ";
print date("D d M Y g:i A", $mtime);
// Sample output: Tue 19 Aug 2003 4:26 PM
```

PHP also enables you to test the change time of a document with the `filectime()` function. On Unix systems, the change time is set when a file's contents are modified or changes are made to its permissions or ownership. On other platforms, the `filectime()` returns the creation date:

```
$ctime = filectime( "test.txt" );
print "test.txt was last changed on ";
print date("D d M Y g:i A", $ctime);
// Sample output: Tue 19 Aug 2003 4:26 PM
```

Creating a Function That Performs Multiple File Tests

Listing 11.8 creates a function that brings the file test functions we have looked at together into one script.

LISTING 11.8   A Function to Output the Results of Multiple File Tests

```
 1: <?php
 2: function outputFileTestInfo( $file ) {
 3:   if ( ! file_exists( $file ) ) {
 4:     print "$file does not exist<br/>";
 5:     return;
 6:   }
 7:   print "$file is ".(    is_file( $file )?"":"not ")."a file<br/>";
 8:   print "$file is ".(     is_dir( $file )?"":"not ")."a directory<br/>";
 9:   print "$file is ".(  is_readable( $file )?"":"not ")."readable<br/>";
10:   print "$file is ".(  is_writable( $file )?"":"not ")."writable<br/>";
11:   print "$file is ".( is_executable( $file )?"":"not ")."executable<br/>";
```

LISTING 11.8   Continued

```
12:    print "$file is ".( filesize($file))." bytes<br/>";
13:    print "$file was accessed on "
14:       .date( "D d M Y g:i A", fileatime( $file ) )."<br/>";
15:    print "$file was modified on "
16:       .date( "D d M Y g:i A", filemtime( $file ) )."<br/>";
17:    print "$file was changed on "
18:       .date( "D d M Y g:i A", filectime( $file ) )."<br/>";
19: }
20: ?>
21: <!DOCTYPE html PUBLIC
22:    "-//W3C//DTD XHTML 1.0 Strict//EN"
23:    "http://www.w3.org/TR/xhtml1/DTD/xhtml1-strict.dtd">
24: <html>
25: <head>
26: <title>Listing 11.8 Multiple File Tests</title>
27: </head>
28: <body>
29: <div>
30: <?php
31: outputFileTestInfo( "test.txt" );
32: ?>
33: </div>
34: </body>
35: </html>
```

Notice that we have used the ternary operator as a compact way of working with some of these tests. Let's look at one of these, found on line 7, in more detail:

```
print "$f is ".(is_file( $f )?"":"not ")."a file<br />";
```

We use the is_file() function as the right expression of the ternary operator. If this returns true, an empty string is returned; otherwise, the string "not " is returned. The return value of the ternary expression is added to the string to be printed with concatenation operators. This statement could be made clearer but less compact, as follows:

```
$is_it = is_file( $f )?"":"not ";
print "$f is $isit a file";
```

We could, of course, be even clearer with an if statement, but imagine how large the function would become if we had used the following:

```
if ( is_file( $f ) ) {
  print "$fi is a file<br>";
} else {
  print "$f is not a file<br>";
}
```

Because the result of these three approaches is the same, the approach you take becomes a matter of preference.

Creating and Deleting Files

If a file does not yet exist, you can create one with the touch() function. Given a string representing a file path, touch() attempts to create an empty file of that name. If the file already exists, the contents are not disturbed, but the modification date is updated to the time at which the function executed:

```
touch("myfile.txt");
```

You can remove an existing file with the unlink() function. Once again, unlink() accepts a file path:

```
unlink("myfile.txt");
```

All functions that create, delete, read, write, or modify files on Unix systems require that the correct file or directory permissions are set.

Opening a File for Writing, Reading, or Appending

Before you can work with a file, you must first open it for reading, writing, or both. PHP provides the fopen() function for this. fopen() requires a string containing the file path, followed by a string containing the mode in which the file is to be opened. The most common modes are read ('r'), write ('w'), and append ('a'). fopen() returns a file resource you will later use to work with the open file. To open a file for reading, you would use the following:

```
$fp = fopen( "test.txt", 'r' );
```

You would use the following to open a file for writing:

```
$fp = fopen( "test.txt", 'w' );
```

To open a file for appending (that is, to add data to the end of a file), you would use this:

```
$fp = fopen( "test.txt", 'a' );
```

fopen() returns false if the file cannot be opened for any reason. Therefore, you should test the function's return value before working with it. You can do this with an if statement:

```
if ( $fp = fopen( "test.txt", "w" ) ) {
  // do something with $fp
}
```

Or you can use a logical operator to end execution if an essential file can't be opened:

```
( $fp = fopen( "test.txt", "w" ) ) or die ("Couldn't open file, sorry");
```

If the fopen() function returns true, the rest of the expression isn't parsed and the die() function (which writes a message to the browser and ends the script) is never reached. Otherwise, the right side of the or operator is parsed and the die() statement is executed.

Assuming that all is well and you go on to work with your open file, you should remember to close it when you have finished. You can do this by calling fclose(), which requires the file resource returned from a successful fopen() call as its argument:

```
fclose( $fp );
```

By the Way

If you are writing a binary file on a Windows system, you should add a 'b' flag to your fopen() mode argument. This tells the operating system that you are working with a binary file and that line endings should not be translated. You can write files in this way:

```
$fp = fopen( "binary_file", "wb" );
```

and read them like this:

```
$fp = fopen( "binary_file", "rb" );
```

By the Way

We often store the resource returned by fopen() in a variable called $fp. This is a convention only. fp stands for file pointer. You might want to use a more descriptive variable name in your projects. As always, it's a matter of balancing brevity and clarity.

Reading from Files

PHP provides a number of functions for reading data from files. These enable you to read by the byte, the line, or even the character.

Reading Lines from a File with fgets() and feof()

After you have opened a file for reading, you often need to access it line by line. To read a line from an open file, you can use fgets(), which requires the file resource returned from fopen() as an argument. You must also pass it an integer as a second argument. This specifies the number of bytes the function should read if it doesn't first encounter a line end or the end of the file. The `fgets()` function reads the file until it reaches a newline character (`"\n"`), the number of bytes specified in the length argument, or the end of the file:

```
$line = fgets( $fp, 1024 ); // where $fp is the file resource returned by fopen()
```

Although you can read lines with `fgets()`, you need some way of telling when you have reached the end of the file. The `feof()` function does this, returning `true` when the end of the file has been reached and `false` otherwise. This function requires a file resource as its argument:

```
feof( $fp ); // where $fp is the file resource returned by fopen()
```

You now have enough information to read a file line by line, as shown in Listing 11.9.

LISTING 11.9 Opening and Reading a File Line by Line

```
 1: <!DOCTYPE html PUBLIC
 2:   "-//W3C//DTD XHTML 1.0 Strict//EN"
 3:   "http://www.w3.org/TR/xhtml1/DTD/xhtml1-strict.dtd">
 4: <html>
 5: <head>
 6: <title>Listing 11.9 Opening and Reading a File Line by Line</title>
 7: </head>
 8: <body>
 9: <div>
10: <?php
11: $filename = "test.txt";
12: $fp = fopen( $filename, "r" ) or die("Couldn't open $filename");
13: while ( ! feof( $fp ) ) {
14:   $line = fgets( $fp, 1024 );
15:   print "$line<br/>";
16: }
17: ?>
18: </div>
19: </body>
20: </html>
```

We call `fopen()` on line 12 with the name of the file we want to read, using the `or` operator to ensure that script execution ends if the file cannot be read. This usually occurs if the file does not exist or (on a Unix system) if the file's permissions won't allow the script read access to the file. The actual reading takes place in the `while` statement on line 14. The `while` statement's test expression calls `feof()` for each iteration, ending the loop when it returns `true`. In other words, the loop continues until the end of the file is reached. Within the code block, we use `fgets()` on line 14 to extract a line (or 1024 bytes) of the file. We assign the result to `$line` and then print it to the browser on line 15, appending a `<br/>` tag for the sake of readability.

Reading Arbitrary Amounts of Data from a File with `fread()`

Rather than reading text by the line, you can choose to read a file in arbitrarily defined chunks. The `fread()` function accepts a file resource as an argument, as well as the number of bytes you want to read. It returns the amount of data you have requested unless the end of the file is reached first:

```
$chunk = fread( $fp, 16 );
```

Listing 11.10 amends our previous example so that it reads data in chunks of 16 bytes rather than by the line.

LISTING 11.10   Reading a File with `fread()`

```
1: <!DOCTYPE html PUBLIC
 2:   "-//W3C//DTD XHTML 1.0 Strict//EN"
 3:   "http://www.w3.org/TR/xhtml1/DTD/xhtml1-strict.dtd">
 4: <html>
 5: <head>
 6: <title>Listing 11.10 Reading a File with fread()</title>
 7: </head>
 8: <body>
 9: <div>
10: <?php
11: $filename = "test.txt";
12: $fp = fopen( $filename, "r" ) or die("Couldn't open $filename");
13: while ( ! feof( $fp ) ) {
14:    $chunk = fread( $fp, 16 );
15:    print "$chunk<br/>";
16: }
17: ?>
18: </div>
19: </body>
20: </html>
```

Although `fread()` enables you to define the amount of data acquired from a file, it doesn't let you decide the position from which the acquisition begins. You can set this manually with the `fseek()` function, which enables you to change your current position within a file. It requires a file resource and an integer representing the offset from the start of the file (in bytes) to which you want to jump:

```
fseek( $fp, 64 );
```

Listing 11.11 uses `fseek()` and `fread()` to output the second half of a file to the browser.

LISTING 11.11 Moving Around a File with `fseek()`

```
 1: <!DOCTYPE html PUBLIC
 2:   "-//W3C//DTD XHTML 1.0 Strict//EN"
 3:   "http://www.w3.org/TR/xhtml1/DTD/xhtml1-strict.dtd">
 4: <html>
 5: <head>
 6: <title>Listing 11.11 Moving Around a File with fseek()</title>
 7: </head>
 8: <body>
 9: <div>
10: <?php
11: $filename = "test.txt";
12: $fp = fopen( $filename, "r" ) or die("Couldn't open $filename");
13: $fsize = filesize($filename);
14: $halfway = (int)( $fsize / 2 );
15: print "Halfway point: $halfway <br/>\n";
16: fseek( $fp, $halfway );
17: $chunk = fread( $fp, ($fsize - $halfway) );
18: print $chunk;
19: ?>
20: </div>
21: </body>
22: </html>
```

We calculate the halfway point of our file by dividing the return value of `filesize()` by 2 on line 14. We can then use this as the second argument to `fseek()` on line 16, jumping to the halfway point. Finally, we call `fread()` on line 17 to extract the second half of the file, printing the result to the browser.

Reading Characters from a File with `fgetc()`

`fgetc()` is similar to `fgets()` except that it returns only a single character from a file every time it is called. Because a character is always 1 byte in size, `fgetc()` doesn't require a length argument. You simply need to pass it a file resource:

```
$char = fgetc( $fp );
```

Listing 11.12 creates a loop that reads the file `test.txt` a character at a time, outputting each character on its own line to the browser.

LISTING 11.12 Reading Characters with `fgetc()`

```
 1: <!DOCTYPE html PUBLIC
 2:   "-//W3C//DTD XHTML 1.0 Strict//EN"
 3:   "http://www.w3.org/TR/xhtml1/DTD/xhtml1-strict.dtd">
 4: <html>
 5: <head>
 6: <title>Listing 11.12 Reading Characters with fgetc()</title>
 7: </head>
 8: <body>
```

LISTING 11.12 Continued

```
 9: <div>
10: <?php
11: $filename = "test.txt";
12: $fp = fopen( $filename, "r" ) or die("Couldn't open $filename");
13: while ( ! feof( $fp ) ) {
14:   $char = fgetc( $fp );
15:   print "$char<br/>";
16: }
17: ?>
18: </div>
19: </body>
20: </html>
```

Reading the Contents of a File with `file_get_contents()`

The file reading functions we have covered so far give you a lot of control. If your objective is to read the contents of a file into a variable, however, there is a nice blunt tool to get the job done. The `file_get_contents()` function requires a string representing the path to a file and returns the file's contents:

```
$contents = file_get_contents( "test.txt" );
```

`file_get_contents()` was introduced with PHP 4.3. If you are using an older version of PHP, you can use the `file()` function to achieve a similar effect. `file()` requires a file path and returns an array, and each element of the returned array contains a line of the file's contents. You can then use the `implode()` function to join all the elements of the array to form a single string:

```
$file_array = file( "test.txt" );
$contents = implode( $file_array );
```

Writing or Appending to a File

The processes for writing to a file and appending to a file are similar. The difference lies in the `fopen()` call. When you write to a file, you should use the mode argument "w" when you call `fopen()`:

```
$fp = fopen( "test.txt", "w" );
```

All subsequent writing occurs from the start of the file. If the file doesn't already exist, it is created. Conversely, if the file already exists, any prior content is destroyed and replaced by the data you write.

When you append to a file, you should use mode "a" in your fopen() call:

```
$fp = fopen( "test.txt", "a" );
```

Any subsequent writes to your file are added to the existing content.

Writing to a File with fwrite() or fputs()

fwrite() accepts a file resource and a string; it then writes the string to the file. fputs() works in exactly the same way:

```
fwrite( $fp, "hello world" );
fputs( $fp, "hello world" );
```

Writing to files is as straightforward as that. Listing 11.13 uses fwrite() to print to a file. We then append a further string to the same file using fputs().

LISTING 11.13   Writing and Appending to a File

```
 1: <!DOCTYPE html PUBLIC
 2:   "-//W3C//DTD XHTML 1.0 Strict//EN"
 3:   "http://www.w3.org/TR/xhtml1/DTD/xhtml1-strict.dtd">
 4: <html>
 5: <head>
 6: <title>Listing 11.13 Writing and Appending to a File</title>
 7: </head>
 8: <body>
 9: <div>
10: <?php
11: $filename = "test2.txt";
12: print "Writing to $filename<br/>";
13: $fp = fopen( $filename, "w" ) or die("Couldn't open $filename");
14: fwrite( $fp, "Hello world\n" );
15: fclose( $fp );
16: print "Appending to $filename<br/>";
17: $fp = fopen( $filename, "a" ) or die("Couldn't open $filename");
18: fputs( $fp, "And another thing\n" );
19: fclose( $fp );
20: ?>
21: </div>
22: </body>
23: </html>
```

Writing Data to a File with file_put_contents()

The file_put_contents() function was introduced with PHP 5. It eliminates the need for opening and closing a file:

```
file_put_contents( "test2.txt", "Hello world\n" );
```

If you need to append to a file, you can pass a FILE_APPEND flag to the function, like so:

```
file_put_contents( "test2.txt", "And another thing\n", FILE_APPEND );
```

A second flag can be used with file_put_contents(). FILE_USE_INCLUDE_PATH creates the function to look in your include directories for the file to write to. This should be used with caution, if at all, because you could find yourself writing somewhere unexpected or undesirable if your include path is changed.

Locking Files with flock()

The techniques you have learned for reading and amending files will work fine if you are presenting your script to only a single user. In the real world, however, you would expect many users to access your projects more or less at the same time. Imagine what would happen if two users were to execute a script that writes to one file at the same moment. The file would quickly become corrupt.

PHP provides the flock() function to forestall this eventuality. flock() locks a file to warn other processes against writing to or reading from a file while the current process is working with it. flock() requires a valid file resource and an integer representing the type of lock you want to set. PHP provides predefined constants for each of the integers you are likely to need. Table 11.1 lists three kinds of locks you can apply to a file.

TABLE 11.1 Integer Arguments to the flock() Function

Constant	Integer	Lock Type	Description
LOCK_SH	1	Shared	Allows other processes to read the file but prevents writing (used when reading a file)
LOCK_EX	2	Exclusive	Prevents other processes from either reading from or writing to a file (used when writing to a file)
LOCK_UN	3	Release	Releases a shared or exclusive lock

You should call flock() directly after calling fopen() and then call it again to release the lock before closing the file:

```
$fp = fopen( "test.txt", "a" ) or die("couldn't open");
flock( $fp, LOCK_EX ); // exclusive lock
// write to the file
flock( $fp, LOCK_UN ); // release the lock
fclose( $fp );
```

Locking with `flock()` is advisory. Only other scripts that use `flock()` will respect a lock you set.

Watch
Out!

Working with Directories

Now that you can test, read, and write to files, let's turn our attention to directories. PHP provides many functions to work with directories. You will look at how to create, remove, and read them.

Creating Directories with `mkdir()`

`mkdir()` enables you to create a directory. `mkdir()` also requires a string representing the path to the directory you want to create and an integer that should be an octal number representing the mode you want to set for the directory. You specify an octal (base 8) number with a leading 0. The mode argument has an effect only on Unix systems. The mode should consist of three numbers between 0 and 7, representing permissions for the directory owner, group, and everyone, respectively. This function returns `true` if it successfully creates a directory, or `false` if it doesn't. If `mkdir()` fails, this is usually because the containing directory has permissions that preclude processes with the script's user ID from writing. If you are not comfortable with setting Unix directory permissions, one of the following examples should fit your needs. Unless you really need your directory to be world writable, you should probably use `0755`, which allows the world to read your directory but not write to it:

```
mkdir( "testdir", 0777 ); // global read/write/execute permissions
mkdir( "testdir", 0755 ); // world and group: read/execute only
             // owner: read/write/execute
```

Removing a Directory with `rmdir()`

`rmdir()` enables you to remove a directory from the file system, if the process running your script has the right to do so and if the directory is empty. `rmdir()` requires only a string representing the path to the directory you want to create:

```
rmdir( "testdir" );
```

Opening a Directory for Reading with `opendir()`

Before you can read the contents of a directory, you must first obtain a directory resource. You can do this with the `opendir()` function, which requires a string representing the path to the directory you want to open. opendir() returns a directory handle unless the directory is not present or readable, in which case it returns false:

```
$dh = opendir( "testdir" );
```

Reading the Contents of a Directory with readdir()

Just as you use gets()to read a line from a file, you can use readdir() to read a file or directory name from a directory. readdir() requires a directory handle and returns a string containing the item name. If the end of the directory has been reached, readdir() returns false. Note that readdir() returns only the names of its items, rather than full paths. Listing 11.14 shows the contents of a directory.

LISTING 11.14   Listing the Contents of a Directory with readdir()

```
 1: <!DOCTYPE html PUBLIC
 2:    "-//W3C//DTD XHTML 1.0 Strict//EN"
 3:    "http://www.w3.org/TR/xhtml1/DTD/xhtml1-strict.dtd">
 4: <html>
 5: <head>
 6: <title>Listing 11.14 Listing the Contents
 7: of a Directory with readdir()</title>
 8: </head>
 9: <body>
10: <div>
11: <?php
12: $dirname = ".";
13: $dh = opendir( $dirname );
14: while ( ! is_bool( $file = readdir( $dh )) ) {
15:    if ( is_dir( "$dirname/$file" ) ) {
16:      print "(D) ";
17:    }
18:    print "$file<br/>";
19: }
20: closedir( $dh );
21: ?>
22: </div>
23: </body>
24: </html>
```

We open our directory for reading with the opendir() function on line 13 and use a while statement to loop through each of its elements on line 11. We call readdir() as part of the while statement's test expression, assigning its result to the $file variable. Within the body of the while statement, we use the $dirname variable in conjunction with the $file variable to create a full file path, which we can then test on line 15. If the path leads to a directory, we print "(D) " to the browser on line 16. Finally, we print the filename on line 18.

We have used a cautious construction in the test of the while statement. Most PHP programmers (myself included) would use something similar to the following:

```
while ( $file = readdir( $dh ) ) {
   print "$file<BR>\n";
}
```

The value returned by readdir() is tested. Because any string other than "0" resolves to true, there should be no problem. Imagine, however, a directory that contains four files: "0", "1", "2", and "3". The output from the preceding code on my system is as follows:

.
..

When the loop reaches the file named "0", the string returned by readdir() resolves to false, causing the loop to end. The approach in Listing 11.14 uses is_bool() in conjunction with the not (!) operator to check that the value returned by readdir() is not a Boolean. As a string, "0" is not recognized as a Boolean, and the loop continues until readdir() returns false.

Summary

In this hour, you learned how to use include() to incorporate files into your documents and execute any PHP code contained in include files. You learned how to use some of PHP's file test functions and explored functions for reading files by the line, by the character, or in arbitrary chunks. You also learned how to write to files, either replacing or appending to existing content. Finally, you learned how to create, remove, and read directories.

Now that you can work with files, you can save and access substantial amounts of data. If you need to look up data from large files, however, your scripts will begin to slow down quite considerably. What you need is some type of database. In the next hour, we will look at PHP's DBA functions, which provide relatively fast access to data on file systems.

Q&A

Q *Will the* `include()` *statement slow down my scripts?*

A Because an included file must be opened and parsed by the engine, it will add some overhead. The benefits of reusable code libraries often outweigh the relatively low performance overhead, however.

Q *Should I always end script execution if a file cannot be opened for writing or reading?*

A You should always allow for this possibility. If your script absolutely depends on the file with which you want to work, you might want to use the `die()` function, writing an informative error message to the browser. In less critical situations, you still need to allow for the failure, perhaps adding it to a log file.

Workshop

Quiz

1. Which functions could you use to add library code to the currently running script?

2. Which function would you use to find out whether a file is present on your file system?

3. How would you determine the size of a file?

4. Which function would you use to open a file for reading or writing?

5. Which function would you use to read a line of data from a file?

6. How can you tell when you have reached the end of a file?

7. Which function would you use to write a line of data to a file?

8. How would you open a directory for reading?

9. Which function would you use to read the name of a directory item after you have opened a directory for reading?

Answers

1. You can use the `require()` or `include()` statement to incorporate PHP files into the current document. You could also use `include_once()` or `require_once()`.

2. You can test for the existence of a file with the `file_exists()` function.

3. The `filesize()` function returns a file's size in bytes.

4. The `fopen()` function opens a file. It accepts the path to a file and a character representing the mode. It returns a file resource.

5. The `fgets()` function reads data up to the buffer size you pass it, the end of the line, or the end of the document, whichever comes first.

6. The `feof()` function returns `true` when the file resource it is passed has reached the end of the file.

7. You can write data to a file with the `fputs()` function.

8. The `opendir()` function enables you to open a directory for reading.

9. The `readdir()` function returns the name of a directory item from an opened directory.

Exercises

1. Create a form that accepts a user's first and second name. Create a script that saves this data to a file.

2. Create a script that reads the data file you created in exercise 1. As well as writing its contents to the browser (adding a `-<br />` tag to each line), print a summary that includes the number of lines in the file and the file's size.

Working with the DBA Functions

What You'll Learn in This Hour:

▶ How to open a database
▶ How to add data to the database
▶ How to extract data from the database
▶ How to change and delete items
▶ How to store more complex types of data in DBM-style databases

Whichever platform you use, you will almost certainly have a DBM-style database system available to you. DBM stands for database manager, and DBM-like systems enable you to store and manipulate name/value pairs on your system.

DBA stands for database abstraction layer, and these functions are designed to provide a common interface to a range of file-based database systems.

Although DBA functions do not offer the power of a SQL database, they are flexible and easy to use. The fact that DBA functions stand above a range of common database systems means that your code is likely to be portable even if the database files themselves might not be.

Beneath the Abstraction

To use the DBA functions, you need to have one of the supported database systems installed. If you are running Linux, you probably have the GNU Database Manager (GDBM) installed. For each system, there is a corresponding compile option that should have been used when PHP was installed. You can see the supported databases and their corresponding compile options in Table 12.1.

TABLE 12.1   DBM Systems Supported by the DBA Functions

Type	Compile Option	Further Information
cdbm	--with-cdbm	Read-only database system
cdb	--with-cdb	Read/write when bundled version is used; no updates allowed
db2	--with-db2	http://www.sleepycat.com/
db3	--with-db3	http://www.sleepycat.com/
db4	--with-db4	http://www.sleepycat.com/ (since PHP 5)
dbm	--with-dbm	The original DBM; deprecated
gdbm	--with-gdbm	GNU Database Manager
ndbm	--with-ndbm	Deprecated
flatfile	--with-flatfile	Backward compatibility; use is discouraged
inifile	--with-inifile	For management of .ini files (for example, php.ini)

If your system and PHP installation support one of these systems, you can use the DBA functions with no problems. Note that support for the cdbm system (which is designed for fast access to static databases) is read-only. If you have not compiled PHP with support for any of the DBA handlers listed in Table 12.1, your script will fail with an error when you attempt to use any of the DBA functions.

You can check the handlers available to you with the dba_handlers() function. This returns an array of handler names. Adding the following to a script gives you a quick listing of available handlers:

```
var_dump( dba_handlers() );
```

You could also use the phpinfo()function. The phpinfo() output page has a section on DBA that lists handlers and confirms that DBA support is enabled.

By the Way

The dba_handlers() function was introduced with PHP 4.3.

We will use the commonly available GDBM system in our examples.

Opening a Database

You can open a DBM-like database with the function dba_open(). This function requires three arguments: the path to the database file, a string containing the flags with which you want to open the database, and a string representing the database manager you want to work with (the "Type" column in Table 12.1). dba_open() returns a DBA resource that you can then pass to other DBA functions to access or manipulate your database. Because dba_open() involves reading from and writing to files, PHP must have permission to write to the directory that will contain your database.

The flags you pass to dba_open()determine the way in which you can work with your database. They are listed in Table 12.2.

TABLE 12.2   Flags for Use with dba_open()

Flag	Description
r	Open a database for reading only
w	Open a database for writing and reading
c	Create a database (or open for read/write access if it exists)
n	Create a new database (truncate the old version if it exists)

The following code fragment opens a database, creating a new one if it does not already exist:

```
$dbh = dba_open( "./data/products", "c", "gdbm" )
        or die( "Couldn't open Database" );
```

Notice that we use a die() statement to end script execution if our attempt to open the database fails.

When you finish working with a database, you should close it using the function dba_close(). This is because PHP locks a database you are working with so that other processes cannot attempt to modify the data you are reading or writing. If you don't close the database, other processes have to wait longer before using the database. dba_close() requires a valid DBA resource:

```
dba_close( $dbh );
```

As of PHP 4.3, you can extend the flag you pass to dba_open() to allow for fine-grained control of database locking. Because basic locking is implemented by default, these details are beyond the scope of this book. You can, however, find more information at http://www.php.net/manual/en/function.dba-open.php.

By the Way

Adding Data to the Database

You can add name/value pairs to your open database with the function dba_insert(), which requires the name of a key, the value you want to store, and a valid DBA resource (as returned by dba_open()). This function returns true if all is well and false if an error occurs (such as an attempt to write to a database opened in read-only mode, or to overwrite an element of the same name). If the element you are attempting to insert already exists, the data is not overwritten.

Listing 12.1 creates or opens a database called products and adds some data to it.

LISTING 12.1   Adding Items to a Database

```
 1: <!DOCTYPE html PUBLIC
 2:   "-//W3C//DTD XHTML 1.0 Strict//EN"
 3:   "http://www.w3.org/TR/xhtml1/DTD/xhtml1-strict.dtd">
 4: <html>
 5: <head>
 6: <title>Listing 12.1 Adding Items to a Database</title>
 7: </head>
 8: <body>
 9: <div>
10:
11: Adding products now...
12:
13: <?php
14: $dbh = dba_open( "./data/products", "c", "gdbm" )
15:      or die( "Couldn't open database" );
16:
17: dba_insert( "Sonic Screwdriver", 23.20, $dbh);
18: dba_insert( "Tricorder", 55.50, $dbh);
19: dba_insert( "ORAC AI", 2200.50, $dbh);
20: dba_insert( "HAL 2000", 4500.00, $dbh);
21:
22:
23: dba_close( $dbh );
24: ?>
25: </div>
26: </body>
27: </html>
```

To add values to the database, we use the dba_insert() functions (lines 17–20). All values are converted to strings when added to the database. We can treat our price strings as floats when we extract them from the database, however. We covered the float data type in Hour 4, "The Building Blocks." Notice that we can use keys that have more than one word.

If we now attempt to call dba_insert() with the same key argument as one of the keys we have already used, dba_insert() returns false and makes no change to the database. A warning is also generated. This level of protection prevents accidental data loss. Sometimes, however, you want to overwrite existing data when you write to the database.

Amending Elements in a Database

You can amend an entry in a database with the dba_replace() function, which requires the name of a key, the new value to add, and a valid DBA resource. It returns true if all goes well and false if an error occurs. Listing 12.2 amends the code in Listing 12.1 so that keys are added regardless of existence.

LISTING 12.2 Adding or Changing Items in a Database

```
 1: <!DOCTYPE html PUBLIC
 2:    "-//W3C//DTD XHTML 1.0 Strict//EN"
 3:    "http://www.w3.org/TR/xhtml1/DTD/xhtml1-strict.dtd">
 4: <html>
 5: <head>
 6: <title>Listing 12.2 Adding or Changing Items
 7:    in a database</title>
 8: </head>
 9: <body>
10: <div>
11: Adding products now...
12: <?php
13: $dbh = dba_open( "./data/products", "c", "gdbm" )
14:        or die( "Couldn't open database" );
15: dba_replace( "Sonic Screwdriver", 25.20, $dbh );
16: dba_replace( "Tricorder", 56.50, $dbh );
17: dba_replace( "ORAC AI", 2209.50, $dbh );
18: dba_replace( "HAL 2000", 4535.50, $dbh );
19: dba_close( $dbh );
20: ?>
21: </div>
22: </body>
23: </html>
```

We have had to change only the function calls from dba_insert() to dba_replace() to change the functionality of the script.

Reading from a Database

Now that you can add data to your database, you need to find a way to fetch it. You can extract an individual element from the database with the dba_fetch() function. dba_fetch() requires the name of the element you want to access and a valid DBA resource, and it returns the value you are accessing as a string. So, to access the price of the "Tricorder" item, you would use the following code:

```
$price = dba_fetch( "Tricorder", $dbh );
```

If the "Tricorder" element does not exist in the database, dba_fetch() returns false.

You won't always know the names of all the keys in the database, however. What would you do if you needed to output every product and price to the browser without hard-coding the product names into your script? PHP provides a mechanism by which you can loop through every element in a database.

You can get the first key in a database with the dba_firstkey() function, which requires a DBA resource and returns the first key. This won't necessarily be the first element you added because DBM-like databases often maintain their own ordering systems. After you've retrieved the first key, you can access each subsequent key with the dba_nextkey()function. dba_nextkey() also requires a DBA resource and returns an element's key. By combining these functions with dba_fetch(), you can now list an entire database.

Listing 12.3 outputs the products database to the browser. We acquire the first key in the database on line 24 using the dba_firstkey() function. We then use a while loop on line 25 to work our way through all the elements in the database. Elements are acquired with the call to dba_fetch() on line 26. After we have written the element to the browser, we use dba_nextkey() on line 29 to acquire the next key and assign it to the $key variable. When there are no more keys to acquire, dba_nextkey() returns false and the test expression on line 25 halts the loop.

LISTING 12.3   Reading All Records from a Database

```
 1: <!DOCTYPE html PUBLIC
 2:    "-//W3C//DTD XHTML 1.0 Strict//EN"
 3:    "http://www.w3.org/TR/xhtml1/DTD/xhtml1-strict.dtd">
 4: <html>
 5: <head>
 6: <title>Listing 12.3 Reading All
 7:    Records from a Database </title>
 8: </head>
 9: <body>
10: <div>
11: <p>
```

LISTING 12.3   Continued

```
12:  Here at the Impossible Gadget Shop
13:  we're offering the following exciting
14:  products:
15:  </p>
16:  <table border="1" cellpadding ="5">
17:  <tr>
18:  <td align="center"> <b>product</b></td>
19:  <td align="center"> <b>price</b> </td>
20:  </tr>
21:  <?php
22:  $dbh = dba_open( "./data/products", "c", "gdbm" )
23:      or die( "Couldn't open database" );
24:  $key = dba_firstkey( $dbh );
25:  while ( $key != false ) {
26:    $value = dba_fetch( $key, $dbh);
27:    print "<tr><td align = \"left\"> $key </td>";
28:    print "<td align = \"right\"> \$".sprintf( "%01.2f", $value )."</td></tr>";
29:    $key = dba_nextkey( $dbh);
30:  }
31:  dba_close( $dbh );
32:  ?>
33:  </table>
34:  </div>
35:  </body>
36:  </html>
```

Figure 12.1 shows the output from Listing 12.3.

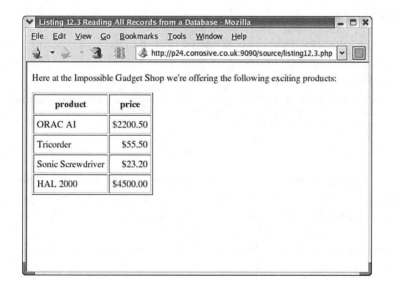

FIGURE 12.1
Reading all records
from a database.

Determining Whether an Item Exists in a Database

Before reading or setting an element in a database, it is sometimes useful to know whether the element exists. You can do this with the dba_exists() function, which requires the name of the element for which you are testing and a valid DBA resource. It returns true if the element exists:

```
if ( dba_exists("Tricorder", $dbh ) )
  print dba_fetch( "Tricorder", $dbh );
```

Deleting an Item from a Database

You can delete an item from a database using the dba_delete() function. dba_delete() requires the name of the element you want to remove from the database and a valid DBA resource. It returns true if the item was successfully deleted and false if the element did not exist to be deleted:

```
dba_delete( "Tricorder", $dbh );
```

Adding Complex Data Structures to a Database

All data in a DBM-like database is extracted in string format, so you are limited to storing integers, strings, and doubles. Any other data type will be lost. Let's try to store an array, for example:

```
$array = array( 1, 2, 3, 4 );
$dbh = dba_open( "./data/test", "c", "gdbm" ) or die("Couldn't open test");
dba_insert("arraytest", $array, $dbh );
print gettype( dba_fetch("arraytest", $dbh) );
// prints "string"
```

We create an array and store it in the variable $array. We then open a database and attempt to insert an element called "arraytest", passing it the $array variable as the value. We then test the return type from dba_fetch() when attempting to access "arraytest" and ascertain that a string has been returned. In fact, if we printed the value stored in the "arraytest" record, we would get the string "Array". That would seem to wrap up any hopes for storing arrays and objects.

Fortunately, PHP provides a feature that enables you to "freeze-dry" values of any data type in string format. The data can then be stored in a database or file until it is needed. You can use this technique to store arrays and even objects in a database.

To convert the array in the previous example to a string, we must use the serialize() function. serialize() requires a value of any type and returns a string:

```
$array = array( 1, 2, 3, 4 );
print serialize( $array );
// prints a:4:{i:0;i:1;i:1;i:2;i:2;i:3;i:3;i:4;}
```

We can now store this string in the database. When we want to resurrect it, we can use the unserialize() function. unserialize() requires a serialized string and returns a value of the appropriate data type.

This enables you to store complex data structures within the relatively simple format allowed by DBM-like databases. Listing 12.4 serializes an associative array for each of the items in our list of products and adds the result to a database.

LISTING 12.4   Adding Complex Data to a Database

```
 1: <!DOCTYPE html PUBLIC
 2:   "-//W3C//DTD XHTML 1.0 Strict//EN"
 3:   "http://www.w3.org/TR/xhtml1/DTD/xhtml1-strict.dtd">
 4: <html>
 5: <head>
 6: <title>Listing 12.4 Adding Complex Data to a Database</title>
 7: </head>
 8: <body>
 9: <div>
10: Adding complex data to database
11: <?php
12: $products = array(
13:     "Sonic Screwdriver" => array( "price"=>22.50,
14:                     "shipping"=>12.50,
15:                     "color"=>"green" ),
16:     "Tricorder"     => array( "price"=>55.50,
17:                     "shipping"=>7.50,
18:                     "color"=>"red" ),
19:     "ORAC AI"       => array( "price"=>2200.50,
20:                     "shipping"=>34.50,
21:                     "color"=>"blue" ),
22:     "HAL 2000"      => array( "price"=>4500.50,
23:                     "shipping"=>18.50,
24:                     "color"=>"pink" )
25:     );
26: $dbh = dba_open( "./data/products2", "c", "gdbm" )
27:       or die( "Couldn't open database" );
28: foreach ( $products as $key => $value ) {
29:   dba_replace( $key, serialize( $value ), $dbh );
30: }
31: dba_close( $dbh );
32: ?>
33: </div>
34: </body>
35: </html>
```

We build a multidimensional array beginning on line 12, containing the product names as keys and four arrays of product information as values. We then open the database on line 26 and loop through the array on line 28. For each element, we pass the product name and a serialized version of the product array to dba_replace() (line 29). We then close the database (line 31).

Listing 12.5 writes the code that extracts this data.

LISTING 12.5   Retrieving Serialized Data from a Database

```
1: <!DOCTYPE html PUBLIC
2:    "-//W3C//DTD XHTML 1.0 Strict//EN"
3:    "http://www.w3.org/TR/xhtml1/DTD/xhtml1-strict.dtd">
4: <html>
5: <head>
6: <title>Listing 12.5 Retrieving Serialized
7:    Data from a Database</title>
8: </head>
9: <body>
10: <div>
11: <p>
12:   Here at the Impossible Gadget Shop
13:   we're offering the following exciting
14:   products:
15: </p>
16: <table border="1" cellpadding ="5">
17: <tr>
18: <td align="center"> <b>product</b> </td>
19: <td align="center"> <b>color</b>   </td>
20: <td align="center"> <b>shipping</b> </td>
21: <td align="center"> <b>price</b>   </td>
22: </tr>
23: <?php
24: $dbh = dba_open( "./data/products2", "c", "gdbm" )
25:      or die( "Couldn't open database" );
26:
27: $key = dba_firstkey( $dbh );
28: while ( $key != false ) {
29:   $prodarray = unserialize( dba_fetch( $key, $dbh) );
30: ?>
31:   <tr><td align="left">
32:     <?=$key?>
33:   </td><td align="left">
34:     <?=$prodarray['color']?>
35:   </td><td align="right">
36:     $<?=sprintf( "%01.2f", $prodarray['shipping'] )?>
37:   </td><td align="right">
38:     $<?=sprintf( "%01.2f", $prodarray['price'] )?>
39:   </td></tr>
40: <?php
41:   $key = dba_nextkey( $dbh );
42: }
43: dba_close( $dbh );
44: ?>
45: </table>
46: </div>
47: </body>
48: </html>
```

Listing 12.5 is similar to the example in Listing 12.3. In this case, though, we are displaying more fields. We open the database on line 24 and then use dba_firstkey() (line 27) and dba_nextkey() (line 41) to loop through each item in the database. We extract the value and use unserialize() to reconstruct the product array on line 29. Then printing each element of the product array to the browser is easy. Notice that we enter HTML mode to write the table rows. We print dynamic information using the short PHP tags in conjunction with an equals sign (=). This construction is very useful for embedding dynamic values in HTML. So

```
<?= $value ?>
```

is equivalent to

```
<?php
echo $value;
?>
```

The former fragment is nicely compact. We are assuming that short open tags are enabled, which can be risky if you expect to deploy your code on servers beyond your control.

Figure 12.2 shows the output from Listing 12.5.

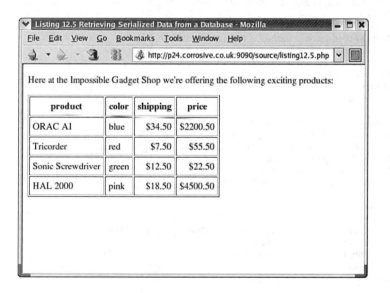

FIGURE 12.2
Retrieving serialized data from a database.

An Example

We now have enough information to build an example using some of the techniques discussed in this hour. Our brief is to build a quick and dirty script to enable a site editor to change the prices in the products database created in Listing 12.2. The administrator should also be able to remove elements from the database and add new ones. The page will not be hosted on a publicly available server, so security is not an issue for this project.

First, we must build a form that incorporates all the elements in the database. The user will be able to change any price using a text field and choose which items to delete using a check box. She will also have two text fields for adding a new item to the database. Listing 12.6 shows the code to create the form.

LISTING 12.6 Building an HTML Form Based on Content from a Database

```
 1: <!DOCTYPE html PUBLIC
 2:   "-//W3C//DTD XHTML 1.0 Strict//EN"
 3:   "http://www.w3.org/TR/xhtml1/DTD/xhtml1-strict.dtd">
 4: <html>
 5: <head>
 6: <title>Listing 12.6 Building an HTML Form Based
 7:   on Content From a Database</title>
 8: </head>
 9: <body>
10: <form method="post" action="<?php print $SERVER['PHP_SELF'] ?>">
11: <table border="1">
12: <tr>
13: <td>delete</td>
14: <td>product</td>
15: <td>price</td>
16: </tr>
17: <?php
18: $dbh = dba_open( "./data/products", "c", "gdbm" )
19:      or die( "Couldn't open database" );
20: $key = dba_firstkey( $dbh );
21: while ( $key != false ) {
22:   $price = dba_fetch( $key, $dbh );
23:
24:   print <<<LIST
25:   <tr><td>
26:     <input type="checkbox" name="delete[]" value="$key" />
27:   </td><td> $key </td><td>
28:     <input type="text" name="prices[$key]" value="$price" />
29:   </td></tr>
30: LIST;
31:
32:   $key = dba_nextkey( $dbh );
33: }
34: dba_close( $dbh );
35: ?>
36: <tr>
```

LISTING 12.6   Continued

```
37: <td> </td>
38: <td><input type="text" name="name_add" /></td>
39: <td><input type="text" name="price_add" /></td>
40: </tr>
41: <tr>
42: <td colspan="3" align="right">
43: <input type="submit" value="amend" />
44: </td>
45: </tr>
46: </table>
47: </form>
48: </body>
49: </html>
```

> In Listing 12.6, we use the 'heredoc' print statement syntax. Using this syntax, print statements look like this:
>
> ```
>     print <<<CHUNK
> contents here
> CHUNK;
> ```
>
> The word CHUNK in the previous fragment is arbitrary. You can use your own word, as long as you are consistent. The document terminator (the second instance of CHUNK) should be flush with the left margin and must be followed by a semicolon and no spaces. This syntax makes printing multiple lines of text easy. Variables are substituted as they are in double-quoted strings with the exception that you do not have to escape double-quote characters within the string.

By the Way

We begin an HTML form that points back to the current page (line 10).

Having written some table headers to the screen on lines 12–16, we open the database and loop through the contents of it using dba_firstkey() (line 20) and dba_nextkey() (line 32) to get each key in turn. We then use dba_fetch() on line 22 to extract the value.

In the first table cell of each row, we create a check box (line 25). Notice that we give all these the name "delete[]". This instructs PHP to construct an array element called delete containing all submitted values that share this name. The delete element is stored in the $_POST array. We use the database element name (stored in $key) as the value for each check box. When the form is submitted, therefore, we should have a delete element available to us in the built-in $_POST array. The $_POST['delete'] array will contain the names of all the database elements we want to delete.

We then print the element name to the browser on line 27 and create another text field on line 29. This field presents the product price to the user, ready for amendment. We name the field 'prices' followed by square brackets containing the name of the database element. When the form is submitted, PHP adds an associative array element called prices to the $_POST superglobal. Each element in the $_POST['prices'] array will be indexed by a database key, and its value will be the user-submitted price data.

We close the database (line 34) and write the final fields (lines 38 and 39). These allow the user to add new product and price combinations. Only two fields are required, and we give them the names name_add and price_add.

Figure 12.3 shows the output from Listing 12.6.

FIGURE 12.3
Building an HTML form based on content from a database.

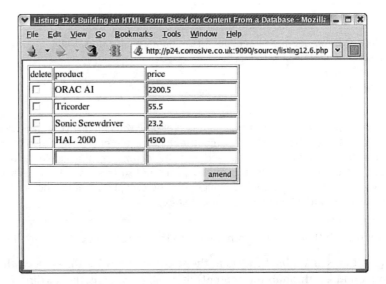

Now that we have created the form, we need to write code to deal with the user input. This is not as difficult as it sounds. There are three possible actions we can take. First, we can delete items from the database; second, we can amend prices in the database; and third, we can add new elements to the database.

User-submitted data is available to us in the superglobal $_POST array. We will work directly with this array in most instances, but we need to save one element to an array variable:

```
$prices = $_POST['prices'];
```

We might need to remove elements from the $prices array. If you need to manipulate user input, it is generally better to work with a local version than directly on the built-in global.

If the form has been submitted, we know which items we need to delete because a $_POST['delete'] array variable will have been made available. We need to loop through this array and delete the elements whose names it contains, like so:

```
if ( ! empty( $_POST['delete'] ) ) {
  foreach( $_POST['delete'] as $val ) {
    unset( $prices[$val]);
    dba_delete( $val, $dbh );
  }
}
```

First, we test that the $_POST['delete'] array exists and has elements. If the user has only just arrived at the page or has not chosen to delete any items, the $_POST array will not have a 'delete' element. If the element exists, we can loop through it. For each string held in the $_POST['delete'] array, we call dba_delete(), removing the element by that name from the database. We also remove the element of the same name from the $prices array.

To update the database according to the user amendments, we have a choice. We could update only those elements that the user has elected to change. We would choose this option if we expected many users to be using the script at the same time or if the database was likely to grow significantly. As it is, this script will be run by a single administrator and is expected to deal with only a few products, so we opt to update every element in the database:

```
if ( ! empty( $prices ) ) {
  foreach ( $prices as $key=>$val ) {
    dba_replace( $key, (float)$val, $dbh );
  }
}
```

We test for the existence of the $prices array, which should contain a new version of the entire database. We then loop through the array, calling dba_replace() for each of its elements.

Finally, we need to check whether the user has submitted a new product for inclusion in the database:

```
if ( ! empty( $_POST['name_add'] ) && ! empty( $_POST['price_add'] ) ) {
  dba_insert( $_POST['name_add'], (float)$_POST['price_add'], $dbh );
}
```

Instead of testing whether $_POST['name_add'] and $_POST['price_add'] are set, we test whether they are empty. This is a subtle but important difference. When the user submits the form we have built, these variables are always set. They can, however, contain empty strings. We do not want to add empty strings to our database, so we execute the code to insert new values only if neither variable is empty.

We use dba_insert() rather than dba_replace() to guard against the user inadvertently overwriting an element that has already been defined.

You can see the complete code in Listing 12.7; you can find the code that handles deletions on lines 6–10. The code to update the database is on lines 13–17. We handle the insertion of new elements on lines 19–21.

LISTING 12.7   The Complete Product Maintenance Code

```
 1: <?php
 2: $dbh = dba_open( "./data/products", "c", "gdbm" )
 3:       or die( "Couldn't open database" );
 4: $prices = $_POST['prices'];
 5:
 6: if ( ! empty( $_POST['delete'] ) ) {
 7:   foreach( $_POST['delete'] as $val ) {
 8:     unset( $prices[$val]);
 9:     dba_delete( $val, $dbh );
10:   }
11: }
12:
13: if ( ! empty( $prices ) ) {
14:   foreach ( $prices as $key=>$val ) {
15:     dba_replace( $key, (float)$val, $dbh );
16:   }
17: }
18:
19: if ( ! empty( $_POST['name_add'] ) && ! empty( $_POST['price_add'] ) ) {
20:   dba_insert( $_POST['name_add'], (float)$_POST['price_add'], $dbh );
21: }
22: ?>
23: <!DOCTYPE html PUBLIC
24:   "-//W3C//DTD XHTML 1.0 Strict//EN"
25:   "http://www.w3.org/TR/xhtml1/DTD/xhtml1-strict.dtd">
26: <html>
27: <head>
28: <title>Listing 12.7 The Complete Product Maintenance Code</title>
29: </head>
30: <body>
31: <form method="post" action="<?php print $SERVER['PHP_SELF'] ?>">
32: <table border="1">
33: <tr>
34: <td>delete</td>
35: <td>product</td>
36: <td>price</td>
37: </tr>
38: <?php
39: $key = dba_firstkey( $dbh );
40: while ( $key != false ) {
41:   $price = dba_fetch( $key, $dbh );
42:
43:   print <<<LIST
44:   <tr><td>
45:     <input type="checkbox" name="delete[]" value="$key" />
46:   </td><td> $key </td><td>
47:     <input type="text" name="prices[$key]" value="$price" />
```

LISTING 12.7   Continued

```
48:    </td></tr>
49: LIST;
50:
51:    $key = dba_nextkey( $dbh );
52: }
53: dba_close( $dbh );
54: ?>
55: <tr>
56: <td> </td>
57: <td><input type="text" name="name_add" /></td>
58: <td><input type="text" name="price_add" /></td>
59: </tr>
60: <tr>
61: <td colspan="3" align="right">
62: <input type="submit" value="amend" />
63: </td>
64: </tr>
65: </table>
66: </form>
67: </body>
68: </html>
```

Summary

In this hour, you learned how to use PHP's powerful DBA functions to store and retrieve data. You learned how to use dba_open() to acquire a DBA resource, which you can use with other DBA functions. You also learned how to add data to a database with dba_insert(), alter it with dba_replace(), and delete it with dba_delete(). You learned how to use dba_fetch() to retrieve data and how to use serialize() and unserialize() to save complex data structures to a database. Finally, you worked through an example that uses many of the techniques we have examined.

The DBA functions are useful for storing relatively small amounts of data that need to be queried only in a simple way. Inevitably, your needs will occasionally be more demanding than this. In the next chapter, we will cover MySQL, an open source SQL database.

Q&A

Q *When should I use a DBM-like database as opposed to a SQL database?*

A A DBM-like database is a good option when you want to store small amounts of relatively simple data (typically name/value pairs). If you want to store larger amounts of data or want to retrieve information based on conditions of any type, you should consider a SQL solution.

Workshop

Quiz

1. Which function would you use to open a database using the DBA functions?

2. Which function would you use to insert a record into a database?

3. Which function would you use to replace a record in a database?

4. How would you access a record from a database by name?

5. How would you get the name (as opposed to the value) of the first element in a database?

6. How would you get subsequent element names?

7. How would you delete a named element from a database?

Answers

1. You can open a database with the dba_open() function.

2. The dba_insert() function adds a record to a database.

3. The dba_replace() function replaces a record in a database.

4. The dba_fetch() function returns an element given a DBA resource and the element's name.

5. dba_firstkey() returns the name of the first element in a DBM-like database.

6. After calling dba_firstkey(), you can get subsequent element names by calling dba_nextkey().

7. You can delete an element with dba_delete().

Exercises

1. Create a database to keep track of usernames and passwords. Create a script that allows users to register their combinations. Don't forget to check for duplications.

2. Create an authentication script that checks a username and password. If the user input matches an entry in the database, present the user with a special message. Otherwise, re-present the login form to the user.

HOUR 13

Database Integration—SQL

What You'll Learn in This Hour:

▶ A few SQL samples

▶ How to connect to a MySQL database server

▶ How to select, insert, and update data with the MySQL functions

▶ How to select, insert, and update data with the SQLite functions

▶ How to work with the PEAR::DB package

One of the defining features of PHP is the ease with which you can connect to and manipulate databases. In this chapter we will look at three database packages that lie at the heart of PHP. MySQL has traditionally been the database of choice for PHP developers. A vast number of scripts have been developed using the so-called triad of PHP, Apache, and MySQL. We will also examine SQLite, which is new with PHP 5. The fact that it is bundled with the PHP distribution and works efficiently with flat files, requiring no separate server, is likely to make it a favorite for developers who require a lightweight solution. Finally, we will examine the PEAR::DB package, which stands above database-specific functions, providing a unified interface that enables the programmer to write a project once and then run it seamlessly with different database applications.

A (Very) Brief Introduction to SQL

SQL stands for Structured Query Language. It provides a standardized syntax by which different types of databases can be queried. Most SQL database products provide their own extensions to the language, just as many browsers provide their own extensions to HTML. Nonetheless, an understanding of SQL enables you to work with a wide range of database products across multiple platforms.

This book cannot describe all the intricacies of SQL. In this section we attempt to cover a little background, however.

Most database applications such as MySQL run as a server daemon to which users on the same or even remote machines can connect. Once connected to the server, you can select a database if you have the privileges to do so.

A database has a varying number of tables of data, and each table is arranged in rows and columns. The intersection between a row and a column is the point at which each item of data you want to store and access sits. Each column accepts only a predefined type of data, INT for integer, for example, or VARCHAR for a variable number of characters up to a defined limit.

To create a new table within a database we have selected, we might use a SQL query like the following:

```
CREATE TABLE people ( first_name VARCHAR(30), second_name VARCHAR(30), age INT);
```

Our new table has three columns. first_name and second_name can contain strings of up to 30 characters, and age can contain any integer.

To add data to this table, we could use an INSERT statement:

```
INSERT INTO mytable
( first_name, second_name, age )
VALUES ( 'John', 'Smith', 36 );
```

The field names to which we want to add data are defined in the first set of parentheses. The values we want to insert are defined in the second.

To acquire all the data in a table, we would use a SELECT statement:

```
SELECT * FROM mytable;
```

The * symbol represents a wildcard, which means "all fields." To acquire the information from a single field, you can use the column name in place of the wildcard:

```
SELECT age FROM mytable;
```

To change the values already stored in a table, you can use an UPDATE statement:

```
UPDATE mytable SET first_name = 'Bert';
```

This changes the first_name field in every row to Bert. We can narrow the focus of the SELECT and UPDATE statements with a WHERE clause. For example

```
SELECT * FROM mytable WHERE first_name = 'Bert';
```

returns only those rows whose `first_name` fields contain the string `Bert`. This next example

```
UPDATE mytable SET first_name = 'Bert' WHERE second_name = 'Baker';
```

changes the `first_name` fields of all rows whose `second_name` fields contain `Baker`.

For more information on SQL, see *Sams Teach Yourself SQL in 21 Days* by Ryan K. Stephens et. al.

Connecting to the MySQL Database Server

MySQL is a popular open-source database. As a consequence, it has become one of the foundations of open-source Web development. PHP no longer bundles MySQL but remains a perfect partner for it.

Because PHP is not bundled with MySQL, you should make certain that it is present on your system. You can get MySQL together with all its installation instructions from `http://www.mysql.com/`.

To ensure that PHP works with MySQL you should configure it using the `--with-mysql` flag, like so:

```
./configure --with-mysql
```

If the previous fragment does not work for you, you may need to specify a path to the MySQL directory, like this:

```
./configure --with-mysql=/path/to/mysql/dir
```

You will need to add your own path, of course, but this should be enough to get MySQL working with PHP.

Before you can begin working with your database, you must first connect to the server. PHP provides the `mysql_connect()` function to do just this. `mysql_connect()` does not require any arguments but accepts up to five. The first three arguments are strings: a hostname, a username, and a password. The fourth optional argument is a Boolean. If you pass `true` for this, every call to `mysql_connect()` returns a new connection. Otherwise, `mysql_connect()` returns the currently open connection for all calls that use the same arguments. The fifth optional argument enables you to pass integer flags directly to the MySQL server.

If you omit these arguments, the function assumes localhost as the host and that no password or username has been set up in the mysql user table, unless defaults have been set up in the php.ini file. Naturally, this is unwise for anything but a test database, so we will always include a username and password in our examples. mysql_connect() returns a link resource if the connection is successful. You can store this return value in a variable so that you can continue to work with the database server.

The following code fragment uses mysql_connect() to connect to the MySQL database server:

```
$link = mysql_connect( "localhost", "p24_user", "cwaffie" );
if ( ! $link ) {
  die( "Couldn't connect to MySQL" );
}
```

If you are using PHP in conjunction with Apache, you could also connect to the database server with mysql_pconnect(). From the coder's perspective, this function works in exactly the same way as mysql_connect(). In fact, there is an important difference. If you use this function, the connection does not die when your script stops executing or if you call mysql_close() (which ends a standard connection to the MySQL server). Instead, the connection is left active, waiting for another process to call mysql_pconnect(). In other words, the overhead of opening a new connection to the server can be saved if you use mysql_pconnect() and a previous call to the script has left the connection open.

Selecting a Database

Now that we have established a connection to the MySQL daemon, we must choose which database we want to work with. You can select a database with the mysql_select_db() function, which requires a database name and optionally accepts a link resource. If you omit this, the resource returned from the last connection to the server is assumed. mysql_select_db() returns true if the database exists and you are able to access it. In the following fragment, we select a database called p24:

```
$database = "p24";
mysql_select_db( $database ) or die ( "Couldn't open $database );
```

Finding Out About Errors

So far, we have tested the return values of the MySQL functions that we have used and called die() to end script execution if a problem occurs. You might, however, want to print more informative error messages to the browser to aid debugging. MySQL sets an error number and an error string whenever an operation fails. You can access the error number with mysql_errno() and the error string with mysql_error(). Listing 13.1 brings our previous examples together into a simple script that connects to the server and selects a database. We use mysql_error() to make our error messages more useful. On line 14 we connect to the database. If this is successful, we then select a database on line 19 before closing the connection on line 22. Notice that we suppress any warnings that might be generated by mysql_connect() and mysql_select_db() using the at character (@).

LISTING 13.1   Opening a Connection and Selecting a Database

```
 1: <!DOCTYPE html PUBLIC
 2:   "-//W3C//DTD XHTML 1.0 Strict//EN"
 3:   "http://www.w3.org/TR/xhtml1/DTD/xhtml1-strict.dtd">
 4: <html>
 5: <head>
 6: <title>Listing 13.1 Opening a Connection to a Database</title>
 7: </head>
 8: <body>
 9: <div>
10: <?php
11: $user = "p24_user";
12: $pass = "cwaffie";
13: $db = "p24";
14: $link = @mysql_connect( "localhost", $user, $pass );
15: if ( ! $link ) {
16:   die( "Couldn't connect to MySQL: ".mysql_error() );
17: }
18: print "<h2>Successfully connected to server</h2>\n\n";
19: @mysql_select_db( $db )
20:   or die ( "Couldn't open $db: ".mysql_error() );
21: print "Successfully selected database \"$db\"<br />\n";
22: mysql_close( $link );
23: ?>
24: </div>
25: </body>
26: </html>
```

If we change the value of the $db variable in line 13 to "unauthorized", we will be attempting to open a nonexistent database. The output of our die() function call therefore looks something like the following:

```
Couldn't open unauthorized: Access denied for user:
➥'p24_user@localhost' to database 'unauthorized'
```

Adding Data to a Table

Now that we have access to our database, we can add information to one of its tables. For the following examples, imagine that we are building a site that allows people to buy domain names.

We have created a table within the p24 database called domains. The table was created with five columns: a primary key field called id that automatically incre-ments an integer as data is added, a domain field that contains a variable number of characters (VARCHAR), a sex field that contains a single character (M or F), and a mail field that contains a user's email address. The following SQL statement was used in the MySQL client to create the table:

```
create table domains (
            id INT NOT NULL AUTO_INCREMENT,
        PRIMARY KEY( id ),
        domain VARCHAR( 200 ),
        sex ENUM('M','F') NOT NULL,
        mail VARCHAR( 200 ) );
```

To add data to this table, we need to construct and execute a SQL query. PHP pro-vides the mysql_query() function for this purpose; it requires a string containing a SQL query and, optionally, a link resource. If the resource is omitted, the query is sent to the database server to which you last connected. mysql_query() returns true if the query is successful. If your query contains a syntax error or you don't have permission to access the database in question, mysql_query() returns false. Listing 13.2 extends our previous examples starting at line 15 and uses mysql_query() (line 17) to send an INSERT statement to the domains table in the p24 database.

LISTING 13.2   Adding a Row to a Table

```
 1: <!DOCTYPE html PUBLIC
 2:   "-//W3C//DTD XHTML 1.0 Strict//EN"
 3:   "http://www.w3.org/TR/xhtml1/DTD/xhtml1-strict.dtd">
 4: <html>
 5: <head>
 6: <title>Listing 13.2 Adding a Row to a Database</title>
 7: </head>
 8: <body>
 9: <div>
10: <?php
11: $user = "p24_user";
12: $pass = "cwaffie";
13: $db = "p24";
14: $link = @mysql_connect( "localhost", $user, $pass );
15: if ( ! $link ) {
16:   die( "Couldn't connect to MySQL: ".mysql_error() );
17: }
```

LISTING 13.2   Continued

```
18: print "<h2>Successfully connected to server</h2>\n\n";
19: @mysql_select_db( $db )
20:    or die ( "Couldn't open $db: ".mysql_error() );
21: print "Successfully selected database \"$db\"<br />\n";
22:
23: $query = "INSERT INTO domains( domain, sex, mail )
24:     values( 'example.com', 'F', 'sharp@example.com' )";
25: print "running query: <br />\n$query<br />\n";
26: mysql_query( $query, $link )
27:    or die ( "INSERT error: ".mysql_error() );
28:
29: mysql_close( $link );
30: ?>
31: </div>
32: </body>
33: </html>
```

Notice that we did not insert a value for the id column in line 15. This field auto-increments.

Of course, every time we reload the script in Listing 13.2, the same data is added to a new row. Listing 13.3 creates a script that enters user input into our database.

LISTING 13.3   Adding User Input to a Database

```
1: <!DOCTYPE html PUBLIC
2:    "-//W3C//DTD XHTML 1.0 Strict//EN"
3:    "http://www.w3.org/TR/xhtml1/DTD/xhtml1-strict.dtd">
4: <html>
5: <head>
6: <title>Listing 13.3 Adding user input to a database</title>
7: </head>
8: <body>
9: <?php
10:
11: if (  ! empty( $_RFQUEST['scx']  ) &&
12:     ! empty( $_REQUEST['domain'] ) &&
13:     ! empty( $_REQUEST['mail']  ) ) {
14:    // check user input here!
15:    $dberror = "";
16:    $ret = add_to_database( $_REQUEST['domain'],
17:               $_REQUEST['sex'],
18:               $_REQUEST['mail'], $dberror );
19:    if ( ! $ret ) {
20:      print "Error: $dberror<br />\n";
21:    } else {
22:      print "Thank you very much<br />\n";
23:    }
24: } else {
25:    write_form();
26: }
27:
```

LISTING 13.3 Continued

```
28: function add_to_database( $domain, $sex, $mail, &$dberror ) {
29:    $domain = mysql_real_escape_string( $domain );
30:    $sex  = mysql_real_escape_string( $sex );
31:    $mail  = mysql_real_escape_string( $mail );
32:    $link  = mysql_pconnect( "localhost", "p24_user", "cwaffie" );
33:    if ( ! $link ) {
34:       $dberror = mysql_error();
35:       return false;
36:    }
37:    if ( ! mysql_select_db( "p24", $link ) ) {
38:       $dberror = mysql_error();
39:       return false;
40:    }
41:    $query = "INSERT INTO domains ( domain, sex, mail )
42:          values( '$domain', '$sex', '$mail' )";
43:    if ( ! mysql_query( $query, $link ) ) {
44:       $dberror = mysql_error();
45:       return false;
46:    }
47:    return true;
48: }
49:
50: function write_form() {
51:    print <<<EOF
52:       <form method="post" action="{$_SERVER['PHP_SELF']}">
53:
54:       <p><input type="text" name="domain" />
55:       The domain you would like</p>
56:
57:       <p><input type="text" name="mail" />
58:       Your mail address</p>
59:
60:       <p><select name="sex">
61:       <option value="F">Female</option>
62:       <option value="M">Male</option>
63:       </select></p>
64:
65:       <p><input type="submit" value="submit!" /></p>
66:       </form>
67: FORM;
68: }
69: ?>
70: </body>
71: </html>
```

To keep the example brief, we have left out one important process in Listing 13.3, testing user input. We are trusting our users. We should, in fact, check any kind of user input to ensure that we are getting sensible values.

We check for the request parameters domain, sex, and mail on line 11. If they exist, we can be fairly certain that the user has submitted data, and we can then call the add_to_database() function on line 16.

The add_to_database() function declared on line 28 requires four arguments: the $domain, $sex, and $mail variables submitted by the user and a string variable called $dberror. We populate this last argument with any error strings we encounter. For this reason, we accept $dberror as a reference to a variable. Any changes made to this string within the function change the original argument rather than a copy. We use the function mysql_real_escape_string() to transform the user-submitted values held by $domain, $sex, and $mail. This adds backslash characters into the string to escape characters such as single and double quotation marks. You should always escape data that is passed in from the user.

We attempt to open a connection to the MySQL server on line 32. If this fails, we assign an error string to $dberror and end the execution of the function by returning false on line 35. We select the database that contains the domains table on line 37 and build a SQL query to insert the user-submitted values. We pass this to mysql_query() on line 43, which makes the query for us. If either mysql_select_db() or mysql_query() fails, we assign the value returned by mysql_error() to $dberror and return false. Assuming that all went well, the function returns true on line 47.

Back in the calling code, we can test the return value from add_to_database() on line 19. If the function returns true, we can be sure that we have added to the database and thank the user on line 22. Otherwise, we write an error message to the browser. We know that the $dberror variable we passed to add_to_database() now contains useful information, so we include it in our error message.

If our initial if statement fails to find domain, sex, or mail request parameters, we can assume that no data has been submitted and call another user-defined function—write_form()—on line 16 to output an HTML form to the browser.

Acquiring the Value of an Automatically Incremented Field

In our previous examples, we have added data to our database without worrying about the id column, which automatically increments as data is inserted. If we need the value of this field for a record at a later date, we can always extract it with a SQL query. What if we need the value immediately, though? It would be wasteful to look it up. Luckily, PHP provides mysql_insert_id(), a function that returns the value of an auto-incremented key field after a SQL INSERT statement has been performed. mysql_insert_id() optionally accepts a link resource as an argument. With no arguments, it works with the most recent link established.

So, if we want to tell a user the number we have allocated to her order, we could call `mysql_insert_id()` directly after adding the user's data to our database:

```
$query = "INSERT INTO domains ( domain, sex, mail ) ";
$query .= "values( '$domain', '$sex', '$mail' )";
mysql_query( $query, $link );
$id = mysql_insert_id();
print "Thank you. Your transaction number is $id.";
```

Accessing Information

Now that we can add information to a database, we need to look at strategies for retrieving the information it contains. As you might guess, you can use `mysql_query()` to make a SELECT query. How do you use this to look at the returned rows, though? When you perform a successful SELECT query, `mysql_query()` returns a result resource. You can pass this resource to other functions to access and gain information about a resultset.

Finding the Number of Rows Found by a Query

You can find the number of rows returned as a result of a SELECT query using the `mysql_num_rows()` function. `mysql_num_rows()` requires a result resource and returns a count of the rows in the set. Listing 13.4 uses a SQL SELECT statement to request all rows in the domains table that have a sex field containing F and then uses `mysql_num_rows()` to determine the result set's size. If we only needed this figure, we could use MySQL's COUNT function. `mysql_num_rows()` is useful when you want to work with a found set and need some summary information before you begin.

LISTING 13.4   Finding the Number of Rows Returned by a SELECT Statement with `mysql_num_rows()`

```
 1: <!DOCTYPE html PUBLIC
 2:   "-//W3C//DTD XHTML 1.0 Strict//EN"
 3:   "http://www.w3.org/TR/xhtml1/DTD/xhtml1-strict.dtd">
 4: <html>
 5: <head>
 6: <title>Listing 13.4 Using mysql_num_rows()</title>
 7: </head>
 8: <body>
 9: <?php
10: $user = "p24_user";
11: $pass = "cwaffie";
12: $db = "p24";
13: $link = mysql_connect( "localhost", $user, $pass );
14: if ( ! $link ) {
15:   die( "Couldn't connect to MySQL: ".mysql_error() );
16: }
```

LISTING 13.4   Continued

```
17:
18: mysql_select_db( $db, $link )
19:   or die ( "Couldn't open $db: ".mysql_error() );
20:
21: $result = mysql_query( "SELECT * FROM domains where sex='F'" );
22: $num_rows = mysql_num_rows( $result );
23:
24: print "<p>$num_rows women have added data to the table</p>\n";
25:
26: // summarise data
27:
28: mysql_close( $link );
29: ?>
30: </body>
31: </html>
```

The mysql_query() function returns a result resource. We then pass this to mysql_num_rows(), which returns the total number of rows found.

We connect to the database on line 13 and select the database on line 18. On line 21 we call mysql_query(), passing it our SQL query. The function returns a result resource that we can then use with mysql_num_rows() on line 22. Having output summary information on line 24, we are ready to begin some more substantial work with our results. We do this in the next section.

Accessing a Resultset

After you have performed a SELECT query and gained a result resource, you can use a loop to access each found row in turn. PHP maintains an internal pointer that keeps a record of your position within a found set. This moves on to the next row as each one is accessed.

You can easily get an array of the fields in each found row with mysql_fetch_row(). This function requires a result resource, returning an array containing each field in the row. When the end of the found set is reached, mysql_fetch_row() returns false. Listing 13.5 outputs selected rows from the domains table to the browser.

LISTING 13.5   Listing All Rows and Fields in a Table

```
1: <!DOCTYPE html PUBLIC
2:   "-//W3C//DTD XHTML 1.0 Strict//EN"
3:   "http://www.w3.org/TR/xhtml1/DTD/xhtml1-strict.dtd">
4: <html>
5: <head>
6: <title>Listing 13.5 Selecting Data</title>
7: </head>
```

LISTING 13.5   Continued

```
 8: <body>
 9: <?php
10: $user = "p24_user";
11: $pass = "cwaffie";
12: $db = "p24";
13: $link = mysql_connect( "localhost", $user, $pass );
14: if ( ! $link ) {
15:   die( "Couldn't connect to MySQL: ".mysql_error() );
16: }
17:
18: mysql_select_db( $db, $link )
19:   or die ( "Couldn't open $db: ".mysql_error() );
20:
21: $result = mysql_query( "SELECT * FROM domains where sex='F'" );
22: $num_rows = mysql_num_rows( $result );
23:
24: print "<p>$num_rows women have added data to the table</p>\n";
25:
26: print "<table border=\"1\">\n";
27: while ( $a_row = mysql_fetch_row( $result ) ) {
28:   print "<tr>\n";
29:   foreach ( $a_row as $field ) {
30:     print "\t<td>".stripslashes($field)."</td>\n";
31:   }
32:   print "</tr>\n";
33: }
34: print "</table>\n";
35: mysql_close( $link );
36: ?>
37: </body>
38: </html>
```

After we have connected to the server and selected the database, we use mysql_query() on line 21 to send a SELECT statement to the database server. We store the returned result resource in a variable called $result and use this to acquire the number of found rows as before.

In the test expression of our while statement on line 27, we assign the result of mysql_fetch_row() to the variable $a_row. Remember that an assignment operator returns the value of its right-hand operand, so the assignment resolves to true as long as mysql_fetch_row() returns a positive value. Within the body of the while statement, we loop through the row array contained in $a_row on line 29, outputting each element to the browser embedded in a table cell.

You can also access fields by name in one of two ways. mysql_fetch_array() returns a numeric array, as does mysql_fetch_row(). It also returns an associative array, with the names of the fields as the keys. The following fragment rewrites the while statement from Listing 13.5, incorporating mysql_fetch_array() (this replaces lines 26–34):

```
print "<table border=\"1\">\n";
while ( $a_row = mysql_fetch_array( $result ) ) {
  print "<tr>\n";
  print "<td>".stripslashes($a_row['mail'])."</td>";
  print "<td>".stripslashes($a_row['domain'])."</td>";
  print "</tr>\n";
}
print "</table>\n";
```

The default behavior of mysql_fetch_array() is to return an array indexed by a string that also contains the same values indexed numerically. This is fine if you want to refer to your fields individually. If, however, you need to dump all the array values and keys, you will not want this duplication. mysql_fetch_array() accepts an optional second argument, and this integer should be one of three built-in constants—MYSQL_ASSOC, MYSQL_NUM, or MYSQL_BOTH. Passing MYSQL_BOTH is redundant in that it enforces the default behavior. Passing MYSQL_ASSOC to mysql_fetch_array() ensures that the return array is indexed by strings only, and passing MYSQL_NUM to mysql_fetch_array() ensures that the return array is numerically indexed.

If you are seeking the functionality provided by

```
mysql_fetch_array( $result, MYSQL_ASSOC );
```

you can use a shortcut function introduced with PHP 4.03. mysql_fetch_assoc() is functionally identical to a call to mysql_fetch_array() with MYSQL_ASSOC.

You can also extract the fields from a row as properties of an object with mysql_fetch_object(). The field names become the names of the properties. The following fragment rewrites the while statement from Listing 13.5, this time incorporating mysql_fetch_object() (this replaces lines 26–34):

```
print "<table border=\"1\">\n";
while ( $a_row = mysql_fetch_object( $result ) ) {
  print "<tr>\n";
  print "<td>".stripslashes($a_row->mail)."</td>";
  print "<td>".stripslashes($a_row->domain)."</td>";
  print "</tr>\n";
}
print "</table>\n";
```

Both mysql_fetch_array() and mysql_fetch_object() make it easier for you to selectively extract information from a row. Neither of these functions takes much longer than mysql_fetch_row() to execute. Which you choose to use is largely a matter of preference, although mysql_fetch_array() is more commonly used.

Changing Data

You can change data using the `mysql_query()` function in conjunction with an UPDATE statement.

A successful UPDATE statement does not necessarily change any rows. You need to use a function to call `mysql_affected_rows()` to discover whether you have changed data in your table. `mysql_affected_rows()` optionally accepts a link resource; if this is missing, the most recent connection is assumed. This function can be used with any SQL query that can alter data in a table row.

Listing 13.6 builds a script that enables an administrator to change any of the values in the domain column of our sample table.

LISTING 13.6 Using `mysql_query()` to Alter Rows in a Database

```
 1: <?php
 2: $user  = "p24_user";
 3: $pass  = "cwaffie";
 4: $db    = "p24";
 5: $link = connect( $user, $pass, $db );
 6:
 7: function connect( $user, $pass, $db ) {
 8:   $link = mysql_connect( "localhost", $user, $pass );
 9:   if ( ! $link ) {
10:     die( "Couldn't connect to MySQL: ".mysql_error() );
11:   }
12:   mysql_select_db( $db, $link )
13:     or die ( "Couldn't open $db: ".mysql_error() );
14:   return $link;
15: }
16:
17: function update( $dblink, $domain, $id ) {
18:   $id     = mysql_real_escape_string( $id     );
19:   $domain = mysql_real_escape_string( $domain );
20:   $query = "UPDATE domains SET domain='$domain' where id=$id";
21:   $result = mysql_query( $query );
22:   print "<h3>Table updated ". mysql_affected_rows() .
23:   " row(s) changed</h3>\n\n";
24: }
25:
26: function getSelect( $dblink, $id ) {
27:   $result = mysql_query( "SELECT * FROM domains" );
28:   $select = "<select name=\"id\">\n";
29:   while( $a_row = mysql_fetch_object( $result ) ) {
30:     $select .= "<option value=\"$a_row->id\"";
31:     if ( $id == $a_row->id ) {
32:       $select .= " selected=\"selected\"";
33:     }
34:     $select .= ">$a_row->mail: $a_row->domain</option>\n";
35:   }
36:   $select .= "</select>\n";
37:   return $select;
```

LISTING 13.6   Continued

```
38: }
39: ?>
40: <!DOCTYPE html PUBLIC
41:    "-//W3C//DTD XHTML 1.0 Strict//EN"
42:    "http://www.w3.org/TR/xhtml1/DTD/xhtml1-strict.dtd">
43: <html>
44: <head>
45: <title>Listing 13.6 Updating Data</title>
46: </head>
47: <body>
48:
49: <h1>Correct domains</h1>
50:
51: <?php
52: if ( ! empty( $_REQUEST['domain'] ) &&
53:      ! empty( $_REQUEST['id'] ) ) {
54:    update( $link, $_REQUEST['domain'], $_REQUEST['id'] );
55: }
56: ?>
57:
58: <form action="<?php print $_SERVER['PHP_SELF'] ?>" method="post">
59: <div>
60: <?php
61: print getSelect( $link, $_REQUEST['id'] );
62: ?>
63: <input type="text" name="domain" />
64: </div>
65: </form>
66: </body>
67: </html>
```

We open a connection to the database server and select a database as normal using the function declared on line 7. We test for the presence of the request arguments, domain and id, on line 17. If these are present, we call the update() function, which is defined on line 17, passing it the database resource acquired from the connect() function and the id and domain request parameters. The update() function builds a SQL UPDATE query on line 20 that changes the value of the domain field where the id field contains the same value as our $id argument. We do not get an error if a nonexistent id is used or if the $domain variable is the same as the current value for domain in the relevant row. Instead, the mysql_affected_rows() simply returns 0. We print this return value (usually 1 in this example) to the browser on lines 22 and 23.

Starting on line 58, we print an HTML form to enable the administrator to make her changes. Most of the work is delegated to the getSelect() function, which is declared on line 26. We use mysql_query() (line 27) again to extract the values of the id and domain columns and incorporate them into an HTML SELECT element (lines 28–36). The administrator uses this pop-up menu to choose which domain to change. If the administrator has already submitted the form and the id value she chose matches the value of the id field we are currently outputting, we add the string selected="selected" to the option element (line 32). This ensures that her changed value will be instantly visible to her in the menu.

SQLite: A Lightweight SQL Engine

PHP version 5 comes bundled with a SQL library that works with flat files, rather than with a database server. This is useful for writing PHP scripts in environments that don't provide access to MySQL or to another third-party SQL server.

In this section we will discuss PHP's SQLite functions. You shouldn't need to do anything special to install SQLite, so let's get straight to it with some code to open or create a new database. Because SQLite works with your file system, you need to work with a directory your script can write to:

```
$db = "data/testdb";
$dbres = sqlite_open($db, 0666, $error);
if ( ! is_resource( $dbres ) ) {
  die( "sqllite error: $error" );
}
```

The sqlite_open() function requires a path to a database file, a mode, and an error variable. The mode argument is not currently used by the SQLite functions, but you should use 0666 as a placeholder so the $error argument can be passed to the sqlite_open() function.

The function returns a resource, which we use to work with SQLite; otherwise, it returns false if an error is encountered. We store the return value in $resource and test it. If $resource contains false, we print the contents of the $error variable, which will have been populated with error information.

Creating a Table in a SQLite Database

Now that we have opened or created a database, we can create a table with which to work. We execute SQL statements with the sqlite_query() function, which requires a SQLite database resource and a string containing the query to execute. For queries that return no resultset, the function returns true if the process was successful and false if an error occurred. Let's drop and create a table:

```
@sqlite_query( $dbres, "DROP TABLE people" );
$create =  "CREATE TABLE people ( id INTEGER PRIMARY KEY,
                firstname varchar(255),
                secondname varchar(255) )";
sqlite_query( $dbres, $create );
```

We use a DROP statement to ensure that no people table is in place when we create one. Notice that we use an @ character in front of our first call to sqlite_query(). This suppresses the error message we will encounter the first time this script is run:

```
Warning: sqlite_query(): no such table: people
```

We then write the table. Although SQLite does not complain about the CREATE statement we use, the VARCHAR types we specify are actually irrelevant. SQLite treats all its fields as strings, regardless of the field declaration. The only exception to this is our first field. We have declared the id field as INTEGER PRIMARY KEY, ensuring that the id field will contain an integer value that will be incremented automatically as rows are entered.

Entering and Updating Data

Now that we have encountered the sqlite_query() function, we are ready to add some data:

```
$insert = array(
      array( "firstname" => "joan",
          "secondname" =>"peel" ),
      array( "firstname" => "mary",
          "secondname" =>"biscuit" )
);

foreach ( $insert as $row ) {
  $insert = "INSERT INTO people ( 'firstname', 'secondname' )
              VALUES( '{$row['firstname']}',
                  '{$row['secondname']}' )";
  sqlite_query( $dbres, $insert );
  print "Inserting {$row['firstname']} {$row['secondname']}: ";
  print "id: ".sqlite_last_insert_rowid( $dbres )."<br />\n";
}
```

In fact, most of the previous example is taken up with the creation of an array and with reporting back to the user. We create a multidimensional array containing two array elements, each containing firstname and secondname elements. We loop through this, building a SQL string for each iteration and passing it to the sqlite_query() function. We use a new function, sqlite_last_insert_rowid(), to get the auto-incremented id for our insert. It is often useful to know the value of an auto-incremented id after we have inserted a row. The sqlite_last_insert_rowid() function saves us the trouble of a second query. The output from the previous fragment confirms that we have acquired id values:

```
Inserting joan peel: id: 1<br />
Inserting mary biscuit: id: 2<br />
```

Of course, we can also run an update query, as shown here:

```
$update = "UPDATE people SET firstname='John' where secondname='peel'";
sqlite_query( $dbres, $update );
```

Selecting Data

We can use the sqlite_query() function to send a SELECT statement to SQLite. When we request data through sqlite_query(), we get a result resource in return. We can use this with other SQLite functions to access our data. After we have a result resource, we can access a row of data with sqlite_fetch_array():

```
$select =  "SELECT * FROM people";
$res = sqlite_query( $dbres, $select );

while ( sqlite_has_more( $res ) ) {
  $row = sqlite_fetch_array( $res );
  print "row: {$row['id']} {$row['firstname']} {$row['secondname']}";
  print "<br />\n";
}
```

We call sqlite_query(), passing it our database resource, and a SELECT statement. We get a result resource in return. In production code, we would test the return value to ensure that it is a valid resource. The sqlite_has_more() function returns true if there is still more data to read in a resultset and false otherwise. We can therefore use it in the test expression of a while loop. sqlite_fetch_array() returns an associative array of the current row in a resultset, and we print the elements of each row to the browser:

```
row: 1 John peel<br />
row: 2 mary biscuit<br />
```

Now that we have finished with our database for this request, we can call sqlite_close(). sqlite_close() requires a database resource and closes the connection to the database, freeing it up for other processes:

```
sqlite_close( $db );
```

Using the PEAR DB Package

The PHP Extension and Application Repository (PEAR) is a collection of powerful and quality-controlled libraries that can be used to extend PHP's functionality. We cover PEAR in much more detail in Hour 23, "PEAR: Reusable Components to Extend the Power of PHP." The DB package, however, is so enormously significant as a database tool, it would be a serious omission to not include it here.

We have looked at two mechanisms for working with SQL. You might have notice how similar the functions we covered are. Yet despite these similarities, shifting a project from one set of database functions to another is time-consuming. You would have to go through your source code and change function names before the transfer would be complete.

Wouldn't it be better to have a library that hides these implementation details behind a common set of functions or methods? When you choose to change a database, you can substitute a different implementation behind the common database interface you are using without disturbing your code. Your code would continue to work with the functions it has always called, and the functions would work with the new database functions on your behalf.

In previous editions of this book, we cooked up our own code to handle database abstraction to a certain extent. Now, however, a standard library exists that is designed precisely for this purpose. The DB package supports a number of databases, including MySQL, Dbase, FrontBase, Interbase, Mini SQL, PostgeSQL, Microsoft SQL Server, ODBC, Informix, SyBase, and, of course, SQLite.

Let's begin to work with the DB package.

Installing the PEAR::DB Package

PEAR::DB should be bundled with your distribution of PHP 5. If you do not have it, though, you can install the PEAR::DB package from the command line with this simple command:

```
pear install DB
```

You also might want to run another PEAR command, like so:

```
pear upgrade DB
```

This updates your DB package and ensures that you have the latest version, as well as support for even more database applications.

Working with the PEAR::DB Package

In this section, we reproduce the code we wrote for SQLite using a MySQL database. The code has only one line of code specific to MySQL.

The first thing we need to do to work with the DB package is acquire a DB object. This is achieved by calling the static connect() method on the DB class. The connect() method requires what is known as a data source name (DSN). A DSN string combines all the information that is needed to identify and establish a connection with a database server.

When assembled, a DSN looks a bit like a Web address. Table 13.1 lists most of the elements of a DSN.

TABLE 13.1 Some of the Parts of a Data Source Name

Part	Description
data_app	One of mysql, pgsql, ibase, msql, mssql, oci8, odbc, sybase, ifx, or fbsql
syntax	SQL syntax (for example, sql92)
protocol	Connection protocols, such as TCP and Unix
user	The username
pass	The password
host:port	Host and port (the port is optional); for example, localhost:3306
database	The database to work with

Table 13.1 shows many more elements than you would probably use in a DSN. They would be put together in the order in which they are listed:

data_app(syntax)://user:pass@protocol+host:port/database

In reality, you will probably use only a few of these parts to make up your DSN. Let's construct a DSN for working with a MySQL database and use it to acquire a database object:

```
require_once("DB.php");
$user = "p24_user";
$pass = "cwaffie";
$host = "localhost";
$database = "p24";

$dsn = "mysql://$user:$pass@$host/$database";
$db = DB::connect($dsn);
```

We assemble our DSN with values for user, password, host, and database. We then pass the assembled string to the DB::connect() method, which is a factory method. That is, it uses the information you pass it to decide which object you need. The object it returns is always a child of DB_common. In our example, we acquire a DB_mysql object, which provides the MySQL-specific functionality we need.

We could, of course, have configured the DB package to work with SQLite, like this:

```
$dsn = "sqlite://./mydb.db";
$db = DB::connect($dsn);
```

After we have connected to the database, our examples should run identically for either database.

If, for some reason, our call to DB::connect() fails, it returns a DB_error() object instead of the object we want. We can test for an error with the DB::isError() method:

```
if ( DB::isError($db) ) {
  die ( $db->getMessage() );
}
```

DB::isError() tests the type of a DB package return value. If it is a DB_error object, the method returns true. DB_error provides the getMessage() method, which enables us to print an informative error message to the browser.

We have set up the p24 database so that it contains a people table:

```
CREATE TABLE people
( id INT PRIMARY KEY,
 firstname VARCHAR(255),
 secondname VARCHAR(255) );
```

Let's clear the table of data, so that we are working with a clean sheet:

```
$delete_query = $db->query( "DELETE FROM people" );
if ( DB::isError( $delete_query ) ) {
  die ($delete_query->getMessage());
}
```

We introduce the query() method, which accepts a SQL query and returns different values according to the type of query it is passed. If the query passed generates a resultset, we expect a DB_result object from query(). If, as in our fragment, we pass a query that does not generate data, query() will return a positive integer. As before, we test for a DB_error object using DB::isError(). You should write code that anticipates all possible error conditions and implement strategies for recovery or failure. This is known as coding *defensively*. To keep our code clear of repetition, we will drop the error tests in future fragments, but you should you test for errors in production code.

So, the query() method enables us to execute SQL statements. Where possible, you should try to keep your SQL as standard as you can. If you use application-specific features, you risk undermining the portability the DB package provides.

Let's add some data to the people database:

```
$insert = array(
     array( "firstname" => "joan",
          "secondname" =>"peel" ),
     array( "firstname" => "mary",
          "secondname" =>"biscuit" )
);

foreach ( $insert as $row ) {
  $id = $db->nextId('people_sequence');
  $row['id'] = $id;
  print "Inserting {$row['firstname']} {$row['secondname']}: $id<br />\n";
  $db->autoExecute( 'people', $row, DB_AUTOQUERY_INSERT );
}
```

We have introduced a few new features of the DB package in the previous fragment. First, we build up some data that we will use to populate our table. We use an array of associative arrays, with each subarray representing a row and containing field values indexed by field names. We loop through our data array, calling a new method—nextID(). nextID() is an example of a **sequence**, which is used to acquire unique IDs for primary keys. nextID() requires a sequence name. This can be any-thing you want, but you should always use the same name for a table if you want to ensure that your ID values are unique. Behind the scenes, our DB_common object has created a sequence table in the p24 database to keep track of the ID values it has generated. We can therefore be sure that we will always get a unique ID as long as we call nextID() with the same name and in relation to the same database.

Why have we used this relatively complicated way of generating a unique ID for our row, when MySQL and SQLite automatically add an ID for us? The reason is portability. By using the interface provided by the DB package to generate ID val-ues, we ensure that we can change our code to work with another database with the minimum of amendment. In fact, we should have to change only the DSN string.

So, we have an ID value that we tack onto the $row array generated for each iter-ation of the foreach loop. This means that $row is an associative array contain-ing the names and values for a complete row of the people table. We could use this to generate an INSERT SQL statement. The DB package, however, provides a useful, convenient method. Let's look at it again:

```
$db->autoExecute( 'people', $row, DB_AUTOQUERY_INSERT );
```

The autoExecute() method accepts a table name, an associative array containing field names and corresponding values, and a mode value. The mode can be one of DB_AUTOQUERY_INSERT and DB_AUTOQUERY_UPDATE. If you want to update a table, you can also pass a WHERE string as a fourth argument (such as id=5). The autoExecute() method constructs a SQL string on your behalf and passes it to the database.

Like query(), the autoExecute() method returns a DB_result object if all goes well or a DB_Error object if a problem exists.

So, we have populated the people table with some sample data. Let's update the table before moving on to listing information:

```
$update_query = "UPDATE people SET firstname='John' WHERE secondname='peel'";
$update_result = $db->query( $update_query );
```

The previous fragment should be familiar to you by now. We simply call the query() method with an UPDATE SQL statement.

Finally, let's work with a SELECT statement:

```
$query = "SELECT * FROM people";
$query_result = $db->query( $query );

while ( $row = $query_result->fetchRow( DB_FETCHMODE_ASSOC ) ) {
  print "row: {$row['id']} {$row['firstname']} {$row['secondname']}";
  print "<br />\n";
}
```

Again, we use the query() method. We are expecting a DB_result object, which we can use to extract our resultset. Don't forget that you should use DB::isError() to test production code.

The DB_result class provides the fetchRow() method that acquires row data from a resultset for us and advances the pointer to the next row. It returns null when the data has all been read. You can pass an integer to fetchRow() to influence the structure of the data it returns. We used DB_FETCHMODE_ASSOC because we want an associative array. Also available is DB_FETCHMODE_ORDERED, which is the default value and causes the row to be returned as a numerically indexed array. You can also pass fetchRow() the DB_FETCHMODE_OBJECT constant to cause an object to be returned containing the row's field names as properties, populated with their respective field values.

Finally, we can free the results of our query from memory and disconnect from the database:

```
$query_result->free();
$db->disconnect();
```

Calling the DB_result::free() method causes the result resource to be released by the DB_result object. The DB_Common::disconnect() method relinquishes our connection to the database.

Database code is frequently a barrier to portability, and switching between database applications can be a real headache. Used carefully, the DB package helps you avoid the issue of migrating from one database solution to another.

Summary

In this hour, you covered some of the basics of storing and retrieving information using SQL.

You learned how to connect to a MySQL database with `mysql_connect()` or `mysql_pconnect()`.

You learned how make SQL queries using `mysql_query()` and how to access data using the result resource this function returns.

You also found out how to use the SQLite functions to store and retrieve data. In particular, you learned how to open databases with `sqlite_open()`, make queries with `sqlite_query()`, and fetch data with `sqlite_fetch_array()`.

Finally, you learned about the PEAR::DB package. You learned how to use a DSN with the `DB::connect()` method to make a connection to a database. You also learned how to make SQL queries with the `DB_common::query()` method and automate data selects with `DB_common::autoExecute()`.

Q&A

Q *Have we covered all the MySQL, SQLite, and PEAR::DB functions?*

A By no means have we covered them all. There has really been space to cover only the basics in this chapter. However, if you are comfortable with the concepts we have covered, you will easily understand the remaining functions. You can read about the MySQL functions at `http://www.php.net/mysql` and find out more about SQLite at `http://www.php.net/sqlite`. The PEAR::DB documentation is available at `http://pear.php.net/manual/en/package.database.php`.

Q *When should I use the PEAR::DB package in preference to working directly with database functions?*

A The `PEAR::DB` functions should be used if your code is likely be deployed in different contexts from that of development. For example, if you are writing a script that you intend to share with other people, why limit your users to a particular setup? On the other hand, if you are writing a quick local script, working directly with MySQL or SQLite might be easier.

Workshop

Quiz

1. How would you open a connection to a MySQL database server?

2. Which MySQL function would you use to select a database?

3. Which function would you use to send a SQL query to a MySQL database?

4. What does the `mysql_insert_id()` function do?

5. How would you declare an auto-increment field for a SQLite database?

6. Which function would you use to execute a SQL statement with the SQLite functions?

7. Which object is returned by `DB::connect()`?

8. How would you get a unique id for a row using the `PEAR::DB` package?

Answers

1. You can connect to a MySQL daemon using the `mysql_connect()` function.

2. The `mysql_select_db()` function attempts to select a database.

3. You can send a SQL query to the database server with the `mysql_query()` function.

4. `mysql_insert_id()` returns the value of an automatically incrementing field after a new row has been added to a table.

5. You can define an auto-increment field in a SQLite database by declaring a field as `INTEGER PRIMARY KEY` in a `CREATE` statement, like so:

```
CREATE TABLE thing ( id INTEGER PRIMARY KEY, name VARCHAR(100) );
```

6. The `sqlite_query()` function executes a SQL statement.

7. `DB::connect()` returns an object of type `DB_common`. This is always a child implementation specific to a database application.

8. The `DB_common::nextID()` method can be used to get a unique id, as shown here:

```
$id = $db->nextId('sequencename');
```

Exercises

1. Create a database with three fields: email (up to 70 characters), message (up to 250 characters), and date (an integer that contains a Unix timestamp). Build a script to allow users to populate the database.

2. Create a script that displays the information from the database you created in exercise 1.

HOUR 14

Beyond the Box

What You'll Learn in This Hour:

▶ More about predefined variables
▶ The anatomy of an HTTP connection
▶ How to acquire a document from a remote server
▶ How to create your own HTTP connection
▶ How to connect to other network services
▶ How to send email from your scripts

In this hour, we will look at some of the functions that enable you to gain information from or interact with the outside world.

Server Variables Revisited

You have already encountered the predefined elements that PHP, in conjunction with your server, stores in the superglobal $_SERVER array. Generally, $_SERVER elements are made available to PHP by the server (or the shell if you are running a script from the command line). If you are running Apache, all the elements we discuss will likely be accessible to you. If you are running another server, there is no guarantee that $_SERVER will have been populated with all the elements discussed in this hour, so you should check before using them in scripts. Table 14.1 lists some of the $_SERVER elements you might be able to use to find out more about your visitors (see Table 10.1 for a more complete list of $_SERVER elements).

TABLE 14.1   Some Useful $_SERVER Elements

Variable	Description
$_SERVER['HTTP_REFERER']	The URL from which the current script was called (the misspelling is deliberate).
$_SERVER['HTTP_USER_AGENT']	Information about the browser and platform the visitor is using.
$_SERVER['REMOTE_ADDR']	The visitor's IP address.
$_SERVER['REMOTE_HOST']	The visitor's hostname.
$_SERVER['QUERY_STRING']	The (encoded) string that can be appended to the URL (in the format ?akey=avalue&anotherkey=anothervalue). These keys and values should become available to your scripts in the $_GET and $_REQUEST superglobal arrays.
$_SERVER['PATH_INFO']	Additional information that can be appended to the URL.

Listing 14.1 builds a script that outputs the contents of these variables to the browser.

LISTING 14.1   Listing Some Server Variables

```
 1: <html>
 2: <head>
 3: <title>Listing 14.1 Listing Some $_Server Elements</title>
 4: </head>
 5: <body>
 6: <?php
 7: $envs = array( "HTTP_REFERER", "HTTP_USER_AGENT", "REMOTE_ADDR",
 8:     "REMOTE_HOST", "QUERY_STRING", "PATH_INFO" );
 9: foreach ( $envs as $env )
10:    print "$env: $_SERVER[$env]<br>";
11: ?>
12: </body>
13: </html>
```

Figure 14.1 shows the output from Listing 14.1. The data in Figure 14.1 was generated as a result of calling the script from a link in another page. The link that called the script looks like this:

```
<a href="listing14.1.php/my_path_info?query_key=query_value">listing14.1</a>
```

As you can see, the link uses a relative path to call listing14.1.php.

FIGURE 14.1
Printing some
$ _SERVER elements
to the browser.

Additional path information (my_path_info) is included after the document name, which becomes available in $_SERVER['PATH_INFO'].

We have hard-coded a query string (query_key=query_value) into the link, which becomes available in $_SERVER['QUERY_STRING']. You will most often encounter a query string when using a form with a GET method argument, but you can also build your own query strings to pass information from page to page. The query string consists of name value pairs separated by ampersand symbols (&). These pairs are URL encoded, which means that any characters that are illegal or have other meanings in URLs are converted to their hexadecimal equivalents. Although you have access to the entire query string in the $_SERVER['QUERY_STRING'] super-global variable, you will rarely need to use this. Each key name is available to you as an element of the $_GET and $_REQUEST arrays ($_GET['query_value'] in our example), and these hold a corresponding decoded value (query_value).

The $_SERVER['HTTP_REFERER'] element can be useful to you if you want to track which hits on your script originate from which links. Beware, though: This and other environment variables can be easily faked. You will see how later in this hour. Because correcting it would cause compatibility problems, we are stuck with the incorrect spelling of 'referrer'. Not all browsers supply this header, so you should avoid relying on it.

You can parse the $_SERVER['HTTP_USER_AGENT'] element to work out the plat-form and browser the visitor is using. Once again, this can be faked. This element can be useful if you need to present different HTML code or JavaScript according to the browser type and version the visitor is using. Hour 8, "Working with

Strings," and Hour 18, "Working with Regular Expressions," give you the tools you need to extract any information you want from this string.

The $_SERVER['REMOTE_ADDR'] element contains the user's IP address and can be used to track unique visitors to your site. Be aware, though, that many Web users do not have a fixed IP address. Instead, their Internet service providers dynamically allocate them an address when they dial up. This means that a single IP address might be used by different visitors to your site and a single visitor might enter using different IP addresses from the same account.

The $_SERVER['REMOTE_HOST'] variable might not be available to you, depending on the configuration of your server. If available, it holds the hostname of the user. The presence of this variable requires that the server look up the hostname for every request, so it is often disabled for the sake of efficiency. If you don't have access to this variable, you can acquire it using the value of the $_SERVER['REMOTE_ADDR'] variable. You will see how to do this later in the hour.

A Brief Summary of an HTTP Client/Server Negotiation

It is beyond the scope of this book to explore all the information exchanged between server and client when a request is made, not least because PHP handles most of these details for you. You should gain a basic understanding of this process, however, especially if you intend to write scripts that fetch Web pages or check the status of Web addresses.

HTTP stands for *Hypertext Transfer Protocol*. It is essentially a set of rules that defines the process by which a client sends a request and a server returns a response. Both client and server provide information about themselves and the data to be transferred. Much of this information becomes available to you in superglobal arrays.

The Request

A client requests data from the server according to a strict set of rules. The request consists of up to three components:

▶ A request line
▶ A header section
▶ An entity body

The request line is mandatory. It consists of a request method, typically GET, HEAD, or POST; the address of the required document; and the HTTP version to be used (HTTP/1.0 or HTTP/1.1). A typical request for a document called mydoc.html might look like this:

```
GET /mydoc.html HTTP/1.0
```

The client is making a GET request. In other words, it is requesting an entire document but sending no data itself (in fact, you *can* send small amounts of data as part of a GET request by adding a query string to the URL). The HEAD method would be used if you wanted only information about a document. The POST method is used to transfer data from a client to the server, usually from an HTML form.

The request line is enough in itself to make a valid GET request. To inform the server that a request is complete, an empty line must be sent.

Most clients follow the request line with a header section in which name/value pairs can be sent to the server. Some of these become available to you as environment variables. Each client header consists of a key and value on one line separated by a colon. Table 14.2 lists a few of these.

TABLE 14.2   **Some Client Headers**

Name	Description
Accept	The media types with which the client can work.
Accept-Encoding	The types of data compression the client can handle.
Accept-Charset	The character sets the client prefers.
Accept-Language	The language the client prefers (en for English).
Host	The host to which a request is being made. Some servers that maintain multiple virtual hosts rely heavily on this header.
Referer	The document from which a request is being made.
User-Agent	Information about the client type and version.

For GET and HEAD methods, the header section ends the request and an empty line is sent to the server. For requests made using the POST method, an empty line is followed by the entity body. An entity body consists of any data to be sent to the server; this is usually a set of URL-encoded name/value pairs similar to those found in a query string.

Listing 14.2 shows a request sent to a server by Mozilla 5.0.

LISTING 14.2   Typical Client Headers Sent by a Mozilla Browser

```
1: GET /index.html HTTP/1.1
2: Host: resources.corrosive.co.uk:9090
3: User-Agent: Mozilla/5.0 (X11; U; Linux i686; en-US; rv:1.2.1) Gecko/20030225
4: Accept: text/xml,application/xml,application/xhtml+xml,text/html;
5: Accept-Encoding: gzip, deflate, compress;q=0.9
6: Accept-Charset: ISO-8859-1, utf-8;q=0.66, *;q=0.66
7: Keep-Alive: 300
8: Connection: keep-alive
```

The Response

After a server has received a client's request, it sends a response to the client. The response usually consists of three parts:

▶ A status line

▶ A header section

▶ An entity body

As you can see, there's a lot of symmetry between a request and a response. In fact, certain headers can be sent by either client or server, especially those that provide information about an entity body.

The status line consists of the HTTP version the server is using (HTTP/1.0 or HTTP/1.1), a response code, and a text message that clarifies the meaning of the response code.

Many response codes are available that a server can send to a browser. Each code provides some information about the success or otherwise of the request. Table 14.3 lists some of the more common response codes.

TABLE 14.3   Some Response Codes

Code	Text	Description
200	OK	The request was successful, and the requested data will follow.
301	Moved Permanently	The requested data no longer exists on the server. A location header will contain a new address.
302	Moved Temporarily	The requested data has been moved. A location header will contain a new address.
404	Not Found	The data could not be found at the supplied address.
500	Internal Server Error	The server or a CGI script has encountered a severe problem in attempting to serve the data.

A typical response line, therefore, might look something like the following:

```
HTTP/1.1 200 OK
```

The header section includes a series of response headers, formatted in the same way as request headers. Table 14.4 lists some headers commonly sent by servers.

TABLE 14.4   Some Common Server Headers

Name	Description
Date	The current date
Server	The server name and version
Content-Type	The MIME type of content in the entity body
Content-Length	The size of the entity in bytes
Location	The full address of an alternative document

Listing 14.3 shows a typical server response. After the headers have been sent (lines 2–6), the server sends an empty line to the client (line 7) followed by the entity body (the document originally requested).

LISTING 14.3   A Server Response

```
 1: HTTP/1.1 200 OK
 2: Date: Mon, 08 Sep 2003 19:24:35 GMT
 3: Server: Apache/2.0.47 (Unix) PHP/5.0.0b1
 4: X-Powered-By: PHP/5.0.0b1
 5: Connection: close
 6: Content-Type: text/html; charset=ISO-8859-1
 7:
 8: <!DOCTYPE html PUBLIC
 9:   "-//W3C//DTD XHTML 1.0 Strict//EN"
10:   "http://www.w3.org/TR/xhtml1/DTD/xhtml1-strict.dtd">
11: <html>
12: <head>
13: <title>Listing 14.3 A server response</title>
14: </head>
15: <body>
16: <div>
17: Hello
18: </div>
19: </body>
20: </html>
```

Getting a Document from a Remote Address

Although PHP is a server-side language, it can act as a client, requesting data from remote servers and making the output available to your scripts. If you are already comfortable reading files from the server, you will have no problem using PHP to acquire information from the Web. In fact, the syntax is exactly the same. You can use fopen() to connect to a Web address in the same way as you would with a file. Listing 14.4 opens a connection to a remote server and requests a page, printing the result to the browser.

LISTING 14.4   Getting and Printing a Web Page with fopen()

```
 1: <!DOCTYPE html PUBLIC
 2:   "-//W3C//DTD XHTML 1.0 Strict//EN"
 3:   "http://www.w3.org/TR/xhtml1/DTD/xhtml1-strict.dtd">
 4: <html>
 5: <head>
 6: <title>Listing 14.4 Getting a Web Page with fopen()</title>
 7: </head>
 8: <body>
 9: <div>
10: <?php
11: $webpage = "http://p24.corrosive.co.uk:9090/source/readthis.php";
12: $fp = fopen( $webpage, "r" ) or die("couldn't open $webpage");
13: while ( ! feof( $fp )) {
14:   print fgets( $fp, 1024 );
15: }
16: ?>
17: </div>
18: </body>
19: </html>
```

To take advantage of this feature, you need to ensure that the allow_url_fopen directive is set to On. This is the default setting.

You most likely won't want to output an entire page to the browser. More commonly, you would parse the document you download.

By the Way

> Prior to PHP 4.0.5, fopen() did not support HTTP redirects. When most modern browsers are sent a 301 or 302 response header, they make a new request based on the contents of the Location header. fopen() now supports this, so URLs that reference directories no longer have to end with a forward slash.

fopen() returns a file resource if the connection is successful and false if the connection cannot be established or the page doesn't exist. After you have a file pointer, you can use it as normal to read the file. PHP introduces itself to the remote server as a client. On my system, it sends the following request:

```
GET /source/readthis.php HTTP/1.0
Host: p24.corrosive.co.uk:9090
```

By the Way

> You can also access remote files using the include() statement. If the allow_url_fopen directive is set to On and a valid URL is passed to include(), then the result of a request for the remote file is incorporated into the script.
>
> Unless you are very sure about what you are doing, you should be cautious of this feature. Including source code from third parties in your own project is a big security risk.

This process is simple and is the approach you will use to access a Web page in most instances. There is more to fopen() than we have covered yet. We look again at the function in the section "An Introduction to Streams," later in this chapter.

Converting IP Addresses and Hostnames

Even if your server does not provide you with a $_SERVER['REMOTE_HOST'] variable, you will probably know the IP address of a visitor from the $_SERVER['REMOTE_ADDR'] environment variable. You can use this in conjunction with the function gethostbyaddr() to get the user's hostname. gethostbyaddr() requires a string representing an IP address and returns the equivalent hostname. If an error occurs, it returns the IP address it was given. Listing 14.5 creates a script that uses gethostbyaddr() to acquire the user's hostname if the $REMOTE_HOST variable is unavailable.

LISTING 14.5 Using gethostbyaddr() to Get a Hostname

```
1: <!DOCTYPE html PUBLIC
 2:   "-//W3C//DTD XHTML 1.0 Strict//EN"
 3:   "http://www.w3.org/TR/xhtml1/DTD/xhtml1-strict.dtd">
 4: <html>
 5: <head>
 6: <title>Listing 14.5 Using gethostbyaddr() to get a host name</title>
 7: </head>
 8: <body>
 9: <div>
10: <?php
11: if ( ! empty( $_SERVER['REMOTE_HOST'] ) ) {
12:   print "Hello visitor at ".$_SERVER['REMOTE_HOST'];
13: } else if ( ! empty( $_SERVER['REMOTE_ADDR'] ) ) {
14:    print "Hello visitor at ";
```

LISTING 14.5 Continued

```
15:     print gethostbyaddr( $_SERVER['REMOTE_ADDR'] );
16: } else {
17:    print "Hello you, wherever you are";
18: }
19: ?>
20: </div>
21: </body>
22: </html>
```

If we have access to the $_SERVER['REMOTE_HOST'] element, we simply print this to the browser on line 12. Otherwise, if we have access to the $_SERVER['REMOTE_ADDR'] element, we attempt to acquire the user's hostname using gethostbyaddr() on line 15. If all else fails, we print a generic welcome message on line 17.

To attempt to convert a hostname to an IP address, you can use gethostbyname(). This function requires a hostname as its argument. It returns an IP address or, if an error occurs, the hostname you provided.

Making a Network Connection

So far, we have had it easy. This is because PHP makes working with a Web page on a remote server as simple as opening a file on your own system. Sometimes, though, you need to exercise a little more control over a network connection or acquire more information about it.

You can make a connection to an Internet server with fsockopen(), which requires a hostname or an IP address, a port number, and two empty variables. The empty variables you pass to fsockopen() are populated to provide more information about the connection attempt should it fail. You can also pass fsockopen() an optional timeout integer, which determines how long fsockopen() will wait (in seconds) before giving up on a connection. If the connection is successful, a resource variable is returned; otherwise, it returns false.

The following fragment initiates a connection to a Web server:

```
$fp = fsockopen( "www.corrosive.co.uk", 80, $errno, errdesc, 30 );
```

80 is the usual port number a Web server listens on.

The first empty variable, $errno, contains an error number if the connection is unsuccessful, and $errdesc might contain more information about the failure.

After you have the file pointer, you can both write to the connection with `fputs()` and read from it with `fgets()` as you might with a file. When you have finished working with your connection, you should close it with `fclose()`.

We now have enough information to initiate our own connection to a Web server. Listing 14.6 makes an HTTP connection, retrieving a page and storing it in a variable.

LISTING 14.6 Retrieving a Web Page Using `fsockopen()`

```
1: <!DOCTYPE html PUBLIC
 2:    "-//W3C//DTD XHTML 1.0 Strict//EN"
 3:    "http://www.w3.org/TR/xhtml1/DTD/xhtml1-strict.dtd">
 4: <html>
 5: <head>
 6: <title>Listing 14.6 Retrieving a Web page using fsockopen()</title>
 7: </head>
 8: <body>
 9: <div>
10: <?php
11: $host = "www.corrosive.co.uk";
12: $page = "/index.html";
13: $fp = fsockopen( "$host", 80, $errno, $errdesc );
14: if ( ! $fp ) {
15:    die ( "Couldn't connect to $host:\nError: $errno\nDesc: $errdesc\n" );
16: }
17:
18: $request = "GET $page HTTP/1.0\r\n";
19: $request .= "Host: $host\r\n";
20: $request .= "Referer: http://www.corrosive.co.uk/refpage.html\r\n";
21: $request .= "User-Agent: PHP test client\r\n\r\n";
22:
23: $page = array();
24: fputs ( $fp, $request );
25: while ( ! feof( $fp ) ) {
26:    $page[] = fgets( $fp, 1024 );
27: }
28: fclose( $fp );
29: print "the server returned ".(count($page))." lines!";
30: ?>
31: </div>
32: </body>
33: </html>
```

Notice the request headers (lines 18–21) we send to the server in line 24. The Webmaster at the remote host sees the value you sent in the User-Agent header in her log file. She also might assume that a visitor to our page connected from a link at `http://www.corrosive.co.uk/refpage.html`. For this reason, you should be cautious of some of the environment variables available to your scripts. Treat them as a valuable guide, rather than a set of facts.

There are some legitimate reasons you might want to fake some headers. You might need to parse some data that will be sent only to Netscape-compatible browsers. One way you can do this is to include the word "Mozilla" in the User-Agent header. Nevertheless, pity the poor Webmaster. Operational decisions are made as a result of server statistics, so try not to distort the information you provide.

The example in Listing 14.6 adds little to PHP's built-in method of acquiring Web pages. Listing 14.7 uses fsockopen() to check the status codes returned by servers when we request a series of pages.

LISTING 14.7   **Outputting the Status Lines Returned by Web Servers**

```
 1: <!DOCTYPE html PUBLIC
 2:   "-//W3C//DTD XHTML 1.0 Strict//EN"
 3:   "http://www.w3.org/TR/xhtml1/DTD/xhtml1-strict.dtd">
 4: <html>
 5: <head>
 6: <title>Listing 14.7 Outputting Server Status Lines</title>
 7: </head>
 8: <body>
 9: <div>
10: <?php
11: $to_check = array (
12:           "www.corrosive.co.uk" => "/index.html",
13:           "www.virgin.com"      => "/notthere.html",
14:           "www.4332blah.com"    => "/nohost.html"
15:         );
16:
17: foreach ( $to_check as $host => $page ) {
18:   print "<p>\n";
19:   $fp = @fsockopen( "$host", 80, $errno, $errdesc, 10);
20:   print "Trying $host<br/>\n";
21:   if ( ! $fp ) {
22:     print "Couldn't connect to $host:<br/>\n";
23:     print "Error: $errno<br/>\n";
24:     print "Desc: $errdesc<br/>\n";
25:   } else {
26:     print "Trying to get $page<br/>\n";
27:     fputs( $fp, "HEAD $page HTTP/1.0\r\n" );
28:     fputs( $fp, "Host: $host\r\n" );
29:     fputs( $fp, "\r\n" );
30:     print fgets( $fp, 1024 );
31:     fclose( $fp );
32:   }
33:   print "</p>\n";
34: }
35:
36: ?>
37: </div>
38: </body>
39: </html>
```

We create an associative array of the server names and page addresses we want to check starting at line 11. We loop through this using a `foreach` statement on line 17. For every element, we initiate a connection using `fsockopen()` (line 19), setting a timeout of 10 seconds. If the connection fails, we print a message to the browser. If the connection is successful, however, we send a request to the server on lines 27–29. We use the HEAD method because we are not interested in parsing an entity body. Notice that we send a Host header, which is required to ensure that the correct site is referenced for a server with multiple virtual hosts. We use `fgets()` on line 30 to get the status line from the server. We are not going to work with server headers for this example, so we close the connection with `fclose()` on line 31 and move onto the next element in the list.

Figure 14.2 shows the output from Listing 14.7.

FIGURE 14.2
A script to print server response headers.

If you are interested in writing sophisticated Web client applications, you should look at the CURL package (`http://curl.haxx.se/`). As of PHP 4.02, support was added for CURL which can handle many of HTTP's more tricky aspects, including user and password authentication, cookies, and POST form submissions. It can also handle secure transactions with HTTPS and a range of other protocols. You can get more details from the PHP manual at `http://www.php.net/manual/en/ref.curl.php`.

Making an NNTP Connection Using fsockopen()

fsockopen() can be used to make a connection to any Internet server. In Listing 14.8, we connect to an NNTP (Usenet) server, select a newsgroup, and list the headers of the first message.

LISTING 14.8   A Basic NNTP Connection Using fsockopen()

```
 1: <!DOCTYPE html PUBLIC
 2:   "-//W3C//DTD XHTML 1.0 Strict//EN"
 3:   "http://www.w3.org/TR/xhtml1/DTD/xhtml1-strict.dtd">
 4: <html>
 5: <head>
 6: <title>Listing 14.8 A basic NNTP Connection Using fsockopen()</title>
 7: </head>
 8: <body>
 9: <?php
10: $server = "news"; // change this to your news server
11: $group = "sci.physics";
12: $line = "";
13: print "<pre>\n";
14: print "-- Trying to connect to $server\n\n";
15:
16: $fp = @fsockopen( "$server", 119, $error, $description, 10 );
17: if ( ! $fp ) {
18:   die("Couldn't connect to $server\n$errno\n$errdesc\n\n");
19: }
20:
21: print "-- Connected to $server\n\n";
22:
23: $line = fgets( $fp, 1024 );
24: $status = explode( " ", $line );
25:
26: if ( $status[0] != 200 && $status[0] != 201 ) {
27:   fputs( $fp, "close" );
28:   die("Error: $line\n\n");
29: }
30:
31: print "$line\n";
32: print "-- Selecting $group\n\n";
33: fputs( $fp, "group $group\n" );
34: $line = fgets( $fp, 1024 );
35: $status = explode( " ", $line );
36:
37: if ( $status[0] != 211 ) {
38:   fputs( $fp, "close" );
39:   die("Error: $line\n\n");
40: }
41:
42: print "$line\n";
43: print "-- Getting headers for first message\n\n";
44: fputs( $fp, "head\n" );
45: $line = fgets( $fp, 1024 );
46: $status = explode( " ", $line );
47: print htmlspecialchars("$line\n");
48:
```

LISTING 14.8   Continued

```
49: if ( $status[0] != 221 ) {
50:   fputs( $fp, "close" );
51:   die("Error: $line\n\n");
52: }
53:
54: while ( ! ( strpos($line, ".") === 0 ) ) {
55:   $line = fgets( $fp, 1024 );
56:   print htmlspecialchars($line);
57: }
58:
59: fputs( $fp, "close\n" );
60: print "</pre>";
61: ?>
62: </body>
63: </html>
```

The code in Listing 14.8 does little more than demonstrate that an NNTP connection is possible with `fsockopen()`. In a real-world example, you would want to handle the line parsing in a function to save repetition and extract more information from the server's output. Rather than reinvent the wheel in this way, you might want to investigate PHP's IMAP functions, which provide POP3 and NNTP connectivity and automate much of this work for you. On the other hand, the example does illustrate the power and potential of PHP as a network-capable language.

We store the hostname of our server in a variable—`$server`—on line 10 and store the group we want to select in `$group` on line 11. If you want to run this script, you should assign the hostname of your ISP's news server to the `$server` variable.

> If your ISP does not allow you access to a news server, you might be able to run this script on a public news server. An excellent resource for public servers can be found at `http://www.newzbot.com/`.

By the Way

We use `fsockopen()` on line 16 to connect to the host on port 119, which is the usual port for NNTP connections. If a valid file resource is not returned, we use `die()` on line 18 to print the error number and description to the browser and end script execution. On connection, the server should have sent us a confirmation message, so we attempt to acquire this with `fgets()` on line 23. If all is well, this string begins with the status code 200. To test this, we use `explode()` (on line 24) to split the `$line` string into an array using the space character as the delimiter. To learn more about the `explode()` function, refer to Hour 8. If the first element of this array is 200 or 201 (the status returned by servers that do not allow posting), we can continue; otherwise, we end the script.

If all is proceeding as expected, we send the news server the "group" command that should select a newsgroup on line 33. If this is successful, the server should return a string beginning with the status code 211. We test this again on line 37 and end execution if we don't get what we are expecting.

Now that we have selected our newsgroup, we send the "head" command to the server on line 44, which requests the headers for the first message in the group. Again, we test the server response on line 49, looking for the status code 221. Finally, we acquire the header itself. The server's listing of a header ends with a single dot (.) on its own line, so we test for this in a while statement on line 49. As long as the server's output line does not begin with a dot, we request and print the next line.

Finally, we close the connection. Figure 14.3 shows a typical output from Listing 14.8.

FIGURE 14.3
Making an NNTP connection.

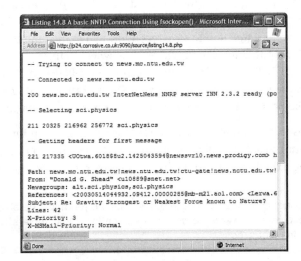

Sending Mail with the mail() Function

PHP can automate the sending of Internet mail for you. The mail() function requires three strings representing the recipient of the mail, the mail subject, and the message. mail() returns false if it encounters an error. In the following fragment, we send an email:

```
$to = "someone@adomain.com";
$subject = "hi";
$message = "just a test message! ";
mail( $to, $subject, $message ) or print "Could not send mail";
```

If you are running PHP on a Unix system, mail() uses a mail application such as Sendmail. On other systems, the function connects to a local or remote SMTP mail server. You should set this using the SMTP directive in the php.ini file.

You are not limited to the mail headers implied by the mail() function's required arguments. You can include as many mail headers as you want in an optional fourth string argument. These should be separated by CRLF characters ('\r\n'). In the following example, we include a From field in our mail message, as well as an X-Priority header that some clients recognize:

```
$to = "someone@example.com";
$from = "book@corrosive.co.uk";
$subject = "hi";
$message = "just a test message! ";
mail( $to, $subject, $message, "From: $from\r\nX-Priority: 1 (Highest)" )
or print "Could not send mail";
```

As of PHP 4.0.5, an additional fifth optional parameter can be used. This enables you to pass command-line-style arguments directly to the mailer.

An Introduction to Streams

A **stream** is a flow of data that can be read from and written to. Streams were introduced with PHP 4.3. You can work with streams using resource variables and define them using specially structured strings. You might be surprised to discover that we have already done quite a lot of work with streams. Let's revisit the fopen() function:

```
$fp = fopen( "/path/to/file.txt", "r" );
$wp = fopen( "http://www.example.com", "r" );
```

We use fopen() to acquire a resource that can then be used with methods such as fgets(). After we have this resource, we can ignore the fact that the source of the stream we are working with is a Web page or a file. It is just a stream.

In the second call to fopen(), the engine provides an HTTP stream rather than a file stream because of the syntax of the path argument. We refer to streams in two parts: the scheme (http in the fragment) and the target (www.example.com). The scheme and the target are separated by the characters '://':

```
scheme://target
http://www.example.com
```

In the first call to fopen(), the scheme was omitted and the engine resorted to the default behavior, providing a file stream. Table 14.4 lists some of the schemes PHP supports.

TABLE 14.4   Some Stream Protocols

`scheme://target`	**Description**
`file://path/file`	The file at `path/file` on the file system
`ftp://host/path`	The object at `host/path` via FTP
`ftp://user:pass@host`	The object at `host/path` via FTP (using `user/pass`)
`ftps://host/path`	The object at `host/path` via secure FTP
`ftps://user:pass@host`	The object at `host/path` via secure FTP (using `user/pass`)
`http://host/path`	The object at `host/path` via HTTP
`http://user:pass@host`	The object at `host/path` via HTTP (with authentication)
`https://host/path`	The object at `host/path` via HTTPS
`https://user:pass@host`	The object at `host/path` via HTTPS (with authentication)
`php://input`	Raw POST data
`php://output`	Output stream to browser or command line

With `fopen()`, we have a function that handles different stream protocols differently according to type. This is possible because each protocol is managed behind the scenes by its own wrapper. A particular wrapper is invoked by a stream function such as `fopen()` according to the scheme provided. The target information after the `'://'` is passed to the wrapper and used to acquire the relevant resource. Also passed to the wrapper are any mode arguments (such as r for read and w for write), options, and an optional context array. Streams sit behind most functions that open flows of data, including `file()`, `file_get_contents()`, `fsockopen()`, and so on. We will deal with `fopen()` in our examples.

Streams and Contexts

PHP provides a mechanism by which stream wrappers can be passed fine-grained parameters to help them with their reading, writing, or appending. Context options take the form of an array whose key should be the name of the wrapper. The array's value should be an associative array of option names and values. Let's define an option array for an HTTP stream:

```
$options = array(
    "http"=>array(
      "user_agent"=>"php24-test-script",
      "header"=>"Referer: http://www.example.com/index.html\r\n"
  )
  );
```

The $options array should be fairly clear. We will be telling our HTTP wrapper to use the Referer header and the user_agent string supplied. Before we can pass these options to fopen(), we must first create a context resource:

```
$context = stream_context_create( $options );
```

Table 14.5 lists all the context options the HTTP wrapper accepts.

TABLE 14.5   The Context Options Supported by the HTTP Wrapper

Key	Description
content	Request information passed after the request header, typically in POST requests
header	One or more request headers; each header should end with a newline
method	The request method, usually GET or POST
user_agent	The User-agent request header (if not overridden by a header option)

In Listing 14.9 we create a simple page that reports on the $_SERVER['HTTP_REFERER'] and $_SERVER['HTTP_USER_AGENT'] elements. We will use this to test our context resource.

LISTING 14.9   Reporting the User Agent and Referrer

```
1: <!DOCTYPE html PUBLIC
2:   "-//W3C//DTD XHTML 1.0 Strict//EN"
3:   "http://www.w3.org/TR/xhtml1/DTD/xhtml1-strict.dtd">
4: <html>
5: <head>
6: <title>Listing 14.9 Reporting User Agent and Referrer</title>
7: </head>
8: <body>
9: <div>
10: <p>
11: Browser: <b><?php print $_SERVER['HTTP_USER_AGENT'] ?></b><br />
12: Referring page: <b><?php print $_SERVER['HTTP_REFERER'] ?></b>
13: </p>
14: </div>
15: </body>
16: </html>
```

Now we can access this page using an HTTP wrapper. If all goes well, we should see our context options in the output. In Listing 14.10 we create a context resource, passing it to fopen() to display the output from Listing 14.9.

LISTING 14.10   Calling `fopen()` with a Context Resource

```
 1: <?php
 2: $url="http://p24.corrosive.co.uk:9090/source/listing14.9.php";
 3: $options = array(
 4:         "http"=>array(
 5:             "user_agent"=>"php24-test-script",
 6:             "header"=>"referer: http://www.example.com/index.html\r\n"
 7:           )
 8:       );
 9:
10: $context = stream_context_create( $options );
11:
12: $res = fopen( $url, 'r', 0, $context ) or
13:     die( "could not open page" );
14:
15: while ( ! feof( $res ) ) {
16:   print fgets( $res, 1024 );
17: }
18:
19: ?>
```

We assign a full URL to the $url variable on line 2. This points to the simple script we created in Listing 14.9. We then create an $options array, passing it to `stream_context_create()` on line 10 to acquire a context resource. We call `fopen()` on line 12, passing it our $url variable, a mode string, a zero integer (meaning that we want to pass no special options), and our context resource. Because the $url string begins with `http://`, an HTTP wrapper is invoked. It makes an HTTP request, using the context options we passed to `fopen()`. On lines 15 and 16, we use `fgets()` and `feof()` to output the stream to the browser. You can see the output from Listing 14.10 in Figure 14.4, confirming that Listing 14.9 reports the headers we set.

FIGURE 14.4
Calling an HTTP wrapper with a context resource.

> You can get a full list of stream wrappers and details of the context options available for each one at `http://uk.php.net/manual/en/wrappers.php`.

By the Way

Summary

In this hour, you saw how to use environment variables to learn more about your visitors. If you don't have access to a user's hostname, you should now be able to use `gethostbyaddr()` to acquire it.

You learned some of the basics about the negotiation that takes place between a client and server when an HTTP connection is made.

You learned how to use `fopen()` to get a document from the Web and how to use `fsockopen()` to make your own HTTP connection. You should also be able to use `fsockopen()` to make connections to other network services. You learned how to use `mail()` to send email from your scripts. Finally, you peeked below the hood to examine streams, the mechanism by which data functions deal transparently with multiple protocols.

So far in this book, we have concentrated on text. In the next hour, we look at some functions that enable us to use PHP to construct and manipulate images.

Q&A

Q *HTTP seems a little esoteric. Do I really need to know about it to write good PHP code?*

A No. You can write excellent code with knowing the intricacies of client/server interaction. On the other hand, a basic understanding of the process is useful if you want to do more than just download pages from remote servers.

Q *If I can send fake headers to a remote server, how suspicious should I be of environment variables myself?*

A You should not trust environment variables such as `$_SERVER['HTTP_REFERER']` and `$_SERVER['HTTP_USER_AGENT']` if their accuracy is essential to the operation of your script. Remember, though, that the vast majority of clients you deal with will tell you the truth. If you are merely ensuring a productive user experience by detecting browser type or gathering overall statistical information, there is no need to distrust this data.

Workshop

Quiz

1. Which server variable might give you the URL of the referring page?

2. Why can you not rely on the $_SERVER['REMOTE_ADDR'] variable to track an individual user across multiple visits to your script?

3. What does HTTP stand for?

4. Which client header line tells the server about the browser that is making the request?

5. What does the server response code 404 mean?

6. Without making your own network connection, which function might you use to access a Web page on a remote server?

7. Given an IP address, which function could you use to get a hostname?

8. Which function would you use to make a network connection?

9. Which PHP function would you use to send an email?

Answers

1. You can often find the URL of the referring page in the $_SERVER['HTTP_REFERER'] variable.

2. Many service providers allocate a different IP address to their users every time they log on, so you cannot assume a user will return with the same address.

3. HTTP stands for Hypertext Transfer Protocol.

4. A client might send a User-Agent header, which tells the server about the client version and operating system that are running.

5. The server response 404 means that the requested page or resource cannot be found on the server.

6. The fopen() function can be used for Web pages on remote machines as well as files on your file system.

7. The gethostbyaddr() function accepts an IP address and returns a resolved hostname.

8. The `fsockopen()` function establishes a connection with a remote server.

9. You can send email with the `mail()` function.

Exercises

1. Create a script that accepts a Web hostname (such as `http://www.microsoft.com`) from user input. Send the host a HEAD request using `fsockopen()` to create the connection. Print the response to the browser. Remember to handle the possibility that no connection can be established.

2. Create a script that accepts a message from the user and mails it to you. Add server variables to the user's message to tell you about her browser and IP address.

HOUR 15

Images On-the-Fly

What You'll Learn in This Hour:

▶ How to create and output an image
▶ How to work with colors
▶ How to draw shapes, including arcs, rectangles, and polygons
▶ How to fill areas with color
▶ How to work with TrueType fonts

The functions included in this hour rely on a library called GD which is bundled with PHP.

The GD library is a set of tools that enables programmers to create and work with images on-the-fly. If PHP is compiled with GD support, you can use PHP's image functions to create dynamic images. Due to licensing issues, the bundled library does not support the GIF image format. We will output images as PNGs because they are available by default with the bundled library and are supported by most browsers. With the GD functions you can create sophisticated graphics on-the-fly.

Checking Your Configuration with gd_info()

Although the GD library is bundled with PHP, some features (such as JPEG support, for example) require external libraries. You can see which features PHP is compiled to support with the gd_info() function. gd_info() requires no arguments and returns an associative array describing your GD setup. Table 15.1 lists the elements of the array returned by gd_info().

TABLE 15.1   The Array Returned by `gd_info()`

Element	Description
GD Version	The version of GD used; `bundled (2.0.15 compatible)`, for example
FreeType Support	Whether FreeType fonts are supported (0 or 1)
FreeType Linkage	The library used to provide FreeType functionality; `with TTF library`, for example.
T1Lib Support	Support for Type 1 fonts
GIF Read Support	Read-only support for the GIF format (0 or 1)
GIF Create Support	Support for creating and manipulating GIF data (0 or 1)
JPG Support	Support for reading, creating, and manipulating JPEG data (0 or 1)
PNG Support	Support for reading, creating, and manipulating PNG data (0 or 1)
WBMP Support	Support for reading, creating, and manipulating wireless bitmap data (0 or 1)
XPM Support	Support for reading, creating, and manipulating X Windows pixmap image data (0 or 1)
XBM Support	Support for reading, creating, and manipulating X Windows bitmap image data (0 or 1)
JIS-mapped Japanese Font Support	Support for Japanese International Standard character set (0 or 1)

We can run `gd_info()` in a script like so:

```
print "<pre>";
print_r( gd_info() );
print "</pre>";
```

Notice that we output the array using `print_r()` and maintain formatting by wrapping our output in a `<pre>` element. On our system the output looks like this:

```
Array
(
  [GD Version] => bundled (2.0.15 compatible)
  [FreeType Support] => 1
  [FreeType Linkage] => with TTF library
  [T1Lib Support] =>
  [GIF Read Support] => 1
  [GIF Create Support] =>
  [JPG Support] => 1
  [PNG Support] => 1
  [WBMP Support] => 1
  [XPM Support] =>
```

```
    [XBM Support] => 1
    [JIS-mapped Japanese Font Support] =>
)
```

We can see from this output that it would be a mistake to attempt to output a GIF file, but we can work with the JPEG and PNG formats.

Creating and Outputting Images

Before you can begin to work with an image, you must acquire an image resource. You can do this using the `imagecreate()` function. `imagecreate()` requires two arguments, one for the image's height and another for its width. It returns an image resource, which you will use with most of the functions we cover in this hour. You should be familiar with resources from your work with files and databases. The image resource returned by `imagecreate()` is a required argument for most of the functions in this book:

```
$image = imagecreate( 200, 200 );
```

Now that you have an image resource, you can allocate a color.

By the Way

If you want to work with an existing image rather than create a new one, PHP provides a range of functions to open files of different types. You can open and work with a JPEG file, for example, by passing its path to `imagecreatefromjpeg()`. You can also open and work with a PNG file by passing a path to `imagecreatefrompng()`. You can then work with the image resource returned by these functions as we do in the examples in this hour. You will need to use `gd_info()` to check that GD is set up to work with the format you want to read.

You can find these and other variations on `imagecreate()` at the Image Functions section of the PHP manual, at `http://www.php.net/gd`.

Acquiring Color

To work with color, you need to acquire a color resource. You can do this with the `imagecolorallocate()` function, which requires an image resource and three integers between 0 and 255 representing red, green, and blue. The function returns an image resource that you can use to define the color of shapes, fills, and text:

```
$red = imagecolorallocate( $image, 255,0,0 );
```

Coincidentally, the first time you call `imagecolorallocate()`, you also set the default color for your image.

Now that you have an image resource and a color allocated, you are nearly ready to output your first image to the browser. To do this, you need to use the imagepng() function, which requires the image resource as an argument. imagepng() also accepts an optional path argument. If you provide a path here, PHP will attempt to write the data to a file rather than to the browser. This can be useful for caching dynamically generated images.

Listing 15.1 uses these functions to create and output an image.

LISTING 15.1   A Dynamically Created Image

```
1: <?php
2: header("Content-type: image/png");
3: $image = imagecreate( 200, 200 );
4: $red = imagecolorallocate( $image, 255, 0, 0 );
5: imagepng($image);
6: ?>
```

Notice that we sent a Content-type header to the browser (line 2) before doing anything else. We need to tell the browser to expect image information; otherwise, it treats the script's output as HTML. This script can now be called directly by the browser, or as part of an IMG element, like so:

```
<img src="listing15.1.php" alt="a PHP generated image">
```

Figure 15.1 shows the output of Listing 15.1.

FIGURE 15.1
A dynamically
created image.

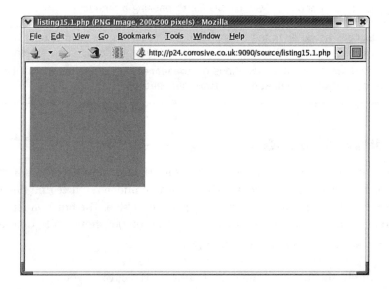

We have created a square, but we have no way as yet of controlling its color.

By the Way

Depending on your setup, you might be able to output image formats other than PNGs. To add JPEG support on a Unix system, for example, you might need an external JPEG library from the Independent JPEG Group at http://www.ijg.org/files/jpegsrc.v6b.tar.gz.

In the following fragment, we unpack the archive and install it from a Linux command line:

```
tar -xvzf jpegsrc.v6b.tar.gz
cd jpeg-6b
./configure
  --enable-shared \
  --enable-static \
  --prefix=/usr
make
make install
```

After the JPEG library is installed, we can ensure that PHP can use it when we run PHP's configure script:

```
./configure --with-apxs=/home/apache/bin/apxs' \
  --with-gd \
  --with-freetype=/usr/include/freetype/ \
  --with-ttf \
  --with-zlib-dir=/usr/include \
  --with-jpeg-dir=/usr/lib
```

After PHP is compiled, we can substitute imagejpeg() for imagepng() to write JPEG rather than PNG data.

Like imagepng(), imagejpeg() accepts an image resource and optional second argument, which you can use to write an image to a file. It also accepts a third integer argument representing the quality of the image you want to output. This can be a value between 1 and 100. If you omit the third argument, a default of 75 is used.

As you read this, you might find that JPEG support is bundled with your version of PHP. Use gd_info() to check your configuration before recompiling.

Drawing Lines

Before you draw a line on an image, you need to determine the points from and to which you want to draw.

You can think of an image as a block of pixels indexed from 0 on both the horizontal and vertical axes. The origin is the upper-left corner of the image.

In other words, a pixel with the coordinates 5, 8 is the sixth pixel along and the ninth pixel down, looking from left to right, top to bottom.

The imageline() function draws a line between one pixel coordinate and another. It requires an image resource, four integers representing the start and end coordinates of the line, and a color resource.

Listing 15.2 adds to the image created in Listing 15.1, drawing a line from corner to corner.

LISTING 15.2   Drawing a Line with imageline()

```
1: <?php
2: header("Content-type: image/png");
3: $image = imagecreate( 200, 200 );
4: $red = imagecolorallocate($image, 255,0,0);
5: $blue = imagecolorallocate($image, 0,0,255 );
6: imageline( $image, 0, 0, 199, 199, $blue );
7: imagepng($image);
8: ?>
```

We acquire two color resources, one for red (line 4) and one for blue (line 5). We then use the resource stored in the variable $blue for the line's color on line 6. Notice that our line ends at the coordinates 199, 199 and not 200, 200; that's because pixels are indexed from 0. Figure 15.2 shows the output from Listing 15.2.

FIGURE 15.2
Drawing a line with imageline().

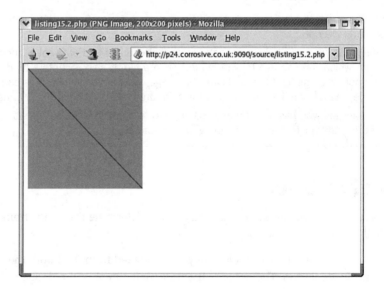

Applying Color Fills

You can fill an area with color using PHP just as you can with your favorite graphics application. The function imagefill() requires an image resource, starting coordinates for the fill it is to perform, and a color resource. It then transforms the starting pixel and all adjacent pixels of the same color. Listing 15.3 adds a call to imagefill() to our script, making the image a little more interesting.

LISTING 15.3   Using imagefill()

```
1: <?php
2: header("Content-type: image/png");
3: $image = imagecreate( 200, 200 );
4: $red = imagecolorallocate($image, 255,0,0);
5: $blue = imagecolorallocate($image, 0,0,255 );
6: imageline( $image, 0, 0, 199, 199, $blue );
7: imagefill( $image, 0, 199, $blue );
8: imagepng($image);
9: ?>
```

The only change we have made to our example is the call to imagefill() on line 7. Figure 15.3 shows the output from Listing 15.3.

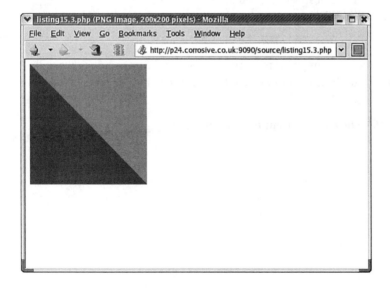

FIGURE 15.3
Using
imagefill().

Drawing an Arc

You can add partial or complete arcs to your images with the imagearc() function. imagearc() requires an image object, coordinates for the center point, an integer for width, an integer for height, a start point and end point (in degrees), and a color resource. Arcs are drawn clockwise starting from 3 o'clock. The following fragment draws a quarter circle:

```
imagearc( $image, 99, 99, 200, 200, 0, 90, $blue );
```

This draws a partial arc, with its center at the coordinates 99, 99. The total height and width are both 200 pixels. Drawing starts at 3 o'clock and continues for 90° (to 6 o'clock).

Listing 15.4 draws a complete circle and fills it with blue.

LISTING 15.4   Drawing a Circle with imagearc()

```
1: <?php
2: header("Content-type: image/png");
3: $image = imagecreate( 200, 200 );
4: $red = imagecolorallocate($image, 255,0,0);
5: $blue = imagecolorallocate($image, 0,0,255 );
6: imagearc( $image, 99, 99, 180, 180, 0, 360, $blue );
7: imagefill( $image, 99, 99, $blue );
8: imagepng($image);
9: ?>
```

As before, we acquire color resources (lines 4 and 5). On line 6, we call imagearc() to draw a complete circle; then the call to imagefill() on line 7 fills our circle with blue.

Figure 15.4 shows the output from Listing 15.4.

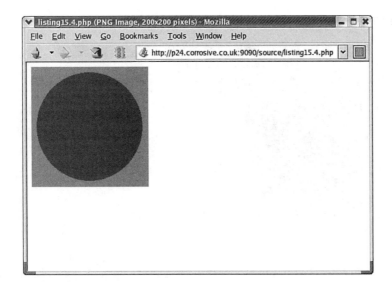

FIGURE 15.4
Drawing a circle
with `imagearc()`.

Drawing a Rectangle

You can draw a rectangle in PHP using the `imagerectangle()` function.
`imagerectangle()` requires an image resource, the coordinates for your rectangle's
upper-left corner, the coordinates for its bottom-right corner, and a color resource.
The following fragment draws a rectangle whose upper-left coordinates are 19, 19
and bottom-right coordinates are 179, 179:

```
imagerectangle( $image, 19, 19, 179, 179, $blue );
```

You could then fill this with `imagefill()`. Because this is such a common operation, however, PHP provides the `imagefilledrectangle()` function, which expects
exactly the same arguments as `imagerectangle()` but produces a rectangle filled
with the color you specify. Listing 15.5 creates a filled rectangle (line 6) and outputs the image to the browser.

LISTING 15.5   Drawing a Filled Rectangle with `imagefilledrectangle()`

```
1: <?php
2: header("Content-type: image/png");
3: $image = imagecreate( 200, 200 );
4: $red = imagecolorallocate($image, 255,0,0);
5: $blue = imagecolorallocate($image, 0,0,255 );
6: imagefilledrectangle( $image, 19, 19, 179, 179, $blue );
7: imagepng( $image );
8: ?>
```

Figure 15.5 shows the output from Listing 15.5.

FIGURE 15.5
Drawing a filled
rectangle with
imagefilled
rectangle().

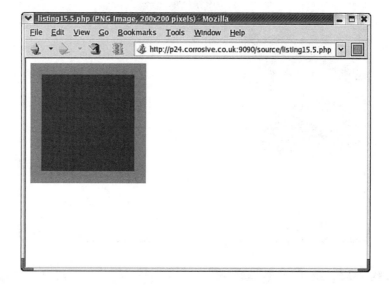

Drawing a Polygon

You can draw more sophisticated shapes using imagepolygon(). This function requires an image resource, an array of point coordinates, an integer representing the number of points in the shape, and a color resource. The array passed to imagepolygon() should be numerically indexed. The first two elements give the coordinates of the first point, the second two give the coordinates of the second point, and so on. imagepolygon() fills in the lines between the points, automatically closing your shape by joining the final point to the first. You can create a filled polygon with the imagefilledpolygon() function.

Listing 15.6 draws a filled polygon, outputting the result to the browser.

LISTING 15.6   Drawing a Polygon with imagefilledpolygon()

```
 1: <?php
 2: header("Content-type: image/png");
 3: $image = imagecreate( 200, 200 );
 4: $red = imagecolorallocate($image, 255,0,0);
 5: $blue = imagecolorallocate($image, 0,0,255 );
 6: $points = array (   10, 10,
 7:        190, 190,
 8:        190, 10,
 9:        10, 190
10:        );
11: imagefilledpolygon( $image, $points, count( $points )/2 , $blue );
12: imagepng($image);
13: ?>
```

After acquiring image and color resources (lines 2–5), we create an array of coordinates on line 6. Notice that when we call `imagefilledpolygon()` on line 11, we tell it the number of points we want to connect by counting the number of elements in the `$points` array and dividing the result by 2. Figure 15.6 shows the output from Listing 15.6.

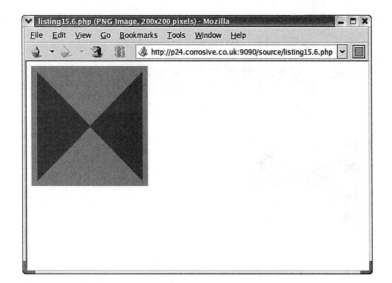

FIGURE 15.6
Drawing a polygon with `imagefilled polygon()`.

Making a Color Transparent

PHP allows you to make selected colors within your image transparent with `imagecolortransparent()`, which requires an image resource and a color resource. When you output your image to the browser, the color you pass to `imagecolortransparent()` is transparent. Listing 15.7 changes our polygon code so that the shape floats on the browser instead of sitting against a background color.

LISTING 15.7 Making Colors Transparent with `imagecolortransparent()`

```
1: <?php
2: header("Content-type: image/png");
3:
4: $image = imagecreate( 200, 200 );
5: $red = imagecolorallocate($image, 255,0,0);
6: $blue = imagecolorallocate($image, 0,0,255 );
7:
8: $points = array (    10, 10,
9:         190, 190,
10:        190, 10,
11:        10, 190
12:        );
```

LISTING 15.7   Continued

```
13:
14: imagefilledpolygon( $image, $points, count( $points )/2 , $blue );
15: imagecolortransparent( $image, $red );
16: imagepng($image);
17: ?>
```

Listing 15.7 is identical to Listing 15.6 except for the call to imagecolortransparent()
on line 15. Figure 15.7 shows the output from Listing 15.7.

FIGURE 15.7
Making colors
transparent with
imagecolor
transparent().

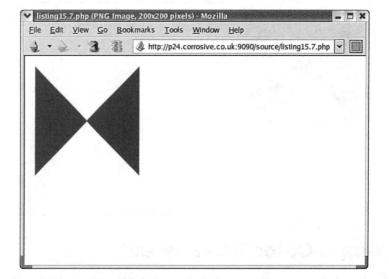

Working with Text

In this section we will work primarily with PHP's TrueType functions, which are
useful for creating sophisticated charts or navigation. For a quick and easy way of
writing to an image, however, the imagestring() function is the perfect tool.

Writing to an Image with the imagestring() Function

The imagestring() function is simple and useful. It requires an image resource, a
font number, an x-axis location, and a y-axis location (with location 0,0 being
the upper-left corner of the image). The function also requires the string you want
to output and a color resource. Of these arguments, only the font numbers should
need much explanation. These are built-in fonts of ascending size. Font 1 is the

smallest in size, font 2 is slightly larger, and so on up to font 5. In the following fragment, we use `imagestring()` to write some text to an image:

```
header("Content-type: image/png");
$image = imagecreate( 200, 200 );
$red = imagecolorallocate($image, 255,0,0);
$blue = imagecolorallocate($image, 0,0,255 );

for ( $x=1; $x<=5; $x++ ) {
  imageString( $image, $x, (20*$x), (20*$x), "Welcome!", $blue );
}

imagepng($image);
```

We output a `Content-type` header and create an image and two color resources as before. Then we use a `for` loop to increment a counter variable, `$x` from 1 to 5. For each iteration of the loop, we call `imagestring()`, passing it our image resource, the font number held by the `$x` variable, and two location coordinates. We use the same string—`Welcome!`—and the color blue for each call to `imagestring()`.

You can see the output from this fragment in Figure 15.8.

FIGURE 15.8
Writing text to an image with `imagestring()`.

Working with TrueType Fonts

If you are working with the GD functions on a Windows system, you probably have access to the TrueType text functions already. If you are working in a Linux context, however, you might need to tell PHP about the TrueType library on your system when you compile it. We cover the installation process for a Linux system in Hour 2, "Installing PHP."

When you have TrueType support, you can use text functions to create image-based charts or navigation elements. PHP even gives you the tool you need to check that any text you write will fit within the space available.

Writing a String with imageTTFtext()

You can write text to your image with the imageTTFtext() function. This requires eight arguments: an image resource, a size argument representing the height of the characters to be written, an angle, the starting coordinates (one argument for the x-axis and another for the y-axis), a color resource, the path to a TrueType font, and the text you want to write.

The start point for any text you write determines where the baseline of the first character in the string will be.

Listing 15.8 writes a string to an image and outputs the result to the browser.

LISTING 15.8　Writing a String with imageTTFtext()

```
 1: <?php
 2: header("Content-type: image/png");
 3:
 4: $image = imagecreate( 400, 200 );
 5: $red = imagecolorallocate($image, 255,0,0);
 6: $blue = imagecolorallocate($image, 0,0,255 );
 7: $font = "luxisri.ttf";
 8:
 9: imageTTFtext( $image, 50, 0, 20, 100, $blue, $font, "Welcome!" );
10:
11: imagepng($image);
12: ?>
```

We create a canvas with a width of 400 pixels and a height of 200 pixels on line 4. We define two colors (lines 5 and 6) and store the path to a TrueType font in a variable called $font (line 7).

Note that font files are likely to be stored in a different directory on your server. If you are not sure where, you could try searching for files with the .ttf extension. If you still cannot find the fonts you need on your system, you should be able to locate TrueType fonts on the Web and upload them to your Web space.

After we have stored the font path in the $font variable, we write the text Welcome! to the image on line 9.

For the call to imageTTFtext(), we define a size of 50, an angle of 0, a starting position of 20 on the x-axis, and a starting position of 100 on the y-axis. We also pass the function the color resource stored in the $blue variable, the font path stored in $font, and (finally) the text we want to output. You can see the result in Figure 15.9.

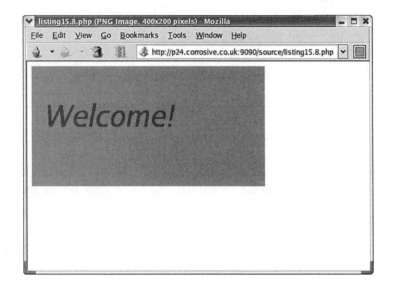

FIGURE 15.9
Writing text with imageTTFtext().

Of course, we have to guess where to put the text at the moment. The size argument does not give us an accurate idea of the text's height, and the width is a mystery. In fact, imageTTFtext() will return dimension information, but by then the deed is done. Luckily, PHP provides a function that enables you to try before you buy.

Testing Text Dimensions with imageTTFbox()

You can get information about the dimensions of text using the imageTTFbox() function, which is so called because it tells you about the text's bounding box. imageTTFbox() requires the font size, the angle, a path to a font file, and the text to be written. It is one of the few image functions that does not require an image resource. It returns an eight-element array, which is explained in Table 15.2.

TABLE 15.2   The Array Returned by `imageTTFbox()`

Index	Description
0	Bottom-left (horizontal axis)
1	Bottom-left (vertical axis)
2	Bottom-right (horizontal axis)
3	Bottom-right (vertical axis)
4	Upper-right (horizontal axis)
5	Upper-right (vertical axis)
6	Upper-left (horizontal axis)
7	Upper-left (vertical axis)

All figures on the vertical axis are relative to the text's baseline, which is 0. Figures for the vertical axis at the top of the text count down from this figure and are therefore usually minus numbers. Figures for the vertical axis at the bottom of the text count up from 0, giving the number of pixels the text drops from the baseline.

So, if you test a string containing a *y* with `imageTTFbbox()`, for example, the return array might have a figure of 3 for element 1 because the tail of the *y* drops 3 pixels below the baseline. It could have a figure of –10 for element 7 because the text is raised 10 pixels above the baseline.

To complicate matters, there seems to be a 2-pixel difference between the baseline as returned by `imageTTFbbox()` and the visible baseline when drawing text. You might need to adjust for this by thinking of the height of the baseline as 2 pixels greater than that returned by the `imageTTFbbox()`.

On the horizontal axis, figures for `imageTTFbbox()` on the left take account of text that begins before the given start point by returning the offset as a minus number in elements 6 and 0. This is usually a small number, so whether you adjust alignment to take account of this depends on the level of accuracy you require.

You can use the information returned by `imageTTFbbox()` to align text within an image. Listing 15.9 creates a script that dynamically outputs text, centering it within our image on both the vertical and horizontal planes.

LISTING 15.9   Aligning Text Within a Fixed Space Using `imageTTFbbox()`

```
1: <?php
2: header("Content-type: image/png");
3: $height = 100;
4: $width = 200;
5: $fontsize = 50;
6: if ( empty ( $_GET['text'] ) ) {
```

LISTING 15.9   Continued

```
 7:   $text = "Change me!";
 8: } else {
 9:   $text = $_GET['text'];
10: }
11: $image = imagecreate( $width, $height );
12: $red = imagecolorallocate($image, 255,0,0);
13: $blue = imagecolorallocate($image, 0,0,255 );
14: $font = "luxisri.ttf";
15: $textwidth = $width;
16: $textheight;
17: while ( true ) {
18:   $box = imageTTFbbox( $fontsize, 0, $font, $text );
19:   $textwidth = abs( $box[2] );
20:   $textbodyheight = ( abs($box[7]) )-2;
21:   if ( $textwidth < $width - 20 )
22:     break;
23:   $fontsize--;
24: }
25: $pngXcenter = (int) ( $width/2 );
26: $pngYcenter = (int) ( $height/2 );
27: imageTTFtext( $image, $fontsize, 0,
28:     (int) ($pngXcenter-($textwidth/2)),
29:     (int) ($pngYcenter+(($textbodyheight)/2) ),
30:     $blue, $font, $text );
31: imagepng($image);
32: ?>
```

We store the height and width of the image in the variables $height and $width (lines 3 and 4) and set a default font size of 50 on line 5. On line 6, we test the built-in $_GET array for the presence of an element called 'text', setting a default on line 9 if it isn't present. In this way, the image can accept data from a Web page, either in the query string of an image URL or from form submission. We use imagecreate() on line 11 to acquire an image resource. We acquire color resources in the usual way and store the path to a TrueType font file in a variable called $font (lines 12–14).

We want to fit the string stored in $text into the available space, but we have no way of knowing yet whether it will. Within a while statement starting on line 17, we pass the font path and string to imageTTFbbox() on line 18, storing the resultant array in a variable called $box. The element $box[2] contains the position of the lower-right corner on the horizontal axis. We take this to be the width of the string and store it in $textwidth on line 21.

We want to center the text vertically, but only account for the area above the text's baseline. We can use the absolute value of $box[7] to find the height of the text above the baseline, although we need to adjust this by 2 pixels. We store this value in $textbodyheight on line 20.

Now that we have a working figure for the text's width, we can test it against the width of the image (less 10 pixels border). If the text is smaller than the width of the canvas we are using, we end the loop on line 22. Otherwise, we reduce the font size on line 23, ready to try again.

Dividing the $height and $width values by 2 (lines 25 and 26), we can find the approximate center point of the image. We write the text to the image on line 27, using the figures we have calculated for the image's center point in conjunction with the text's height and width to calculate the offset.

Finally, we write the image to the browser on line 31. Figure 15.10 shows the output from Listing 15.9.

FIGURE 15.10
Aligning text within
a fixed space using
imageTTFbbox().

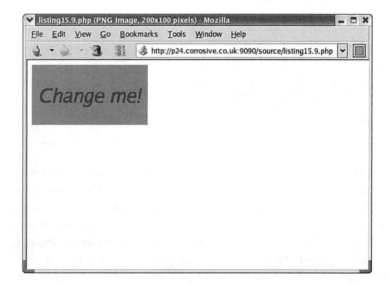

This code can now be called from another page as part of an img element. The following fragment writes some simple code that enables a user to add his own string to be included in the image:

```php
<?php
$text = ( empty( $_GET['text'] ) )?"Dynamic":$_GET['text'];
?>
<form action="<?php print $_SERVER['PHP_SELF'] ?>" method="get">
<input type="text" name="text" />
</form>
<p>
<img src="listing15.9.php?text=<?php print urlencode($text) ?>" />
</p>
```

When we call the script in Listing 15.9 on line 10, we append a query string that includes the text to be added to the image. You can learn more about this technique for passing information from script to script in Hour 19, "Saving State with Cookies and Query Strings."

Bringing It Together

Let's build an example that uses some of the functions we have examined in this hour. Suppose that we have been asked to produce a dynamic bar chart that compares a range of labeled numbers. The bar chart must include the relevant label below each bar. Our client must be able to change the number of bars on the chart, the height and width of the image, and the size of the border around the chart. The bar chart will be used for consumer votes, and all that is needed is an at-a-glance representation of the data. A more detailed breakdown will be included in the HTML portion of the containing page.

To make our code reasonably reusable, we create a class called `SimpleBar`.

Before we even reach the constructor, we can set up some values that we don't intend to make changeable by the client. We declare them private, like so:

```
private $xgutter = 20; // left/right margin
private $ygutter = 20; // top/bottom margin
private $bottomspace = 30; // gap at the bottom
private $internalgap = 10; // space between bars
private $cells = array(); // labels/amounts for bar chart
```

The $xgutter and $ygutter properties determine the margin around the chart horizontally and vertically. $internalgap determines the space between the bars, and the $bottomspace property contains the space available to label the bars at the bottom of the screen.

In the constructor, we assign some values to properties we want the client coder to be able to influence:

```
function __construct( $width, $height, $font ) {
  $this->totalwidth = $width;
  $this->totalheight = $height;
  $this->font = $font;
}
```

The constructor is called with a width, height, font, and properties set accordingly. Now we have most of the parameters in place, except for the data to be displayed.

The easiest way of storing labels and values is in an associative array. Our class will have a property called $cells, and we will allow client code to add to this array through a method called addBar():

```
function addBar( $label, $amount ) {
  $this->cells[ $label ] = $amount;
}
```

With our parameters in place, we can define a draw() method to work with them:

```
function draw() {
    $image = imagecreate( $this->totalwidth, $this->totalheight );
    $red = ImageColorAllocate($image, 255, 0, 0);
    $blue = ImageColorAllocate($image, 0, 0, 255 );
    $black = ImageColorAllocate($image, 0, 0, 0 );
//...
```

First, we acquire an image resource and set up some colors. We won't make color a factor that client code can change, although we could consider this for the future:

```
$max = max( $this->cells );
$total = count( $this->cells );
$graphCanX = ( $this->totalwidth - $this->xgutter*2 );
$graphCanY = ( $this->totalheight - $this->ygutter*2
        - $this->bottomspace );
$posX = $this->xgutter;
$posY = $this->totalheight - $this->ygutter - $this->bottomspace;
$cellwidth = (int)(( $graphCanX -
  ( $this->internalgap * ( $total-1 ) )) / $total) ;
$textsize = $this->getTextSize( $cellwidth );
```

First, we cache the maximum value in our cells property and the number of elements it contains. We calculate the graph canvas (the space in which the bars are to be written). On the x-axis, this is the total width minus twice the size of the margin. On the y-axis, we also need to take account of the $bottomspace property to leave room for the labels.

$posX stores the point on the x-axis at which we will start drawing the bars, so we set this to the same value as $xgutter, which contains the value for the margin on the $x axis. $posY stores the bottom point of our bars; it is equivalent to the total height of the image less the margin and the space for the labels stored in $bottomheight.

$cellwidth contains the width of each bar. To arrive at this value, we must calculate the total amount of space between bars, take this from the chart width, and divide this result by the total number of bars.

Before we can create and work with our image, we need to determine the text size. Our problem is that we don't know how long the labels will be, and we want to ensure that each of the labels will fit within the width of the bar above it. We call a private method—getTextSize()—and pass it the $cellwidth variable we have calculated:

```
private function _getTextSize( $cellwidth ) {
  $textsize = (int)($this->bottomspace);
  if ( $cellwidth < 10 ) {
    $cellwidth = 10;
  }
  foreach ( $this->cells as $key=>$val ) {
    while ( true ) {
      $box = ImageTTFbBox( $textsize, 0, $this->font, $key );
      $textwidth = abs( $box[2] );
      if ( $textwidth < $cellwidth ) {
        break;
      }
      $textsize--;
    }
  }
  return $textsize;
}
```

We then loop through the $cells property array to calculate the maximum text size we can use.

For each of the elements, we begin a loop, acquiring dimension information for the label using imageTTFbbox(). We take the text width to be $box[2] and test it against the $cellwidth variable, which contains the width of a single bar in the chart. We break the loop if the text is smaller than the bar width; otherwise, we decrement $textsize and try again. $textsize continues to shrink until every label in the array fits within the bar width. We can now return a value for use in the draw() method.

Finally, we can create an image resource and begin to work with it:

```
//...
  foreach ( $this->cells as $key=>$val ) {
    $cellheight = (int)(($val/$max) * $graphCanY);
    $center = (int)($posX+($cellwidth/2));
    imagefilledrectangle( $image, $posX, ($posY-$cellheight),
      ($posX+$cellwidth), $posY, $blue );
    $box = imageTTFbBox( $textsize, 0, $this->font, $key );
    $tw = $box[2];
    ImageTTFText( $image, $textsize, 0, ($center-($tw/2)),
        ($this->totalheight-$this->ygutter), $black,
        $this->font, $key );
    $posX += ( $cellwidth + $this->internalgap);
  }
  imagepng( $image );
```

Once again, we loop through our $cells array and calculate the height of the bar, storing the result in $cellheight. We calculate the center point (on the x-axis) of the bar, which is $posX plus half the width of the bar.

Next, we draw the bar, using imagefilledrectangle() and the variables $posX, $posY, $cellheight, and $cellwidth.

To align our text, we use imageTTFbbox() again, storing its return array in $box. We use $box[2] as our working width and assign this to a temporary variable, $tw. We now have enough information to write the label. We derive our x position from the $center variable minus half the width of the text and derive our y position from the image's height minus the margin.

We increment $posX to start working with the next bar.

Finally, we output the image.

Although our basic bar chart class has some ugly internals, its interface code is simplicity itself from the point of view of a client coder:

```
$graph = new SimpleBar( 500, 300, "luxisri.ttf" );
$graph->addBar( "liked", 200 );
$graph->addBar( "hated", 400 );
$graph->addBar( "ok", 900 );
$graph->draw();
```

You can see the complete script in Listing 15.10 and sample output in Figure 15.11.

FIGURE 15.11
A dynamic bar chart.

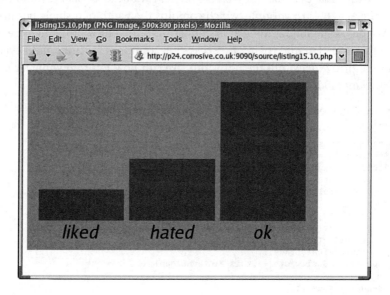

LISTING 15.10   A Dynamic Bar Chart

```php
1: <?php
2: header("Content-type: image/png");
3:
4: class SimpleBar {
5:   private $xgutter = 20; // left/right margin
6:   private $ygutter = 20; // top/bottom margin
7:   private $bottomspace = 30; // gap at the bottom
8:   private $internalgap = 10; // space between bars
9:   private $cells = array(); // labels/amounts for bar chart
10:  private $totalwidth; // width of the image
11:  private $totalheight; // height of the image
12:  private $font; // the font to use
13:
14:  function __construct( $width, $height, $font ) {
15:    $this->totalwidth = $width;
16:    $this->totalheight = $height;
17:    $this->font = $font;
18:  }
19:
20:  function addBar( $label, $amount ) {
21:    $this->cells[ $label ] = $amount;
22:  }
23:
24:  private function _getTextSize( $cellwidth ) {
25:    $textsize = (int)($this->bottomspace);
26:    if ( $cellwidth < 10 ) {
27:      $cellwidth = 10;
28:    }
29:    foreach ( $this->cells as $key=>$val ) {
30:      while ( true ) {
31:        $box = ImageTTFbBox( $textsize, 0, $this->font, $key );
32:        $textwidth = abs( $box[2] );
33:        if ( $textwidth < $cellwidth ) {
34:          break;
35:        }
36:        $textsize--;
37:      }
38:    }
39:    return $textsize;
40:  }
41:
42:  function draw() {
43:    $image = imagecreate( $this->totalwidth, $this->totalheight );
44:    $red = ImageColorAllocate($image, 255, 0, 0);
45:    $blue = ImageColorAllocate($image, 0, 0, 255 );
46:    $black = ImageColorAllocate($image, 0, 0, 0 );
47:
48:    $max = max( $this->cells );
49:    $total = count( $this->cells );
50:    $graphCanX = ( $this->totalwidth - $this->xgutter*2 );
51:    $graphCanY = ( $this->totalheight - $this->ygutter*2
52:                  - $this->bottomspace );
53:    $posX = $this->xgutter;
54:    $posY = $this->totalheight - $this->ygutter - $this->bottomspace;
55:    $cellwidth = (int)(( $graphCanX -
```

LISTING 15.10   Continued

```
56:        ( $this->internalgap * ( $total-1 ) )) / $total) ;
57:        $textsize = $this->_getTextSize( $cellwidth );
58:
59:        foreach ( $this->cells as $key=>$val ) {
60:          $cellheight = (int)(($val/$max) * $graphCanY);
61:          $center = (int)($posX+($cellwidth/2));
62:          imagefilledrectangle( $image, $posX, ($posY-$cellheight),
63:            ($posX+$cellwidth), $posY, $blue );
64:          $box = imageTTFbBox( $textsize, 0, $this->font, $key );
65:          $tw = $box[2];
66:          ImageTTFText( $image, $textsize, 0, ($center-($tw/2)),
67:            ($this->totalheight-$this->ygutter), $black,
68:            $this->font, $key );
69:          $posX += ( $cellwidth + $this->internalgap);
70:        }
71:
72:        imagepng( $image );
73:    }
74: }
75:
76: $graph = new SimpleBar( 500, 300, "luxisri.ttf" );
77: $graph->addBar( "liked", 200 );
78: $graph->addBar( "hated", 400 );
79: $graph->addBar( "ok", 900 );
80: $graph->draw();
81: ?>
```

Summary

PHP's support for the GD library enables you to produce dynamic charts and navigation elements with relative ease.

In this hour, you learned how to use imagecreate() and imagepng() to create and output an image. You learned how to acquire color resources with imagecolorallocate() and to use color resources with imagefill() to fill areas with color. You also learned how to use line and shape functions to create outline and filled shapes. You learned how to use PHP's support for the FreeType library to work with TrueType fonts and worked through an example that wrote text to an image. Finally, you worked through a bar chart example that brought some of these techniques together into a single script.

Our next hour is timely indeed. It discusses dates and the many useful functions PHP provides to help you work with them.

Q&A

Q *Are there any performance issues with regard to dynamic images?*

A A dynamically created image is slower to arrive at the browser than an image that already exists. Depending on the efficiency of your script, the impact is not likely to be noticeable to the user if you use dynamic images sparingly.

Remember that functions such as `imagepng()` and `imagejpeg()` accept an optional path argument that causes the image to be written to a file. You can use this to cache your dynamic images, changing them only when the information they present changes.

Workshop

Quiz

1. Which header should you send to the browser before building and out-putting a PNG image?

2. Which function could you use to acquire an image resource that you can use with other image functions?

3. Which function would you use to output your PNG after building it?

4. Which function could you use to acquire a color resource?

5. With which function would you draw a line on a dynamic image?

6. Which function would you use to fill an area in a dynamic image?

7. Which function might you use to draw an arc?

8. How might you draw a rectangle?

9. How would you draw a polygon?

10. Which function would you use to write a string to a dynamic image?

Answers

1. To output a PNG image, you should use the `header()` function to send the line `"Content-type: image/png"` to the browser.

2. The `imagecreate()` function, returns an image resource. Functions such as `imagecreatefrompng()` can also be used to acquire an image resource from a file on the server.

3. You can output a PNG file with the `imagepng()` function.

4. You can acquire a color resource with the `imagecolorallocate()` function.

5. The `imageline()` function draws a line.

6. The `imagefill()` function fills an area with color.

7. You can draw an arc with the `imagearc()` function.

8. You can draw an outline rectangle with the `imagerectangle()` function. If you want to draw a filled rectangle, you can use `imagefilledrectangle()`.

9. You can draw a polygon with either `imagepolygon()` or `imagefilledpolygon()`.

10. You can write a string to a dynamic image with the `imageTTFtext()` function. You could also use the `imagestring()` function if you needed less control over positioning, size, and font.

Exercises

1. Write a script that creates a progress bar that could be used on a fundraising site to indicate how much money has been raised in relation to the target.

2. Write a script that writes a headline image based on input from a form or query string. Allow user input to determine the canvas size, background and foreground colors, and the presence and offset of a drop shadow.

HOUR 16

Working with Dates and Times

What You'll Learn in This Hour:

▶ How to acquire the current date and time
▶ How to get information about a date
▶ How to format date information
▶ How to test dates for validity
▶ How to set dates
▶ How to build a simple calendar script
▶ How to build a class library to generate date pull-downs in HTML forms

Dates are so much a part of everyday life that it becomes easy to work with them without thinking. The quirks of your calendar can be difficult to work with in programs, though. Fortunately, PHP provides powerful tools for date arithmetic that make manipulating dates easy.

Getting the Date with `time()`

PHP's `time()` function gives you all the information you need about the current date and time. It requires no arguments but returns an integer. This number is a little hard on the eyes, for us humans, but extremely useful nonetheless:

```
print time();
// sample output: 1061577460
```

The integer returned by `time()` represents the number of seconds elapsed since midnight GMT on January 1, 1970. This moment is known as the **Unix epoch**, and the number of seconds that have elapsed since then is referred to as a **timestamp**. PHP offers excellent tools to convert a timestamp into a form that humans are comfortable with. Even so, isn't a timestamp a needlessly convoluted way of storing a date? In fact, the opposite is true. From just one number, you can extract enormous amounts of information. Even better, a timestamp can make date arithmetic much easier than you might imagine.

Think of a homegrown date system in which you record days of the month, as well as months and years. Now imagine a script that needs to add one day to a given date. If this date happened to be December 31, 1999, rather than add 1 to the date, you would have to write code to set the day of the month to 1, the month to January, and the year to 2000. Using a timestamp, you need only add a day's worth of seconds to your current figure, and you are done. You can convert this new figure into something more friendly at your leisure.

Converting a Timestamp with `getdate()`

Now that you have a timestamp to work with, you must convert it before you present it to the user. `getdate()` optionally accepts a timestamp and returns an associative array containing information about the date. If you omit the timestamp, it works with the current timestamp as returned by `time()`. Table 16.1 lists the elements contained in the array returned by `getdate()`.

TABLE 16.1   The Associative Array Returned by `getdate()`

Key	Description	Example
seconds	Seconds past the minute (0–59)	28
minutes	Minutes past the hour (0–59)	7
hours	Hours of the day (0–23)	12
mday	Day of the month (1–31)	20
wday	Day of the week (0–6)	4
mon	Month of the year (1–12)	1
year	Year (four digits)	2004
yday	Day of year (0–365)	19
weekday	Day of the week (name)	Thursday
month	Month of the year (name)	January
0	Timestamp	948370048

Listing 16.1 uses getdate() (line 11) to extract information from a timestamp, using a foreach statement to print each element (line 12). You can see a typical output example in Figure 16.1. getdate() returns the date according to the local time zone.

LISTING 16.1   Acquiring Date Information with getdate()

```
1: <!DOCTYPE html PUBLIC
2:    "-//W3C//DTD XHTML 1.0 Strict//EN"
3:    "http://www.w3.org/TR/xhtml1/DTD/xhtml1-strict.dtd">
4: <html>
5: <head>
6: <title>Listing 16.1 Acquiring Date Information with getdate()</title>
7: </head>
8: <body>
9: <div>
10: <?php
11: $date_array = getdate(); // no argument passed so today's date will be used
12: foreach ( $date_array as $key => $val ) {
13:    print "$key = $val<br/>";
14: }
15: ?>
16: <hr/>
17: <p>
18: <?
19: print "Today's date: ";
20: print $date_array['mon']."/".$date_array['mday']."/".$date_array['year'];
21: ?>
22: </p>
23: </div>
24: </body>
25: </html>
```

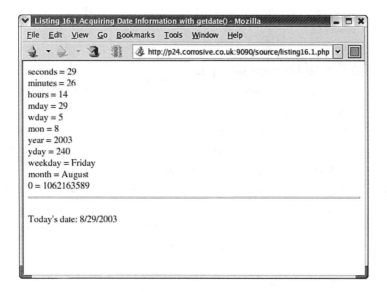

FIGURE 16.1
Using getdate().

Converting a Timestamp with date()

You can use getdate() when you want to work with the elements it outputs. Sometimes, though, you only want to display the date as a string. The date() function returns a formatted string representing a date. You can exercise an enormous amount of control over the format that date() returns with a string argument you must pass to it. In addition to the format string, date() optionally accepts a timestamp. Table 16.2 lists the codes a format string can contain; any other data you include in the format string passed to date() is included in the return value.

TABLE 16.2   Format Codes for Use with date()

Format	Description	Example
a	*am* or *pm* lowercase	pm
A	*AM* or *PM* uppercase	PM
B	Swatch beat (timezone-free 'Internet time')	771
d	Day of month (number with leading zeroes)	08
D	Day of week (three letters)	Wed
F	Month name	October
g	Hour (12-hour format—no leading zeroes)	6
G	Hour (24-hour format—no leading zeroes)	18
h	Hour (12-hour format—leading zeroes)	06
H	Hour (24-hour format—leading zeroes)	18
i	Minutes	31
I	Daylight savings time (Boolean value)	1
j	Day of the month (no leading zeroes)	8
l	Day of the week (name)	Wednesday
L	Leap year (1 for yes, 0 for no)	0
m	Month of year (number—leading zeroes)	10
M	Month of year (three letters)	Oct
n	Month of year (number—no leading zeroes)	10
O	Offset in hours from GMT (in [+-]HHMM format)	+0100
r	Full date standardized to RFC 822 (http://www.faqs.org/rfcs/rfc822.html)	Wed, 8 Oct 2003 18:31:15+0100
s	Seconds, with leading zeroes	15
S	English suffix for date in month (e.g. 20th)	th

TABLE 16.2 Continued

Format	Description	Example
t	Number of days in the given month	31
T	Timezone setting on the machine used	BST
U	Unix timestamp	1065634275
w	Day of week (number indexed from Sunday = 0)	3
W	Week of year	41
y	Year (two digits)	03
Y	Year (four digits)	2003
z	Day of year (0–366)	280
Z	Offset in seconds from GMT	3600

Listing 16.2 puts a few format codes to the test.

LISTING 16.2 Formatting a Date with date()

```
 1: <!DOCTYPE html PUBLIC
 2:    "-//W3C//DTD XHTML 1.0 Strict//EN"
 3:    "http://www.w3.org/TR/xhtml1/DTD/xhtml1-strict.dtd">
 4: <html>
 5: <head>
 6: <title>Listing 16.2 Formatting a Date with date()</title>
 7: </head>
 8: <body>
 9: <div>
10: <?php
11: print date("m/d/y G.i:s", time());
12: // 10/08/03 19.17:42
13: print "<br/>";
14: print "Today is ";
15: print date("jS of F Y, \a\\t g.i a", time());
16: // Today is 8th of October 2003, at 7.17 pm
17: ?>
18: </div>
19: </body>
20: </html>
```

In Listing 16.2 we call date() twice—the first time on line 11 to output an abbreviated date format, the second on line 15 for a longer format.

Although the format string looks arcane, it is easy to build. If you want to add a string to the format containing letters that are format codes, you can escape them by placing a backslash (\) in front of them. For characters that become control characters when escaped, you must escape the backslash that precedes them.

"\n" should become "\\n", for example, if you want to include an *n* in the format string. date() returns information according to your local time zone. If you want to format a date in GMT, you should use the gmdate() function, which works in exactly the same way.

Creating Timestamps with mktime()

You can already get information about the current time, but you cannot yet work with arbitrary dates. mktime() returns a timestamp you can then use with date() or getdate(). mktime() accepts up to six integer arguments in the following order:

> hour
>
> minute
>
> second
>
> month
>
> day of month
>
> year

Listing 16.3 uses mktime() to get a timestamp that we then use with the date() function.

LISTING 16.3   Creating a Timestamp with mktime()

```
 1: <!DOCTYPE html PUBLIC
 2:   "-//W3C//DTD XHTML 1.0 Strict//EN"
 3:   "http://www.w3.org/TR/xhtml1/DTD/xhtml1-strict.dtd">
 4: <html>
 5: <head>
 6: <title>Listing 16.3 Creating a Timestamp with mktime()</title>
 7: </head>
 8: <body>
 9: <div>
10: <?php
11: // make a timestamp for 1/5/04 at 2.30 am
12: $ts = mktime( 2, 30, 0, 5, 1, 2004 );
13: print date("m/d/y G.i:s", $ts);
14: // 05/01/04 2.30:00
15: print "<br/>";
16: print "The date is ";
17: print date("jS of F Y, \a\\t g.i a", $ts );
18: // The date is 1st of May 2004, at 2.30 am
19: ?>
20: </div>
21: </body>
22: </html>
```

We call `mktime()` on line 12, assigning the returned timestamp to the `$ts` variable. We can then use `date()` on lines 13 and 17 to output formatted versions of the date using `$ts`. You can choose to omit some or all of the arguments to `mktime()`, and the value appropriate to the current time will be used instead. `mktime()` also adjusts for values that go beyond the relevant range, so an hour argument of 25 translates to 1.00am on the day after that specified in the month, day, and year arguments.

Testing a Date with `checkdate()`

You might need to accept date information from user input. Before you work with this date or store it in a database, you should check that the date is valid. `checkdate()` accepts three integers: month, day, and year. `checkdate()` returns `true` if the month is between 1 and 12, the day is acceptable for the given month and year (accounting for leap years), and the year is between 0 and 32767. Be careful, though, because a date might be valid but not acceptable to other date functions. For example, the following line returns `true`:

```
checkdate( 4, 4, 1066 )
```

If you were to attempt to build a date with `mktime()` using these values, you would end up with a timestamp of -1. As a rule of thumb, do not use `mktime()` with years before 1902 and be cautious of using date functions with any date before 1970.

An Example

Let's bring most of these functions together into an example. We are going to build a calendar that can display the dates for any month between 1980 and 2010. The user will be able to select both month and year with pull-down menus, and the dates for that month will be organized according to the days of the week. If the input is invalid or absent, we will default to the first day of the current month. To develop our calendar, we will create three classes.

The `DateIterator` Class

The `DateIterator` class in Listing 16.4 is responsible for setting a pointer to the beginning of the given month and counting each of its days.

LISTING 16.4 The DateIterator Class

```php
1: <?php
2: class DateIterator {
3:   public static $ADAY = 86400;
4:   private $pointer;
5:
6:   function __construct( $month, $day, $year ) {
7:     $this->pointer= mktime ( 0, 0, 0, $month, $day, $year );
8:   }
9:
10:   function incrementDay() {
11:     $this->pointer += (DateIterator::$ADAY);
12:   }
13:
14:   function getMonthStartWDay() {
15:     $date_array = $this->getPointerArray();
16:     $date = mktime ( 0, 0, 0,
17:       $date_array['mon'],
18:       1, $date_array['year'] );
19:     $array = getdate( $date );
20:     return $array['wday'];
21:   }
22:
23:   function getPointer() {
24:     return $this->pointer;
25:   }
26:
27:   function getPointerArray() {
28:     return getDate( $this->pointer );
29:   }
30: }
31: ?>
```

The DateIterator class includes a useful static property on line 3. DateIterator::
$ADAY contains the number of seconds in a day, and this value is used to move a
DateIterator object's pointer forward day by day. The constructor accepts three integer arguments for month of year, day of month, and year, respectively. We construct
a timestamp representing the required date on line 7 using the mktime() function.

The real business of the class takes place in the incrementDay() method (line 10).
It simply advances the pointer forward by one day.

The getMonthStartWDay() method on line 14 returns the day of the week index
for the first day of the current month. This is used later to work out whether a calendar cell should be filled.

The getPointer() method returns the current date timestamp. getPointerArray()
uses the getDate() function to return an associative array for the same date.

This simple class enables us to tick through the days in a month and is used by a
QuickCalendar object.

The QuickCalendar **Class**

The QuickCalendar class steps through a calendar grid. The grid is indexed on the x-axis by days of the week and on the y-axis by discrete weeks. You can see the class in Listing 16.5.

LISTING 16.5   The QuickCalendar **Class**

```php
 1: <?php
 2: include_once( "listing16.4.php" );
 3:
 4: class QuickCalendar {
 5:    private $cellno=0;
 6:    private $month;
 7:    private $year;
 8:    private $dateIterator;
 9:
10:    function __construct( $month, $year ) {
11:      if ( empty( $month ) || empty( $year ) ) {
12:        $nowArray = getdate();
13:        $year = $nowArray['year'];
14:        $month = $nowArray['mon'];
15:      }
16:
17:      $this->dateIterator = new DateIterator( $month, 1, $year );
18:      $this->month = $month;
19:      $this->year = $year;
20:    }
21:
22:    function getCurrentArray() {
23:      return $this->dateIterator->getPointerArray();
24:    }
25:
26:    function cellBeforeMonthStart() {
27:      return ( $this->cellno < $this->dateIterator->getMonthStartWDay() );
28:    }
29:
30:    function cellAfterMonthEnd() {
31:      $current = $this->getCurrentArray();
32:      if ($this->month == 12) {
33:        return ( $this->year < $current['year'] );
34:      }
35:      return ( $this->month < $current['mon'] );
36:    }
37:
38:    function endOfRow() {
39:      return ( ! ( $this->cellno % 7 ) );
40:    }
41:
42:    function endOfGrid() {
43:      return ( $this->cellAfterMonthEnd() && $this->endOfRow() );
44:    }
45:
46:    function nextCell() {
47:      if ( $this->endOfGrid() ) {
```

LISTING 16.5   Continued

```
48:        $ret = null;
49:      } else if ( $this->cellBeforeMonthStart() ||
50:            $this->cellAfterMonthEnd() ) {
51:        $ret = array();
52:      } else {
53:        $ret = $this->getCurrentArray();
54:        $this->dateIterator->incrementDay();
55:      }
56:      $this->cellno++;
57:      return $ret;
58:   }
59: }
60: ?>
```

The constructor accepts month and year integers and instantiates a DateIterator object. If these arguments are empty, we use the current date and derive the month and year from that. We cache the starting month and year on lines 18 and 19.

The getCurrentArray() on line 22 returns the DateIterator object's pointer as an associative array (as derived from getDate()).

Each cell can have a number of statuses. Our grid starts on a Sunday, so if the first day of a month is a Wednesday, the cells between Sunday and Tuesday are empty. For these cells, the cellBeforeMonthStart() method (line 26) returns true. By the same token, the last day of a month might not fall on the final cell in the grid. The cellAfterMonthEnd() method returns true for each cell that is within the grid but after the end of the month. Every seventh cell is the last in a row (that is, the end of a week). For these, the endOfRow() method returns true. Finally, for the last cell in a grid, the endOfGrid() method returns true.

These tests are all used by the nextCell() method, which iterates a $cellno property and calls on the DateIterator object's iterateDay() method. nextCell() returns an empty array for cells that fall before the start of a month or after the end of a month. It returns a date array as returned by getCurrentArray() for cells within the month. Finally, when the grid is finished, it returns null. Client code can call this method repeatedly and call on the test method endOfRow() to determine when to break a row.

This class is not easy to grasp at a sitting. Let's look at the client code that uses it to get a sense of the interface:

```
<table border="1" cellpadding="5">
<tr>
<?php
$cal = new QuickCalendar( );
while ( ! is_null( $cell = $cal->nextCell() ) ) {
```

```
    if ( empty( $cell ) ) {
      print "<td> - </td>";
    } else {
      print "<td>".$cell['mday']." ".$cell['month']."</td>";
    }
    if ( $cal->endOfRow() && ! $cal->endOfGrid() ) {
      print "</tr><tr>";
    }
}
?>
</tr>
</table>
```

The client code instantiates a `QuickCalendar` object and calls `nextCell()` until it returns null. If `getCell()` returns an empty array, it displays an empty cell; otherwise, it displays a cell containing a date. At the end of each iteration, the code uses the `QuickCalendar` object's `endOfRow()` method to test whether it should end the table row and begin a new one. This is all it takes to convert the virtual grid managed by `QuickCalendar` into a real grid. Because the display is entirely divorced from the logic of the calendar, you could output calendar grids in different formats very easily.

Now that you can output a calendar, you need to build a mechanism with which the user can select a month and a year. You will need to generate two pull-downs and headings for the HTML grid. Rather than embed it directly in HTML markup, you'll tuck code to generate pull-downs into a helper class.

The `DateViewHelper` Class

This simple class consists of two static methods for generating pull-downs and two arrays that hold the days of the week and months of the year. You can see the `DateViewHelper` class in Listing 16.6.

LISTING 16.6   The `DateViewHelper` Class

```
 1: <?php
 2: class DateViewHelper {
 3:    static $MONTHS = array(
 4:          "January", "February", "March", "April",
 5:          "May", "June", "July", "August", "September",
 6:          "October", "November", "December");
 7:    static $DAYS = Array(
 8:          "Sunday", "Monday", "Tuesday", "Wednesday",
 9:          "Thursday", "Friday", "Saturday");
10:
11:    static function yearPulldown( $from, $to, $selected ) {
12:       $ret = "";
13:       for ( $x = $from; $x <= $to; $x++ ) {
14:          $ret .= "<option";
```

LISTING 16.6   Continued

```
15:        $ret .= ($x == $selected )?' selected="selected"':"";
16:        $ret .= ">$x</option>\n";
17:     }
18:     return $ret;
19:   }
20:
21:   static function monthPulldown( $selected ) {
22:     for ( $x=1; $x <= 12; $x++ ) {
23:        $ret .= "<option value=\"$x\"";
24:        $ret .= ($x == $selected )?' selected="selected"':"";
25:        $ret .= ">".dateViewHelper::$MONTHS[$x-1]."</option>\n";
26:     }
27:     return $ret;
28:   }
29: }
30: ?>
```

The yearPulldown() method on line 11 requires starting and ending years as well as a selected year. It uses a for loop to iterate through all the numbers between $from and $to, adding <option> elements to a return string as it does so. The monthPulldown() method on line 21 is similar: It loops through the static $MONTHS array property to generate a string of <option> elements.

These three classes are now ready to be used to output a calendar.

The Client Code

It is now really only a matter of working with the classes we have created and formatting the output. We do this in Listing 16.7.

LISTING 16.7   The Calendar Client Code

```
 1: <?php
 2: include_once( "listing16.5.php" );
 3: include_once( "listing16.6.php" );
 4:
 5: $cal = new QuickCalendar( $_REQUEST['month'],
 6:           $_REQUEST['year'] );
 7: $current = $cal->getCurrentArray( );
 8: ?>
 9:
10: <!DOCTYPE html PUBLIC
11:    "-//W3C//DTD XHTML 1.0 Strict//EN"
12:    "http://www.w3.org/TR/xhtml1/DTD/xhtml1-strict.dtd">
13: <html>
14: <head>
15: <title>Calendar: <?php print $current['month']." ".
16:           $current['year'] ?></title>
17: </head>
18: <body>
19:
```

LISTING 16.7   Continued

```
20: <h1>Calendar: <?php print $current['month']." ".
21:          $current['year'] ?></h1>
22:
23: <form method="post" action="<?php echo $_SERVER['PHP_SELF'] ?>">
24: <div>
25: <select name="month">
26: <?php print DateViewHelper::monthPulldown(
27:          $current['mon'] ); ?>
28: </select>
29:
30: <select name="year">
31: <?php print DateViewHelper::yearPulldown( 1980, 2010,
32:          $current['year'] ); ?>
33: </select>
34:
35: <input type="submit" value="Go!" />
36: </div>
37: </form>
38:
39: <table border="1" cellpadding="5">
40: <tr><td><b>
41: <?php print implode( "</b></td><td><b>",
42:          DateViewHelper::$DAYS ); ?>
43: </b></td></tr>
44: <tr>
45: <?
46: while ( ! is_null( $cell = $cal->nextCell() ) ) {
47:   if ( empty( $cell ) ) {
48:      print "<td> - </td>";
49:   } else {
50:      print "<td>".$cell['mday']." ".$cell['month']."</td>";
51:   }
52:   if ( $cal->endOfRow() && ! $cal->endOfGrid() ) {
53:      print "</tr><tr>";
54:   }
55: }
56: ?>
57: </tr>
58: </table>
59: </body>
60: </html>
```

We first include the QuickCalendar and DateViewHelper classes on lines 2 and 3. We instantiate a QuickCalendar object, passing it the submitted parameters 'month' and 'year' on line 5. We then assign it to the variable $cal. If we are visiting this page for the first time, the 'month' and 'year' arguments have not yet been filled. Our QuickCalendar object deals with this for us, though, by working to the current date.

We call the QuickCalendar object's getCurrentArray() method to get a date array for the first day of the month in question. We use this to output a descriptive title detailing the month and year we will be displaying.

Between lines 25 and 28, we output a pull-down of months, calling the
DateViewHelper class's static monthPulldown() method. Notice that we do not not
need to instantiate a DateViewHelper object to call a static method on the class.
Between lines 30 and 33, we do the same thing for a month's pull-down by calling the DateViewHelper class's yearPulldown() method.

We need our grid to be labelled with the days of the week. We could type them
out, but we have opted to save typing by accessing the DateViewHelper class's
static $DAYS array, calling the implode() function to output the day strings, sepa-
rated by table cell element tags.

Finally, we work with our QuickCalendar object to output the cells in a loop starting on line 46. We have already looked at this fragment, which calls on the
nextCell(), endOfRow(), and endOfGrid() methods to format the output.

You can see the output from a call to this script in Figure 16.2.

FIGURE 16.2
The calendar
script.

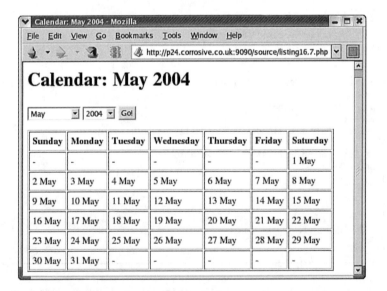

A Date Pull-down Library

Because dates are so ubiquitous in Web interfaces and because working with
dates is often comparatively nontrivial, now would seem to be a good time to
look at a class library to automate some of the work that dates can present.
Along the way we will revisit some of the techniques we have already covered.

The simple `date_pulldown` library was born during the creation of a freelance job listing site. The project necessarily involved the presentation of multiple date pull-downs allowing employers to select both the start and end of contract periods, and for candidates to indicate periods of availability. A date pull-down, in this instance, is three separate `select` elements—one for day of the month, one for month, and another for year.

When a user submits a page, the script checks his input. If a problem exists, the page must be represented with the user's input still in place. This is easy to accomplish with text boxes but is more of a chore with pull-down menus. Pages that display information pulled from a database present a similar problem. Data can be entered straight into the value attributes of text type input elements, but dates need to be split into month, day, and year values and then the correct option elements must be selected.

The `date_pulldown` class makes date pull-downs **sticky** (to remember settings from page to page) and easy to set.

To create our class, we first need to declare it and create a constructor. We can also declare some class properties, like so:

```
class date_pulldown {
  private $name;
  private $timestamp = -1;
  private $months = array("Jan", "Feb", "Mar", "Apr", "May", "Jun",
            "Jul", "Aug", "Sep", "Oct", "Nov", "Dec");
  private $yearstart = -1;
  private $yearend = -1;

  function __construct( $name ) {
    $this->name = $name;
  }
// ...
```

We declare the `$name` property, which is used to name the HTML `select` elements. The `$timestamp` property holds a Unix timestamp, and the `$months` array property contains the strings we will display in our month pull-down. `$yearstart` and `$yearend` are both set to `-1` pending initialization. They will eventually hold the first and last years of the range that will be presented in the year pull-down.

The constructor is simple: It accepts a string, which we then use to assign to the `$name` property.

Now that we have the basis of our class, we need a set of methods by which the client code can set the date:

```
// ...
  function setDate_request( ) {
    if ( ! $this->setDate_array( $_REQUEST[$this->name] ) ) {
      return $this->setDate_timestamp( time() );
    }
    return true;
  }

  function setDate_timestamp( $time ) {
    $this->timestamp = $time;
    return true;
  }

  function setDate_array( $inputdate ) {
    if ( is_array( $inputdate ) &&
      isset( $inputdate['mon'] ) &&
      isset( $inputdate['mday'] ) &&
      isset( $inputdate['year'] ) ) {
      $this->timestamp = mktime( 11, 59, 59,
        $inputdate['mon'], $inputdate['mday'], $inputdate['year'] );
      return true;
    }

    return false;
  }
// ...
```

Of these methods, setDate_timestamp() is the simplest. It requires a Unix time-stamp and assigns it to the $timestamp property.

setDate_array() expects an associative array with at least three keys: 'mon', 'mday', and 'year'. These fields contain data in the same format as in the array returned by getdate(). This means that setDate_array() accepts a hand-built array such as

```
array( 'mday'=> 5, 'mon'=>7, 'year' => 1999 );
```

or the result of a call to getDate() such as

```
getdate( 931172399 );
```

It is no accident that the pull-downs we will be building later will be constructed to produce an array containing 'mon', 'mday', and 'year' fields. The method uses the mktime() function to construct a timestamp that is then assigned to the $timestamp variable.

The setDate_request() method is called by default. It attempts to find a request argument (as held in the superglobal $_REQUEST array) with the same name as the object's $name property. This is passed to setDate_array(). If a global variable of the right structure is discovered, it is used to create the $timestamp variable. Otherwise, the current date is used.

The range for days and months is fixed, but years are a different matter. We create a few methods to allow the client coder to set her own range of years (although we also provide default behavior):

```
// ...
  function setYearStart( $year ) {
    $this->yearstart = $year;
  }

  function setYearEnd( $year ) {
    $this->yearend = $year;
  }

  function getYearStart() {
    if ( $this->yearstart < 0 ) {
      $nowarray = getdate( time() );
      $this->yearstart = $nowarray['year']-5;
    }
    return $this->yearstart;
  }

  function getYearEnd() {
    if ( $this->yearend < 0 ) {
      $nowarray = getdate( time() );
      $this->yearend = $nowarray['year']+5;
    }
    return $this->yearend;
  }
// ...
```

The setYearStart() and setYearEnd() methods are straightforward. A year is directly assigned to the appropriate property, and getYearStart() tests whether the $yearstart property has been set. If the property is not set, it assigns a $yearstart 5 years before the current year. getYearEnd() performs a similar operation. We're now ready to create the business end of the class:

```
// ...
  function output( ) {
    if ( $this->timestamp < 0 ) {
      $this->setDate_request();
    }
    $datearray = getdate( $this->timestamp );
    $out = $this->day_select( $this->name, $datearray );
    $out .= $this->month_select( $this->name, $datearray );
    $out .= $this->year_select( $this->name, $datearray );
    return $out;
  }
```

```
function day_select( $fieldname, $datearray ) {
  $out = "<select name=\"$fieldname"."[mday]\">\n";
  for ( $x=1; $x<=31; $x++ ) {
    $selected = ($datearray['mday']==($x)?
      ' selected="selected"':"");
    $out .= "<option value=\"$x\"$selected>".sprintf("%02d", $x );
    $out .= "</option>\n";
  }
  $out .= "</select>\n";
  return $out;
}

function month_select( $fieldname, $datearray ) {
  $out = "<select name=\"$fieldname"."[mon]\">\n";
  for ( $x = 1; $x <= 12; $x++ ) {
    $selected = ($datearray['mon']==($x)?
      ' selected="selected"':"");
    $out .= "<option value=\"$x\"$selected>".$this->months[$x-1];
    $out .= "</option>\n";
  }
  $out .= "</select>\n";
  return $out;
}

function year_select( $fieldname, $datearray ) {
  $out = "<select name=\"$fieldname"."[year]\">";
  $start = $this->getYearStart();
  $end = $this->getYearEnd();
  for ( $x= $start; $x < $end; $x++ ) {
    $selected = ($datearray['year']==($x)?
      ' selected="selected"':"");
    $out .= "<option value=\"$x\"$selected>$x";
    $out .= "</option>\n";
  }
  $out .= "</select>\n";
  return $out;
}
}
```

The output() method orchestrates most of this code. It first checks the $timestamp property. Unless the client coder has called one of the setDate methods, it is set to -1 and setDate_global() is called by default. The timestamp is passed to the getdate() function to construct a date array, and a method is called for each pull-down to be produced.

day_select() simply constructs an HTML select element with an option element for each of the 31 possible days in a month. The object's 'current' date is stored in the $datearray argument variable, which is used during the construction of the element to set the selected attribute of the relevant option element. Notice that we use sprintf() to format the day number, adding a leading zero to days 1–9. month_select() and year_select() use similar logic to construct the month and year pull-downs.

In Listing 16.8, we create some code that calls the library class.

LISTING 16.8   Using the `date_pulldown` Class

```
 1: <!DOCTYPE html PUBLIC
 2:   "-//W3C//DTD XHTML 1.0 Strict//EN"
 3:   "http://www.w3.org/TR/xhtml1/DTD/xhtml1-strict.dtd">
 4: <html>
 5: <head>
 6: <title>Listing 16.8 using the date_pulldown class</title>
 7: </head>
 8: <?php
 9: include("date_pulldown.class.php");
10: $date1 = new date_pulldown("fromdate");
11: $date2 = new date_pulldown("todate");
12: $date3 = new date_pulldown("foundingdate");
13: $date3->setYearStart(1971);
14: if ( empty( $_REQUEST['foundingdate'] ) ) {
15:    $date3->setDate_array( array( 'mday'=>26, 'mon'=>4, 'year'=>1984 ) );
16: }
17: ?>
18: <body>
19: <div>
20:
21: <form action="<?php echo $PHP_INFO ?>" method="post">
22: <p>
23: From:<br/>
24: <?php print $date1->output( ); ?>
25: </p>
26:
27: <p>
28: To:<br/>
29: <?php print $date2->output( ); ?>
30: </p>
31:
32: <p>
33: Company founded:<br/>
34: <?php print $date3->output( ); ?>
35: </p>
36:
37: <p>
38: <input type="submit" value="do it" />
39: </p>
40: </form>
41:
42: </div>
43: </body>
44: </html>
```

Notice that we've tucked the class itself away in a library file called `date_pulldown.class.php`, which we access using the `include()` statement on line 9. We use the class's default behavior for all the pull-downs except for `'foundingdate'`. For this object, we override the default year start, setting it to 1972 on line 13. We also define an arbitrary date on line 14 for this pull-down that will be displayed until the form is submitted (see Figure 16.3).

FIGURE 16.3
The pull-downs generated by the date_pulldown class.

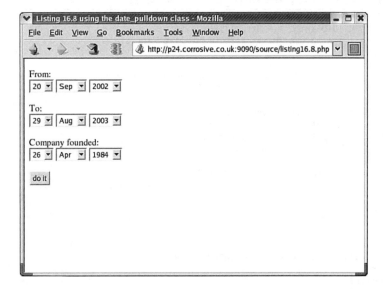

Summary

In this hour, you learned how to use `time()` to get a date stamp for the current date and time. You learned how to use `getdate()` to extract date information from a timestamp and `date()` to convert a timestamp into a formatted string. You also learned how to create a timestamp using `mktime()` and how to test a date for validity with `checkdate()`. You worked through an example script, which applies some of the tools you have looked at, and built a class library that automates some of the more tedious aspects of working with dates in forms.

Q&A

Q *Are there any functions for converting between different calendars?*

A Yes. PHP provides an entire suite of functions that covers alternative calendars. You can read about these in the official PHP manual at `http://www.php.net/manual/ref.calendar.php`.

Workshop

Quiz

1. How would you acquire a Unix timestamp representing the current date and time?

2. Which function accepts a timestamp and returns an associative array representing the given date?

3. Which function would you use to format date information?

4. How would you acquire a timestamp for an arbitrary date?

5. Which function could you use to check the validity of a date?

Answers

1. The `time()` function returns the current date in timestamp format.

2. The `getdate()` function returns an associative array whose elements contain aspects of the given date.

3. The `date()` function is used to format a date.

4. Given arguments representing the hour, minute, second, month, day of month, and year, the `mktime()` function returns a Unix timestamp.

5. You can check a date with the `checkdate()` function.

Exercise

1. Create a birthday count-down script. Given form input of month, day, and year, output a message that tells the user how many days, hours, minutes, and seconds until the big day.

HOUR 17

Advanced Objects

What You'll Learn in This Hour:

► How to define class constants
► How to define and work with static properties and methods
► How to overload calls to object properties and methods
► How to prevent a child class from overriding a method
► How to automate clean-up when an object is discarded
► How to handle error conditions
► How to define types using abstract classes and interfaces

In Hour 9, "Objects," we covered the least you should know to work with objects in PHP. In this hour, we are going to look at objects in more detail. We will look especially at some of the many new features that PHP 5 has introduced. With PHP 5, the language became much more amenable to object-oriented design. In this hour, we will discover how the language has changed and what you can do to take advantage of the new features.

Objects and Constants

In Hour 4, "The Building Blocks," we looked at defining global constants. Remember that constants hold values that cannot be changed during script execution. You define global constants using the define() function.

As of PHP 5, you can define constants within classes. You declare a constant using the const keyword at the top of your class:

```
class MyClass {
        const PI = 3.14;
//...
```

Constants are available via the class rather than an object:

```
print MyClass::PI;
```

This aspect makes a class constant useful when the value it contains applies equally to all objects of the type and when the value should be fixed and unchangeable.

Let's work through a simple example. In Listing 17.1, we present a fragment of an Item class. An Item in this example is an item of stock in a shop. We want to store an integer $status property for every Item. This single integer will combine multiple flags. We want the flags to be available globally, and we need them to be read-only.

LISTING 17.1   A Class That Uses Class Constants

```php
 1: <?php
 2:
 3: class Item {
 4:    const DISCONTINUED = 1;
 5:    const PROMOTIONAL = 2;
 6:    const STOCKED_OFFSITE = 4;
 7:    private $status = 0;
 8:
 9:    public function addStatus( $num ) {
10:       $this->status |= $num;
11:    }
12:
13:    public function isPromotional() {
14:       return ( Item::PROMOTIONAL & $this->status )?true:false;
15:    }
16:
17:    public function isDiscontinued() {
18:       return ( Item::DISCONTINUED & $this->status )?true:false;
19:    }
20:
21:    public function isOffsiteItem() {
22:       return ( Item::STOCKED_OFFSITE & $this->status )?true:false;
23:    }
24: }
25:
26: $item = new Item();
27: $item->addStatus( Item::STOCKED_OFFSITE );
28: $item->addStatus( Item::PROMOTIONAL );
29: $item->addStatus( Item::DISCONTINUED );
30:
31: if ( $item->isOffsiteItem() ) {
32:    print "This item is stocked at our warehouse. Delivery within 4 days";
33: }
34: ?>
```

We define three class constant flags on lines 4 to 6. It's easiest to think of these flags in binary terms:

```
001 = 1
010 = 2
100 = 4
```

The idea is that we can combine each of those numbers in a single $status property by using the binary or (¦) operator. This process sets the bits that are set in either one operand or the other:

```
1 ¦ 2 == 3
001 or 010 equals 011
```

We perform the operation to combine flags in the addStatus() method on line 9. We call addStatus() on lines 27 to 29, setting all the available bits. Notice how we access the status flags using the class name and not the object handle.

The rest of the class consists of methods to check the $status array. Let's look at isDiscontinued() on line 17. We use the binary and (&) operator to compare $status with the constant flag Item::DISCONTINUED. This test compares the bits in the two operands and resolves to a new number that contains only the bits that the two numbers have in common:

```
111  $status
001  DISCONTINUED
001  result of 'and' operation
```

The effect of this operation is that isDiscontinued() will only return true if Item::DISCONTINUED has been passed to addStatus().

Another common use for class constants is to store error codes that can be set and tested when an object fails in an operation.

Static Properties

Static properties were also introduced with PHP 5. They are similar in some senses to class constants in that a static property is available via the class rather than the object. Static properties can be changed at runtime, however, making them useful when greater flexibility is required.

We declare a static variable with the static keyword:

```
class Item {
  public static $SALES_TAX=9;
  //...
```

Notice that we can also determine the access level for a static property. We access the static class property via the class name:

```
print "the tax to be levied on all items is ";
print Item::$SALES_TAX;
print "%";
```

We could change Item::$SALES_TAX at any time, and the value would change for all instances of Item and for all client code.

Static Methods

It is not only properties that can be declared static. As of PHP 5, you can declare a method static:

```
static function doOperation() {
//...
```

Some classes make static the utility methods that do not depend upon member variables, to make the tool more widely available. We might supply a calcTax() method in Item, for example:

```
class Item {
  public static $SALES_TAX=10;
  private $name;
  public static function calcTax( $amount ) {
    return ( $amount + ( $amount/(Item::$SALES_TAX/100)) );
  }
}
```

The calcTax() method uses the static $SALES_TAX property to calculate a new total given a starting amount. Crucially, this method does not attempt to access any standard properties. Because static methods are called outside of object context (that is, using the class name and not an object handle), they cannot use the $this pseudo-variable to access methods or properties. Let's use the calcTax() method:

```
$amount = 10;
print "given a cost of $amount, the total will be ";
print Item::calcTax( $amount );
// prints " given a cost of 10, the total will be 110"
```

The benefit of using a static method in this example was that we did not need to create or acquire an Item object to gain access to the functionality in calcTax().

Let's look at another common use for static methods and properties. In Listing 17.2, we create a Shop class. Our system design calls for a central Shop object. We want client code to be able to get an instance of this object at any time, and we want to ensure that only one Shop object is created during the life of a script execution. All objects requesting a Shop object will be guaranteed to get a reference to the same object and will therefore work with the same data as one another.

LISTING 17.2 Using Static Methods and Properties to Limit Instances of a Class (PHP 5 Only)

```
 1: <?php
 2:
 3: class Shop {
 4:    private static $instance;
 5:    public $name="shop";
 6:
 7:    private function __construct() {
 8:      // block attempts to instantiate
 9:    }
10:
11:    public static function getInstance() {
12:       if ( empty( self::$instance ) ) {
13:       self::$instance = new Shop();
14:       }
15:       return self::$instance;
16:    }
17: }
18:
19: // $s = new Shop();
20: // would fail because __construct() is declared private
21:
22: $first = Shop::getInstance();
23: $first->name="Acme Shopping Emporium";
24:
25: $second = Shop::getInstance();
26: print $second->name;
27: // prints "Acme Shopping Emporium"
28: ?>
```

Listing 17.2 shows an example of a design pattern called **singleton**. It is intended to ensure that only one instance of a class exists in a process at any time and that any client code can easily access that instance. We declare a private static property called $instance on line 4. On line 5, we declare and assign to a property called $name. We will use it to test our class later. Notice that we declared the constructor private on line 7. This declaration makes it impossible for any external code to create an instance of the Shop object. We declare a static method called getInstance() on line 11. Because it is static, getInstance() can be called through the class rather than the object instance:

```
Shop::getInstance();
```

As a member function, getInstance() has privileged status. It can set and get the static $instance property. It can also create a new instance of the shop object using new. We test $instance and assign a Shop object to it if it is empty. After the test, we can be sure that we have a Shop object in the $instance property, and we return it to the user on line 15.

We use the self keyword to access the $instance property. self refers to the current class in the same way that $this refers to the current object.

We call getInstance() on line 25, acquiring a Shop object. To test the class, we change the $name property on line 23 and then call getInstance() once again on line 25. We confirm that the $second variable contains a reference to the same instance of Shop on line 26 by printing $shop->name.

Intercepting Calls to Object Properties and Methods

PHP 5 introduces three built-in methods that you can use to trap messages to your objects and alter default behavior.

Usually, if an undefined method is called, a fatal error will be generated and your script will fail. If you define a __call() method in your class, however, you can catch the message and decide what to do with it. Every time an undeclared method is called on your object, the __call() method will be invoked. Two arguments will automatically be populated for you: a string variable holding the name of the method that was called and an array variable holding any arguments that were passed. Anything you return from __call() is returned to the client code as if the undefined method existed. Let's put some code together to illustrate this point:

```
class TestCall {
  function __call( $method, $args ) {
    $ret = "method '$method' called<br />\n";
    $ret .= "<pre>\n";
    $ret .= print_r( $args, true );
    $ret .= "</pre>";
    return $ret;
  }
}
$item = new TestCall();
print $item->arbitrary( "a", "b", 1 );
```

We create a class called TestCall and give it a __call() method. __call() expects the method name and an array of method arguments. It assigns a string quoting the contents of both of these to a variable, $ret, and returns it to the calling code. We call the nonexistent $test->arbitrary() method and print the result:

```
method 'arbitrary' called<br />
<pre>
```

```
Array
(
  [0] => a
  [1] => b
  [2] => 1
)
</pre>
```

The output from this code fragment illustrates that __call() intercepted our method call and accessed both the method name and arguments. As Harry Fuecks points out in his article at http://www.phppatterns.com/index.php/article/article-view/ 28/1/2, one of the best uses of __call() is in the construction of wrapper objects, which provide object-based interfaces to built-in or third-party standalone functions.

Let's look at an example. In Listing 17.3, we simulate a procedural third-party library provided by an online store called Bloggs. We cannot change these functions, which add items from our shop to the Bloggs store, but we would like to be able to tell an Item object to add itself to or remove itself from the Bloggs store using our object interface. We could create methods that mirror each of the functions. If however there are a lot of functions to mirror, and the functions expect similar arguments, then we can create virtual methods to map to functions dynamically.

LISTING 17.3   Intercepting Method Calls with the __call() Method (PHP 5 Only)

```
 1: <?php
 2:
 3: // third party function
 4: function bloggsRegister( $item_array, $immediately=false ) {
 5:   return "Registering item with Bloggs stores<br />\n";
 6: }
 7:
 8: // third party function
 9: function bloggsRemove( $item_array, $immediately=false ) {
10:   return "Removing item from Bloggs stores<br />\n";
11: }
12:
13:
14: class Item {
15:   public $name = "item";
16:   public $price = 0;
17:
18:   function __call( $method, $args ) {
19:     $bloggsfuncs = array ( "bloggsRegister", "bloggsRemove" );
20:     if ( in_array( $method, $bloggsfuncs ) ) {
21:       array_unshift( $args, get_object_vars( $this ) );
22:       return call_user_func( $method, $args );
23:     }
24:   }
25: }
26:
```

LISTING 17.3   Continued

```
27: $item = new Item();
28: print $item->bloggsRegister( true );
29: print $item->bloggsRemove( true );
30: ?>
```

We set up two fake third-party methods, bloggsRegister() and bloggsRemove() on lines 4 and 8. They do nothing but report that they have been called. We create an Item class on line 14, providing some sample properties. The heart of the class is the __call() method on line 18. We set up an array of acceptable methods on line 19 and store it in the local $bloggsfuncs variable. We don't want to work with methods that we know nothing about, so we test whether the method name used by the client code is stored in the $bloggsfuncs array. If the method name is found in the array, we call the standalone function of the same name, passing it an array consisting of the Item object's properties and the first user-defined argument (extracted from the $args array). We return the function's return value.

On lines 28 and 29, we test our dynamic methods. When we call the bloggsRegister() method, __call() is invoked because the Item class does not define bloggsRegister(). The string "bloggsRegister" is passed to __call() and stored in the $method argument. Because the string is found in $bloggsfuncs, the bloggsRegister() function is called.

With just two functions in our example, there is little gain, but if you imagine a Bloggs API with tens of utility functions, we could create an effective object wrapper quickly and easily.

You might want to do something similar with built-in functions. You might, for example, bundle a suite of file-related methods into a single MyFile class.

The __get() and __set() methods are similar in nature to __call(). __get() is called whenever client code attempts to access a property that is not explicitly defined. It is passed the name of the property accessed:

```
function __get( $prop ) {
        print "property $prop was accessed";
}
```

__set() is called when client code attempts to assign a value to a property that has not been explicitly defined. It is passed a string argument containing the name of the property and a mixed argument (an argument of any type) containing the value the client code attempted to set:

```
function __set( $prop, $val ) {
        print "client wishes to store $val in $prop";
}
```

In Listing 17.4, we use these methods to create a read-only property that always holds the current date array.

LISTING 17.4　Intercepting Property Access with __get() and __set() (PHP 5 Only)

```
 1: <?php
 2: class TimeThing {
 3:   function __get( $arg ) {
 4:     if ( $arg == "time" ) {
 5:       return getdate();
 6:     }
 7:   }
 8:
 9:   function __set( $arg, $val ) {
10:     if ( $arg == "time" ) {
11:       trigger_error( "cannot set property $arg" );
12:       return false;
13:     }
14:   }
15: }
16:
17: $cal = new TimeThing();
18: print $cal->time['mday']."/";
19: print $cal->time['mon']."/";
20: print $cal->time['year'];
21:
22: // illegal call
23: $cal->time = 555;
24: ?>
```

We create a class called TimeThing on line 2. The __get() method on line 3 tests the property name provided by the client code. If the string is "time"—that is, if the client coder has attempted to access a $time property—then the method returns the date array as generated by getdate() on line 5. When we access the $time property on lines 18 to 20, we see that it is automatically populated with the date array.

We don't want the client coder to be able to override the $time property, so we implement a __set() method on line 9. If we detect an attempt to write to $time, we trigger an error message. We block all attempts to set nonexistent properties by providing no further implementation. To allow dynamic setting of properties we would have included the following line:

$this->$arg=$val;

Final Methods

Sometimes, you do not want subclasses to be able to override methods that you define or implement. Perhaps the functionality you define there is exactly the way things should be:

```
class Item {
  private $id = 555;
  final function getID() {
    return $this->id;
  }
}
```

By declaring the getID() method final in this example, we ensure that any attempt to override it in a subclass will cause an error. Notice the following code:

```
class PriceItem extends Item {
  function getID() {
    return 0;
  }
}
```

It generates the following error:

```
Fatal error: Cannot override final method item::getid()
```

On the whole, you should use final sparingly. Your class might fit uses that you do not yet know about, and flexibility is worth maintaining.

Cleaning Up Using Destructors

In Hour 9, we saw that PHP 5 provides the __construct() method to help us set up an object upon instantiation. Objects have their allotted span, and PHP 5 provides us with a means of easing their passing as well as welcoming their arrival. The __destruct() method is automatically called when an object is about to be expunged from memory. This generally happens when no part of your script process holds a reference to the object any longer. The process enables you to handle any last-minute clean-up that your object might need to take care of, such as closing database handles.

In Listing 17.5, we set up another Item scenario. We invent an ItemUpdater class. In theory, this class generates objects responsible for saving Item objects. An Item object will hold a reference to its own updater. Such structures are useful ways of ensuring that objects focus on their core responsibilities. Item objects are responsible for managing information concerning shop items. ItemUpdater objects are responsible for saving Item objects. All that an Item object knows about an ItemUpdater is that it has an update() method. It does not know whether it is going to be saved to an XML file by XmlItemUpdater or to a database by MysqlItemUpdater.

LISTING 17.5   Cleaning Up with the __destruct Method (PHP 5 Only)

```
 1: <?php
 2:
 3: class ItemUpdater {
 4:    public function update( Item $item ) {
 5:      print "updating.. ";
 6:      print $item->name;
 7:    }
 8: }
 9:
10: class Item {
11:    public $name = "item";
12:    private $updater;
13:
14:    public function setUpdater( ItemUpdater $update ) {
15:      $this->updater=$update;
16:    }
17:    function __destruct() {
18:      if ( ! empty( $this->updater )) {
19:        $this->updater->update( $this );
20:      }
21:    }
22: }
23:
24: $item = new Item();
25: $item->setUpdater( new ItemUpdater() ) ;
26: unset( $item );
27: ?>
```

We create an ItemUpdater class on line 3. It has a single method, update() which demands an Item object. In our example, it merely writes a message to the browser announcing its intention of saving the Item it has been passed. We create an Item class on line 10 containing a setUpdater() method on line 14. setUpdater() simply caches an ItemUpdater object for later use. On line 17, we define our __destruct() method. It tests whether an ItemUpdater object has been cached in the $updater property. If an ItemUpdater object is available, we call its update() method.

We test our classes on line 24 by creating a new Item object, setting an ItemUpdater object. We then cruelly unset the Item object, effectively destroying it. When this code is run, the __destruct() method is called, invoking the ItemUpdater object's update method. The following is written to the browser:

updating.. item

Managing Error Conditions with Exceptions

Although it was possible to set a custom error handler in PHP 4, most scripts prior to PHP 5 made do with relatively crude error handling. Methods that ran into trouble would generally choose between using die() to end script execution completely or returning a flag value such as false or -1.

PHP 5 introduces exceptions, allowing methods to hand responsibility back to client code when particular errors are encountered.

An **exception** is an object that can be automatically populated with information about the error that has occurred and its script context. You must instantiate Exception objects yourself with the new keyword just as you would with any object. Once you have an Exception object, you can literally throw it back to the client code:

```
function doThing() {
  // uh oh. Trouble!
  throw new Exception( "A generic error", 666 );

  print "this will never be executed";
}
```

The Exception class's constructor optionally accepts an error string and an error code. When the Exception is thrown with the throw keyword, method execution ends abruptly. Responsibility for handling the problem is passed back to the calling code.

Suppose we were to call the doThing() method as normal:

```
$test = new ThingDoer();
$test->doThing();
```

We run into the following error:

```
Fatal error: Uncaught exception 'exception'! in Unknown on line 0
```

When you throw an exception in an invoked method, you must make sure that you catch it in the calling code. To do so, you need at least two clauses, try and catch. Within the try block, you attempt to execute the code that might generate an error. Within the catch block, you handle the error condition should it arise:

```
try {
  $test = new ThingDoer();
  $test->doThing();
} catch ( Exception $e ) {
  print $e->getMessage();
}
```

You must declare an argument in the catch clause, as you would in a method declaration. The $e argument in the preceding fragment is automatically populated with an Exception object that you can work with. Notice that we use a hint to make the type of object that we are expecting explicit. The reason this step is necessary will become clear in a little while.

An Exception object has the following methods:

```
function exception( $message, $errorcode );
function getmessage();
function getcode();
function getfile();
function getline();
```

You can use them to construct error messages.

If you fail to catch an exception from within a method, then that method will implicitly throw the uncaught exception. It is then up to the method that invoked the current one to catch the exception, and so on. Your script fails if the exception is not handled at some point up the chain.

Defining Custom Exception Classes

Although the default Exception object is useful, you can make it more so by subclassing it and adding your own enhancements. The value can be as much in the names of your subclasses as in any additional methods you define.

Let's extend Exception to report on all its fields:

```
class MyException extends Exception {
  public function summarize() {
    $ret = "<pre>\n";
    $ret .=  "msg: ".$this->getMessage()."\n"
          ."code: ".$this->getCode()."\n"
          ."line: ".$this->getLine()."\n"
          ."file: ".$this->getFile()."\n";
    $ret .= "</pre>\n";
    return $ret;
  }
}
```

In this fragment, we define a class called MyException that extends Exception. We create a new method called summarize() which collates the output of all the Exception object's reporting methods.

In Listing 17.6, we take exception handling a stage further by using two additional custom Exception classes. Notice that we gain value from them without adding any further functionality at all.

LISTING 17.6   Using Custom Exceptions to Handle Different Circumstances

```
 1: <?php
 2:
 3: class MyException extends Exception {
 4:   public function summarize() {
 5:     $ret = "<pre>\n";
 6:     $ret .= "msg: ".$this->getMessage()."\n"
 7:           ."code: ".$this->getCode()."\n"
 8:           ."line: ".$this->getLine()."\n"
 9:           ."file: ".$this->getFile()."\n";
10:     $ret .= "</pre>\n";
11:     return $ret;
12:   }
13: }
14:
15: class FileNotFoundException extends MyException { }
16:
17: class FileOpenException extends MyException { }
18:
19: class Reader {
20:   function getContents( $file ) {
21:     if ( ! file_exists( $file ) ) {
22:       throw new FileNotFoundException( "could not find '$file'" );
23:     }
24:     $fp = @fopen( $file, 'r' );
25:     if ( ! $fp ) {
26:       throw new FileOpenException( "unable to open '$file'" );
27:     }
28:     while ( ! feof( $fp ) ) {
29:       $ret .= fgets( $fp, 1024 );
30:     }
31:     fclose( $fp );
32:     return $ret;
33:   }
34: }
35:
36: $reader = new Reader();
37: try {
38:   print $reader->getContents( "blah.txt" );
39: } catch ( FileNotFoundException $e ) {
40:   print $e->summarize();
41: } catch ( FileOpenException $e ) {
42:   print $e->summarize();
43: } catch ( Exception $e ) {
44:   die("unknown error");
45: }
46: ?>
```

We define the MyException class on line 3 and then extend it on line 15 and line 17, creating the empty FileNotFoundException and FileOpenException classes. On line 19, we define a class called Reader, which will use our Exception classes. Its getContents() method is designed to read and return the contents of a text file. It requires the path to a file as its sole argument. If a file cannot be found in that path, we throw a `FileNotFoundException` object on line 22. We then attempt to open the file. If we are unable to acquire a file resource, we throw a `FileOpenException` on line 26. Assuming we pass these hurdles, we go on to read the file and return its contents.

We try to work with the `Reader` class on line 36 and onward. Because we know `getContents()` is liable to throw `Exception` objects, we wrap our call to the method in a `try` clause. On line 39, we catch a `FileNotFoundException`, printing the return value of the `summarize()` method we defined in the `MyException` class to the browser. On line 41, we catch the `FileOpenException`. This is where the empty custom `Exceptions` come into their own. We are able to provide different behaviors according the type of `Exception` thrown. If the `getContents()` method throws a `FileNotFoundException`, then the relevant `catch` clause is invoked. We might give a user the chance to re-enter some data in this clause but give up altogether in confusion if the `FileOpenException` `catch` clause is invoked. On line 43, we catch a plain `Exception` object. This line is our backstop; we will deal with any exceptions we have not planned for here. There should be no unexpected `Exception` objects in our example, but it is often a good idea to keep a backstop in place anyhow, in case new exceptions are added during development.

Exceptions are a great way of keeping your methods clear. You can return the data type your client code expects without confusing matters by returning error flags when things go wrong. Your method can focus on the task at hand, ignoring special cases without damaging the design of your script. You also benefit by forcing client code to take responsibility for error conditions, making for less buggy code. Finally, using multiple `catch` clauses, you can build up sophisticated responses to errors.

Tools for Building Object Hierarchies

In this section, we delve even deeper into object-oriented design issues. We have already seen how useful the hints are in method arguments introduced with PHP 5. Hints are important because we can be sure that when using them we will be working with an object of a particular type. We encountered this earlier in this hour:

```
public function update( Item $item ) {
  print "updating.. ";
  print $item->name;
}
```

The update() method knows that it has an Item object and can go ahead and work with the $name property that it knows will be accessible. So by constraining the type of the argument passed to the method, we ensure the interface of the object.

Abstract classes and interfaces are ways of doing a similar thing. Each ensures the availability of features for client code.

Abstract Classes

Abstract classes are deceptively simple but very useful. You must define an abstract class using the abstract keyword:

```
abstract class ItemUpdater {
}
```

The effect is that it is now impossible to directly instantiate an ItemUpdater object. Notice the following line:

```
$updater = new ItemUpdater();
```

It results in the following error:

```
Fatal error: Cannot instantiate abstract class itemupdater
```

An abstract class is a template for its children, rather than a functional class in its own right. Let us assume that all ItemUpdater objects should have update(), delete(), and retrieve() methods. We can enforce this rule within the abstract ItemUpdater() class by declaring abstract methods:

```
abstract class ItemUpdater {
  abstract public function update( Item $item );
  abstract public function retrieve( $identifier );
  abstract public function delete( Item $item );
}
```

Now, if we subclass ItemUpdater, we are required to take on the responsibilities the parent has laid down. Let's try dodging our duty:

```
class XmlItemUpdater extends ItemUpdater {
}
```

PHP will not let us create a concrete XMLItemUpdater class that extends ItemUpdater but does not implement its methods:

```
Fatal error: Class xmlitemupdater contains 3 abstract methods
➥and must therefore be declared abstract (itemupdater::update,
➥[itemupdater::retrieve, itemupdater::delete, ...)
```

We could, if we want, defer the problem by declaring XmlItemUpdater abstract as well. Instead, let's provide a concrete subclass for ItemUpdater that reports when the update() method is invoked. We can also create two further subclasses, as shown in Listing 17.7, and use them to revisit our __destruct() example in Listing 17.5.

LISTING 17.7   An Abstract Class and Concrete Implementations

```
1: <?php
2:
3: class Item {
4:   public $name = "item";
5:   private $updater;
6:
7:   public function setUpdater( ItemUpdater $update ) {
8:     $this->updater=$update;
9:   }
10:   function __destruct() {
11:     if ( ! empty( $this->updater )) {
12:       $this->updater->update( $this );
13:     }
14:   }
15: }
16:
17: abstract class ItemUpdater {
18:   abstract public function update( Item $item );
19:   abstract public function retrieve( $identifier );
20:   abstract public function delete( Item $item );
21: }
22:
23: class ReportItemUpdater extends ItemUpdater {
24:
25:   public function update( Item $item ) {
26:     print get_class( $this )."::update(): $item->name<br />\n";
27:     return true;
28:   }
29:
30:   public function retrieve( $id ) {
31:     print get_class( $this )."::retrieve(): id $id<br />\n";
32:     return new Item();
33:   }
34:
35:   public function delete( Item $item ) {
36:     print get_class( $this )."::delete(): id $id<br />\n";
37:     return true;
38:   }
39: }
40:
41: class XmlItemUpdater extends ReportItemUpdater { }
42:
43: class MysqlItemUpdater extends ReportItemUpdater { }
44:
45: $item = new Item();
46: $item->setUpdater( new XmlItemUpdater );
```

LISTING 17.7   Continued

```
47: unset( $item );
48: // prints "xmlitemupdater::update(): item<br />"
49:
50: $item = new Item();
51: $item->setUpdater( new MysqlItemUpdater );
52: unset( $item );
53: // prints "mysqlitemupdater::update(): item<br />"
54: ?>
```

For convenience, we re-present the Item class from Listing 17.4. The key features to note are the setUpdater() method on line 7 and the __destruct() method on line 10. setUpdater() requires an ItemUpdater object, which it stores in the private $updater property. The __destruct() method is automatically invoked before an Item object is destroyed and calls on the ItemUpdater object's update() method.

We define the abstract ItemUpdater on line 17 and a concrete subclass ReportItemUpdater on line 23. ReportItemUpdater does nothing but report on calls to its methods: implementations of update(), retrieve(), and delete(). We subclass ReportItemUpdater on lines 41 and 43, creating an empty XmlItemUpdater class and an empty MysqlUpdater class. Were this production code, we would of course implement both MysqlItemUpdater and XmlItemUpdater to write, delete, and retrieve Item objects. For this example, any method call through objects of these types will default to the ReportItemUpdater implementation, printing a report to the browser so that we can see what is going on.

On line 45, we instantiate an Item object and then pass an XmlItemUpdater object to its setUpdater() method. We destroy the Item object on line 47 by calling the unset() function. This step invokes its __destruct() method, thereby causing it to call XmlItemupdater::update(). This is confirmed by script output.

On line 50, we repeat the process with a MysqlItemUpdater object. The point of this exercise is to demonstrate the interchangeable nature of our ItemUpdater objects. The Item object does not know or care how it is being saved and retrieved. It knows only that it has been passed an ItemUpdater object for storage and use. The abstract ItemUpdater base class ensures that there will be an implemented update() method but leaves the implementation details up to its subclasses. This model, with variable functionality in different subclasses hidden behind a common ancestry and interface, is known as **polymorphism**.

So we can use argument hints in conjunction with an abstract class to ensure that a particular interface will be available in an object passed to a method.

We also use abstract classes to fix the definition of a method. Not only did we ensure the presence of a update() method when we defined ItemUpdater, but also we ensured that the update() method would always expect an Item object as its argument.

Unfortunately, PHP does not provide you with a way of defining a return type when you define an abstract. We can demand that all implementations of delete() must be passed an Item object, but we can't demand that all implementations of retrieve() return an Item object. There are still some things that we must take on trust.

Although our ItemUpdater class contained no implementation, a partial implementation is allowed in abstract classes. This is useful when all subclasses are likely to want to share the same implementation of a method. The best place to put it is usually in the base class. You will often see methods in abstract classes calling their own abstract methods:

```
abstract class OutputComponent {

    abstract function getComponentText();
    abstract function filterComponentText( $txt );
    abstract function writeComponentText();

    function doOutput() {
        $txt = $this->getComponentText();
        $txt = $this->filterComponentText( $txt );
        $this->writeComponentText( $txt );
    }
}
```

So in the preceding fragment, we define three abstract methods. In doOutput(), we work with the methods, leaving the details of implementation to subclasses. This neat trick (documented as the "template method" design pattern) illustrates once again the value of the interface in object-oriented programming. Different OutputComponent subclasses use different techniques to access text and apply different kinds of filters. Subclasses can generate output in different ways from one another. For all this potential for difference, the doOutput() method remains valid, ignoring the details hidden behind the interface. Template methods are often declared final, ensuring that all subclasses work in the same way.

Interfaces

We have talked a lot about a type's interface during this hour. To confuse matters, we are now going to discuss a language feature called an **interface**. An interface is similar in some ways to an abstract class. It allows you to define a set of methods that a related class is obligated to implement.

There are some key differences between abstract classes and interfaces. You declare interfaces with the `interface` keyword:

```
interface Serializable {
  function writeObject();
}
```

You are not allowed to add any implementation at all to an interface, only properties and method definitions. You do not have to declare your method definitions abstract; it is done for you implicitly.

Classes do not *extend* interfaces; they *implement* them. A class can extend another class and implement as many interfaces as you want. By implementing an interface, a class becomes that type, in addition to its type by inheritance:

```
class User extends Person implements Costable {
  // ...
}
```

So in the preceding example, the `User` class must implement any methods defined by the `Costable` interface. Any `User` objects will be of both type `'Person'` and type `'Costable'`. This means that we can use interfaces to aggregate objects that derive from different roots but share common facets. In Listing 17.8, we define an interface called `Serializable` and define two classes that implement it.

LISTING 17.8   Defining and Using an Interface

```
 1: <?php
 2:
 3: interface Serializable {
 4:    public function writeObject();
 5: }
 6:
 7: class Point implements Serializable {
 8:    public $x;
 9:    public $y;
10:
11:    public function writeObject() {
12:      return serialize( $this );
13:    }
14: }
15:
16: class Item implements Serializable {
17:    public function writeObject() {
18:      return serialize( $this );
19:    }
20: }
21:
22: class Serializer {
23:    private $sArray = array();
24:
```

LISTING 17.8   Continued

```
25:    function register( Serializable $obj ) {
26:       $this->sArray[] = $obj;
27:    }
28:
29:    function output() {
30:       foreach ( $this->sArray as $obj ) {
31:          print $obj->writeObject()."\n";
32:       }
33:    }
34: }
35:
36: $serializer = new Serializer();
37: $serializer->register( new Item() );
38: $serializer->register( new Point() );
39: print "<pre>";
40: $serializer->output();
41: print "</pre>";
42: ?>
```

We define our interface, Serializable, on line 3. We define a method
writeObject() on line 4 that implementing classes must include. We set up two
test classes, Point (line 7) and Item (line 16), both of which implement
Serializable. In each case, the writeObject() method merely calls and returns
PHP's serialize() function (lines 12 and 18).

We set up a demonstration class called Serializer on line 22. Serializer has a
register() method that will only accept Serializable objects. Any object passed
to register() is saved in the private $sObjects property. The output() method
on line 29 loops through $sArray, calling writeObject() on each object in the
array. We know that we can call writeObject() because the only mechanism we
have provided for populating $sArray is the update() method.

On lines 36 through 41, we run Serializer through its paces, instantiating a
Serializer object, registering Item and Point objects, and then calling
Serializer::output(). Because they both implement Serializable, the Item and
Point objects are recognized as type Serializable, and the update() method's
type hinting causes no problems. The output() method prints the results to the
browser:

```
0:4:"item":0:{}
0:5:"point":2:{s:1:"x";N;s:1:"y";N;}
```

Passing and Assigning Objects

Before we leave the subject of PHP and objects, it is important to stress a particular difference between PHP 4 and PHP 5. In PHP 4, objects were passed to and from functions by value. Let's pass an object around a bit to test this process:

```php
class PassObj {
  function PassObj( $item ) {
    $item->name="harry";
  }
}

class Item {
  var $name = "bob";
}

$item = new Item();
$pass = new PassObj( $item );
print $item->name;
```

The PassObj class in the fragment has a constructor that accepts an Item object. It changes the $name property of the Item object and does nothing else. If we were to run this code with PHP 4, a copy of an Item object would be passed to the PassObj constructor. The original object would not be affected by the change, and the script would output "bob", the default $name value for Item objects.

If we were to run the code fragment in PHP 5, the script would output "harry". PHP 5 passes and assigns objects by reference rather than value. There would be only one Item object in the script, and different handles would refer to it. This behavior is more natural for an object-oriented language.

To forcibly pass and assign by reference in PHP 4, you need to do so explicitly, using the ampersand (&) character. The following fragment of PHP 4 code passes, assigns, and returns a variable by reference:

```php
function & addItem( &$item ) {
  $this->items[] = &$item;
  return $item;
}
```

We tell the function to return by reference by placing an ampersand before the function name. We enforce pass by reference in the method definition by placing the ampersand before the argument variable, and we assign by reference by placing the ampersand after the assignment operator. Failure to do all of these things would result in at least one copy of the Item object being made. PHP 5 would require no ampersands to get the same result.

Summary

As we have seen, with version 5, PHP has dramatically enhanced its object support. We have now covered most of PHP's object-oriented features. If you are excited by the prospect of working with objects and PHP, realize that this chapter is not even the end of the beginning. Object-oriented design is a vast subject but very rewarding. It is likely that PHP 5 will encourage a small revolution in design books for PHP, so keep your eyes on the bookshop shelves.

In this hour, you learned about class constants and explored a trick for using constant flags to store status settings. You learned how to use static properties and methods to control access to an object. You used the __call(), __get(), and __set() methods to overload object calls and the __destruct() method to handle the end of an object's life. You learned how to define, throw, and catch exceptions. Finally, you defined type functionality using abstract classes and interfaces.

Q&A

Q *You mentioned books about object-oriented design. Can you be more specific?*

A Because PHP 5 is so new, there are few books focusing on object-oriented design with PHP at the time of writing. This will probably not be the case as you read this sentence, so you might consider a visit to your local bookstore. If you have any knowledge of C++, we recommend a book called *Design Patterns: Elements of Reusable Object-Oriented Software* by Erich Gamma *et al.* If you have a background in Java, we recommend *Design Patterns Explained* by Alan Shalloway and James R. Trott. The magazine *PHP|architect* focuses on objects in many of its articles (http://www.phparchitect.com). Another good source for object-oriented information is *phpPatterns* at http://www.phppatterns.com.

Q *Is there any way of simulating abstract classes or interfaces in PHP 4?*

A It would be hard to emulate an interface with PHP 4. Abstract classes, however, can be simulated. Define a base class, and ensure that every "abstract" method contains a die() statement:

```
function doThing() {
    die( "doThing() is abstract and must be overridden" );
}
```

This is clearly not as satisfactory as PHP 5's abstract classes, but it can be deployed quite effectively nevertheless.

Workshop

Quiz

1. What keyword would you use to define a class constant?

2. A static property cannot be changed at runtime. True or false?

3. Can a static method access normal object properties using the $this pseudo variable?

4. What built-in method could you implement to catch an attempt to access a nonexistent property?

5. How would you prevent a method being overridden?

6. What built-in method will be called when an object is about to be destroyed?

7. What keyword would you use to send an exception to client code?

8. What clause would you define to handle a specific exception in client code?

9. How would you instantiate an abstract class?

Answers

1. You would define a class constant with the const keyword:

   ```
   const DJ="John Peel"
   ```

2. False. A static property can be changed throughout script operation. Statics are properties that are set at class rather than object level.

3. No. Static methods have no direct access to object properties because they do not exist in object context.

4. You can implement the __get() method to catch attempts to read nonexistent properties.

5. You can prevent a method from being overridden by declaring it final:

   ```
   final function getDJ() {
     return "john peel";
   }
   ```

6. The __destruct() method is called when an object is about to be destroyed.

7. You can send an exception to calling code with the `throw` keyword:

```
throw new WrongDjException("not John Peel");
```

8. You can handle a specific exception using a `catch` clause:

```
try {
  getRightDJ();
} catch ( WrongDjException $e ) {
  print "Sorry an error occurred";
}
```

9. This is a trick question. You cannot instantiate an abstract class; you must subclass it and instantiate a concrete child class.

Exercises

1. Take a look at your own projects. Can you find anything that would benefit from an object-oriented approach? Is there any functionality that you could extract and develop as a reusable class?

2. We covered the database abstraction (DBA) layer functions in Hour 12, "Working with the DBA Functions." Write a class for reading and writing with DBA functions. What exceptions might you need to throw?

HOUR 18

Working with Regular Expressions

What You'll Learn in This Hour:

▶ How to match patterns in strings using regular expressions
▶ The basics of regular expression syntax
▶ How to replace text in strings using regular expressions
▶ How to use regular expressions to split a string into an array

Regular expressions are a powerful way of examining and modifying text. They enable you to search for patterns within a string, extracting matches flexibly and precisely. Be warned that because they are more powerful, they are also slower than the more basic string function examined in Hour 8, "Working with Strings." You should use string functions, therefore, if you don't need the extra power afforded by the use of a regular expression function.

PHP supports two flavors of regular expressions. It has a set of functions that emulate regular expressions as employed in Perl and a set of functions that support the more limited POSIX regular expressions. Because Perl-compatible regular expressions are the more powerful of the two, we will concentrate on them.

Perl Compatible Regular Expressions

Perl is a powerful scripting language. It was originally designed as a replacement for more limited Unix shell tools, and one of its core features is an extended regular expression engine. PHP provides support for the Perl regular expression syntax, giving you a suite of flexible tools for managing and transforming text.

A **regular expression** is a combination of symbols that match a pattern in text. Learning how to use regular expressions, therefore, is much more than learning the arguments and return types of PHP's regular expression functions. We will begin with the functions and use them to introduce regular expression syntax.

Matching Patterns with `preg_match()`

`preg_match()` accepts four arguments: a regular expression string, a source string, an array variable (which stores matches), and an optional fourth flag argument. `preg_match()` returns 0 if a match is found and 1 otherwise. These numbers represent the number of matches the function can make in a string. Your regular expression string should be enclosed by delimiters, conventionally forward slashes, although you can use any character that isn't alphanumeric (apart from the backslash character).

Let's search the string "aardvark advocacy" for the letters "aa":

```
print "<pre>\n";
print preg_match("/aa/", "aardvark advocacy", $array) . "\n";
print_r( $array );
print "</pre>\n";

// output:
// 1
// Array
// (
//    [0] => aa
// )
```

The letters aa exist in aardvark, so `preg_match()` returns 1. The first element of the $array variable is also filled with the matched string, which we print to the browser. This might seem strange given that we already know the pattern we are looking for is "aa". We are not, however, limited to looking for predefined characters. We can use a single dot (.) to match any character:

```
print "<pre>\n";
print preg_match("/d./", "aardvark advocacy", $array);
print "</pre>\n";
print_r( $array );

// output:
// 1
// Array
// (
//    [0] => dv
// )
```

d. matches "d" followed by any character. We don't know in advance what the second character will be, so the value in $array[0] becomes useful.

If you pass an integer constant flag, PREG_OFFSET_CAPTURE, to preg_match() as the fourth argument, matches in the $array variable are returned as two element arrays, with the first element containing the match and the second containing the number of characters from the start of the search string where the match was found. Suppose we amend our previous call to preg_match():

```
preg_match("/d./", "aardvark advocacy", $array, PREG_OFFSET_CAPTURE );
```

$array will contain a subarray, containing the matched string "dv" and the number 3, representing the number of characters before the match:

```
// Array
// (
//    [0] => Array
//        (
//            [0] => dv
//            [1] => 3
//        )
//
// )
```

Using Quantifiers to Match a Character More Than Once

When you search for a character in a string, you can use a quantifier to determine the number of times this character should repeat for a match to be made. The pattern a+, for example, will match at least one "a" followed by "a" zero or more times. Let's put this to the test:

```
if ( preg_match("/a+/","aaaa", $array) ) {
  print "<pre>\n";
  print_r( $array );
  print "</pre>\n";
}

// output:
// Array
// (
//    [0] => aaaa
// )
```

Notice that this regular expression greedily matches as many characters as it can. Table 18.1 lists the quantifiers you can use to test for a recurring character.

TABLE 18.1 Quantifiers for Matching a Recurring Character

Symbol	Description	Example
*	Zero or more instances	a*
+	One or more instances	a+
?	Zero or one instance	a?

TABLE 18.1   Continued

Symbol	Description	Example
{*n*}	*n* instances	a{3}
{*n*,}	At least *n* instances	a{3,}
{,*n*}	Up to *n* instances	a{,2}
{*n*1,*n*2}	At least *n*1 instances, no more than *n*2 instances	a{1,2}

The numbers between braces in Table 18.1 are called bounds. **Bounds** define the number of times a character or range of characters should be matched in a regular expression. You should place your upper and lower bounds between braces after the character you want to match:

```
a{4,5}
```

This line matches no fewer than four and no more than five instances of the character a.

PCREs and Greediness

By default, regular expressions attempt to match as many characters as possible. Notice the following line:

```
"/p.*t/"
```

It will find the first "p" in a string and match as many characters as possible until the last possible "t" character is reached. So this regular expression matches the entire test string in the following fragment:

```
$text = "pot post pat patent";
if ( preg_match( "/p.*t/", $text, $array ) ) {
  print "<pre>\n";
  print_r( $array );
  print "</pre>\n";
}

// output:
// Array
// (
//    [0] => pot post pat patent
// )
```

By placing a question mark (?) after any quantifier, you can force a PCRE to be more frugal. Notice the following line:

```
"p.*t"
```

It means "p followed by as many characters as possible followed by t." But now notice the next line:

```
"p.*?t"
```

It means "p followed by as few characters as possible followed by t."

The following fragment uses this technique to match the smallest number of characters starting with "p" and ending with "t":

```
$text = "pot post pat patent";
if ( preg_match( "/p.*?t/", $text, $array ) ) {
  print "<pre>\n";
  print_r( $array );
  print "</pre>\n";
}

// output:
// Array
// (
//   [0] => pot
// )
```

Matching Ranges of Characters with Character Classes

Until now, we have either matched specified characters or used . to match any character. **Character classes** enable you to match any one of a group of characters. To define a character class, you surround the characters you want to match in square brackets. [ab] will match "a" or "b." After you define a character class, you can treat it as if it were a character. So [ab]+ will match "aaa," "bbb," or "ababab."

You can also match ranges of characters with a character class: [a-z] will match any lowercase letter, [A-Z] will match any uppercase letter, and [0-9] will match any number. You can combine ranges and individual characters into one character class, so [a-z5] will match any lowercase letter or the number 5.

In the following fragment, we are looking for any lowercase alphabetical character or the numbers 3, 4, and 7:

```
if ( preg_match("/[a-z347]+/","AB dkfd773sxFF", $array) ) {
  print "<pre>\n";
  print_r( $array );
  print "</pre>\n";
}

// output:
// Array
// (
//   [0] => dkfd773sx
// )
```

You can also negate a character class by including a caret (^) character after the opening square bracket: [^A-Z] will match anything apart from an uppercase character.

Let's negate the characters in the character class we defined in the previous example:

```
if ( preg_match("/[^a-z347]+/","AB dkfd773sxFF", $array) ) {
  print "<pre>\n";
  print_r( $array );
  print "</pre>\n";
}

// output:
// Array
// (
//    [0] => AB
// )
```

PCREs and Backslashed Characters

You can escape certain characters with PCREs, just as you can within strings. \t, for example, represents a tab character, and \n represents a newline. PCREs also define some escape characters that will match entire character types. Table 18.2 lists these backslash characters.

TABLE 18.2 Escape Characters That Match Character Types

Character	Matches
\d	Any number
\D	Anything other than a number
\s	Any kind of whitespace
\S	Anything other than whitespace
\w	Alphanumeric characters (including the underscore character)
\W	Anything other than an alphanumeric character or an underscore

These escape characters can vastly simplify your regular expressions. Without them, you would be forced to use a character class to match ranges of characters. Compare the following valid methods for matching word characters:

```
preg_match( "/p[a-zA-Z0-9_]+t/", $text, $array );
preg_match( "/p\w+t/", $text, $array );
```

Both the examples match "p" followed by one or more alphanumeric characters followed by "t." The second example is easier to write and read, however.

PCREs also support a number of escape characters that act as anchors. **Anchors** match positions within a string, without matching any characters. They are listed in Table 18.3.

TABLE 18.3   Escape Characters That Act As Anchors

Character	Matches
\A	Beginning of string
\b	Word boundary
\B	Not a word boundary
\Z	End of string (matches before final newline or at end of string)
\z	End of string (matches only at very end of string)

Let's put the word boundary character to the test:

```
$text = "pot post pat patent";
if ( preg_match( "/\bp\w+t\b/", $text, $array ) ) {
  print "<pre>\n";
  print_r( $array );
  print "</pre>\n";
}

// output:
// Array
// (
//   [0] => pot
// )
```

The preg_match() call in the previous fragment will match the character "p" but only if it is at a word boundary, followed by any number of word characters, followed by "t," but only if it is at a word boundary. The word boundary escape character does not actually match a character; it merely confirms that a boundary exists for a match to take place.

You can also escape characters to turn off their meanings. To match a "." character, for example, you should add a backslash to the character in your regular expression string:

```
preg_match( "/\./", $string, $array );
```

Working with Subpatterns

A **subpattern** is a pattern enclosed in parentheses (sometimes referred to as an atom). After you define a subpattern, you can treat it as if it were itself a character or character class. In other words, you can match the same pattern as many times as you want using the syntax described in Table 18.1.

Subpatterns are also used to change the way a regular expression is interpreted, usually by limiting the scope of a set of alternatives.

Finally, you can use subpatterns to save the results of a submatch within a regular expression for later use.

In the next fragment, we define a pattern and use parentheses to match individual elements within it:

```
$test = "Whatever you do, don't panic!";
if ( preg_match( "/(don't)\s+(panic)/", $test, $array ) ) {
  print "<pre>\n";
  print_r( $array );
  print "</pre>\n";
}

// output:
// Array
// (
//    [0] => don't panic
//    [1] => don't
//    [2] => panic
// )
```

The first element of the array variable that is passed to preg_match() contains the complete matched string. Subsequent elements contain each individual atom matched. This means that you can access the component parts of a matched pattern as well as the entire match.

In the following code fragment, we match an IP address and access not only the entire address, but also each of its component parts:

```
$test = "158.152.55.35";
if ( preg_match( "/(\d+)\.(\d+)\.(\d+)\.(\d+)/", $test, $array ) ) {
  print "<pre>\n";
  print_r( $array );
  print "</pre>\n";
}

// output:
// Array
// (
//    [0] => 158.152.55.35
//    [1] => 158
//    [2] => 152
//    [3] => 55
//    [4] => 35
// )
```

Notice that we used a backslash (\) to escape the dots in the regular expression. By doing so, we signal that we want to strip . of its special meaning and treat it as a specific character. You must do the same for any character that has a function in a regular expression if you want to refer to it.

Branches

You can combine patterns with the pipe (¦) character to create **branches** in your regular expressions. A regular expression with two branches will match either the first pattern or the second. This process adds yet another layer of flexibility to regular expression syntax. In the next code fragment, we match either .com or .co.uk in a string:

```
$test = "www.example.com";
if ( preg_match( "/www\.example(\.com¦\.co\.uk)/", $test, $array ) ) {
  print "it is a $array[1] domain<br/>";
}
// output:
// it is a .com domain
```

We illustrate two aspects of a subpattern in the preceding example. First, we capture the match of .com or .co.uk, making it available in $array[1], and second, we define the scope of the branch. Without the parentheses, we would match either www.example.com or .co.uk, which is not what we want at all.

Anchoring a Regular Expression

Not only can you determine the pattern you want to find in a string, you also can decide where in the string you want to find it. To test whether a pattern is at the beginning of a string, prepend a caret (^) symbol to your regular expression. ^a will match "apple," but not "banana."

To test that a pattern is at the end of a string, append a dollar ($) symbol to the end of your regular expression. a$ will match "flea" but not "dear."

Finding Matches Globally with `preg_match_all()`

It is a feature of `preg_match()` that it only matches the first pattern it finds in a string. So searching for words beginning with "p" and ending with "s," we will match only the first found pattern. Let's try it out:

```
$text = "I sell pots, plants, pistachios, pianos and parrots";
if ( preg_match( "/\bp\w+s\b/", $text, $array ) ) {
  print "<pre>\n";
  print_r( $array );
  print "</pre>\n";
}
```

```
// output:
// Array
// (
//   [0] => pots
// )
```

As we would expect, the first match, "pots," is stored in the first element of the $array variable. None of the other words are matched.

We can use preg_match_all() to access every match in the test string in one call. preg_match_all() accepts a regular expression, a source string, and an array variable and will return true if a match is found. The array variable is populated with a multidimensional array, the first element of which will contain every match to the complete pattern defined in the regular expression.

Listing 18.1 tests a string using preg_match_all(), the print_r() function to output the multidimensional array of results.

LISTING 18.1 Using preg_match_all() to Match a Pattern Globally

```
 1: <!DOCTYPE html PUBLIC
 2:   "-//W3C//DTD XHTML 1.0 Strict//EN"
 3:   "http://www.w3.org/TR/xhtml1/DTD/xhtml1-strict.dtd">
 4: <html>
 5: <head>
 6: <title>Using preg_match_all() to Match a Pattern Globally</title>
 7: </head>
 8: <body>
 9: <?php
10: $text = "I sell pots, plants, pistachios, pianos and parrots";
11: if ( preg_match_all( "/\bp\w+s\b/", $text, $array ) ) {
12:   print "<pre>\n";
13:   print_r( $array );
14:   print "</pre>\n";
15: }
16:
17: // output:
18: // Array
19: // (
20: //   [0] => Array
21: //     (
22: //       [0] => pots
23: //       [1] => plants
24: //       [2] => pistachios
25: //       [3] => pianos
26: //       [4] => parrots
27: //     )
28: //
29: // )
30:
31: ?>
32: </body>
33: </html>
```

The first and only element of the $array variable that we passed to preg_match_all() on line 11 has been populated with an array of strings. This array contains every word in the test string that begins with "p" and ends with "s."

preg_match_all() populates a multidimensional array to store matches to subpatterns. The first element of the array argument passed to preg_match_all() will contain every match of the complete regular expression. Each additional element will contain the matches that correspond to each atom (subpattern in parentheses). Notice the following call to preg_match_all():

```
$text = "01-05-99, 01-10-99, 01-03-00";
preg_match_all( "/(\d+)-(\d+)-(\d+)/", $text, $array );
```

$array[0] will store an array of complete matches:

```
$array[0][0]: 01-05-99
$array[0][1]: 01-10-99
$array[0][2]: 01-03-00
```

$array[1] will store an array of matches that corresponds to the first subpattern:

```
$array[1][0]: 01
$array[1][1]: 01
$array[1][2]: 01
```

$array[2] will store an array of matches that corresponds to the second subpattern:

```
$array[2][0]: 05
$array[2][1]: 10
$array[2][2]: 03
```

And so on. We can change this behavior by passing a constant integer flag, PREG_SET_ORDER, to preg_match_all() as its optional fourth argument:

```
$text = "01-05-99, 01-10-99, 01-03-00";
preg_match_all( "/(\d+)-(\d+)-(\d+)/", $text, $array, PREG_SET_ORDER );
```

This will change the structure of $array. Each element will be an array as before. Of the subarrays in $array, the first element of each will be a complete match, and each subsequent element will be a submatch. So the first element of $array will contain all aspects of the first match:

```
$array[0][0]: 01-05-99
$array[0][1]: 01
$array[0][2]: 05
$array[0][3]: 99
```

The second array will contain all aspects of the second match:

```
$array[1][0]: 01-10-99
$array[1][1]: 01
$array[1][2]: 10
$array[1][3]: 99
```

And so on.

Using `preg_replace()` to Replace Patterns

Until now, we have searched for patterns in a string, leaving the search string untouched. `preg_replace()` enables you to find a pattern in a string and replace it with a new substring. `preg_replace()` requires three strings: a regular expression, the text with which to replace a found pattern, and the text to modify. It optionally accepts a fourth integer argument, which sets a limit to the number of replacements the function should perform. `preg_replace()` returns a string, including the modification if a match was found or an unchanged copy of the original source string otherwise. In the following fragment, we search for the name of a club official, replacing it with name of her successor:

```
$test = "Our Secretary, Sarah Williams is pleased to welcome you.";
print preg_replace("/Sarah Williams/", "Rev. P.W. Goodchild", $test);
// output:
// Our Secretary, Rev. P.W. Goodchild is pleased to welcome you.
```

Note that although `preg_match()` will only match the first pattern it finds, `preg_replace()` will find and replace every instance of a pattern, unless you pass a limit integer as a fourth argument.

Using Back References with `preg_replace()`

Back references make it possible for you to use part of a matched pattern in the replacement string. To use this feature, you should use parentheses to wrap any elements of your regular expression that you might want to use. The text matched by these subpatterns will be available to the replacement string if you refer to them with a dollar character ($) and the number of the subpattern ($1, for example). Subpatterns are numbered in order, outer to inner, left to right, starting at $1. $0 stores the entire match.

The following fragment converts dates in dd/mm/yy format to mm/dd/yy format:

```
$test = "25/12/2000";
print preg_replace("¦(\d+)/(\d+)/(\d+)¦", "$2/$1/$3", $test);
// output:
// 12/25/2000
```

Notice that we used a pipe (¦) symbol as a delimiter. This is to save us from having to escape the forward slashes in the pattern we want to match.

Instead of a source string, you can pass an array of strings to preg_replace(), and it will transform each string in turn. In this case, the return value will be an array of transformed strings.

You can also pass arrays of regular expressions and replacement strings to preg_replace(). Each regular expression will be applied to the source string, and the corresponding replacement string will be applied. The following fragment transforms date formats as before but also changes copyright information in the source string:

```
$text = "25/12/99, 14/5/00. Copyright 2003";
$regs = array( "¦\b(\d+)/(\d+)/(\d+)\b¦", "/([Cc]opyright) 2003/" );
$reps = array( "$2/$1/$3",        "$1 2004" );
$text = preg_replace( $regs, $reps, $text );
print "$text<br />";
// output:
// 12/25/99, 5/14/00. Copyright 2004<br />
```

We create two arrays. The first, $regs, contains two regular expressions, and the second, $reps, contains replacement strings. The first element of the $regs array corresponds to the first element of the $reps array, and so on.

If the array of replacement strings contains fewer elements than the array of regular expressions, patterns matched by those regular expressions without corresponding replacement strings will be replaced with an empty string.

If you pass preg_replace() an array of regular expressions but only a string as replacement, the same replacement string will be applied to each pattern in the array of regular expressions.

Modifiers

PCREs allow you to modify the way that a pattern is applied through the use of pattern modifiers.

A **pattern modifier** is a letter that should be placed after the final delimiter in your PCRE. It will refine the behavior of your regular expression.

Table 18.4 lists some PCRE pattern modifiers.

TABLE 18.4   PCRE Modifiers

Pattern	Description
/i	Case insensitive.
/e	Treats replacement string in `preg_replace()` as PHP code.
/m	$ and ^ anchors match at newlines as well as the beginning and end of the string.
/s	Matches newlines (newlines are not normally matched by .).
/x	Whitespace outside character classes is not matched to aid readability. To match whitespace, use \s, \t, or \ .
/A	Matches pattern only at start of string (this modifier is not found in Perl).
/E	Matches pattern only at end of string (this modifier is not found in Perl).
/U	Makes the regular expression ungreedy; the minimum number of allowable matches is found (this modifier is not found in Perl).

Where they do not contradict one another, you can combine pattern modifiers. You might want to use the x modifier to make your regular expression easier to read, for example, and also the i modifier to make it match patterns regardless of case. Note the following line:

```
/ b \S* t /ix
```

It will match "bat" and "BAT" but not "B A T," for example. Unescaped spaces in a regular expression modified by x are there for aesthetic reasons only and will not match any patterns in the source string.

The m modifier can be useful if you want to match an anchored pattern on multiple lines of text. The anchor patterns ^ and $ match the beginning and end of an entire string by default. The following fragment uses the m modifier to change the behavior of $:

```
$text = "name: matt\noccupation: coder\neyes: blue\n";
if ( preg_match_all( "/^\w+:\s+(.*)$/m", $text, $array ) ) {
  print "<pre>\n";
  print_r( $array );
  print "</pre>\n";
}

// output:
// Array
// (
//    [0] => Array
//       (
//          [0] => name: matt
//          [1] => occupation: coder
```

```
//          [2] => eyes: blue
//      )
//
//    [1] => Array
//      (
//          [0] => matt
//          [1] => coder
//          [2] => blue
//      )
//
//  )
```

We create a regular expression that will match any word characters followed by a colon and any number of space characters. We then match any number of characters followed by the end of string ($) anchor. Because we have used the m pattern modifier, $ matches the end of every line rather than the end of the string.

The s modifier is useful when you want to use . to match characters across multiple lines. The following fragment attempts to access the first and last words of a string:

```
$text = "start with this line\nand you will reach\na conclusion in the end\n";
if ( preg_match( "/^(\w+).*?(\w+)$/", $text, $array ) ) {
  print "<pre>\n";
  print_r( $array );
  print "</pre>\n";
}
```

This code will print nothing. Although the regular expression will find word characters at the beginning of the string, the . will not match the newline characters embedded in the text. The s modifier will change this:

```
$text = "start with this line\nand you will reach\na conclusion in the end\n";
if ( preg_match( "/^(\w+).*?(\w+)$/s", $text, $array ) ) {
  print "<pre>\n";
  print_r( $array );
  print "</pre>\n";
}
```

```
// output:
// Array
// (
//   [0] => start with this line
// and you will reach
// a conclusion in the end
//   [1] => start
//   [2] => end
// )
```

The e modifier can be particularly powerful. It allows you to treat the replacement string in `preg_replace()` as if it were PHP. You can pass back references to functions as arguments, for example, or process lists of numbers. In the following example, we use the e modifier to pass matched numbers in dates to a function that returns the same date in a new format:

```
function convDate( $month, $day, $year ) {
  $year = ($year < 70 )?$year+2000:$year;
  $time = ( mktime( 0,0,0,$month,$day,$year) );
  return date("l d F Y", $time);
}

$dates = "3/18/03<br />\n7/22/04";
$dates = preg_replace( "/([0-9]+)\/([0-9]+)\/([0-9]+)/e",
    "convDate($1,$2,$3)", $dates);
print $dates;

// output:
// Tuesday 18 March 2003<br />
// Thursday 22 July 2004
```

We match any set of three numbers separated by slashes, using parentheses to capture the matched numbers. Because we are using the e modifier, we can call the user-defined function `convDate()` from the replacement string argument, passing the three back references to the function. `convDate()` simply takes the numerical input and produces a more verbose date, which replaces the original. Because in our example, we are matching numbers, we do not need to enclose the backreferences in quotes. If we were matching strings, quotes would be necessary around each string backreference.

Using `preg_replace_callback()` **to Replace Patterns**

`preg_replace_callback()` allows you to assign a callback function that will be called for every full match your regular expression finds. `preg_replace_callback()` requires a regular expression, a reference to a callback function, and the string to be analyzed. Like `preg_replace()`, it also optionally accepts a limit argument.

The callback function should be designed to accept a single array argument. It will contain the full match at index 0 and each submatch in subsequent positions in the array. Whatever the callback function returns will be incorporated into the string returned by `preg_replace_callback()`.

We can use `preg_replace_callback()` to rewrite our date-replacement example:

```
function convDate( $matches ) {
  $year = ($year < 70 )?$matches[3]+2000:$matches[3];
  $time = ( mktime( 0,0,0,$matches[1],$matches[2],$matches[3]) );
  return date("l d F Y", $time);
}

$dates = "3/18/03<br />\n7/22/04";
$dates = preg_replace_callback( "/([0-9]+)\/([0-9]+)\/([0-9]+)/",
     "convDate", $dates);
print $dates;

// output:
// Tuesday 18 March 2003<br />
// Thursday 22 July 2004
```

This example calls the `convDate()` function twice, once for each time the regular expression matches. The day, month, and year figures are then easy to extract from the array that is passed to `convDate()` and stored in the $matches argument variable.

Using `preg_split()` to Break Up Strings

In Hour 8, you saw that you could split a string of tokens into an array using `explode()`. This is powerful but limits you to a single set of characters that can be used as a delimiter. PHP's `preg_split()` function enables you to use the power of regular expressions to define a flexible delimiter. `preg_split()` requires a string representing a pattern to use as a delimiter and a source string. It also accepts an optional third argument representing a limit to the number of elements you want returned and an optional flag argument. `preg_split()` returns an array.

The following fragment uses a regular expression with two branches to split a string on a comma followed by a space or the word and surrounded by two spaces:

```
$text = "apples, oranges, peaches and grapefruit";
$fruitarray = preg_split( "/, | and /", $text );
print "<pre>\n";
print_r( $fruitarray );
print "</pre>\n";

// output:
// Array
// (
//   [0] => apples
//   [1] => oranges
//   [2] => peaches
//   [3] => grapefruit
// )
```

Summary

Regular expressions are a huge subject, and we've really only scraped the surface of their power in this hour. Nevertheless, you should now be able to use regular expression functions to find and replace complex patterns in text.

You should be able to use the `preg_match()` regular expression function to find patterns in strings and the `preg_replace()` function to replace all instances of a pattern in a string. You should be able to find ranges of characters using character classes, multiple patterns using quantifiers, and alternative patterns using branches. You should be able to extract subpatterns and refer to them with backreferences. You should be able to use escape characters to anchor patterns or to match character types. You should be able to use modifiers to change the way in which PCREs work.

In the next hour, we will examine some core techniques for creating environments that can retain information across multiple requests.

Q&A

Q *Regular expressions seem very powerful. Is there anywhere I can find out more about them?*

A The relevant section in the PHP manual at `http://www.php.net/pcre` will offer some information about regular expression syntax. You can also find some useful information at `http://www.perldoc.com`—in particular, an introduction to Perl regular expressions at `http://www.perldoc.com/perl5.8.0/pod/perlretut.html`. For a challenging but comprehensive guide to regular expressions, you should acquire *Mastering Regular Expressions* by Jeffrey Friedl.

Workshop

Quiz

1. What regular expression function would you use to match a pattern in a string?

2. What regular expression syntax would you use to match the letter "b" at least once but not more than six times?

3. How would you specify a character range between "d" and "f?"

4. How would you negate the character range you defined in question 3?

5. What syntax would you use to match either any number or the word "tree?"

6. What regular expression function would you use to replace a matched pattern?

7. The regular expression

   `.*bc`

   will match greedily; that is, it will match "abc000000bc" rather than "abc." How would you make the preceding regular expression match only the first instance of a pattern it finds?

8. What backslash character will match whitespace?

9. What function could you use to match every instance of a pattern in a string?

10. Which modifier would you use in a PCRE function to match a pattern independently of case?

Answers

1. You can use the `preg_match()` function to find a pattern in a string.

2. You can use braces containing the minimum and maximum instances (the bounds) of a character to match:

   `b{1,6}`

3. You can specify a character range using square brackets:

   `[d-f]`

4. You can negate a character range with the caret symbol:

   `[^d-f]`

5. You can match alternative branches with the pipe (¦) character:

   `[0-9]¦tree`

6. You can use the `preg_replace()` function to replace a matched pattern with a given alternative.

7. By adding a question mark to a quantifier, you can force the match to be nongreedy:

   ```
   /.*?bc/
   ```

8. \s will match whitespace in a PCRE.

9. The preg_match_all() function will match every instance of a pattern in a string.

10. The /i modifier will make a PCRE function match independently of case.

Exercise

1. Use regular expressions to extract email addresses from a file. Add them to an array and output the result to the browser. Refine your regular expression across a number of files.

HOUR 19

Saving State with Cookies and Query Strings

What You'll Learn in This Hour:

▶ What cookies are and how they work
▶ How to read a cookie
▶ How to set a cookie
▶ How to use cookies to store site usage information in a database
▶ About query strings
▶ How to build a function to turn an associative array into a query string

HTTP is a stateless protocol. Therefore, every page a user downloads from your server represents a separate connection. On the other hand, Web sites are perceived by users and publishers alike as environments, as spaces within which a single page is part of a wider whole. It's not surprising, therefore, that strategies to pass information from page to page are as old as the Web itself.

In this hour, we will examine two methods of storing information on one page that can then be accessed on subsequent pages.

Cookies

Netscape originated the "magic cookie" back in the days of Netscape 1. The origin of the name is the subject of some debate, although it seems reasonable to assume that the fortune cookie might have played a role in the thinking behind it. Since then, the standard has been embraced by other browser producers.

A **cookie** is a small amount of data stored by the user's browser in compliance with a request from a server or script. A host can request that up to 20 cookies be stored by a user's browser. Each cookie consists of a name, a value, and an expiry date, as well as host and path information. An individual cookie is limited to 4KB.

After a cookie is set, only the originating host can read the data, ensuring that the user's privacy is respected. Furthermore, the user can configure his browser to notify him of all cookies set or even to refuse all cookie requests. For this reason, cookies should be used in moderation and should not be relied on as an essential element of an environment design without first warning the user.

Having said that, cookies can be an excellent way of saving small amounts of information about a user from page to page or even from visit to visit.

The Anatomy of a Cookie

Cookies are usually set in an HTTP header (although JavaScript can also set a cookie directly on a browser). A PHP script that sets a cookie might send headers that look something like this:

```
HTTP/1.1 200 OK
Date: Mon, 25 Aug 2003 13:40:22 GMT
Server: Apache/2.0.47 (Unix) PHP/5.0.0b1
X-Powered-By: PHP/5.0.0b1
Set-Cookie: vegetable=artichoke; expires=Mon, 25-Aug-2003 14:40:27 GMT; path=/;
domain=corrosive.co.uk
Connection: close
Content-Type: text/html; charset=ISO-8859-1
```

As you can see, the Set-Cookie header contains a name value pair, a GMT date, a path, and a domain. The name and value are URL encoded. The expires field is an instruction to the browser to forget the cookie after the given time and date. The path field defines the position on a Web site below which the cookie should be sent back to the server, whereas the domain field determines the Internet domains to which the cookie should be sent. The domain cannot be different from the domain from which the cookie was sent, but it can nonetheless specify a degree of flexibility. In the preceding example, the browser sends the cookie to the server corrosive.co.uk. You can read more about HTTP headers in Hour 14, "Beyond the Box."

If the browser is configured to store cookies, it keeps this information until the expiry date. If the user points the browser at any page that matches the path and domain of the cookie, it resends the cookie to the server. The browser's headers might look something like this:

```
GET /phpbook/source/listing19.1.php HTTP/1.1
Host: matt.corrosive.co.uk:9090
User-Agent: Mozilla/5.0 (X11; U; Linux ppc; en-US; rv:1.2.1) Gecko/20030228
Accept: text/xml,application/xml,application/xhtml+xml,text/html ...
Accept-Language: en-us, en;q=0.50
Accept-Encoding: gzip, deflate, compress;q=0.9
Accept-Charset: ISO-8859-1, utf-8;q=0.66, *;q=0.66
Keep-Alive: 300
Connection: keep-alive
Cookie: vegetable=artichoke
Cache-Control: max-age=0
```

A PHP script then has access to the cookie in the superglobal array variable $_COOKIE["vegetable"]:

```
print $_COOKIE['vegetable']."<br/>"; // prints "artichoke"
```

Setting a Cookie with PHP

You can set a cookie in a PHP script in two ways. You can use the header() function to set the Set-Cookie header. You encountered the header() function in Hour 10, "Working with Forms." header() requires a string that is included in the header section of the server response. Because headers are sent automatically for you, header() must be called before any output is sent to the browser:

```
header ("Set-Cookie: vegetable=artichoke; expires=Wed,
➥25-Aug-04 14:39:58 GMT; path=/; domain=corrosive.co.uk ");
```

Although not difficult, this method of setting a cookie requires you to build a function to construct the header string. Formatting the date as in this example and URL encoding the name/value pair would not be a particularly arduous task. It would, however, be an exercise in wheel reinvention because PHP provides a function that does just that.

setcookie() does what the name suggests—it outputs a Set-Cookie header. For this reason, it should be called before any other content is sent to the browser. The function accepts the cookie name, cookie value, expiry date in Unix epoch format, path, domain, and integer (which should be set to 1 if the cookie is to be sent only over a secure connection). All arguments to this function are optional apart from the first (cookie name) parameter.

Listing 19.1 uses setcookie() to set a cookie.

LISTING 19.1   Setting and Printing a Cookie Value

```php
1: <?php
2: setcookie( "vegetable", "artichoke", time()+3600, "/",
3:      "corrosive.co.uk", 0 );
4: ?>
5: <!DOCTYPE html PUBLIC
6:     "-//W3C//DTD XHTML 1.0 Strict//EN"
7:     "http://www.w3.org/TR/xhtml1/DTD/xhtml1-strict.dtd">
8: <html>
9: <head>
10: <title>Listing 19.1 Setting and Printing a Cookie Value</title>
11: </head>
12: <body>
13: <?php
14: if ( isset( $_COOKIE['vegetable'] ) ) {
15:   print "<p>Hello again, your chosen vegetable is ";
16:   print "{$_COOKIE['vegetable']}</p>";
17: } else {
18:   print "<p>Hello you. This may be your first visit</p>";
19: }
20: ?>
21: </body>
22: </html>
```

By the Way

If you want Listing 19.1 to run on your server, you must change the setCookie() function's host argument to match your domain, like so:

```php
setcookie( "vegetable", "artichoke", time()+3600, "/",
"example.com", 0 );
```

You can also omit the last two arguments completely, and your current domain will be used implicitly:

```php
setcookie( "vegetable", "artichoke", time()+3600, "/" );
```

Even though we set the cookie (line 2) when the script is run for the first time, the $vegetable variable is not created at this point. A cookie is read only when the browser sends it to the server, which doesn't happen until the user revisits a page in your domain. We set the cookie name to "vegetable" on line 2 and the cookie value to "artichoke". We use the time() function to get the current time stamp and add 3600 to it (there are 3600 seconds in an hour). This total represents our expiry date. We define a path of "/", which means a cookie should be sent for any page within our server environment. We set the domain argument to "corrosive.co.uk", which means a cookie will be sent to any server in that group (www.corrosive.co.uk as well as dev.corrosive.co.uk, for example). If you want the cookie returned only to the server hosting your script, you can use the $_SERVER['SERVER_NAME'] server variable instead of hard-coding the server name. The added advantage of this is that your code will work as expected even if you move it to a new server. Finally, we pass 0 to setcookie() signaling that cookies can be sent in an insecure environment.

Although you can omit all but the first argument, you should include all the arguments with the exception of the domain and the secure flag. This is because the path argument is required by some browsers for cookies to work as they should. Additionally, without the path argument the cookie is sent only to documents in the current directory or its subdirectories.

Passing `setcookie()` an empty string (`""`) for string arguments or `0` for integer fields causes these arguments to be skipped.

Deleting a Cookie

Officially, to delete a cookie, you should call `setcookie()` with the name argument only:

```
setcookie( "vegetable" );
```

This does not always work well, however, and should not be relied on. It is safest to set the cookie with a date that has already expired:

```
setcookie( "vegetable", "", time()-60, "/", "corrosive.co.uk", 0);
```

You should also be sure to pass `setcookie()` the same path, domain, and secure parameters as you did when originally setting the cookie.

Creating Session Cookies

To create a cookie that lasts only as long as the user is running her browser, pass `setcookie()` an expiry argument of `0`. While the user's browser continues to run, the cookie is returned to the server. The browser does not remember the cookie, however, after it has been quit and restarted.

This can be useful for scripts that validate a user with a cookie, allowing continued access to personal information on multiple pages after a password has been submitted. You will not want the browser to have continued access to these pages after it has been restarted because you can't be sure that it has not been taken over by a new user:

```
setcookie( "session_id", "55435", 0 );
```

An Example—Tracking Site Usage

Imagine that we have been given a brief by a site publisher to use cookies and SQLite to gather statistics about visitors to the site. The client wants to get figures for the number of individual visitors to the site, average number of hits per visit for each visitor, and average time spent on the site for each user.

Our first duty will be to explain the limitations of cookies to the client. First, not all users will have cookies enabled on their browsers. If not passed a cookie by a browser, a cookie script is likely to assume that this is the user's first visit. The figures are therefore likely to be skewed by browsers that won't or can't support cookies. Furthermore, you cannot be sure that the same user will use the same browser all the time or that a single browser won't be shared by multiple users.

Having done this, we can move on to fulfilling the brief. In fact, we can produce a working example in fewer than 100 lines of code!

We need to create a database table with the fields listed in Table 19.1.

TABLE 19.1   Database Fields

Name	Type	Description
id	integer	An autoincremented field that produces and stores a unique ID for each visitor
first_visit	integer	A timestamp representing the moment of the first page request made by a visitor
last_visit	integer	A timestamp representing the moment of the most recent page request made by a visitor
num_visits	integer	The number of distinct sessions attributed to the visitor
total_duration	integer	The estimated total time spent on the site (in seconds)
total_clicks	integer	The total number of requests made by the visitor

Rather than create it manually we will embed the code to generate our table in the script itself. Once we have a table to work with, we need to write the code that will open a database connection and check for the existence of a cookie. If the cookie does not exist, we need to create a new row in our table, setting up the initial values for the fields we will maintain. We create this code in Listing 19.2.

LISTING 19.2   A Script to Add New User Information to a SQLite Database

```
 1: <?php
 2: $GLOBALS['dbres'] = connect( "data/testdb" );
 3: $GLOBALS['visit_id'] = $_COOKIE['visit_id'];
 4:
 5: if ( empty( $visit_id ) ) {
 6:   newuser( );
 7:   print "<p>Welcome, first time user!</p>";
 8: } else {
 9:   print "<p>Welcome back $visit_id</p>";
10: }
```

LISTING 19.2   Continued

```
11:
12: function newuser( ) {
13:    $visit_data = array (
14:          'first_visit' => time(),
15:          'last_visit' => time(),
16:          'num_visits' => 1,
17:          'total_duration' => 0,
18:          'total_clicks' => 1
19:          );
20:
21:    insert_visit( $visit_data );
22:    setcookie( "visit_id", $visit_data['id'],
23:         time()+(60*60*24*365*10), "/" );
24:    return $visit_data;
25: }
26:
27: function connect( $db ) {
28:    $dbres = sqlite_open($db, 0, $error);
29:    if ( ! is_resource( $dbres ) ) {
30:       die( "sqllite error: $error" );
31:    }
32:    $create = "CREATE TABLE track_visit (
33:          id INTEGER PRIMARY KEY,
34:          first_visit INTEGER,
35:          last_visit INTEGER,
36:          num_visits INTEGER,
37:          total_duration INTEGER,
38:          total_clicks INTEGER)";
39:    @sqlite_query( $dbres, $create );
40:    return $dbres;
41: }
42:
43: function insert_visit( &$visit_data ) {
44:    $query = "INSERT INTO track_visit ( ";
45:    $query .= implode( ", ", array_keys( $visit_data ) );
46:    $query .= " ) VALUES( ";
47:    $query .= implode(", ", array_values( $visit_data ) );
48:    $query .= " );";
49:    $result = sqlite_query( $GLOBALS['dbres'], $query );
50:    $visit_data['id'] = sqlite_last_insert_rowid( $GLOBALS['dbres'] );
51: }
52: ?>
```

We generate an SQLite resource variable using a convenience function called connect(), declared on line 27. This opens the database file on line 28, checking that a valid resource has been created on line 29 (you can read more about working with SQLite in Hour 13, "Database Integration—SQL"). We also create the 'track_visit' table on line 39 by passing a SQL CREATE statement to the sqlite_query() function. If the table already exists, a warning is generated, so we suppress this by adding an "at" character to the function call, like so:

```
@sqlite_query( $dbres, $create );
```

The connect() function returns a SQLite resource value that is stored in a global variable called $GLOBALS['dbres']. This is accessed by all functions that work with the database. On line 3, we attempt to extract the 'visit_id' element from the $_COOKIE array and assign it to a variable: $visit_id. On line 4, we test $visit_id. If the variable is empty, we assume that we are dealing with a new user, calling a function we have named newuser().

newuser() is declared on line 12, requires no arguments, and returns an array of the values we will add to our table. Within the function, we create an array called $visit_data on line 13. We set the first_visit and last_visit elements to the current time in seconds. Because this is the first visit, we set the num_visits and total_clicks elements to 1. No time has elapsed in this visit, so we set total_duration to 0.

On line 21 we call the insert_visit() function (declared on line 43) that accepts the $visit_data array and uses its elements to create a new row in our table, setting each field to the value of the element of the same name. Notice that we use the built-in implode() function on line 45 to construct our SQL statement. Because the id field autoincrements, this does not need to be inserted. We can subsequently access the value set for id using the sqlite_last_insert_rowid () function on line 50. Now that we have an ID for our new visitor, we add this to our $visit_data array, which then accurately reflects the visitor's row in the SQLite table. The $visit_data array was passed to insert_visit() by reference, so the array we manipulate here is also referenced from the variable of the same name in the calling newuser() function.

Finally, in the newuser() function, we use setcookie() on line 22 to set a visit_id cookie and return the $visit_data array to the calling code on line 24.

The next time our visitor hits this script, the $visit_id variable will have been populated with the value of the visit_id cookie. Because this variable is set, the user will be welcomed and no action will be taken.

In fact, we will need to update information in the track_visit table if we detect the return of a known visitor. We will need to test whether the current request is part of an ongoing visit or represents the beginning of a new visit. We do this with a global variable that defines a time in seconds. If the time of the last request added to this interval is greater than the current time, we assume that the current request is part of a session in progress. Otherwise, we are welcoming back an old friend.

Listing 19.3 adds new functions to the code created in Listing 19.2.

LISTING 19.3   A Script to Track Users Using Cookies and a SQLite Database

```
 1: <?php
 2: $GLOBALS['slength']  = 300;
 3: $GLOBALS['dbres']    = connect( "data/testdb" );
 4: $GLOBALS['visit_id'] = $_COOKIE['visit_id'];
 5: $GLOBALS['user_stats'];
 6:
 7: if ( empty( $visit_id ) ) {
 8:   $user_stats = newuser( );
 9:   print "<p>Welcome, first time user!</p>";
10: } else {
11:   print "<p>Welcome back $visit_id</p>";
12:   $user_stats = olduser( $visit_id );
13: }
14:
15: function newuser( ) {
16:   $visit_data = array (
17:         'first_visit' => time(),
18:         'last_visit' => time(),
19:         'num_visits' => 1,
20:         'total_duration' => 0,
21:         'total_clicks' => 1
22:         );
23:
24:   insert_visit( $visit_data );
25:   setcookie( "visit_id", $visit_data['id'],
26:         time()+(60*60*24*365*10), "/" );
27:   return $visit_data;
28: }
29:
30: function olduser( $visit_id ) {
31:   $now = time();
32:   $visit_data = get_visit( $visit_id );
33:   if ( ! $visit_data ) {
34:     return newuser( );
35:   }
36:   $visit_data['total_clicks']++;
37:   if ( ( $visit_data['last_visit'] + $GLOBALS['slength'] ) > $now ) {
38:     $visit_data['total_duration'] +=
39:           ( $now - $visit_data['last_visit'] );
40:   } else {
41:     $visit_data['num_visits']++;
42:   }
43:   $visit_data['last_visit'] = $now;
44:   update_visit( $visit_data );
45:   return $visit_data;
46: }
47:
48: function connect( $db ) {
49:   $dbres = sqlite_open($db, 0, $error);
50:   if ( ! is_resource( $dbres ) ) {
51:     die( "sqlite error: $error" );
52:   }
53:   $create = "CREATE TABLE track_visit (
54:         id INTEGER PRIMARY KEY,
55:         first_visit INTEGER,
56:         last_visit INTEGER,
```

LISTING 19.3 Continued

```
57:           num_visits INTEGER,
58:           total_duration INTEGER,
59:           total_clicks INTEGER)";
60:    @sqlite_query( $dbres, $create );
61:    return $dbres;
62: }
63:
64: function get_visit( $visit_id ) {
65:    $query = "SELECT * FROM track_visit WHERE id=$visit_id";
66:    $result = sqlite_query( $GLOBALS['dbres'], $query );
67:
68:    if ( ! sqlite_num_rows( $result ) ) {
69:      return false;
70:    }
71:    return sqlite_fetch_array( $result, SQLITE_ASSOC );
72: }
73:
74: function update_visit( &$visit_data ) {
75:    $update_pairs = array();
76:    foreach( $visit_data as $field=>$val ) {
77:      if ( ! is_int( $field ) ) {
78:        array_push( $update_pairs, "$field=$val" );
79:      }
80:    }
81:    $query = "UPDATE track_visit SET ";
82:    $query .= implode( ", ", $update_pairs );
83:    $query .= " WHERE id=".$visit_data['id'];
84:    sqlite_query( $GLOBALS['dbres'], $query );
85: }
86:
87: function insert_visit( &$visit_data ) {
88:    $query = "INSERT INTO track_visit ( ";
89:    $query .= implode( ", ", array_keys( $visit_data ) );
90:    $query .= " ) VALUES( ";
91:    $query .= implode(", ", array_values( $visit_data ) );
92:    $query .= " );";
93:    $result = sqlite_query( $GLOBALS['dbres'], $query );
94:    $visit_data['id'] = sqlite_last_insert_rowid( $GLOBALS['dbres'] );
95: }
96: ?>
```

By the Way

Remember that you can alter the length of a session timeout in Listing 19.3 by changing the value of $GLOBALS['slength'] on line 2. This global variable defines the interval of time (in seconds) that the script will accept before declaring one visit over and another started. Although the value of 300 that we use would be acceptable in a real-world situation, you might want to set a smaller value (such as 30) for testing purposes, like this:

```
$GLOBALS['slength'] = 30;
```

We add a new global variable to the script called $slength on line 2. This defines the interval after which we assume that a new visit is taking place. If the

$visit_id variable contains a value, we know that the cookie was in place. We call the olduser() function on line 10, passing it the $visit_id variable.

Within the olduser() function, we first acquire visit data by calling the get_visit() function on line 32. get_visit() is declared on line 64 and requires the visit ID, which it stores in an argument variable called $visit_id. This is used to extract the relevant row from the track_visit table using sqlite_query() on line 66. Assuming we have located the row in our table that matches the visit_id cookie, we use sqlite_fetch_array() on line 71 to populate to return an associative array. The calling code on line 32 assigns this associative array to the $visit_data variable. The olduser() function should now have a populated $visit_data array containing fields for all the columns in our table. If not, we give up and call newuser() (line 34), which adds a row to the database.

On line 37, we test whether the value of the $visit_data['last_visit'] element added to the interval stored in $GLOBALS['slength'] is greater than the current time. If so, fewer than $GLOBALS['slength'] seconds have elapsed since the last hit and we can assume that this request is part of a current session. We therefore add the time elapsed since the last hit to the $visit_data['total_duration'] element on line 38.

If the request represents a new visit, we increment $visit_data['num_visits'] on line 41.

Finally, we pass $visit_data to update_visit() on line 44. update_visit() is declared on line 67 and constructs a SQL UPDATE statement by looping through the altered values in the array. The statement is passed to sqlite_query() on line 84 to update the user's row in the track_visit table. olduser(), the function that called update_visit() on line 44, returns the altered $visit_data array to the calling code.

Now that we've created the code, we should create a quick function to demonstrate it in action. The outputStats() function simply calculates the current user's averages and prints the result to the browser. In reality, you would probably want to create some analysis screens for your client, which would collate overall information. Listing 19.4 creates the outputStats() function. The code from previous examples is incorporated into this script using an include() statement.

LISTING 19.4   A Script to Output Usage Statistics Gathered in Listing 19.3

```
1: <?php
2: include("listing19.3.php");
3: outputStats();
4: function outputStats() {
5:   global $user_stats;
6:   $clicks = sprintf( "%.2f",
7:        ($user_stats['total_clicks']/$user_stats['num_visits']) );
8:   $duration = sprintf( "%.2f",
```

LISTING 19.4   Continued

```
 9:            ($user_stats['total_duration']/$user_stats['num_visits']) );
10:    print "<p>Hello! Your id is ".$user_stats['id']."</p>\n\n";
11:    print "<p>You have visited
12:            ".$user_stats['num_visits']." time(s)</p>\n\n";
13:    print "<p>Av clicks per visit: $clicks</p>\n\n";
14:    print "<p>Av duration of visit: $duration seconds</p>\n\n";
15: }
16: ?>
```

Figure 19.1 shows the output from Listing 19.4. We use an include() statement on line 2 to call the tracking code we have written. We will be including a similar line on every page of our client's site. The outputStats() function called on line 3 and declared on line 4 works with the global $user_stats array variable. This was returned by either newuser() or olduser() and contains the same information as our user's row in the track_visit table.

On line 6, to calculate the user's average number of clicks, we divide the $user_stats['total_clicks'] element by the number of visits we have detected. Similarly on line 8, we divide the $user_stats['total_duration'] element by the same figure. We use sprint() to round the results to two decimal places. All that remains is to write a report to the browser.

FIGURE 19.1
Reporting usage
statistics

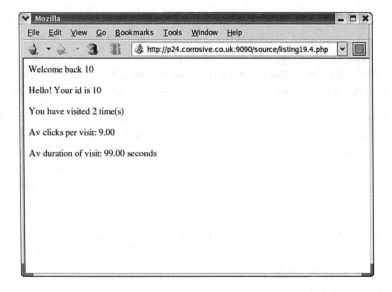

We could, of course, extend this example to track user preference on a site, as well as to log browser types and IP addresses. Imagine a site that analyzes a user's movements and emphasizes content according to the links he chooses.

Working with the Query String

The great drawback of the cookie is its dependence on the client. Not only are you at the mercy of the user, who might choose not to allow cookies, but you must also rely on the browser's implementation of the standard. Some browsers have documented bugs concerning the way they deal with cookies. If you want to save state only for a single session, you might decide to use a more traditional approach.

When you submit a form using the GET method, its fields and values are URL encoded and appended to the URL to which the form is sent. They then become available to the server and your scripts. Assuming a form with two fields, user_id and name, the query string should end up looking something like the following:

```
http://p24.corrosive.co.uk/qstring.php?name=344343&user_id=matt+zandstra
```

Each name and value is separated by an equals (=) sign, and each name/value pair is separated by an ampersand (&). PHP decodes this string and makes each of the pairs available in the superglobal $_GET array which stores all arguments submitted via a GET request. So, to access the user_id GET parameter, you would use the $_GET array like this:

```
$_GET['user_id'];
```

You are not limited to using forms to send query strings. You can build your own relatively easily and in so doing pass substantial amounts of information from page to page.

Creating a Query String

To create a query string, you need to be able to URL encode the keys and values you want to include. Assume that we want to pass a URL to another page as part of a query string. The forward slashes and the colon in a full URL would create ambiguity for a parser. We must therefore convert the URL into hexadecimal characters. We can do this using PHP's urlencode() function, which accepts a string and returns an encoded copy:

```
print urlencode("http://p24.corrosive.co.uk");
// prints http%3A%2F%2Fp24.corrosive.co.uk
```

Now that you can URL encode text, you can build your own query string. The following fragment builds a query string from two variables:

```
<?php
$interest = "arts";
$homepage = "http://p24.corrosive.co.uk";
$query = "homepage=".urlencode( $homepage );
```

```
$query .= "&interest=".urlencode( $interest );
?>
<a href="newpage.php?<?php print $query ?>">Go</a>
```

The URL in the link reaches the browser including an encoded query string:

```
newpage.php?homepage=http%3A%2F%2Fp24.corrosive.co.uk&interest=arts
```

The `homepage` and `interest` parameters become available within `newpage.php` as global variables.

This approach is clumsy, however. Because we have hard-coded variable names into the query string, we cannot reuse the code easily. To pass information effectively from page to page, we need to make it easy to embed names and values into a link and generate a query string automatically. This is especially important if we are to maintain the benefit of PHP that it is easy for a nonprogrammer to work around.

As of PHP 5, a new function was introduced to automate this process: `http_build_query()` accepts an associative array or object and returns a URL-encoded string suitable for adding to a URL in your script.

In Listing 19.5, we use the `http_build_query()` method to build a query string dynamically.

LISTING 19.5   A Function to Build Query Strings

```
 1: <!DOCTYPE html PUBLIC
 2:    "-//W3C//DTD XHTML 1.0 Strict//EN"
 3:    "http://www.w3.org/TR/xhtml1/DTD/xhtml1-strict.dtd">
 4: <html>
 5: <head>
 6: <title>Listing 19.5 Using http_build_query() to Build Query Strings</title>
 7: </head>
 8: <body>
 9: <?php
10: $q = array (
11:     'name' => "Arthur Harold Smith",
12:     'interest' => "Cinema (mainly art house)",
13:     'homepage' => "http://p24.corrosive.co.uk/harold/"
14:     );
15: $query = http_build_query( $q );
16: print $query;
17:
18: // prints name=Arthur+Harold+Smith&interest=Cinema+%28mainly+art+house
19: //    %29&homepage=http%3A%2F%2Fp24.corrosive.co.uk%2Fharold%2F
20:
21: ?>
22: <p>
23: <a href="anotherpage.php?<?php print $query ?>">Go!</a>
24: </p>
25: </body>
26: </html>
```

We construct an array on line 10 with elements 'name', 'interest', and 'homepage'. We then pass the array to http_build_query() on line 15, storing the returned string in a variable called $query. As a test, we print $query to the browser before using the query string in a link on line 23.

Using this function, we can pass information between pages with the minimum of PHP code within HTML elements.

Summary

This hour looked at the two ways of passing information between requests. You can use these to create multiscreen applications and sophisticated environments that respond to user preferences.

You learned how to use the setcookie() function to set cookies on the user's browser. Developing this, you saw how a database could be used in conjunction with cookies to store information about a user between sessions. You learned about query strings and how to encode them, and you developed a function to automate their creation.

PHP is nothing if not versatile, and in the next hour you will examine some built-in functions for automating many of the tasks in this chapter.

Q&A

Q *Are any serious security or privacy issues raised by cookies?*

A A server can access only a cookie set from its own domain. Although a cookie can be stored on the user's hard drive, there is no other access to the user's file system. You can, however, set a cookie in response to a request for an image. So, if many sites include images served from a third-party ad server or counter script, the third party might be able to track a user across multiple domains.

Q *The query string looks ugly in the browser window. Would it be true to say that cookies are the neatest way of saving state?*

A Unfortunately, it isn't that simple. At best, cookies are a transparent way of saving state. Some users, however, set their browsers to warn them every time a cookie is set. These users are likely to find a site that saves state information frequently somewhat frustrating.

Workshop

Quiz

1. Which function is designed to allow you to set a cookie on a visitor's browser?

2. How would you delete a cookie?

3. Which function could you use to escape a string for inclusion in a query string?

4. Which element in the $_SERVER array can contain the raw query string?

5. The name/value pairs submitted as part of a query string will be included in a built-in associative array. What is its name?

Answers

1. The setcookie() function enables you to set a cookie (although you could also output a Set-Cookie header using the header() function).

2. You can delete a cookie by calling setcookie() with a date that has already passed.

3. The urlencode() function translates a string so that it can be included in a query string.

4. The entire query string is made available to you in the $_SERVER['QUERY_STRING'] element.

5. The $_GET array contains the name/value pairs submitted as part of a query string.

Exercises

1. Create a user preference form in which a user can choose a page color and enter a name. Use a cookie to ensure that the user is greeted by name on subsequent pages and that the page is set to the color of her choice.

2. Amend the scripts you created in exercise 1 so that the information is stored in a query string rather than a cookie.

HOUR 20

Saving State with Session Functions

What You'll Learn in This Hour:

- ▶ What session variables are and how they work
- ▶ How to start or resume a session
- ▶ How to work with variables in a session
- ▶ How to destroy a session
- ▶ How to unset session variables

In the previous hour, we looked at saving state from page to page, using a cookie or a query string. Once again, PHP is one step ahead of us. As of PHP 4, functions for managing user sessions were built in to the language. These use techniques similar to those explored in the previous hour but build them into the language, making saving state as easy as calling a function.

What Are Session Functions?

Session functions implement a concept you have already seen. That is the provision to users of a unique identifier, which can then be used from access to access to acquire information linked to that ID. The difference is that most of the work is already done for you. When a user accesses a session-enabled page, she will either be allocated a new identifier or reassociated with one that has already been established for her in a previous access. Any variables that have been associated with the session become available to your code. If the `php.ini` `register_globals` directive is set, session data becomes available in the global namespace. Otherwise, you can access them through the superglobal `$_SESSION` associative array. Remember that `register_globals` is disabled by default, so it is generally the best policy to work with the `$_SESSION` array.

Both the techniques for transmitting information from request to request that you looked at in the previous hour are automatically supported by PHP's session functions. Cookies are used by default, but you can ensure success for all clients by encoding the session ID into all links in your session-enabled pages.

Session state is usually stored in a temporary file, although you can implement database storage using a function called `session_set_save_handler()`. `session_set_save_handler()` is beyond the scope of this book, but you can get more information at `http://www.php.net/manual/en/function.session-set-save-handler.php`.

Starting a Session with `session_start()`

You need to explicitly start or resume a session unless you have changed your `php.ini` configuration file. By default, sessions do not start automatically. In `php.ini`, you will find a line containing the following:

```
session.auto_start = 0
```

By changing the value of `session.auto_start` to 1, you ensure that a session is initiated for every PHP document. If you don't change this setting, you need to call the `session_start()` function.

PHP uses files to store session data between requests so you should also check the `session.save_path` directive in your `php.ini` file. `session.save_path` defines the directory on your filesystem to which session files are saved. You should ensure that it exists and that your PHP process has permission to write to it:

```
session.save_path = "/tmp"
```

After a session has been started, you instantly have access to the user's session ID via the `session_id()` function. `session_id()` allows you to either set or get a session ID. Listing 20.1 starts a session and prints the session ID to the browser.

LISTING 20.1   Starting or Resuming a Session

```
1: <?php
2: session_start();
3: ?>
4: <!DOCTYPE html PUBLIC
5:    "-//W3C//DTD XHTML 1.0 Strict//EN"
6:    "http://www.w3.org/TR/xhtml1/DTD/xhtml1-strict.dtd">
7: <html>
8: <head>
9: <title>Listing 20.1 Starting or Resuming a Session</title>
```

LISTING 20.1   Continued

```
10: </head>
11: <body>
12: <?php
13: print "<p>Welcome, your session ID is ".session_id()."</p>\n\n";
14: ?>
15: </body>
16: </html>
```

When this script is run for the first time from a browser, a session ID is generated by the session_start() function call on line 2. If the page is later reloaded or revisited, the same session ID is allocated to the user. This presupposes, of course, that the user has cookies enabled on his browser. If you examine headers output by the script in Listing 20.1, you can see the cookie being set:

```
HTTP/1.1 200 OK
Date: Tue, 26 Aug 2003 16:54:44 GMT
Server: Apache/2.0.47 (Unix) PHP/5.0.0b1
X-Powered-By: PHP/5.0.0b1
Set-Cookie: PHPSESSID=b3228ce5e66834bc2ced42a899328796; path=/
Expires: Thu, 19 Nov 1981 08:52:00 GMT
Cache-Control: no-store, no-cache, must-revalidate, post-check=0, pre-check=0
Pragma: no-cache
Connection: close
Content-Type: text/html; charset=ISO-8859-1
```

Because start_session() attempts to set a cookie when initiating a session for the first time, you need to call it before you output anything else to the browser. Notice that no expiry date is set in the cookie that PHP sets for the session. This means that the session remains current only as long as the browser is active. When the user restarts his browser, the cookie is not stored. You can change this behavior by altering the session.cookie_lifetime setting in your php.ini file. This defaults to 0, but you can set an expiry period in seconds. This causes an expiry date to be set for any session cookies sent to the browser.

Working with Session Variables

Accessing a unique identifier on each of your PHP documents is only the start of PHP's session functionality. You can set any number of variables as elements of the superglobal $_SESSION array. After these are set, they are available to future requests in the session.

Listing 20.2 registers two variables with a session (lines 10 and 11).

LISTING 20.2 Registering Variables with a Session

```
 1: <?php
 2: session_start();
 3: ?>
 4: <!DOCTYPE html PUBLIC
 5:   "-//W3C//DTD XHTML 1.0 Strict//EN"
 6:   "http://www.w3.org/TR/xhtml1/DTD/xhtml1-strict.dtd">
 7: <html>
 8: <head>
 9: <title>Listing 20.2 Registering Variables with a Session</title>
10: </head>
11: <body>
12: <div>
13: <?php
14: $_SESSION['product1'] = "Sonic Screwdriver";
15: $_SESSION['product2'] = "HAL 2000";
16: print "The products have been registered";
17: ?>
18: </div>
19: </body>
20: </html>
```

The magic in Listing 20.2 will not become apparent until the user moves to a new page. Listing 20.3 creates a separate PHP script that accesses the variables registered in Listing 20.2 (line 11).

LISTING 20.3 Accessing Session Variables

```
 1: <?php
 2: session_start();
 3: ?>
 4: <!DOCTYPE html PUBLIC
 5:   "-//W3C//DTD XHTML 1.0 Strict//EN"
 6:   "http://www.w3.org/TR/xhtml1/DTD/xhtml1-strict.dtd">
 7: <html>
 8: <head>
 9: <title>Listing 20.3 Accessing Session Variables</title>
10: </head>
11: <body>
12: <div>
13: <?php
14: print "Your chosen products are:\n\n";
15: ?>
16: <ul>
17: <li><?php print $_SESSION['product1'] ?></li>
18: <li><?php print $_SESSION['product2'] ?></li>
19: </ul>
20: </div>
21: </body>
22: </html>
```

Figure 20.1 shows the output from Listing 20.3. As you can see, you have access to the product1 and product2 elements of the $_SESSION array in an entirely new page.

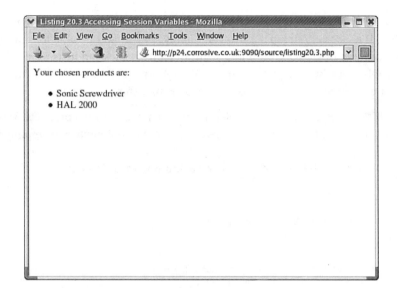

FIGURE 20.1
Accessing session variables.

So, how does the magic work? Behind the scenes, PHP is writing to a temporary file. You can find out where this is being written on your system with the session_save_path() function, which optionally accepts a path to a directory and then writes all session files to this. If you pass it no arguments, it returns a string representing the current directory to which session files are saved. On my system

```
print session_save_path();
```

prints /tmp. A glance at my /tmp directory reveals a number of files with names like the following:

```
sess_2638864e9216fee10fcb8a61db382909
sess_76cae8ac1231b11afa2c69935c11dd95
sess_bb50771a769c605ab77424d59c784ea0
```

Opening the file that matches the session ID I was allocated when I first ran Listing 20.1, I can see how the registered variables have been stored:

```
product1¦s:17:"Sonic Screwdriver";product2¦s:8:"HAL 2000";
```

When an element is added to the $_SESSION array, PHP writes the element name and value to a file. This can be read later, and the element resurrected.

After you have created a session element, you can amend it at will during the execution of your script, and the altered value is reflected in the session file.

The example in Listing 20.2 demonstrates the process of registering elements with a session. It is not very flexible, however. Ideally, you should be able to register a varying number of values. You might want to let users pick products from a list, for example. Luckily, $_SESSION elements do not have to be scalars. You can add arrays or even objects and their data is encoded and stored for you.

Listing 20.4 creates a form that enables a user to choose multiple products. You should then be able to use session elements to create a rudimentary shopping cart.

LISTING 20.4   Registering an Array Variable with a Session

```
 1: <?php
 2: session_start();
 3:
 4: if ( empty( $_SESSION['products'] ) ) {
 5:   $_SESSION['products']=array();
 6: }
 7:
 8: if ( is_array( $_REQUEST['form_products'] ) ) {
 9:   $_SESSION['products'] = array_unique(
10:     array_merge( $_SESSION['products'],
11:           $_REQUEST['form_products'] )
12:   );
13: }
14: ?>
15: <!DOCTYPE html PUBLIC
16:   "-//W3C//DTD XHTML 1.0 Strict//EN"
17:   "http://www.w3.org/TR/xhtml1/DTD/xhtml1-strict.dtd">
18: <html>
19: <head>
20: <title>Listing 20.4 Registering an Array Element with a Session</title>
21: </head>
22: <body>
23: <div>
24: <h1>Product Choice Page</h1>
25: <form action="<?php print $_SERVER['PHP_SELF']?>" method="post">
26: <p>
27: <select name="form_products[]" multiple="multiple" size="3">
28: <option>Sonic Screwdriver</option>
29: <option>Hal 2000</option>
30: <option>Tardis</option>
31: <option>ORAC</option>
32: <option>Transporter bracelet</option>
33: </select>
34: </p>
35: <p>
36: <input type="submit" value="choose" />
37: </p>
38: </form>
39: <a href="listing20.5.php">A content page</a>
40: </div>
41: </body>
42: </html>
```

We begin an HTML form on line 25 and, on line 27, create a `select` element named `form_products[]`, which contains `option` elements for several products. HTML form elements that allow multiple selections should have square brackets appended to the value of their `name` arguments. This makes the user's choices available in an array.

We start or resume a session with `session_start()` on line 2. This should give us access to any previously set session elements. We test the `$_SESSION['products']` element on line 4, setting it as an empty array if it does not already exist. We then test the superglobal `$_REQUEST` array for the presence of the `form_products` array element (line 8). If the array is present, we can assume that the form has been submitted and go on to assign any new items to the `$_SESSION['products']` array. We do this in a single statement, merging the `$_REQUEST['form_products']` array with `$_SESSION['products']` and assigning the unique elements back to `$_SESSION['products']` (lines 9–11). Note that in this example code, we do not check user input. In a real-world situation, we would not blindly assign user input to a session but would first check all input against an array of acceptable values.

At the end of Listing 20.4 (line 39), a link to another script is used to demonstrate our access to the products the user has chosen. We create this new script in Listing 20.5.

LISTING 20.5   Accessing Session Variables

```
 1: <?php
 2: session_start();
 3: ?>
 4: <!DOCTYPE html PUBLIC
 5:   "-//W3C//DTD XHTML 1.0 Strict//EN"
 6:   "http://www.w3.org/TR/xhtml1/DTD/xhtml1-strict.dtd">
 7: <html>
 8: <head>
 9: <title>Listing 20.5 Accessing Session Elements</title>
10: </head>
11: <body>
12: <div>
13: <h1>A Content Page</h1>
14: <?php
15: if ( is_array( $_SESSION['products'] ) ) {
16:   print "<b>Your cart:</b><ol>\n";
17:   foreach ( $_SESSION['products'] as $p ) {
18:     print "<li>$p</li>";
19:   }
20:   print "</ol>";
21: }
22: ?>
23: <a href="listing20.4.php">Back to product choice page</a>
24: </div>
25: </body>
26: </html>
```

Again, we use `session_start()` to resume the session (line 2). We test for the presence of the `products` session element on line 15. If it exists, we loop through it on line 17, printing each of the user's chosen items to the browser.

For a real shopping cart program, of course, you would keep product details in a database and test user input, rather than blindly storing and presenting it, but Listings 20.4 and 20.5 demonstrate the ease with which you can use session functions to access array variables set in other pages.

Destroying Sessions and Unsetting Elements

You can use `session_destroy()` to end a session, erasing all session variables. `session_destroy()` requires no arguments. You should have an established session for this function to work as expected. The following code fragment resumes a session and abruptly destroys it:

```
session_start();
session_destroy();
```

When you move on to other pages that work with a session, the session you have destroyed will not be available to them, forcing them to initiate new sessions of their own. Any variables that have been registered will have been lost.

However, `session_destroy()` does not instantly destroy elements of the $_SESSION array. These remain accessible to the script in which `session_destroy()` is called (until it is reloaded). The following code fragment resumes or initiates a session and registers a session element called `test`, which we set to 5. Destroying the session does not destroy the registered variable:

```
session_start();
$_SESSION['test'] = 5;
session_destroy();
print $_SESSION['test']; // prints 5
```

To remove all $_SESSION elements, you should simply assign an empty array to the variable, like so:

```
session_start();
$_SESSION['test'] = 5;
session_destroy();
$_SESSION=array();
print $_SESSION['test']; // prints nothing. The test element is no more
```

You can remove individual elements by calling unset() on them, like so:

```
unset( $_SESSION['test'] );
```

Passing Session IDs in the Query String

So far, you have relied on a cookie to save the session ID between script requests.
On its own, this is not the most reliable way of saving state because you cannot
be sure that the browser will accept cookies. You can build in a failsafe, however,
by passing the session ID from script to script embedded in a query string. PHP
makes a name/value pair available in a constant called SID if a cookie value for
a session ID cannot be found. You can add this string to any HTML links in session-enabled pages:

```
<a href="anotherpage.html?<?php print SID; ?>">Another page</a>
```

will reach the browser as

```
<a href="anotherpage.html?
➥PHPSESSID=08ecedf79fe34561fa82591401a01da1">Another page</a>
```

The session ID passed in this way is automatically recognized in the target page
when session_start() is called, and you have access to session variables in the
usual way.

If the php.ini directive session.use_trans_sid is set to on, this query string is
automatically added to every link in your pages. This option is disabled by
default, however, so explicitly adding the SID constant to links makes your scripts
more portable.

There are security issues with regard to session IDs in query strings. Links pasted
into emails by users or left in the history of a browser could be hijacked by third
parties. If you use session IDs in URLs, you should be aware of this risk. Consider
implementing an expiry scheme for sessions that have been idle for longer than a
fixed length of time, or even requiring your users to enable cookies.

Encoding and Decoding Session Variables

You have already seen the way in which PHP encodes and saves (serializes) session variables when you peeked into a session file. You can, in fact, gain access to
the encoded string at any time with session_encode(). This can be useful in
debugging your session-enabled environments. You can use session_encode() to
reveal the state of all session variables:

```
session_start();
print session_encode()."<br/>";
// sample output: products¦a:2:{i:0;s:8:"Hal 2000";i:1;s:6:"Tardis";}
```

From the sample output in the previous fragment, you can see the session variables that are stored. You can use this information to check that variables are being registered and updated as you expect. session_encode() is also useful if you need to freeze-dry session variables for storage in a database or file.

After having extracted an encoded string, you can decode it and resurrect its values using session_decode(). The following code fragment demonstrates this process:

```
session_start();
$_SESSION = array(); // there should now be no session variables
session_decode( "products¦a:2:{i:0;s:8:\"Hal 2000\";i:1;s:6:\"Tardis\";}" );
foreach ( $_SESSION['products'] as $p ) {
  print "$p<br/>\n";
}
// Output:
// Hal 2000
// Tardis
```

We start a session as usual. To ensure that we are working with a blank canvas, we clear all session elements by assigning an empty array to $_SESSION. We then pass an encoded string to session_decode(). Rather than returning values, session_decode() populates the $_SESSION array with the unserialized variables. We confirm this by looping through the newly resurrected $_SESSION['products'] array.

Summary

In this hour and the previous hour, you learned different ways of saving state in a stateless protocol. All methods use some combination of cookies and query strings, sometimes combined with the use of files or databases. These approaches all have their benefits and problems.

A cookie is not intrinsically reliable and cannot store much information. On the other hand, it can persist over a long period of time.

Approaches that write information to a file or database involve some cost to speed that might become a problem on a popular site. Nonetheless, a simple ID can unlock large amounts of data stored on disk.

A query string is unlikely to persist as a cookie will and looks ugly in the location window. Even so, it can pass relatively large amounts of information from request to request. The choice you make depends on the circumstances of your project.

In this hour, you learned how to initiate or resume a session with session_start(). Once in a session, you can register variables with it using the $_SESSION array and access session elements from request to request. You should be able to destroy a session with session_destroy().

To ensure that as many users as possible get the benefit of your session-enabled environment, you can now use the SID constant to pass a session ID to the server as part of a query string.

In the next hour, you examine ways that you can use PHP to access other tools on your server.

Q&A

Q *Are there any pitfalls with session functions I should be aware of?*

A The session functions are generally reliable. However, remember that cookies cannot be read across multiple domains, so if your project uses more than one domain name on the same server (perhaps as part of an e-commerce environment), you might need to consider disabling cookies for sessions by setting the session.use_cookies directive to 0 in the php.ini file.

Workshop

Quiz

1. Which function would you use to start or resume a session?

2. Which function contains the current session's ID?

3. How can you associate a variable with a session?

4. How would you end a session and erase all traces of it for future visits?

5. How would you destroy session variables both within the current script and the session?

6. What does the SID constant return?

Answers

1. You can start a session with the `session_start()` function.

2. You can access the session's ID with the `session_id()` function.

3. You set an element in the superglobal `$_SESSION` array.

4. The `session_destroy()` function removes all traces of a session for future requests.

5. You can unset session elements by unsetting all elements of the `$_SESSION` array, like so:

   ```
   $_SESSION = array();
   ```

6. If cookies are not available, the `SID` constant contains a name/value pair that can be incorporated in a query string. This will pass the session ID from script request to script request.

Exercises

1. In the previous hour's "Exercises" section, you created a script that uses a cookie or query string to save user preferences from page to page. Each page in the environment should display a user-defined background color and greet the user by name. Re-create this using PHP's session functions.

2. Create a script that uses session functions to remember which pages in your environment the user has visited. Provide the user with a list of links on each page to make it easy for her to retrace her steps.

Working with the Server Environment

What You'll Learn in This Hour:

▶ How to pipe data to and from external applications

▶ Other ways of sending shell commands and displaying the results on the browser

▶ The security implications of interprocess communication from a PHP script

In previous hours, we have looked at techniques for communicating with remote machines and gaining input from the user. In this hour, we look outward again, this time at some techniques for running external programs on your own machine. The examples in this hour are designed for Unix operating systems, but most of the principles hold true for Windows.

Opening Pipes to and from Processes with popen() and proc_open()

Just as you open a file for writing or reading with fopen(), you can open a pipe to a process with popen(). popen() requires the path to a command and a string representing a mode (read or write). It returns a file pointer that can be used similarly to the file pointer returned by fopen(). You can pass popen() one of two mode flags: "w" to write to the process and "r" to read from it. You cannot, however, both read and write to a process in the same connection.

When you have finished working with the file handle returned by popen(), you must close the connection by calling pclose(), which requires a valid file handler.

Reading from popen() is useful when you want to parse the output from a process on a line-by-line basis. Listing 21.1 opens a connection to the GNU version of the who command and parses its output, adding a mailto link to each username.

LISTING 21.1   Using popen() to Read the Output of the Unix who Command

```
 1: <!DOCTYPE html PUBLIC
 2:   "-//W3C//DTD XHTML 1.0 Strict//EN"
 3:   "http://www.w3.org/TR/xhtml1/DTD/xhtml1-strict.dtd">
 4: <html>
 5: <head>
 6: <title>Listing 21.1 Using popen() to Read the
 7:    Output of the Unix 'who' Command</title>
 8: </head>
 9: <body>
10: <div>
11: <h1>Administrators currently logged on to the server</h1>
12: <?php
13: $ph = popen( "who", "r" )
14:    or die( "Couldn't open connection to 'who' command" );
15: $host="corrosive.co.uk";
16: while ( ! feof( $ph ) ) {
17:    $line = fgets( $ph, 1024 );
18:    if ( strlen( $line ) <= 1 ) {
19:      continue;
20:    }
21:    $line = preg_replace( "/^(\S+).*/",
22:        "<a href=\"mailto:$1@$host\">$1</a><br />\n",
23:        $line );
24:    print "$line";
25: }
26: pclose( $ph );
27: ?>
28: </div>
29: </body>
30: </html>
```

We acquire a file pointer from popen() on line 13 and then use a while statement on line 16 to read each line of output from the process. If the output is a single character, we skip the rest of the current iteration (lines 14 and 15). Otherwise, we use preg_replace() on line 21 to add an HTML link to the string before printing the line on line 24. Finally, we close the connection with pclose() on line 26. Figure 21.1 shows sample output from Listing 21.1.

You can also use a connection established with popen() to write to a process. This is useful for commands that accept data from standard input in addition to command-line arguments. Listing 21.2 opens a connection to the column application using popen().

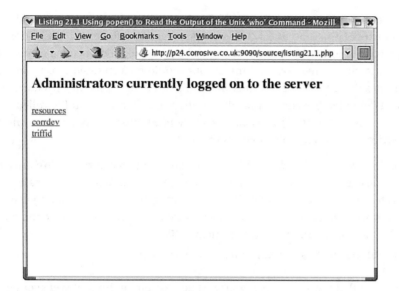

FIGURE 21.1
Reading the output
of the Unix who
command.

LISTING 21.2   Using `popen()` to Pass Data to the `column` Application

```
1: <!DOCTYPE html PUBLIC
2:    "-//W3C//DTD XHTML 1.0 Strict//EN"
3:    "http://www.w3.org/TR/xhtml1/DTD/xhtml1-strict.dtd">
4: <html>
5: <head>
6: <title>Listing 21.2 Using popen() to Pass
7:    Data to the 'column' Command</title>
8: </head>
9: <body>
10: <div>
11: <?php
12: $products = array(
13:     array( "HAL 2000", 2, "red" ),
14:     array( "Tricorder", 3, "blue" ),
15:     array( "ORAC AI", 1, "pink" ),
16:     array( "Sonic Screwdriver", 1, "orange"  )
17:     );
18: $ph = popen( "column -tc 3 -s / > purchases/user3.txt", "w" )
19:   or die( "Couldn't open connection to 'column' command" );
20: foreach ( $products as $prod ) {
21:    fputs( $ph, join('/', $prod)."\n");
22: }
23: pclose( $ph );
24: ?>
25: </div>
26: </body>
27: </html>
```

The purpose of the script in Listing 21.2 is to take the elements of a multidimensional array (defined on line 12) and output them to a file as an ASCII table. We open a connection to the `column` command on line 18, adding some command-line arguments. `-t` requires that the output should be formatted as a table, `-c 3` determines the number of columns we require, and `-s /` sets the "/" character as the field delimiter. We ensure that the results will be written to a file called `user3.txt`. Note that the `purchases` directory must exist on your system and that your script must be capable of writing to it.

Notice that we are doing more than one thing with this command. We are calling the `column` command and writing its output to a file. In fact, we are issuing commands to a noninteractive shell. This means that, in addition to piping content to a process, we can initiate other processes as well. We could even have the output of the `column` command mailed to someone, like so:

```
popen( "column -tc 3 -s / | mail matt@corrosive.co.uk", "w" )
```

This level of flexibility can open your system to a grave threat if you ever pass user input to a PHP function that issues shell commands. We will look at precautions you can take later in the hour.

Having acquired a pipe resource, we loop through the `$product` array on line 20. Each value is itself an array, which we convert to a string using the `join()` function on line 21. Rather than joining on a space character, we join on the delimiter we established as part of our command-line arguments. Using the "/" character to join the array is necessary because the spaces in the product array would otherwise confuse the `column` command. Having joined the array, we pass the resultant string and a newline character to the `fputs()` function.

Finally, we close the connection. Taking a peek into the `user3.txt` file, we should see the table neatly formatted:

```
HAL 2000        2 red
Tricorder       3 blue
ORAC AI         1 pink
Sonic Screwdriver 1 orange
```

We could have made the code more portable by formatting the text using the `sprintf()` function. This would be the preferred approach. Listing 21.2 illustrates a technique that can be useful either for working with third-party commands that have no equivalent within PHP or when you want to build a quick, nonportable script that uses system commands.

In some situations, you will need finer control of a child process. The proc_open()
function allows you to spawn a process, write to it, read from it, and read its error
output. proc_open() requires a string representing the process to start, an array of
descriptors that define modes of communication with the process, and an array
that's populated with pipes.

The array of descriptors should consist of three elements. Each element should
itself take the form of an array containing the string 'pipe' or 'file'. If the first
element is 'pipe', this descriptor represents a read or write pipe between the
process and the script and the second element should be either of 'r' for read or
'w' for write. If the first element is 'file', the descriptor represents a read from,
or write to, a file and the second element should be a path to a file. The third element should be 'r' for read, 'w' for write, or 'a' for append. Here's an example:

```
$descriptors = array( 0 => array( "pipe", r ),
            1 => array( "pipe", w ),
            2 => array( "file", "errors.txt", a )
          );
$proc = proc_open( "my_cmd", $descriptors, $pipes );
```

The $descriptors array in the previous fragment initializes two pipes. The first
pipe represents the standard input from which the process reads, and the second
pipe represents the standard output to which the process writes. The third element
represents a standard error. In this case, the process appends errors to file called
errors.txt. Notice that reading, writing, and appending are all defined from the
point of view of the process and not the script. We call proc_open(), passing it a
string pointing to a command called 'my_cmd', the $descriptor array, and an as-
yet-empty variable called $pipes. The proc_open() function returns a resource
and populates $pipes with an array of resources that mirror the $descriptors
array. We can write to $pipes[0] and read from $pipes[1] just as we would with
file resources. Errors are written to the 'errors.txt' file without our intervention:

```
fwrite( $pipes[0], "some input text" );
while ( ! feof( $pipes[1] ) ) {
  print fgets( $pipes[1], 1024 );
}
```

After we have written to our command and read from it we should close any
open pipes (in this case, the read and write pipes) before calling proc_close.
proc_close() requires a single argument: the resource returned by proc_open().
Here's the code:

```
fclose( $pipes[0] );
fclose( $pipes[1] );
proc_close( $proc );
```

Listing 21.3 creates a small class called Grepper that uses proc_open() to work with the standard Unix grep command.

LISTING 21.3   A Class That Uses proc_open()

```
 1: <?php
 2:
 3: class Grepper {
 4:   private static $descriptors = array( 0 => array( "pipe", r ),
 5:                         1 => array( "pipe", w ),
 6:                         2 => array( "pipe", w )
 7:                   );
 8:
 9:   static function grep ( $in, $arg ) {
10:     $proc = proc_open( "grep $arg", self::$descriptors, $pipes );
11:     if ( ! is_resource( $proc ) ) {
12:       throw new Exception( "proc_open did not return a resource" );
13:     }
14:     fwrite( $pipes[0], $in );
15:     fclose( $pipes[0] );
16:     while ( ! feof( $pipes[1] ) ) {
17:       $ret .= fgets($pipes[1], 1024);
18:     }
19:     fclose( $pipes[1] );
20:     try {
21:       self::checkError( $pipes[2] );
22:     } catch( Exception $e ) {
23:       throw $e;
24:     }
25:     proc_close( $proc );
26:     return $ret;
27:   }
28:
29:   static private function checkError( $pipe ) {
30:     $ret = "";
31:     while ( ! feof( $pipe ) ) {
32:       $ret .= fgets( $pipe );
33:     }
34:     fclose( $pipe );
35:     if ( $ret ) {
36:       throw new Exception( $ret );
37:     }
38:     return false;
39:   }
40: }
41:
42: $string = "mary had a little lamb\n";
43: $string .= "it's fleece was white as snow\n";
44: $string .= "and everywhere that mary went\n";
45: $string .= "the lamb was sure to go\n";
46:
47: try {
48:   print ( Grepper::grep( $string, "mary" ));
49: } catch ( Exception $e ) {
50:   print "error: ".$e->getMessage();
51: }
52: ?>
```

The Grepper class uses proc_open() to call the Unix command grep, which performs a fast search for patterns in strings or files. We set up our descriptors array on line 3, making the $descriptors property private and static. We make $descriptors static because we are going to allow our class to be called statically (that is without the need for creating a Grepper object). Notice that in this example, we are using a pipe for standard error rather than a file. The class has only one public method—grep()—which starts on line 9. The method requires a string to be searched, $in, and a string representing the pattern to find, $arg. Notice that we have declared it static. This means that client coders can call the grep() method using the Grepper class rather than a Grepper object, like this:

```
Grepper::grep( "search for gold", "gold" );
```

We call proc_open() on line 10, passing it the grep command and the client-supplied argument in a single string. We pass it the $descriptors property and an uninitialized $pipes variable.

We check that proc_open() returned a valid resource on line 11. If not, we throw an exception and thereby end method execution.

On line 14, we write the string to be searched to $pipe[0], passing the data to the grep command. We have nothing more to say to grep, so we close the pipe on line 15.

On lines 16–18 we read any output from grep, storing it in a return variable before closing the read pipe.

We call a method named checkError() on line 21, passing it our last remaining pipe: the error descriptor. The checkError() method simply reads from the pipe it is supplied (line 31). If it finds any content, it instantiates and throws an Exception object, which would be rethrown in the grep() method (line 23). In fact, we do not need to manually rethrow an exception. By failing to catch an exception in a method, we implicitly throw it back to the calling code. In Listing 21.3 we catch any Exception object thrown by checkError() and throw it manually to make our code clearer.

Assuming that checkError() does not throw an exception, the grep() method calls proc_close() on line 25 and returns the output it has gathered.

We test the class on line 42, creating a nursery rhyme string and passing it to the grep() method together with the search string "mary". We wrap the call to grep() in a try clause. If an exception is thrown, we output its message to the browser on line 50; otherwise, we print the results of the grep() method on line 48.

Running Commands with exec()

exec() is one of many functions that enable you to pass commands to the shell. The function requires a string representing the path to the command you want to run. It also optionally accepts an array variable that is populated with the command's output and a scalar variable that is populated with the command's return value.

To get a listing for the current working directory, for example, you might pass exec() the command "ls -al .". We do this in Listing 21.4 (line 7), printing the result to the browser.

LISTING 21.4   Using exec() to Produce a Directory Listing

```
 1: <!DOCTYPE html PUBLIC
 2:   "-//W3C//DTD XHTML 1.0 Strict//EN"
 3:   "http://www.w3.org/TR/xhtml1/DTD/xhtml1-strict.dtd">
 4: <html>
 5: <head>
 6: <title>Listing 21.4 Using exec() to Produce a Directory Listing</title>
 7: </head>
 8: <body>
 9: <div>
10: <?php
11: exec( "ls -al .", $output, $return );
12: print "<p>Returned: $return</p>";
13: foreach ( $output as $file ) {
14:   print "$file<br />";
15: }
16: ?>
17: </div>
18: </body>
19: </html>
```

Figure 21.2 shows the output from Listing 21.4.

Notice that the ls command returns 0 on success. If it were unable to find or read the directory passed to it, it would have returned 1.

Once again, we have reinvented the wheel to a certain extent with this example. We could have used the opendir() and readdir() functions to acquire a directory listing. Sometimes, however, a command on your system can achieve an effect that would take a long time to reproduce using PHP's functionality. You might have created a shell or Perl script that performs a complex task. If speed of development is an important factor in your project, you might decide that it is worth calling the external script instead of porting it to PHP, at least in the short term. Remember, though, that calling an external process always adds an overhead to your script in terms of both time and memory usage.

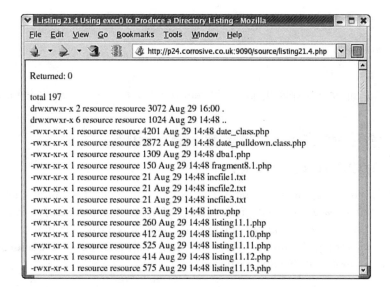

FIGURE 21.2
Using exec() to produce a directory listing.

Running External Commands with system() or the Backtick Operator

The system() function is similar to the exec() function in that it launches an external application. It requires the path to a command and, optionally, a variable, which is populated with the command's return value. system() prints the output of the shell command directly to the browser. The following code fragment prints the manual page for the man command itself:

```php
<?php
print "<pre>";
system( "man man | col -b", $return );
print "</pre>";
?>
```

We print pre tags to the browser to maintain the formatting of the page. We use system() to call man, piping the result through another application called col, which reformats the text for viewing as ASCII. We capture the return value of our shell command in the $return variable, and system() returns its output.

You can achieve a similar result by using the backtick operator. This involves surrounding a shell command in backtick (`) characters. The enclosed command is executed and any output is returned. You can print the output or store it in a variable.

We can re-create the previous example using backticks:

```
print "<pre>";
print `man man | col -b`;
print "</pre>";
```

Note that you must explicitly print the return value from the backtick operator.

Plugging Security Holes with
escapeshellcmd()

Before looking at escapeshellcmd(), let's examine the danger it guards against. We want to allow users to type in the names of manual pages and view output online. Now that we can output one manual page, it is a trivial matter to output any available page. Do not install the code in Listing 21.5; we are deliberately leaving a major security gap unplugged.

LISTING 21.5   Calling the man Command

```
 1: <!DOCTYPE html PUBLIC
 2:   "-//W3C//DTD XHTML 1.0 Strict//EN"
 3:   "http://www.w3.org/TR/xhtml1/DTD/xhtml1-strict.dtd">
 4: <html>
 5: <head>
 6: <title>Listing 21.5 Calling the 'man' Command.
 7:    This Script is NOT Secure</title>
 8: </head>
 9: <body>
10: <div>
11: <form action="<?php print $PHP_SELF ?>" method="post">
12: <p>
13: <input type="text" value="<?php print $_REQUEST['manpage'] ?>"
name="manpage" />
14: </p>
15: </form>
16: <pre>
17: <?php
18: if ( isset( $_REQUEST['manpage'] ) ) {
19:   system( "man ".$_REQUEST['manpage']." | col -b" );
20: }
21: ?>
22: </pre>
23: </div>
24: </body>
25: </html>
```

We extend our previous examples a little by adding a text field on line 13 and including the value from the form submission to the shell command we pass to the system() function on line 19. We are being trusting, however. On a Unix system, a malicious user could add his own commands to the manpage field, thus gaining limited access to the server. Figure 21.3 shows a simple hack that could be applied to this script.

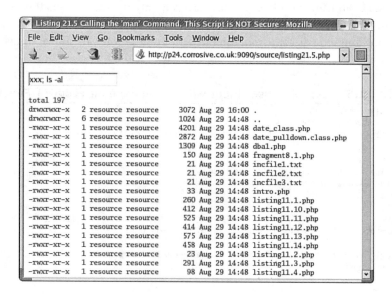

FIGURE 21.3
Calling the man command.

The malicious user has submitted the value xxx; ls -al via the form. This value is stored in the $_REQUEST['manpage'] element. After we combine this text with the shell command string we pass to system(), we end up with the following string:

```
"man xxx; ls -al ¦ col -b"
```

This instructs the shell to fetch the manual page for xxx, which doesn't exist. It then performs a full directory listing, running the output through the col command. If you think that this is as bad as it gets, think again. An unfriendly visitor can list any readable directory on your system. He can even read your /etc/passwd file by adding the following line to the form field:

```
xxx; cat /etc/passwd
```

> **By the Way**
>
> Vulnerabilities due to programming errors or omissions are very common on the Internet. Large, well-resourced companies and organizations have famously left their systems open to attackers by failing to check user input or leaving administration tools open to the public.
>
> It is easy to become complacent. As you code, try to keep security issues in mind at all times.

This clearly represents a grave breach in security and we cannot allow it to happen. The safest way of protecting against this is never to pass user input directly to a shell. You can make yourself a little safer, though, by using the escapeshellcmd() function to add backslashes to any metacharacters the user might submit. escapeshellcmd() requires a string and returns a converted copy. We can now amend our code, making our script a little safer, as shown in Listing 21.6.

LISTING 21.6   Escaping User Input with the escapeshellcmd() **Function**

```
 1: <!DOCTYPE html PUBLIC
 2:   "-//W3C//DTD XHTML 1.0 Strict//EN"
 3:   "http://www.w3.org/TR/xhtml1/DTD/xhtml1-strict.dtd">
 4: <html>
 5: <head>
 6: <title>Listing 21.5 Escaping user input with
 7:    the escapeshellcmd() function</title>
 8: </head>
 9: <body>
10: <div>
11: <form action="<?php print $PHP_SELF ?>" method="post">
12: <p>
13: <input type="text" value="<?php print $_REQUEST['manpage'] ?>"
➥name="manpage" />
14: </p>
15: </form>
16: <pre>
17: <?php
18: if ( isset( $_REQUEST['manpage'] ) ) {
19:    $manpage = escapeshellcmd( $_REQUEST['manpage'] );
20:    system( "man $manpage ¦ col -b" );
21: }
22: ?>
23: </pre>
24: </div>
25: </body>
26: </html>
```

The only addition to this example is the use of escapeshellcmd() on line 19. If the user attempts to enter "xxx; cat /etc/passwd " now, it is amended to "xxx\; cat /etc/passwd ", preventing a new command from being issued. In fact, he will be presented with the manual page for the cat command rather than our password file!

Although you can improve security by using escapeshellcmd(), avoid passing user-submitted content to the shell. You could make your script even safer by compiling a list of all valid manual pages on your system and testing user input against this before calling system(). We do something similar in the next section.

Running External Applications with
passthru()

passthru() is similar to system() except that any output from the shell command you send is not buffered. This makes it suitable for running commands that produce binary as opposed to text data. passthru() accepts a shell command and an optional variable, which is filled with the return value of the command.

Let's construct an example. We want to create a script that outputs images as thumbnails and that can be called from HTML or PHP pages. We are going to let external applications do all the work so that our script will be simple. Listing 21.7 shows the code that locates the image and outputs the data to the browser.

LISTING 21.7   Using passthru() to Output Binary Data

```
 1: <?php
 2: if ( isset( $_REQUEST['image'] ) && file_exists( $_REQUEST['image'] ) ) {
 3:   header( "Content-type: image/gif" );
 4:   $image = $_REQUEST['image'];
 5:   passthru(  "giftopnm $image |
 6:         pnmscale -xscale .5 -yscale .5 |
 7:         ppmquant 256 | ppmtogif" );
 8: } else {
 9:   print "The image ".$_REQUEST['image']." could not be found";
10: }
11: ?>
```

Notice that we have not used escapeshellcmd(). Instead, we have tested the user input against our file system on line 2 using the file_exists() function. We will not pass the $_REQUEST['image'] argument to the shell if the image requested does not exist. For additional security, we could also limit the extension we will accept and the directory that can be accessed.

In the call to passthru() on line 5, we issue a command that calls four commands. Note that for this script to work on your system, you must have these commands installed, and they must be available in your path. First, we call giftopnm, passing it the $image variable. This reads a GIF image and outputs data in portable anymap format. This output is piped to pnmscale, which scales the image to 50% of its original size. The output from pnmscale is in turn piped to ppmquant and ppmtogif, which convert the data to GIF palette and format. This data is finally output to the browser.

We can now call this script from any Web page:

```
<img src="listing21.7.php?image=<?php print urlencode("/path/to/image.gif") ?>">
```

Calling an External CGI Script with the `virtual()` Function

If you are converting a site from plain HTML to PHP-enabled pages, you might have noticed that your server-side includes no longer work. If you are running PHP as an Apache module, you can use the `virtual()` function to call CGI scripts, such as Perl or C Web counters, and include their output in your pages. Any CGI script you write must output HTTP headers.

Let's write a simple Perl CGI script. If you don't know Perl, don't worry about this. It simply outputs an HTTP header and all the environmental variables available to it:

```
#!/usr/bin/perl -w
print "Content-type: text/html\n\n";
foreach ( keys %ENV ){
  print "$_: $ENV{$_}<br />\n";
}
```

Assuming that this script is saved in an executable file called `test.pl` in a `cgi-bin` directory, you can now call it with the `virtual()` function, including its output in your PHP document:

```
<?php
virtual("/cgi-bin/test.pl");
?>
```

Summary

In this hour, you learned how to communicate with the shell and through it with external applications. PHP is a powerful language, but it sometimes is faster to call on an application than it is to create similar functionality yourself.

You learned how to pipe data to and from a command using the `popen()` function. This approach is useful for applications that accept data on standard input and when you want to parse data as it is sent to you by an application.

You learned how to use `exec()`, `system()`, and the backtick operator to pass commands to the shell and to acquire user input. You learned about the dangers of passing user input to the shell and examined the `escapeshellcmd()` function, which will afford you some protection from malicious input. You learned how to use the `passthru()` function to accept binary data resulting from a shell command. Finally, you learned how to emulate server-side includes with the `virtual()` function.

In the next hour, we will examine PHP's support for XML. In addition to the stable PHP parser functions, we will explore some functions that were so new at the time of writing that they were still under development!

Q&A

Q *You've mentioned security a lot in this hour. Where can I go to get more information about security on the Web?*

A Probably the most authoritative introduction to Web security is the Frequently Asked Questions document by Lincoln Stein (author of the famous Perl module, CGI.pm). You can find this at http://www.w3.org/Security/Faq/.

Q *When should I consider calling an external process rather than re-creating its functionality in a script?*

A The issues you should consider when weighing this are portability, speed of development, and efficiency.

If you build functionality into your script instead of relying on an external process, your script should run easily on different platforms or on systems that don't include the third-party application you would be calling. For simple tasks (such as obtaining a directory listing), handling the problem within your code is probably more efficient, saving you the overhead of spawning a second process every time your script is called.

On the other hand, some tasks can be difficult to achieve in PHP or slow to complete (grepping a large file, for example). In these cases, you might need to use a tool specifically designed for the job.

Workshop

Quiz

1. Which function would you use to open a pipe to a process?

2. How would you read data from a process after you have opened a connection?

3. How can you write data to a process after you have opened a connection to it?

4. Will the exec() function print the output of a shell command directly to the browser?

5. What does the `system()` function do with the output from an external command it executes?

6. What does the backtick operator return?

7. How can you escape user input to make it a little safer before passing it to a shell command?

8. How might you execute an external CGI script from within your script?

Answers

1. You open a connection to a process with the function `popen()`.

2. You can read from a process you have opened with `popen()` as you would from a file. In other words, you can use functions such as `feof()` and `fgets()`.

3. You can write to a process as you could with a file, usually with the `fputs()` function.

4. The `exec()` function accepts an array variable, which it fills with the output of the shell command it makes. Output is not sent directly to the browser.

5. The `system()` function prints the output of the external command directly to the browser.

6. The backtick operator returns the output of the external command it calls. This can be stored, parsed, or printed.

7. You can escape user input to make it safer using the `escapeshellcmd()` function. The safest way to execute shell commands, though, is to refrain from passing user input at all.

8. The `virtual()` function calls an external CGI script.

Exercises

1. Create a script that uses the Unix `ps` command to output the currently running processes to the browser. Given that knowledge is power, it might not be good idea to make this script available to your users!

2. Check the `ps` man page for command-line arguments for the `ps` command. Add a form to your script to enable users to choose from a range of command-line arguments to `ps` so they can change the information output. Do not send *any* user input directly to the command line.

HOUR 22

XML

What You'll Learn in This Hour:

▶ Some basics about XML
▶ How to parse XML documents with the XML Parser functions
▶ How to create XML documents with the DOM functions
▶ How to traverse an XML data structure
▶ How to use an XSL document to transform XML
▶ How to parse XML documents with the SimpleXML extension

It would have been hard to miss the buzz created by XML in recent years. XML is fast becoming a tremendously important tool for sharing data between applications and separating logic from presentation in larger projects. Since the first release of this book, PHP has continued to improve its support for XML. With PHP and Zend increasingly at the heart of larger e-business applications, reliable support for XML is essential. For the Web programmer, too, an understanding of XML is no longer an optional extra.

As of version 5, PHP's XML support has been enhanced in two ways. First, PHP has bundled a very reliable and efficient XML library (Gnome's libxml2) upon which all its XML functions are now based. Second, PHP 5 now provides an extremely easy tool for working with XML, called SimpleXML.

What Is XML?

XML stands for Extensible Markup Language, and its very flexibility makes it notoriously hard to define. It is beyond the scope of this book to provide a complete introduction to XML, but we can cover some of the basics. If you would like to read more about XML, please read *Sams Teach Yourself XML in 24 Hours* (ISBN 0-672-32213-7). For a formal definition, see http://www.w3.org/XML/.

XML is a markup language that enables you to define your own markup languages. In fact, it is more a set of rules than a language in itself. These rules determine the ways in which you can define tags and elements (similar to HTML elements). As long as you obey the rules, you have complete freedom to create languages that fulfill a whole range of functions. Because the rules are strict, XML interpreters can easily read XML documents and make their contents available to scripts that can then act on the instructions they contain.

An XML document usually starts with an XML declaration, like so:

```
<?xml version="1.0"?>
```

It also might refer to a document type declaration (DTD). DTDs are beyond the scope of this book, but they define which elements a document can contain, and in what order. Here's an example of one:

```
<!DOCTYPE rootel SYSTEM "http://www.corrosive.co.uk/sample.dtd">
```

The rest of an XML document is made up primarily of tags that combine to form elements and attributes. XML elements look very similar to HTML elements. An XML element is made up of starting and ending tags that can surround text or other elements.

A starting tag consists of a less than sign (<) followed by an element name followed by a greater than sign (>). Open tags can also contain attributes that consist of an attribute name and a quoted attribute value separated by an equals sign. The following fragment illustrates an open tag containing an attribute:

```
<newsitem type="world">
```

Both attribute and element names must begin with a letter or an underscore followed by any combination of letters and numbers. No element name can begin with the letters *xml*.

A closing tag consists of a less than sign (<), a forward slash (/) followed by an element name followed by a greater than sign (>), as shown here:

```
</newsitem>
```

As you can see, XML elements look pretty familiar. One variation you might not be used to, however, is the empty element. These are compressed into a single tag, so

```
<nothinghere></nothinghere>
```

would become

```
<nothinghere />
```

Listing 22.1 pulls all this together into a sample XML document. This is a shortened version of the XML document that we will be working on throughout the chapter.

LISTING 22.1 An XML Document

```
 1: <?xml version="1.0"?>
 2: <banana-news>
 3:     <newsitem type="world">
 4:         <headline>Banana sales reach all time high</headline>
 5:         <image>/res/high.gif</image>
 6:         <byline>William Curvey</byline>
 7:         <article>Research published today by the World Banana
 8:             Tribunal suggests that we have never had it so
 9:             good banana-wise...</article>
10:     </newsitem>
11:
12:     <newsitem type="home">
13:         <headline>Domestic banana use beggars belief</headline>
14:         <image>/res/use.gif</image>
15:         <byline>Charles Split</byline>
16:         <article>Bananas are for more than eating it seems. Local
17:             Innovation Centers have been showcasing some
18:             exciting banana related technologies...</article>
19:     </newsitem>
20: </banana-news>
```

Although Listing 22.1 looks a little like an HTML document, you can see that it contains entirely made-up element names. That is the point of XML. It hands the control and the responsibility over to the developer. An XML interpreter validates syntax and lets you easily access the elements, but it is up to you to write code to act on the information received.

In our example we have illustrated a structure for news items. The entire document is enclosed by a single element, <banana-news> (lines 2–20). This is called the **root** element. A document must have a single root element that encloses all other elements in a document, and every subsequent element must completely enclose any children it might have. Any elements that overlap generate an error in any compliant XML parser, as shown here:

<a><b></a></b>

Am XML document is often represented as a tree of data. Listing 22.1 is drawn out in this way in Figure 22.1. <banana-news> is at the root, branching out to two sibling <newsitem> elements. The <newsitem> elements further divide, leading to the deepest elements.

FIGURE 22.1
An XML document represented as a tree.

So, what is XML for? Well, the short answer is that it is up to you. But in practical terms, XML documents tend to fulfill a range of purposes, including

▶ To structure data logically for sharing (as in Listing 22.1)

▶ To format data (as in XHTML)

▶ To send instructions to an interpreter (whether local or remote)

In this chapter we will concentrate on the first use. Our banana news structure is designed to provide structures that enable us and our partners to easily work with news items.

XML Parser Functions

In this section, we will examine PHP's event-based XML parser functions. Prior to PHP 5, these were based on Jim Clarke's Expat library (XML Parser Toolkit), which is available from http://www.jclark.com/xml/expat.html. As of PHP 5, all PHP's XML functions use libxml2 (http://www.xmlsoft.org/). Event-based models for parsing XML are not the easiest to use, but they can be very efficient. Handler functions are invoked as XML elements are encountered, whereas alternatives such as DOM require that entire documents are modeled in memory before you work with them.

Acquiring a Parser Resource

To begin parsing a document, you need a parser resource. You can acquire one of these with the xml_parser_create() function. xml_parser_create() does not require any arguments and returns a parser resource if all goes well; otherwise, it returns `false`. The function optionally accepts a string containing one of three character encodings: ISO-8859-1, which is the default; US-ASCII; and UTF-8. We will stick to the default:

```
$parser = xml_parser_create();
```

When you have finished working with the parser resource, you might want to free up the memory it is using to reduce your script's overhead. `xml_parser_free()` requires a valid parser resource and returns a boolean—`true` if the operation was successful, and `false` otherwise:

```
xml_parser_free( $parser );
```

Setting XML Handlers

Seven XML events can be associated with a handler; of these, we will cover the three you are most likely to use frequently. That is, the start and end of an element and character data.

To associate a function with element events, you should use the `xml_set_element_handler()` function. This requires three arguments: a valid parser resource, the name of handler for start elements, and the name of a handler for end elements.

You should build the functions in question, designing the start element handler to accept three arguments. The first is a parser resource, the second is a string containing the element's name, and the third is an associative array of attributes. The end element handler should be designed to accept two arguments—the parser resource and the name of the element. Unless you have specified otherwise, all element and attribute names are converted to uppercase characters:

```
// ...
xml_set_element_handler( $parser, "start_handler", "end_handler" );
// ...
function start_handler( $parser, $el_name, $attribs ) {
  print "START: $el_name: <br />\n";
  foreach( $attribs as $at_name=>$at_val ) {
    print "\t$at_name=>\"$at_val\"<br />\n";
  }
}

function end_handler( $parser, $el_name ) {
  print "END: $el_name<br />\n";
}
```

The previous fragment illustrates two very simple element handlers. The start element handler prints the element name and a list of attribute names and values.

This is called for the beginning of every element encountered in an XML document. The end handler merely prints the element name again.

Now that we know where elements begin and end, it would be nice to access any text they might contain. We can do this by setting up a character handler with the xml_set_character_data_handler() function, which requires a valid parser resource and the name of a handler function. The handler function should be designed to accept a parser resource and the found string, like so:

```
function char_data( $parser, $data ) {
  print "\tchar data:<i>".trim($data)."</i><br />\n";
}
```

You can read about the other XML events supported by PHP at the appropriate PHP manual page (http://www.php.net/manual/en/ref.xml.php). You can also see the complete list in Table 22.1.

TABLE 22.1   **The XML Handler Functions**

Function	Trigger Event
xml_set_character_data_handler()	Character data
xml_set_default_handler()	Events not covered by specific handlers
xml_set_element_handler()	Element start and end
xml_set_external_entity_ref_handler()	External entities
xml_set_notation_decl_handler()	Notation declaration
xml_set_processing_instruction_handler()	Processing instructions
xml_set_unparsed_entity_decl_handler()	Unparsed entity (NDATA)

xml_parser_set_option()

I mentioned that element names are passed to handlers as uppercase strings by default. This is not advisable because element names should be case sensitive. You can turn off this feature using the xml_parser_set_option() function. This function requires a parser resource, an integer that determines which option is to be set, and the value for the option itself. To turn off the feature that renders element names uppercase (also called **case folding**), you can use the built-in constant XML_OPTION_CASE_FOLDING and pass 0 to the function:

```
xml_parser_set_option( $parser, XML_OPTION_CASE_FOLDING, 0 );
```

You can also change the target character encoding using this function. To do this, you call `xml_parser_set_option()` with a `$parser` resource, the constant `XML_OPTION_TARGET_ENCODING`, and a string value set to one of ISO-8859-1, US-ASCII, or UTF-8. This makes the parser convert character encoding before passing data to your handlers. By default, the target encoding is the same as that set for the source encoding (ISO-8859-1 by default, or whatever you set with the `xml_parser_create()` function).

Parsing the Document

So far, we've merely been setting the correct conditions for a parse. To actually begin the parse process, we need a function called `xml_parse()`. `xml_parse()` requires a valid parser resource and a string containing the XML to be parsed. You can call `xml_parse()` repeatedly, and it will treat additional data as part of the same document. If you want to inform the parser that it should treat any subsequent call to `xml_parse()` as the start of a new document, you should pass it a positive integer as an optional third argument:

```
$xml_data="<?xml version=\"1.0\"?><banana-news><test /></banana-news>";
xml_parse( $parser, $xml_data, 1 );
```

`xml_parse()` returns a boolean—`true` if the parse was successful and `false` if an error was encountered.

Reporting Errors

When parsing an XML document, you should make allowances for the possibility of errors in the document. If an error is encountered, the parser stops working with your document, but it does not output a message to the browser. It is up to you to generate an informative error message, including the nature of the error and line number at which it occurred.

The parser only reports errors in well-formedness—that is, errors in XML syntax. It is not capable of validating an XML document against a DTD.

We can detect whether an error has occurred by testing the return value of `xml_parse()`. If a failure has occurred, the parser stores an error number, which you can access with the `xml_get_error_code()` function. `xml_get_error_code()` requires a valid parser resource:

```
$code = xml_get_error_code( $parser );
```

The code is an integer that should match an error constant provided for you by PHP, such as XML_ERROR_TAG_MISMATCH. Rather than work our way through all the relevant constants to produce an error message, we can simply pass the code to another function, xml_error_string(). xml_error_string() requires only an XML error code and produces a clear error report:

```
$str = xml_error_string( $code );
```

Now all we need is to find the line number at which the error occurred. We can do this with xml_get_current_line_number(), which requires a parser resource and returns the current line number. Because the parser stops at any error it finds, the current line number is the line number at which the error is to be found:

```
$line = xml_get_current_line_number( $parser );
```

We can now create a function to report on errors:

```
function format_error( $p ) {
    $code = xml_get_error_code( $p );
    $str = xml_error_string( $code );
    $line = xml_get_current_line_number ( $p );
    return "XML ERROR ($code): $str at line $line";
}
```

All the previous fragments are brought together in Listing 22.2.

LISTING 22.2   Parsing an XML Document

```
 1: <?php
 2: $parser = xml_parser_create();
 3:
 4: xml_parser_set_option( $parser, XML_OPTION_CASE_FOLDING, 0 );
 5: xml_set_element_handler( $parser, "start_handler", "end_handler" );
 6: xml_set_character_data_handler( $parser, "char_data" );
 7:
 8: $xml_str = file_get_contents( "listing22.1.xml", 0 );
 9:
10: xml_parse( $parser, $xml_str )
11:    or die( format_error( $parser ) );
12:
13: function start_handler( $parser, $el_name, $attribs ) {
14:    print "START: $el_name: <br />\n";
15:    foreach( $attribs as $at_name=>$at_val ) {
16:      print "\t$at_name=>\"$at_val\"<br />\n";
17:    }
18:    print "\t<blockquote><div>\n";
19: }
20:
21: function end_handler( $parser, $el_name ) {
22:    print "\t</div></blockquote>\n";
23:    print "END: $el_name<br />\n";
24: }
```

LISTING 22.2   Continued

```
25:
26: function char_data( $parser, $data ) {
27:   print "\tchar data:<i>".trim($data)."</i><br />\n";
28: }
29:
30: function format_error( $p ) {
31:   $code = xml_get_error_code( $p );
32:   $str = xml_error_string( $code );
33:   $line = xml_get_current_line_number ( $p );
34:   return "XML ERROR ($code): $str at line $line";
35: }
36: ?>
```

We create a parser on line 2 and establish our handlers (lines 5 and 6). We also declare the handler functions themselves, `start_handler()` on line 13, `end_handler()` on line 21, and `char_data()` on line 26. Listing 22.2 simply dumps all the data it encounters to the browser. This illustrates the parser code in action, but it is not very useful. In the next section, we will discuss a small script that outputs something more sensible.

An Example

We are running a banana-related news site. Our partner provides us with a news feed, consisting of an XML document. We would like to extract only the headlines and article authors for display on our site.

We already have all the tools we need to achieve this. The only new feature we will be introducing is a technique. You can see the code in Listing 22.3.

LISTING 22.3   An Example: Parsing an XML Document

```
1: <?php
2: $open_stack = array();
3: $parser = xml_parser_create();
4: xml_set_element_handler( $parser, "start_handler", "end_handler" );
5: xml_set_character_data_handler( $parser, "character_handler");
6: xml_parser_set_option( $parser, XML_OPTION_CASE_FOLDING, 0 );
7: xml_parse( $parser, file_get_contents( "listing22.1.xml" ))
8:   or die( format_error( $parser ) );
9: xml_parser_free( $parser );
10:
11: function start_handler( $p, $name, $atts ) {
12:   global $open_stack;
13:   $open_stack[] = array($name, "");
14: }
15:
16: function character_handler( $p, $txt ) {
17:   global $open_stack;
18:   $cur_index = count($open_stack)-1;
```

LISTING 22.3   Continued

```
19:     $open_stack[$cur_index][1] =
20:       $open_stack[$cur_index][1].$txt;
21: }
22:
23: function end_handler( $p, $name ) {
24:     global $open_stack;
25:     $el = array_pop( $open_stack );
26:     if ( $name == "headline") {
27:       print "<p><b>$el[1]</b><br />\n";
28:     }
29:     if ( $name == "byline") {
30:       print "<i>$el[1]</i></p>\n\n";
31:     }
32: }
33:
34: function format_error( $p ) {
35:     $code = xml_get_error_code( $p );
36:     $str = xml_error_string( $code );
37:     $line = xml_get_current_line_number ( $p );
38:     return "XML ERROR ($code): $str at line $line";
39: }
40:
41: ?>
```

We begin by establishing a global array variable, $open_stack, on line 2. We will be treating this as a way of determining the current enclosing element at any time. The parser is initialized and the handlers are set, as you have already seen (lines 3–6). When an element is encountered, start_handler() (declared on line 11) is called. We create a two-element array consisting of the element name and an empty string and add it to the end of the $open_stack() array on line 13. As character data is encountered, the character_handler() function is called. We can access the most recently opened XML element by looking at the last array element in $open_stack. We add the character data to the second element of the array representing the currently open XML element (line 19). When the end of an element is encountered, the end_handler() function (declared on line 23) is called. We first remove the last element of the $open_stack array on line 25. The array returned to us should contain two elements—first, the name of the XML element that has just been closed and, second, any character data that was contained by that element. If the element in question is one we want to print, we can do so, adding any formatting we want.

You can see the output from Listing 22.3 (using a more substantial XML document) in Figure 22.2.

FIGURE 22.2
XML input parsed
and formatted for
output.

An Introduction to the DOM XML Functions

The XML Parser functions are event based—that is, the document is read from top to bottom and handlers are triggered as and when the relevant features are encountered. The document object model (DOM) approach is tree-based. The entire XML document is read and rendered as a tree of objects. This means you can traverse the tree at your leisure, manipulating its nodes if you want. You can also construct your own document trees that can then be output to XML text.

PHP support for DOM was still undergoing some development at the time of writing, and the PHP manual (http://www.php.net/manual/en/ref.domxml.php) was temporarily out of date. However, the syntax is being brought into line with the official W3C specification for DOM at http://www.w3.org/TR/2003/WD-DOM-Level-3-Core-20030226/, so if in doubt, you can always go directly to the rule book! If you have worked with the DOM functions and objects in previous versions of PHP, the main change you will notice is that most method or property names have been altered now to use camel case—that is, firstChild rather than first_child, for example.

The DOM functions rely on the libxml2 library, which is bundled with the PHP 5 distribution. You shouldn't have to specify any configuration settings to gain access to DOM.

The first thing you need if you are going to work with the DOM functions is a DomDocument object. The DomDocument object is a container for all elements, which are themselves represented by objects.

Acquiring a DomDocument **Object**

You can create a DomDocument object directly using the new keyword. The constructor accepts a string containing the XML version number with which you will be working. This is always 1.0, so you can omit the argument altogether and the parser will provide the default for you:

```
$doc = new DomDocument();
```

Before we construct our own tree of XML elements, let's look briefly at the mechanism for loading XML from a file:

```
$doc = new DomDocument();
$doc->loadXML( file_get_contents("listing22.1.xml"));
print $doc->saveXML();
```

In the previous fragment, we create a DomDocument() method and call a method named loadXML(), which accepts an XML string and builds a model of it in memory. We then output raw XML again by calling saveXML(), which builds an output string from the XML tree.

In the following examples, we will not load XML from a document. We will instead use the DOM methods to construct our own tree of XML element.

The Root Element

Just as the DOM model provides an analog for an XML document, it also provides an object to represent an element. The DomElement and DomDocument objects derive from a common parent class (DomNode) and are therefore similar in structure.

To create a root element in our document, we must first acquire a DomElement object and then add it. The DomDocument object acts as a factory, generating DomElement objects on request:

```
$rootel = $doc->createElement("banana-news");
```

We use the createElement() method, which accepts a string and generates an element named accordingly. Acquiring an element is not enough on its own. We must add any element we acquire with DomDocument::createElement() to a parent node in the same tree. In this case, we want to add $rootel to the document node itself:

```
$doc->appendChild( $rootel );
```

The `DomNode::appendChild()` method accepts an element and adds it to the end of the node's children. So, we have created a root element and added it as a child of the document object. Remember that the `DomDocument` class extends `DomNode`, which is why we can call `appendChild()` on our `$doc` object. Let's bring that all together:

```
$doc = new DomDocument();
$rootel = $doc->createElement("banana-news");
$doc->appendChild( $rootel );
print $doc->saveXML();
```

We do nothing new in the previous fragment. We create a `DomDocument` object and then use it to generate a `DomElement` object, which we add as the root element of the document using the `appendChild()` method. Finally, we write the minimal XML document to the browser. The output should look like this:

```
<?xml version="1.0"?>
<banana-news/>
```

Adding New `DomElement` Objects to the Tree

Now that we have a root element, we can repeat the mechanism we covered previously to add new elements to the XML document:

```
$headline = $doc->createElement("headline");
$rootel->appendChild( $headline );
```

We create a new <headline> element using `DomDocument::createElement()`. We then add the element to the root (<banana-news>) element. So far, we have worked with only two kinds of nodes: elements and documents. We need to add some text to the <headline> element. To do this we must create a text node:

```
$text = $doc->createTextNode("Banana related disasters");
$headline->appendChild( $text );
```

The `DomDocument::createTextNode()` method automates this process. We are given a `DomText` object, which extends `DomNode`, so we can add it to an element in the normal way.

We now have enough information to use the DOM functions to create the XML document in Listing 22.1. We use data from an associative array (declared on line 2), but it could just as easily have been pulled from a database. You can see the code in Listing 22.4.

LISTING 22.4   Constructing an XML Document with the DOM Functions

```
 1: <?php
 2:
 3: $news = array(
 4:   array( "headline" => "arf arf, mcGraph",
 5:     "image" => "/res/high.gif",
 6:     "byline" => "William Curvey",
 7:     "article" => "Research published today by...",
 8:     "type" => "world"
 9:     ),
10:
11:   array( "headline" => "Banana sales",
12:     "image" => "/res/high.gif",
13:     "byline" => "William Curvey",
14:     "article" => "Research published today by...",
15:     "type" => "world"
16:     ),
17:   array( "headline" => "Domestic banana use beggars belief",
18:     "image" => "/res/use.gif",
19:     "byline" => "Charles Split",
20:     "article" => "Bananas are for more than eating...",
21:     "type" => "world"
22:     )
23: );
24:
25:
26: $doc = new DomDocument("1.0");
27: $root = $doc->appendChild( $doc->createElement("banana-news") );
28: foreach( $news as $newselement ) {
29:     $item = $root->appendChild( $doc->createElement("newsitem") );
30:     $item->setAttribute( "type", $newselement['type'] );
31:     foreach( array("headline", "image", "byline") as $tagname ) {
32:
33:       // PHP 5 let's us do this in one unreadable line:
34:       // $item->appendChild( $doc->createElement( $tagname ) )
35:       //    ->appendChild(
36:       //      $doc->createTextNode( $newselement[$tagname] ) );
37:       // But we will use temporary variables:
38:
39:       $el = $doc->createElement( $tagname );
40:       $item->appendChild( $el );
41:       $text = $doc->createTextNode( $newselement[$tagname] );
42:       $el->appendChild( $text );
43:
44:   }
45: }
46:
47: print $doc->saveXML( );
```

There is very little that is new in Listing 22.4. On line 3 we set up an associative array to hold our news data. On line 26 we instantiate a DomDocument() before adding a <banana-news> root element on line 27. We then loop through our news array, using the createElement(), createTextNode(), and appendChild() elements to build up our tree.

We do introduce a new method on line 30—the setAttribute() function is defined in the DomElement class. It requires name and value arguments and adds an attribute node to the element. An **attribute** modifies an element in some way, consisting of a name/value pair included in the element tag. In this case we are adding the type="world" attribute to <headline> elements.

Getting Information from DomElement Objects

Usually, the first thing you will want to know about a DomElement is its name. This is stored in the $tagName property:

```
print "I am a ".$el->tagName." element";
```

After you know the name of an element, you will want to know whether it has any attributes, which are stored in DomAttr objects. You can acquire an array of DomAttr objects associated with an element by accessing the DomNode::attributes property. This property is an associative array, the keys of which are attribute names, and the values of which are DomAttr objects:

```
$type_attr = $el->attributes['type'];
```

To access the name and value of each DomAttr object, you can use the conveniently named $name and $value properties:

```
$atts = $el->attributes;

if ( ! empty( $atts ) ) {
  foreach( $atts as $name=>$att_ob ) {
    print $att_ob->name.": ".$att_ob->value."<br />\n";
  }
}
```

To navigate an XML tree, you must take advantage of the methods that DOM objects provide about their place in the structure.

Given a DomElement object, you can discover whether it has child elements with the hasChildNodes() method. This method returns a boolean:

```
if ( $el->hasChildNodes() ) {
  print "I am blessed with progeny";
}
```

If the element has children, you can access the first child with the $firstChild property. If the element does not have children, $firstChild contains null, as shown here:

```
if ( $el->hasChildNodes() ) {
    $child = $el->firstChild;
}
```

You can traverse the tree vertically, but what about horizontally? Elements know about their siblings as well. You can access an element's next sibling with the $nextSibling property and its previous sibling with the $previousSibling property. Both of these properties contains null if there is no sibling to be found:

```
$sib = $el->firstChild;
do {
  print $sib->tagName."<br />";
} while( $sib = $sib->nextSibling );
```

A parent, of course, can access all its children. The $childNodes property contains an array of DomNode objects, but if the element is childless, it contains null:

```
$kids = $el->childNodes;
foreach( $kids as $child ) {
  print $child->tagName."<br />";
}
```

Children also know about their parents. The $parentNode property contains an element's parent element.

Examining Text Nodes

Armed with the methods we have covered, we can now swing about an XML tree pretty well. But we haven't gotten down to the most important features of the tree. An element is not the only kind of node we want to deal with. Among its children are text nodes, comment nodes, and others beyond the scope of this book.

Our main concern is text nodes, which we use to acquire document content. The first thing we need to be able to do is to distinguish between DomElement objects and DomText objects. The DomElement and DomText classes share a common parent class: DomNode. All DomNode objects have a $nodeType property that contains an identifying integer. These integers can be tested using built-in constants. For DomElement and DomText objects, we use XML_ELEMENT_NODE and XML_TEXT_NODE, respectively:

```
if ( $child->nodeType == XML_ELEMENT_NODE ) {
  // work with the element
} elsif ( $child->nodeType == XML_TEXT_NODE ) {
  // work with the text node
}
```

After we have located a text node, we still need to access its contents. We can do this with the $nodeValue method:

```
if ( $child->nodeType == XML_TEXT_NODE ) {
  print $child->nodeValue;
}
```

Traversing a Tree: Two Approaches

We now have enough information to work our way through a tree, but how do we go about it? In this section, we examine two approaches to this task.

The first approach is designed to do the work of acquiring each node in turn and return it to the calling code. Listing 22.5 demonstrates.

LISTING 22.5   Traversing a Tree of XML Nodes Using On-Demand Functions

```
 1: <?php
 2:
 3: $doc = new DomDocument("1.0");
 4: $doc->loadXML( file_get_contents("listing22.1.xml") );
 5: $root = $doc->firstChild;
 6: $pointer = $root;
 7:
 8: do {
 9:   print $pointer->tagName."<br />\n";
10: } while ( $pointer = next_element( $pointer ) );
11:
12: function next_element( DomNode $pointer ) {
13:   while ( $pointer = next_node( $pointer ) ) {
14:     if ( $pointer->nodeType == XML_ELEMENT_NODE ) {
15:       return $pointer;
16:     }
17:   }
18:   return false;
19: }
20:
21: function next_node( DomNode $pointer ) {
22:   if ( $pointer->hasChildNodes() ) {
23:     return $pointer->firstChild ;
24:   }
25:   if ( $next = $pointer->nextSibling ) {
26:     return $next;
27:   }
28:   while( $pointer = $pointer->parentNode ) {
29:     if ( $next=$pointer->nextSibling ) {
30:       return $next;
31:     }
32:   }
33: }
34: ?>
```

As you can see, the real work is done by the next_node() function on line 21. This accepts a node object and tests it to see whether it has any children. If so, it returns the first one on line 23. If the node has no children, we then look for a sibling, returning it on line 26 if it is found. If the node has no children or siblings, we then climb back up the tree in a while loop starting on line 28, looking for siblings as we go. As soon as we find a sibling object on our climb, we return it on line 26. By repeatedly calling next_node(), we will eventually traverse the entire tree.

The next approach traverses the tree in the same way. It differs from the previous example in that the calling code does not repeatedly request the next node. Instead, the traversing function calls itself recursively until the tree has been completely explored. You can see this in action in Listing 22.6.

LISTING 22.6 Traversing a Tree of XML Nodes Using Recursion

```
 1: <?php
 2:
 3: $doc = new DomDocument("1.0");
 4: $doc->loadXML( file_get_contents("listing22.1.xml") );
 5: $root = $doc->firstChild;
 6: traverse( $root );
 7:
 8: function traverse( DomNode $node, $level=0 ){
 9:   handle_node( $node, $level );
10:   if ( $node->hasChildNodes() ) {
11:     $children = $node->childNodes;
12:     foreach( $children as $kid ) {
13:       if ( $kid->nodeType == XML_ELEMENT_NODE ) {
14:         traverse( $kid, $level+1 );
15:       }
16:     }
17:   }
18: }
19:
20: function handle_node( DomNode $node, $level ) {
21:   for ( $x=0; $x<$level; $x++ ) {
22:     print " ";
23:   }
24:   if ( $node->nodeType == XML_ELEMENT_NODE ) {
25:     print $node->tagName."<br />\n";
26:   }
27: }
28: ?>
```

The traverse() function on line 6 does all the work. Passed a node object, it looks for children. If children are present, it then works through them using a foreach loop on line 12, calling itself recursively with each child node in turn. Every time traverse() is called, it calls handle_node() (declared on line 20) where application-specific code can work with the node.

XSL: A Brief Discussion

Extensible Stylesheet Language (XSL) is a templating system for XML documents, and with it you can process an XML document for output. With the same XML source, you might apply different XSL documents to format for the Web, PDAs, interactive television, and mobile phones.

Unfortunately, the details of XSL are beyond the scope of this book, but we can briefly examine PHP's support for it.

PHP and XSL

PHP's support for XSL is also currently in flux. The underlying library that PHP 5 now uses is libxslt (`http://xmlsoft.org/XSLT/`). This is a radical departure from previous versions of PHP, which worked with the Sablotron XSLT processor. Because work is not yet complete, everything covered in this section is subject to change. Before using XSL in projects, you should visit the PHP manual (`http://www.php.net/manual/en/ref.xslt.php`) to check the current stability of support for the technology.

Although at the time of writing, XSL support is flagged as experimental and documentation is nonexistent, an easy-to-use and nicely integrated XSLT parser class is already available. Because libxslt is built on the libxml2 library that the DOM and Parser functions already use, PHP's XSL support now works directly with `DomDocument` objects.

At the time of writing, the libxslt library was not bundled with PHP 5; however, you can download it from `http://xmlsoft.org/XSLT`. You also might need to compile PHP with XSL support. You should include the argument

```
--with-xsl
```

when you run the configure script.

An XSL Document

In Listing 22.7, we apply a simple XSL document to the XML we created in Listing 22.1. It outputs a table for each article, adding formatting and changing the order of two of the siblings.

LISTING 22.7 An XSL Document

```
 1: <?xml version="1.0"?>
 2: <xsl:stylesheet
 3:   version="1.0"
 4:   xmlns:xsl="http://www.w3.org/1999/XSL/Transform">
 5:
 6: <xsl:output method="html" />
 7: <xsl:template match="banana-news">
 8:   <table border="1">
 9:     <xsl:apply-templates select="newsitem" />
10:   </table>
11: </xsl:template>
12:
13: <xsl:template match="newsitem">
14:   <tr><td>
15:     <i><xsl:value-of select="byline" /></i>
16:     <br />
17:     <xsl:text> writes</xsl:text>
18:     <b><xsl:value-of select="headline" /></b>
19:   </td></tr>
20: </xsl:template>
21: </xsl:stylesheet>
```

Without getting in too deep with XSL, the purpose of this document should be relatively clear with a close look. Take a look at the first line. An XSL document is also an XML document! The root element

```
<xsl:stylesheet
version="1.0"
xmlns:xsl="http://www.w3.org/1999/XSL/Transform">
```

should always take this form. It establishes the XSL namespace and version number.

The `<xsl:template>` element on line 7 attempts to match the root element. After the match occurs, we establish some basic formatting and with `<xsl:apply-templates>` on line 9 we attempt to match `<newsitem>` elements and generate formatted XHTML for each one.

The HTML you see in Listing 22.7 is subject to the same rules as any XML document, which means that failure to close a `<tr>` or `<td>` element would cause a parser to generate an error message. The `<xsl:value-of>` tags (lines 15 and 18) are substituted by the value of the elements stipulated in their select attribute (`<byline>` and `<headline>`). Notice that we have switched the positions of byline and headline elements we are matching. XSL gives you control over the structure of data in output as well as its format.

Applying XSL to XML with PHP

Now that we have an XSL document, we can use it to transform our XML. In fact, to do this we only need to use a few functions. Listing 22.8 introduces them.

LISTING 22.8   Using XSL to Transform an XML Document

```
 1: <?php
 2: $xslt = new xsltprocessor();
 3:
 4: $xml_doc = new DomDocument();
 5: $xml_doc->loadXML( file_get_contents("./listing22.1.xml") );
 6:
 7: $xsl_doc = new DomDocument();
 8: $xsl_doc->loadXML( file_get_contents("./listing22.7.xsl") );
 9:
10: $xslt->importStylesheet( $xsl_doc );
11: print $xslt->transformToXml( $xml_doc );
12: ?>
```

In Listing 22.8 we use the new XsltProcessor class to work with an XSL document and an XML document to produce formatted text. We initialize DomDocument objects to store our XSL and XML on lines 4 and 7. We then use the loadXML() method to acquire XML data on lines 5 and 8.

We now have an XsltProcessor object and two primed DomDocument objects. On line 10 we call XsltProcessor::importStylesheet(), passing it the DomDocument object containing our XSL. Finally, on line 11 we call transform_to_xml(), passing the method the DomDocument containing the XML to be transformed. The transformToXml() method returns the results of the transformation as a string we print.

Introducing SimpleXML

Do the examples in this chapter seem like a lot of hard work to you? XML is powerful, and DOM in particular contains complexities that must be followed to build compliant parsers. Sometimes, however, you might want to trade off power for ease of use. SimpleXML is just that, an easy and quick way of accessing and amending XML data.

At the time of writing, just two functions are available for SimpleXML: simplexml_load_file() and simplexml_load_string(). The first expects a file path, and the second an XML string. Both functions parse XML and return a simplexml_element object that contains properties named according to the elements found. So, in our banana example, it would contain a property called $newsitem. If more than one element with that name exists at the same level, $newsitem contains an array; otherwise, it holds a value. If the element in question contains other elements, the property contains an additional `simplexml_element` object (or array of objects). Finally, if the element in question contains text, the property contains a string (or array of strings).

This sounds much more complicated than it is in practice. Let's revisit the banana news example (see Listing 22.9).

LISTING 22.9 Parsing an XML Document with SimpleXML

```
1: <?php
2: $simple_element = simplexml_load_file("listing22.1.xml");
3:
4: foreach ( $simple_element->newsitem as $item ) {
5:   print "<b>{$item->headline}</b><br />\n";
6:   print "<i>{$item->byline}</i><br />\n\n";
7: }
8: ?>
```

Listing 22.9 is certainly simple! We acquire a `simplexml_element` object by calling the `simplexml_load_file()` function, passing it the path to an XML file. We then loop through the `$newsitem` property that we know had been made available, printing text elements to the browser. In a real-world example, we would have tested the `$simple_element` object before working with it.

SimpleXML is very much under development. As this book goes to press, it is not yet stable and clearly does not contain all the functions it will. Some examples refer to a `simplexml_save_document_file()` function that should let you save amended data back to an XML file. This has been removed from early distributions of PHP 5, although it is likely that it, or something like it, will reappear. You should look out for SimpleXML documentation on the PHP manual at `http://www.php.net/manual/en`.

Summary

XML is a large topic, worthy of a book in its own right, as the bookstore shelves testify. It would be impossible to cover all its intricacies in a single chapter. However, you should already be able to see some of the possibilities that XML offers programmers.

In this hour you learned how to parse XML documents using the XML Parser functions. You explored the DOM objects and methods and learned how to use them to build an XML document. You learned two simple techniques for traversing a DOM structure. You examined an XSL template and learned how to use it with an XSLT processor and `DomDocument` objects to transform an XML document. Finally, you encountered SimpleXML, a promising but incomplete addition to the PHP XML user's toolkit.

Q&A

Q *Discussions about XML seem to be everywhere at the moment. Is it all hype?*

A People do love a bandwagon, but XML remains an excellent way of sharing data and making larger projects more durable and extensible. The fact that you can define standards using DTDs also means you can build lightweight interpreters that do not need to waste time on error checking. If you have ever tried to download a browser from the Web, you will know how enormous they have become. One of the reasons XHTML—the XML version of HTML—is so important is the likely rise of lightweight browsers in cell phones, PDAs, and other devices that simply will not have the processing power available to handle HTML unless it conforms to a standard. You can read more about XHTML at `http://www.w3.org/TR/xhtml1/`.

Q *Throughout this hour, you warned that many XML features are not yet stable. Is it worth working with XML in PHP?*

A The answer is emphatically yes. PHP's support for XML is in transition at the moment to ensure compliance with standards and bring the various XML extensions together using the same libraries. This means that some functionality is still under development (as this book goes to press) and some function names might be subject to change. The end result, however, should be a powerful and stable suite of tools for working with XML in PHP. You should keep an eye on the manual at `http://www.php.net` to monitor developments. I will try to mention any necessary amendments to this chapter on my site at `http://p24.corrosive.co.uk`.

Workshop

Quiz

1. How would you acquire a parser resource?

2. Which arguments will the XML parser pass to an element start handler?

3. How would you turn off the feature that converts all element names to uppercase characters?

4. How would you get a current line number while an XML document is being parsed?

5. How would you get a `DomDocument` object using an existing XML file?

6. Given an DomElement object, how would you add a child element to your tree?

7. Which object would you use to apply XSL to an XML document?

Answers

1. You can get a parser resource with the xml_parser_create() function, like so:

```
$parser = xml_parser_create();
```

2. The user-defined element start handler function automatically is passed a parser resource, the name of the element which is starting, and an array of attributes.

3. You can use the xml_parser_set_option() function to disable case folding, like so:

```
xml_parser_set_option( $parser, XML_OPTION_CASE_FOLDING, 0 );
```

4. The xml_get_current_line_number() function returns the current line number.

5. You can instantiate a DomDocument object directly using the new keyword. You can then use the loadXML() method to import XML from a file. Here's how:

```
$xml_doc = new DomDocument("1.0" );
$xml_doc->loadXML( file_get_contents("./listing22.1.xml") );
```

6. You can use the appendChild() method to add an element to a tree of objects, as shown here:

```
$doc = new DomDocument();
$rootel = $doc->createElement("banana-news");
$doc->appendChild( $rootel );
```

7. The XsltProcessor class returns an object that can be used to process XSLT.

Exercises

1. Create a script that uses the daily XML news feed provided at http://slashdot.org/slashdot.xml and outputs an HTML version. Create another script to output a neatly formatted text version.

2. Repeat exercise 1, using XSLT to handle the output.

PART IV

Extending PHP

PEAR: Reusable Components to Extend the Power of PHP

What You'll Learn in This Hour:

▶ About the PEAR project and its structure

▶ How to install PEAR packages

▶ How to use the Auth package to password-protect pages

▶ How to automate documentation with the PhpDocumentor package

▶ How to manipulate configuration files with the Config package

PEAR stands for the PHP Extension and Application Repository. It is a large collection of interdependent packages, which add even more power to the PHP language. When you start work on a project, PEAR should be one of your first stops. You might find that much of your job is already done for you, and done well.

In this hour we will take an introductory look at PEAR. Through some of PEAR's packages, you will get a sense of the repository's power and usefulness. We will also consider some of the guiding design principles that underlie PEAR packages and could well be applied to your own work.

What Is PEAR?

At its core, PEAR is a collection of useful, quality-controlled, open source packages that you can include in your projects. The aim of the quality control is not only to ensure that you can rely on the code, but also that packages are interoperable—that is, that they work well with one another. So, when you download one package to help with a project, it might work with any number of other PEAR packages. In the best traditions of object-oriented design, all PEAR packages are designed to be as flexible and extensible as possible.

By the Way

> PEAR is also home for C extensions to PHP. This aspect of the PEAR project is called the PHP Extension Code Library (PECL). This is beyond the scope of this book, but in common with everything else we discuss in this chapter, you can get the details from `http://pear.php.net`.

PEAR is as much about design principles and quality control as it is about the packages themselves.

There are two other important aspects to the PEAR project. First are the repository and the accompanying Web site at `http://pear.php.net` (and various mirror sites). The site provides documentation for all packages, installation instructions, and much more. The server is the central location for packages. Rather than make the download of PHP bigger than it already is, all but a small core of the repository is placed online rather than in the distribution.

This brings us to another important aspect of PEAR. Rather than force you to download packages, unpack them, and install them in the right place, the pear command line tool is bundled with PHP as part of the base PEAR installation. It makes the installation process for individual packages a matter of a single command. What's more, the PEAR package manager handles dependencies for you. If a package you are installing requires another, pear tells you about it.

Installing PEAR

In short, you shouldn't have to do anything to get the PEAR base installation because it is bundled with PHP. As of version 4.3.0, this base installation has included the PEAR package manager, which we will be using in this chapter to install individual packages.

PEAR and Packages

PEAR **packages** are individual subprojects within the PEAR project. They are descriptively named, so the authentication package we will be looking at later this hour is called Auth. By installing Auth, you will be placing a directory called Auth containing a file called Auth.php in your include path. If you are using the PEAR package manager, you will not have to worry about the mechanics of this. After you have installed it, you will simply use a require_once() call in your scripts to use Auth classes, like so:

```
require_once( "Auth/Auth.php" );
```

Installing a Package

Having talked at some length about the PEAR package manager, perhaps we should try to use it. Let's install the Auth package, since we will be working with it shortly. From the command line, type

```
pear install Auth
```

And that should be that! In some cases, you will get a report of a failed dependency—that is, that your required package uses another PEAR package. So, if we were installing a package called `Bibble`, we might encounter the following error:

```
pear install Bibble
downloading Bibble-1.0.3.tar ...
...done: 15,111 bytes
requires package `Bib_core'
Bibble: Dependencies failed
```

The package manager reports that we need a package called `Bib_core`. All we have to do is install `Bib_core` before going back to install `Bibble` again:

```
pear install Bib_core
```

We should be ready now to work with some PEAR packages. Remember, you should stop by `http://pear.php.net` to look at all the packages and get an idea of what is available.

Some PEAR Packages in Action

In this section, we will work with a number of PEAR packages, starting with the Auth package we have already installed. We will also look at a package for documenting your code and a package for working with configuration files.

The Auth Package

Auth is an object-oriented package designed to help you add password protection to your projects. Adding users, avoiding duplicate usernames, logging users in, and authenticating users after they are logged in are all tasks the Web programmer encounters repeatedly. Auth handles the donkey work, leaving you free to concentrate on your project's logic.

In this section we will look at the Auth class and its methods. We will also use Auth with some procedural code to build a simple password-protected environment.

It is important to note that the packages we cover were written for PHP 4 and do not use PHP 5 features such as exceptions and abstract classes. New features will likely be introduced over time, and you should keep an eye on the documentation to see whether anything has changed.

Installing Auth

We have already looked at the procedure for downloading Auth:

```
pear install Auth
```

Auth uses the File_Passwd package, which in turn requires the Crypt_CHAP package. So, we should install these, too:

```
pear install Crypt_CHAP
pear install File_Passwd
```

Now we should be ready to work with the Auth package.

Working with the Auth Class

Now that we have Auth, we can jump in and instantiate an Auth object:

```
require_once("Auth/Auth.php");
$auth = new Auth("File", "./passfile.txt", "write_login" );
```

We use require_once() to make Auth available to our script and then instantiate an Auth object. The Auth class's constructor first requires a storage driver string as its first argument, storage-specific options for its second argument, and the name of a function to use to display a login screen if authentication fails.

Let's look more closely at the storage container issue. Rather than force you to use a specific mechanism for storing and retrieving passwords, Auth works transparently with several storage mechanisms, including files, databases, and even POP mail servers. If we had installed the DB package, for example, we could have used the following syntax to instantiate an Auth object:

```
$auth = new Auth("DB", "mysql://dbuser:dbpass@host/db", "write_login" );
```

We tell the Auth class's constructor that we are using a database and pass it a data source name (DSN) in the option argument. The Auth package uses the DB package to work with a database, and we need to think no more about it (assuming we have configured a database server to have the correct database, table, and fields).

A detailed examination of storage drivers is beyond our scope, but you can read more about them at `http://pear.php.net/manual/en/package.authentication.auth.intro-storage.php`. For our example, we will use the File driver, which uses the File_Passwd package we have already installed.

Now that we have an `Auth` object, it is our responsibility to create a function called `write_login()` that presents a login form. This is automatically called when authorization fails. In fact, if we had omitted the third argument to the Auth constructor, the object would write a form for us automatically, which can be handy for testing purposes. We will create our own function, however:

```
require_once("Auth/Auth.php");
$auth = new Auth("File", "./mypass.txt", "write_login" );
$auth->start();
$auth->addUser( "bob", "bobpass" );

function write_login() {
  print <<<BLOCK
  <form method="post" action="{$_SERVER['PHP_SELF']}">
  <p>User<br /><input type="text" name="username" /></p>
  <p>Pass<br /><input type="password" name="password" /></p>
  <p><input type="submit" value="login" /></p>
  </form>
BLOCK;
}
```

In this fragment we again instantiate an `Auth` object. We create a function called `write_login()` that prints a form if authorization fails. Notice the technique we use for printing multiple lines: This syntax is similar to using double quotation marks in that variables are interpreted, but with the important differences that we don't have to escape double quotation marks inside the string and that we can work with multiple lines of text. The form is straightforward, presenting username and password input text boxes. The names of the fields, username and password, are mandatory; apart from that, we can present the form any way we please.

Notice some new methods in the previous fragment. `Auth::start()` kicks off the authentication process. You should call it for any pages you want to password protect. Because it uses session functions behind the scenes, you should ensure that no text has been sent to the browser before using it.

We also introduce the `Auth::addUser()` method, which accepts username and password string arguments and adds a user to the system. If the user in question exists, `Auth::addUser()` returns a PEAR_Error object. Otherwise, it returns `true` to signal that the user has been added to the system.

PEAR_Error objects contain useful debugging information, in particular, $code and $message properties that detail the nature of the error in question. In the previous fragment, the addUser() method generates a PEAR_Error object every time the script is called apart from the first. This is because the user, bob, already exists after the first request.

So, if we test the previous fragment, the user is presented with a login form until he finally types in an acceptable username and password. Thereafter, he is presented with a blank screen. How can we welcome bob to the private area of our site? Here's how:

```
if ( $auth->getAuth() ) {
  print "</h1>Welcome, {$auth->getUsername()}</h1>";
}
```

The Auth::getAuth() method returns true if the user has been authorized, and false otherwise. So, we can use it to present members-only content. We can use Auth::getUsername() to personalize our message.

Finally, let's be really safe and force bob to log in for every request he makes:

```
$auth->logout();
```

Clearly, we would allow bob to choose to log out, rather than logging him out for every request. But we have given the main Auth package methods an airing here. In the next section, we use Auth to build a more useful example.

An Example

We will use procedural rather than object-oriented code to keep this example compact. We will, however, introduce a couple of useful techniques. In particular, we are going to completely separate our presentation code, the HTML output, from our script logic. In Listing 23.1 you can see an output page that displayed if authentication fails.

LISTING 23.1   The Login View for the Authentication Example

```
1: <!DOCTYPE html PUBLIC
2:   "-//W3C//DTD XHTML 1.0 Strict//EN"
3:   "http://www.w3.org/TR/xhtml1/DTD/xhtml1-strict.dtd">
4: <html>
5: <head>
6: <title>login</title>
7: </head>
8: <body>
9: <h1>Login</h1>
10:
11: <?php include( "listing23.2.php" ); ?>
12:
```

LISTING 23.1   Continued

```
13: <div>
14: <form method="post" action="<?php echo $_SERVER['PHP_SELF'] ?>">
15: <p>Username<br />
16: <input type="text" name="username"
17:   value="<?php echo $_REQUEST['username'] ?>" />
18: </p><p>Pass<br />
19: <input type="password" name="password" />
20: </p><p>
21: <input type="submit" value="login" />
22: </p>
23: </form>
24: </div>
25:
26: </body>
27: </html>
```

Listing 23.1 is almost entirely presentation. We call a presentation helper, listing23.2.php on line 11. Apart from that, we simply present a login form. This script is not designed to be called directly. Instead it is included by a controlling script. Listing 23.2 shows the script we included on line 11.

LISTING 23.2   The Navigation Helper for the Authentication Example

```
 1: <?php
 2: if ( ! empty( $GLOBALS['PAGE']['msg'] )) {
 3:   print "<h2>".$GLOBALS['PAGE']['msg']."</h2>";
 4: }
 5: ?>
 6: <p>
 7: <a href="?cmd=main">home</a>
 8:
 9: <?php
10: if ( $GLOBALS['PAGE']['AUTH']->getAuth() ) {
11:   print ' ¦ <a href="?cmd=logout">logout</a>';
12: } else {
13:   print ' ¦ <a href="?cmd=signup">signup</a>';
14: }
15: ?>
16: </p>
```

The script in Listing 23.2 provides some functionality for navigation and feedback. It is a little more interesting than Listing 23.1, in that it uses a global variable called $PAGE. All views in this script can expect to have access to the $PAGE array and to find it populated with an 'AUTH' element containing an Auth object.

On line 2 we test for a $PAGE['msg'] element, and if it exists, we print it to the browser. By this means, all views can send messages to the user.

On line 10 we use the `Auth` object contained in `$PAGE['AUTH']` to call the `Auth::getAuth()` method. If the user has been authenticated, we print navigation for logging out. Otherwise, we offer the opportunity for the user to sign up. Notice that we don't reference any views directly, but pass a `cmd` request argument to the current script.

As far as the views are concerned, that is all that is of interest for now. Now let's look at the controller at the heart of this system. The controller is responsible for authentication and deciding which views should be presented to the user. All requests should be routed directly through this central script, and the views are displayed using the `include()` function. You can see the controller script in Listing 23.3.

LISTING 23.3 The Controller Script for the Authentication Example

```php
 1: <?php
 2: require_once "Auth/Auth.php";
 3:
 4: $LEGAL_FUNCS = array( "main", "signup", "logout" );
 5: $PAGE['AUTH'] = new Auth("File", "../data/passfile.txt", "write_login" );
 6: $PAGE['msg'] = "";
 7:
 8: switchboard();
 9: function switchboard() {
10:     $comms = $GLOBALS['LEGAL_FUNCS'];
11:     $cmd = $_REQUEST['cmd'];
12:     if ( empty($cmd) || ! in_array( $cmd, $comms ) ) {
13:         $cmd = $comms[0];
14:     }
15:     $page = $cmd();
16:     if ( ! empty( $page ) ) {
17:         @include( $page );
18:     }
19: }
20:
21: function setMessage( $msg ) {
22:     $GLOBALS['PAGE']['msg'] .= "$msg<br />";
23: }
24:
25: // auth functions ///////////////////////
26:
27: function authenticate() {
28:     $auth = $GLOBALS['PAGE']['AUTH'];
29:     $auth->start();
30:     if ( ! $auth->getAuth() ) {
31:         exit();
32:     }
33:
34:     return true;
35: }
36:
37: function write_login() {
```

LISTING 23.3 Continued

```
38:    $auth = $GLOBALS['PAGE']['AUTH'];
39:    if ( $auth->getStatus() == AUTH_EXPIRED ) {
40:      setMessage("Your session has expired");
41:    } else if ( $auth->getStatus() == AUTH_WRONG_LOGIN ) {
42:      setMessage("Login failed. Try again or sign up");
43:    }
44:    // include login
45:    include_once( "listing23.1.php" );
46: }
47:
48: // page functions ////////////////////////
49:
50: function signup() {
51:    if ( empty( $_REQUEST['username'] ) ) {
52:      // return sign up page
53:      return "listing23.signup.php";
54:    }
55:    $signup = $GLOBALS['PAGE']['AUTH']->addUser(
56:      $_REQUEST['username'], $_REQUEST['password'] );
57:    if ( $signup instanceof pear_error ) {
58:      setMessage( $signup->message );
59:      // return sign up page
60:      return "listing23.signup.php";
61:    }
62:    setMessage( "Signup successful" );
63:    return main();
64: }
65:
66: function logout() {
67:    $auth=$GLOBALS['PAGE']['AUTH'];
68:    authenticate();
69:    $auth->logout();
70:    setMessage($auth->getUsername()." logged out");
71:    return write_login();
72: }
73:
74: function main() {
75:    authenticate();
76:    // return main page
77:    return "listing23.main.php";
78: }
79: ?>
```

We set up a global array called $LEGAL_FUNCS on line 4. This contains strings
that we will accept in the cmd request parameter. We need to check the user
input because we will be calling functions dynamically. On line 5 we initialize
our Auth object and store it in $PAGE['AUTH']. Remember that the $PAGE array is
our notice board where we place information the views will use. We must
ensure that both the data directory and the passfile.txt file are writeable by
the server process.

On line 6 we initialize another $PAGE element. $PAGE['msg'] contains any feed-back we want to send to the user. It can be populated from anywhere in the script by calling the setMessage() function on line 21.

The core of the script lies in the switchboard() function on line 9. This attempts to extract a value from $_REQUEST['cmd'], assigning it to the local $cmd variable. If there is no $_REQUEST['cmd'] element or its value is not found in the global $LEGAL_FUNCS array, we assign a default value to $cmd: the first element of the $LEGAL_FUNCS array. In this way we will always have a $cmd variable that is non-empty and legal. We can now dynamically call one of our command functions—that is, one of main(), logout(), and signup().

Command functions optionally return page strings, and if such a string is returned, we use the include() function to display the document on line 17. This provides us with a crude dispatch mechanism. The signup() function, for exam-ple, can choose whether to keep the user on the sign-up screen (by returning the sign-up document's name) or forward her elsewhere.

The authenticate() function on line 27 is the policeman of the script: It stops script execution dead if the user is not valid. We get the Auth object on line 28 and call Auth::start() on line 29. If Auth::getAuth() fails, we call exit(), ending the script. We know, however, that the write_login() function on line 37 has been called by the Auth object before we end the script.

write_login() has two responsibilities. First, it calls a new method for us, Auth::getStatus(), which returns an error flag if problems have occurred. We test the value returned by the getStatus() method against the constants AUTH_EXPIRED and AUTH_WRONG_LOGIN; then we send feedback to the user if one of them matches. Finally, we include the login page on line 45.

The default function is main() on line 74. This is because it is the first function listed in the $LEGAL_FUNCS global array. main() is called by the switchboard() function if the client does not provide a cmd request parameter (accessible from $_REQUEST['cmd']) or if the cmd parameter contains the string 'main'. The main() function calls authenticate(). If the user is new or unauthorized, authenticate() hijacks the script, causing write_login() to be called and ending execution. Otherwise, main() returns the name of our protected page on line 77. The switchboard() function calls include() with this return value, and the user sees the view contained in this page.

The remaining command methods are signup() and logout(). The signup() func-tion on line 50 is called by the switchboard() function if a cmd request parameter is present and contains the string 'signup'. We test for the username request parameter on line 51, using it as a flag to test whether our sign-up form has been submitted. If the parameter is not present, we decide that the user has arrived freshly at the sign-up page and return the document name of the sign-up view on line 53. The view is almost identical to the login screen in Listing 23.1, except it includes a hidden form field:

```
<input type="hidden" name="cmd" value="signup" />
```

This ensures that script flow returns to the signup() function when the form is submitted. If the username parameter is present, we know that the form has been submitted. We therefore call the Auth::addUser() method on line 55, passing it our user input. We test the return value from Auth::addUser() on line 57. If we have received an instance of the PEAR_Error class, we know that all has not gone well. So, we extract the error message from PEAR_Error::message and pass it back to the user by calling setMessage() on line 58. We return the sign-up page's name on line 60, requiring the user to attempt another sign-up.

Assuming that the function has not yet returned a value, we can celebrate a successful sign-up. We set a success message on line 62 and hand control over to the main() function. Remember that main() authenticates and then allows the user through to our protected data.

The final command function is logout() on line 66. This is invoked by the switchboard() function if the cmd parameter contains the string 'logout'. We cannot log out a user without first authenticating him, so we call our authenticate() function on line 68. If authentication fails, the user is sent to the login view, which is the desired result in any case. Assuming that authentication was successful, we call setMessage() on line 70 to feed back to the user and call the write_login() method to present the login page.

Listing 23.3 is a crude but effective model for writing small scripts. We can now easily add a new page command to the $LEGAL_FUNCS array on line 4, creating a function with the same name. The script will automatically recognize and call our new function. Simply by adding authenticate() to our new function it will be protected from unregistered users. In the next hour, we will look at an altogether more sophisticated method for organizing projects.

The PhpDocumentor Package

So, your project is a success. It has grown in size and power, and you are well pleased. Next, it is time to bring in another developer to work with you. She takes a look at your code and sees directory after directory, file after file of undocumented code. You both quickly realize that it will take weeks of unraveling your code before she can contribute fully. Perhaps it is time to consider PhpDocumentor.

It is a cliché that developers dislike documentation, but in common with many clichés there is a grain of truth to it. Documentation is often seen as a luxury, eating into production time. In a competitive market, the time taken to document a project can eat into one's margins. On the other hand, the cost in errors and misconfigurations, and in the steep learning curve for developers taking on a project, can considerably outweigh the costs of documentation.

You can also lessen the effort involved in documenting by doing it as you code, rather than waiting until the end of your project and despairing!

PhpDocumentor is an enormously powerful tool for documenting PHP projects. It has two great uses. First, it produces developer-level documentation generated from within source files. Second, it uses the DocBook XML format to produce user-level tutorial files that can be transformed to resemble documentation like PHP's own manual at `http://www.php.net/manual`. Even with a whole hour at our disposal, we could barely scratch the PhpDocumentor package's full functionality, so we will look here at inline documentation aimed at developers.

The idea of automated documentation using PhpDocumentor is derived from a Java tool called JavaDoc. JavaDoc reads java source files and generates a series of Web pages based on the contents, using hyperlinks to enable the reader to navigate the elements of the source. PhpDocumentor works in the same way: It reads the source files in a directory and builds a tree of pages. It recognizes and documents language elements such as classes, methods, and properties and handles relationships such as inheritance. This is useful, but it only lays bare the basic structure of a project. PhpDocumentor looks for special comment blocks and reads text and tags from within them. It incorporates the information it gleans from these **DocBlocks** into the Web pages it generates. The result is a set of detailed and easily navigable documents for your project.

As with all PEAR packages, installation is easy:

```
pear install phpdocumentor
```

This creates a `PhpDocumentor` library package directory in PHP's library directory and a command-line script called `phpdoc` that you can run to generate documentation from your source code.

By the Way

At the time of writing, PhpDocumentor did not yet handle the advanced object-oriented features introduced with PHP 5.

DocBlocks

PhpDocumentor parses your source files looking for DocBlocks. These are special blocks of code that look like this:

```
/**
 * A DocBlock
 */
```

The DocBlock looks very much like a standard multiline comment. The required additions are the second asterisk in the comment opening and the asterisks that begin each line within the comment.

DocBlocks break down into three parts: a summary, a description, and tags. **Tags** are instructions to PhpDocumentor and provide information about the element being described. Tags take the form of an at character (@) followed by a keyword. Each tag then requires further arguments.

Let's look at an example. In the fragment shown here, we add a class-level DocBlock to a project:

```
/**
 * A class to list directories.
 *
 * This class works with DirectoryFilter class to list the
 * the contents of a directory.
 *
 * @see    DirectoryFilter
 * @author  Matt Zandstra
 * @package FileUtil
 */
class DirectoryList {
  //...
}
```

We introduce our class with a summary line and then go into more detail with our description. We use a number of tags. @see is followed by the name of another class in the project. The class referenced automatically becomes a hyperlink in the documentation output. @see can also be followed by a filename, a class and method in the form MyClass::Method(), a property in the form MyClass::$property, and a standalone function in the form function(). The value that you use for @package defines an organizing principle for a set of classes. I usually organize my classes into directories and use the directory name as my package name. When the documentation is output, the class in the example will be grouped under a FileUtil link with others that share that @package value. The @author tag should be self-explanatory.

You can see a sample PhpDocumentor output for our fragment in Figure 23.1.

FIGURE 23.1
PhpDocumentor
output for a class-
level DocBlock.

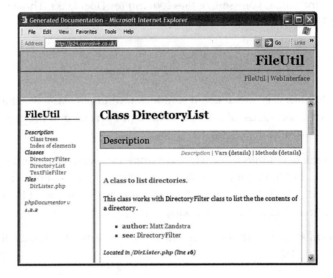

Table 23.1 details some standard tags that are available for all DocBlocks.

TABLE 23.1 **Standard PhpDocumentor Tags**

Tag	Argument/Description
@access	public/private/public
@author	Author name
@copyright	Company/author name
@deprecated	Version at which the feature was deprecated
@example	URL path to a sample file; it imports the syntax-highlighted source
@ignore	No argument; it suppresses output for the element
@internal	No argument; it hides the element from public output
@link	URL path to the document; it creates a hypertext link
@see	Class/Class::method()/Class::$property/function/ filename.ext
@since	The version number or date that the element was introduced
@version	Version information

Now that we have introduced a class, we can provide documentation for our class's properties:

```
class DirectoryList {

/**
 * The directory to examine
 * @access  public
 * @var     String
 */
  var $directory;
```

Notice that we are using PHP 4 syntax in this fragment. PhpDocumentor is incapable of handling PHP 5 elements at the time of writing, although this might well have changed by the time you read this. You can discover the current status of PhpDocumentor and find the complete documentation for it at `http://phpdocu.sourceforge.net`.

We use the `@access` tag to signal to PhpDocumentor that we regard the property as public. We also state the data type of the property using the `@var` tag. This is important because PHP is loosely typed, so there is no constraint as to what can be stored in a property. Your documentation should therefore be as explicit as possible as to which property should store which data type.

If we had declared the `$directory` property as private in the `@access` tag, it would not be displayed in documentation by default. This is also true of any DocBlocks containing the `@internal` tag. I often override this rule, however, to produce developer documentation. So, in Figure 23.2, you can see the output for our public `$directory` property and for a private `$filter` property. Notice that the `$filter` property has been declared to be of type `DirectoryFilter`. Because the `DirectoryFilter` class exists within the documentation, the type is displayed as a hyperlink.

Finally, let's look at a DocBlock for a method.

```
/**
 * Accept a string and return true if the filename should be included
 *
 * This base class always returns 'true'
 *
 * @param  String   The string to check
 * @return Boolean  true if the file is acceptable for inclusion
 */
  function check( $txt ) {
    return true;
  }
```

FIGURE 23.2
PhpDocumentor
output for a property-
level DocBlock.

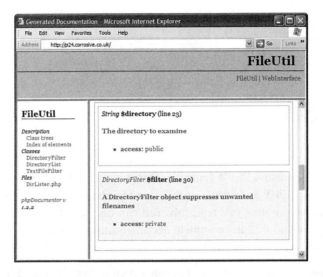

We include both a summary line and additional information. The @param tag provides information about arguments to the method. You should include one @param tag on its own line for each argument in order. The first parameter to the @param tag is the data type of the method argument, and the second parameter is a description of the argument and its purpose. The @return tag is used to describe the return value from a method. Again, the first parameter should be the expected data type, and the second should be a description.

You can see the output for the method DocBlock in Figure 23.3.

FIGURE 23.3
Documentation for
a method.

Generating Documentation

So far, we have discussed the DocBlock comments, and you have seen PhpDocumentor's output, but we have not talked about the mechanism for generating the output. There are a number of ways of doing this, but we will concentrate on using the command-line tool. The command phpdoc is automatically installed when you install PhpDocumentor. It is likely that you will find it in your path. In other words, you should be able to run it by simply typing

phpdoc

To generate your documentation, phpdoc needs a minimum amount of information from you. You pass this to the script using flags. The -d flag is used to pass the name of the directory to document, whereas the -t flag is used to pass the target, or destination, directory. Finally, I like to see my private properties and methods, so I pass the script a special flag, -pp, with the argument 'on'. pp stands for **parse privates**, and the flag causes private elements to be shown in documentation. Putting all this together, a typical call to phpdoc might look like this:

phpdoc -d myproject -pp on -t /home/me/htdocs/mydocs/

There are many more flags to phpdoc. You can find a summary of them at http://phpdoc.org/docs/HTMLSmartyConverter/default/phpDocumentor/ tutorial_phpDocumentor.howto.pkg.html. That is a painful address to type into your browser, but if you are keen to work further with PhpDocumentor, it might well be worth the trouble. You will find a full description of available tags, more examples, and command-line instructions for Windows users.

PhpDocumentor cannot make documentation painless, but it makes incorporating it into you programming routine easier. As your libraries grow in size and scope, you will have cause to be grateful that you developed the documentation habit.

Editing Configuration Files with the Config Package

Writing code to use a configuration file is one of those programming tasks that you find yourself doing time and time again as a programmer. The simplest solution is to use a PHP file to contain configuration directives for your scripts. This can work well, but it can break down if your script needs to share configuration with other systems or you require nonprogrammers to edit it.

The Config package is an extremely flexible way of building configuration files in a wide range of formats.

First of all, we must install Config:

```
pear install xml_util
pear install config
```

Config depends on the XML_Util package, so we install that first.

Now, let's map out a configuration example. Let's imagine that we have created a forum application and want an administrator to be able to control its behavior from a configuration file. The Config package can generate a file for us, but first we need to construct the data tree.

The Config package consists of a tree of element types that can be one of 'directive', 'section', 'comment', and 'blank'. Of these, 'section' can contain items of the other types. This is a lot easier than it sounds: You can create a section, add another section to it, and then add a comment and some directives (name/value pairs) to that.

To get an element that we can work with, we need to instantiate a Config_Container object and pass it a type and name:

```
require_once("Config.php");
$root_container = new Config_Container("section", "forum-configuration");
```

This gives us an object of type "section" called "forum-configuration". The Config_Container class provides us with tools for creating other Config_Container objects of different types. We might want to add a name directive to our forum-configuration section, like so:

```
$root_container->createDirective( "forum-name", "Matt's Forum" );
```

Config_Container::createDirective() requires the name of the directive and its value. The method both returns a new Config_Container object of the directive type and adds it to the current object. We now have a section that contains a directive. Let's add some more to our configuration file:

```
$perm_sec = $root_container->createSection("permissions");
$perm_sec->createDirective("allow-html-tags", "no");
$perm_sec->createDirective("uploads", "55");
$perm_sec->createDirective("allow-pictures", "yes");

$content_sec = $root_container->createSection("content");
$content_sec->createDirective("filter-obscenity", "no");
$content_sec->createDirective("inlude-newsfeeds", "yes");
```

We call a new method, Config_Container::createSection(), which requires a name argument and—like createDirective()—returns another Config_Container object, adding it to the tree. So, our $root_container object now contains a directive and a section. We have a reference to the latest section in the $perm_sec variable, and we use it to create three directives. We then add another section to our $root_container, which we also populate. In addition to Config_Container::createDirective(), we also have access to these methods: createComment(), which requires a string containing the comment text, and createBlank(), which requires no argument and represents a blank line within a configuration file.

Additional arguments to these methods can be used to determine where the elements are added, but this is beyond our scope here.

Now that we have some sample data, we can write our configuration file. To do this, we can create a Config object:

```
$conf = new Config();
$conf->setRoot( $root_container );
$conf->writeConfig("./out.txt", "inifile" );
```

The Config class is principally used for directing the reading and writing of configuration data. We load it up with our $root_container Config_Container object and then call writeConfig() to write the data to a file. Config::writeConfig() requires a path to the file to write to and a config type string. This can be one of the following: 'apache', 'genericconf', 'inifile', 'inicommented', 'phparray', and 'xml'. In our example, we have chosen to output using the 'inifile' type.

Let's take a look at the file we have written:

```
[forum-configuration]
forum-name=Matt's Forum
[permissions]
allow-html-tags=no
uploads=55
allow-pictures=yes
[content]
filter-obscenity=no
include-newsfeeds=yes
```

If we change the config type from 'inifile' to 'xml' and run our script again, our output changes radically:

```
<?xml version="1.0" encoding="ISO-8859-1"?>
<forum-configuration>
 <forum-name>Matt&apos;s Forum</forum-name>
 <permissions>
  <allow-html-tags>no</allow-html-tags>
  <uploads>55</uploads>
```

```
  <allow-pictures>yes</allow-pictures>
 </permissions>
 <content>
  <filter-obscenity>no</filter-obscenity>
  <include-newsfeeds>yes</include-newsfeeds>
 </content>
</forum-configuration>
```

So far, we have concentrated on writing configuration files. Although this is useful, it is only half the story. Let's write some code to read our configuration file back into memory:

```
require_once("Config.php");
$conf = new Config();
$root = $conf->parseConfig("./out.txt", "inifile" );
print $root->toString('phparray', array( "name" => "my_conf" ) );
```

We instantiate a Config object and call a new method, parseConfig(), which is the mirror image of writeConfig(). We are working with a file of type 'inifile', which is a standard Windows configuration format and the type that PHP uses. The method returns a Config_Container object if all goes according to plan. If we were to add error checking to our fragment, we would need to test for a PEAR_Error object. This is the return value we would expect if an error were encountered.

We assume that all is well, however, and call another new method. Config_Container::toString() outputs a string representation of a Config_Container object's contained data according to the config type it is passed. The second argument is an optional array of options. We have passed in an array with the name element set to 'my_conf'. You can see the effect of this here:

```
$my_conf['forum-configuration']['forum-name'] = 'Matt's Forum';
$my_conf['permissions']['allow-html-tags'] = '';
$my_conf['permissions']['uploads'] = '55';
$my_conf['permissions']['allow-pictures'] = '1';
$my_conf['content']['filter-obscenity'] = '';
$my_conf['content']['include-newsfeeds'] = '1';
```

If we had not provided the option array, the default name of conf would have been used for the output. Remember that the output in the previous fragment is a string representation of an array that can be written to a file and read back later.

We work with the data we have acquired using Config::parseConfig, though, by using the Config_Container::toArray() method. By calling $root->toArray(), we acquire an array that we can work with before writing again to a configuration file.

Now we can read from a configuration file, write to a configuration file, and output configuration data to a string. But how can we work with our data after we have acquired it? There are two approaches: We can use Config package methods to traverse and manipulate the tree of `Config_Container` objects, or we can convert our configuration into an array, manipulate the array, and then convert the array back to a Config data structure. This is the approach we are going to take now.

Let's read in the configuration file we created earlier, and work with its contents:

```
require_once("Config.php");
$conf = new Config();
$root = $conf->parseConfig("./out.txt", "inicommented" );
$conf_array = $root->toArray();

$conf_array['root']['content']['filter-obscenity']=1;
$conf_array['root']['content']['max-article-length']=500;

$conf = new Config();
$root = $conf->parseConfig($conf_array['root'], "phparray" );
print $root->toString( "inicommented" );
```

We use `ParseConfig()` as before to acquire the configuration data. We then use a new method, `Config_Container::toArray()`, to get an array representation of the information. This is quick and easy to work with. An interesting thing to note about the `inifile` and `inicommented` formats is that they flatten out your data structure. You need to be aware of this when you convert between configuration formats. We started off with a structure that had a root container called `forum-configuration`. In reading back the same data, we find that this has become the first child container and the Config package has had to create a new default root container, called `root`. The other thing to note is that if you want to preserve data as it was input, it is generally safer to use `inicommented` as your config type. This causes the invocation of a slower but more faithful parser. If speed is an issue, however, you should use the `inifile` config type in your `parseConfig()` call.

We manipulate the array passed back to us by `toArray()`. We change the `filter-obscenity` directive and create a new directive called `max-article-length`.

We pass our array to the `parseConfig()` method of a new `Config` object. We need to pass the `phparray` config type to tell the `Config` object to parse our array rather than a file. Finally, we output our new information to check that we have made the changes we wanted:

```
[forum-configuration]
forum-name=Matt's Forum
[permissions]
allow-html-tags=no
uploads=55
```

```
allow-pictures=yes
[content]
filter-obscenity=1
include-newsfeeds=yes
max-article-length=500
```

We have only scratched the surface of the Config package, but you might already see the hours of programming it could save you in your own projects. Even if you are never going to write or read a configuration file in your coding career, these examples should illustrate the usefulness of the PEAR project. PEAR is a database of quality-controlled, continually updated tools. It is designed to take the sweat and duplication out of working on PHP projects. It is very big, and it is growing all the time.

PEAR and Your Own Code

If you are starting out on your path as a PHP programmer, it might be a little too soon to start talking about authoring your own PEAR package. Remember, though, that every package has its own maintainer and contributors, so there is plenty of opportunity to get involved. If you are interested, you should read the relevant PEAR documentation at
`http://pear.php.net/manual/en/developers.contributing.php`.

Coding Standards

Whether you intend to contribute code to PEAR, you might be interested in the style guide to which contributors must adhere. The strictures might not all be to your taste, but there are some very good practices. The PEAR standards encourage programmers to use parentheses even where not strictly required, for example. So, leaving out the parentheses in an `if` statement that has only one execution line is perfectly legal, as shown here:

```
if ( $length=5 )
  endLine();
```

However, it is safer and more readable to use the parentheses:

```
if ( $length = 5 ) {
  endLine();
}
```

As you glance through your code, picking out control structures is much easier if they are formatted consistently.

The style guide also advocates the use of meaningful return values, even from functions that do not need to return a value to perform their task. A Boolean is a good choice here, returning `true` upon successful completion and `false` upon error.

One principle that is not in the guide is as follows: Where possible, you should always return the same data type from a function or method. This was impossible with PHP 4. PHP 4 PEAR classes often return a `PEAR_Error` object when a problem occurs. Over time, PEAR libraries will likely throw exceptions in these circumstances, allowing functions to return cleanly.

The guide recommends that you always use `<?php ?>` opening and closing tags. These are the only combinations that you can be absolutely certain will be available with every PHP installation you encounter. You should code defensively.

By convention, you will find that C and Java comments (`//` and `/* */`) are favored over Perl/Shell-style comments (`#`).

You can read the full PEAR style guide at `http://pear.php.net/manual/en/standards.php`.

Summary

The popularity of programming cookbooks is a testament to the amount of repetitive donkey work we all have to do to support our projects. PEAR provides a fantastic resource upon which we can build. Don't forget to check `http://pear.php.net` before you begin your next project. If you don't find what you need, perhaps you could consider writing it yourself and submitting it to PEAR.

In this hour you learned about PEAR, the PHP Extension and Application Repository. You learned how to install PEAR packages on your system using the Pear package manager. You learned how to use the Auth package to control access to your site. You also learned about the PhpDocumentor package and how to add comments to your code to automate documentation. You learned about the Config package, which is used to write, manipulate, and read Configuration files. Finally, you looked at some of the coding standards to which PEAR programmers adhere.

Q&A

Q *Are the PEAR packages stable?*

A PEAR packages are being developed at different rates by many different developers, and PHP is a constantly changing environment. Therefore, some packages are more mature than others. All code in PEAR packages is of a high standard, but you should check the changelog of a package when you use it to get a sense of the extent to which it is under development. Every package has its own page on the PEAR site, which includes a link to the changelog.

Q *How will the advent of PHP 5 impact PEAR?*

A Many, if not all, of the PEAR packages are object-oriented, so the advent of PHP 5 is very exciting. In particular, PEAR programmers are likely to begin using abstract classes, interfaces, and private and protected methods. This does mean that there might be a period of transition for some packages as they are modified. The end result should be more stable and powerful code. In particular, the PHPUnit package for automated testing has already been completely rewritten for PHP 5.

Workshop

Quiz

1. From the Unix command line, how would you install an imaginary PEAR package called MyPack?

2. Which method of the Auth class would you use to commence authentication?

3. What is the name of the PEAR object that some methods we have encountered return to indicate a problem with execution?

4. Which tag would you use in a PhpDocumentor comment to describe an argument to a method?

5. Which flag would you pass to the `phpdoc` command-line script to ensure that private methods and properties are documented?

6. A tree of configuration objects in the Config packages will all be of the same type. What is the name of the class from which they will all be instantiated?

7. The PEAR style guide recommends that you should drop parentheses from control structures where it is legal to do so. True or false?

Answers

1. To install a package called MyPack using the command line, you would use `pear install` as follows:

```
pear install MyPack
```

2. The `Auth::start()` method is used to commence authentication with the Auth package.

3. The `PEAR_Error` object is often returned by a PEAR method when an error occurs.

4. The `@param` tag is used to document method arguments.

5. You would pass the flag `-pp` to `phpdoc` to ensure that private elements are documented, like so:

```
phpdoc -s from -pp on -t target
```

6. The Config package builds trees of `Config_Container` objects.

7. The PEAR style guide recommends that you include parentheses in control structures, even when you don't strictly have to.

Exercises

1. Look at the packages at `http://pear.php.net`. How many of them solve problems that you have had to address yourself? How many will solve problems in your upcoming projects?

2. Choose a package that might be useful in your projects. Write a test script to try it. If the documentation on the PEAR site could be more up-to-date, run PhpDocumentor on the source and look at the freshest documentation there is.

Toward a Framework for Larger Projects

What You'll Learn in This Hour:

▶ How to manage client requests with a controller class

▶ How to find and run command classes based on a client request

▶ How to select and serve views based on the return value of a Command class

▶ How to implement views that work with the wider framework

With the introduction of PHP 5, there has been an explosion of interest in object-oriented design for PHP. There has been much debate about the relevance to PHP of design patterns developed in the context of strongly typed object-oriented languages such as C++ and Java. In this chapter we sidestep the theoretical discussion and look under the hood of a simple open-source PHP implementation of the Front Controller pattern. In plain English, that means we are going to look at some techniques for creating an object-oriented framework that could be used as the basis for larger PHP projects.

Principles and Problems

If you have worked for any length of time with PHP, you are bound to have encountered the problem of structuring larger projects. Because embedding PHP in HTML code is easy, the temptation is often to mix the logic of your application with its presentation.

This soon causes a number of problems, however. You tend to find that you are copying and pasting code between files, as the views in your project increase. When you add to your code, you suddenly find that you must repeat your amendments across many pages. Some parts of your project might rapidly fall out of synchronization with others, especially if you are working as part of a team.

Another problem of binding your logic and presentation is the difficulty for designers. You might be a master of all trades, but on larger projects team members typically specialize. Designers want to concentrate on designing without negotiating too many forests of control structures and thickets of quotation marks.

Most PHP programmers define a central set of code libraries and application functions and minimize the amount of code that lives within the PHP pages themselves. The question remains, though, as to how a request flows. Should it flow from the PHP presentation, up to a bank of functions? Many environments work in this way. The trouble with this approach lies in duplication. Even if every PHP page delegates responsibility for handling the client's request to a library function, you must still reproduce this delegation (the function call) and embed it in every page.

Many developers are now deploying an alternative structure, which is commonly used in object-oriented languages such as Java. The so-called MVC (model-view-controller) pattern splits an application into tiers. The controller tier is responsible for managing the messaging of an application. In a Web context, it handles an incoming request, delegates objects to act on the request, and then delegates a view to present the response to the user. So, a request always is routed to the same place—a controller object—and views vary according the nature of the request and of the success of the script in responding to it.

To keep the structure flexible, you don't want the controller to be all-knowing about your application. If you had to program in every action the system might need to take and every page the system will present, the controller object would quickly become hard to manage. So, the MVC pattern presents some challenges. How do we interpret a request and select an action? How do we use this flexibly, so that our code can be reused in different projects, and so we can add new actions to our project with the minimum of difficulty?

Another challenge lies in dispatch. After the system has responded to a request, our controller needs to delegate to the view tier. Somehow we need to map the actions the system takes, and the success (or otherwise) of those actions, to views.

In this chapter, we concentrate on the challenges of the controller and view parts of the MVC pattern and address these problems of command and dispatch. We will write some library code to demonstrate potential solutions, as well as some toy code to illustrate our framework in action.

Along the way, we will take in a lot of PHP's new, advanced object-oriented features.

The Controller Object

In this hour we focus on a particular implementation of the MVC pattern. The so-called front controller pattern places a single controller class at the heart of the system, where it fields requests, invokes commands, and dispatches views.

Although a controller object lies at the heart of our MVC system, it is also simple. Let's take a look at one. Listing 24.1 shows a stripped-down controller object, called Controller.php. We are going to maintain a crude package system based on the directories that enclose our scripts. Controller.php belongs in the controller package.

LISTING 24.1   The Controller Class

```
 1: <?
 2: // controller/Controller.php
 3: // qframe license: http://resources.corrosive.co.uk/pkg/qframe/license.txt
 4: require_once 'controller/ApplicationResources.php';
 5: require_once 'controller/RequestHelper.php';
 6: require_once 'command/CommandFactory.php';
 7:
 8: class Controller {
 9:    private $applicationResources;
10:
11:    function __construct( ApplicationResources $res ) {
12:       $this->applicationResources = $res;
13:       $res->init();
14:    }
15:
16:    function handleRequest() {
17:       $command;
18:       $requestHelper = new RequestHelper( );
19:       $com_factory = $this->applicationResources->getCommandFactory();
20:       try {
21:          $command = $com_factory->getCommand( $requestHelper );
22:          $command->execute( $requestHelper );
23:          $this->applicationResources->getDispatcher()
24:                ->dispatch( $requestHelper );
25:       } catch ( Exception $e ) {
26:          throw $e;
27:       }
28:    }
29: }
30: ?>
```

Similar to the main() function in a C program, the Controller class sits above the action, commanding in broad sweeps and letting lesser objects busy themselves in pursuit of detail. It is invoked by a simple index.php file that instantiates a Controller object and calls handleRequest():

```
try {
    $controller = new Controller( new ApplicationResourcesImpl() );
    $controller->handleRequest();
} catch ( Exception $e ) {
  print "\n\nException reported: <br />\n<pre>\n";
  print_r( $e );
  print "\n</pre>\n\n";
}
```

By the Way

Because the code in this hour is derived from a project that programmers at Corrosive (my employer) have been working on, the code is itself open source.

Every page shown contains a link to a license notice at http://resources.corrosive.co.uk/pkg/qframe/license.txt.

You can also download the full code listing at http://resources.corrosive.co.uk/pkg/qframe/qframe.tar.gz even though the code is not designed for full deployment.

I said that Listing 24.1 had been stripped down. So, what's missing? The comments have been removed. Library code usually has comments for every class function and property. In many libraries, comments take as much as 30% of the total source code.

Notice also that the catch clause on line 25 does nothing but rethrow the exception it catches. Letting all exceptions that are generated by our system bubble right to the surface during development is useful. We don't want bugs hidden behind a graceful failure, which is why we use print_r() in our index.php script to display any exception generated. We could have omitted the try/catch clauses completely to achieve the same effect because uncaught exceptions are automatically rethrown if they are not caught. However, we leave the catch clause in place as a reminder that we want to implement more error handling.

So, what is going on in our Controller class? On line 11 our constructor requires an ApplicationResources object. We use a subclass of ApplicationResources to initialize the system. It handles details such as setting up the username and password for database access, as well as configuring a class that handles view dispatch. The ApplicationResources class itself is declared abstract. The only thing the Controller class knows about is that it is guaranteed to have an init() method, which kicks off configuration, and two methods for acquiring useful objects. These are the `getDispatcher()` method, which returns a `Dispatcher` object, and the `getCommandFactory()` method, which returns a `CommandFactory` object. Devoid of comments, the `ApplicationResources` class looks like this:

```
abstract class ApplicationResources {
  public abstract function init();
  public abstract function getDispatcher();
  public abstract function getCommandFactory();
}
```

We will look at our application-specific implementation later in the hour.

The `Controller::handleRequest()` method deals with the real business of the script. First, we instantiate a `RequestHelper` object on line 18. `RequestHelper` acts as a context for the work that is done in the controller tier and caches the contents of the `$_REQUEST` array, so request parameters can be overridden in tests or in a non-Web context. Commands use `RequestHelper` to register their statuses and save information for use by views. The dispatcher logic uses the record held by the `RequestHelper` object to determine which view to serve. We will look at the `RequestHelper` in more detail shortly.

We get an instance of a `CommandFactory` object from the `ApplicationResources` object on line 21. A `CommandFactory` is responsible for examining a client's request and finding a `Command` to execute in response. If the `CommandFactory` fails to generate a `Command` object, it throws an exception and flow moves to our catch block before we attempt to work with the return value of the `getCommand()` method on line 22. Assuming that we are furnished with a `Command` object, we call `execute()`. `Command::execute()` requires a `RequestHelper` object. `Command` objects leave a record of their names and return values with the `RequestHelper`; this information is used by a `Dispatcher` object on line 24 to decide which page to serve.

If that summary leaves you confused, don't worry! We are going to discuss all these classes in this chapter. If you get lost at any point, remember that the key to it all lies with the `Controller` object. You should be able to remind yourself where a class fits at any time by returning to this example.

Let's get started with the `RequestHelper` class.

The `RequestHelper` and `DataStore` Classes

The `RequestHelper` class acts like a notice board for our application. Different objects leave messages on it that others might find useful. This is a useful solution to the problem of sharing information between applications and tiers because we allow information to move between objects that might otherwise have no knowledge of one another. Listing 24.2 shows our RequestHelper class.

LISTING 24.2   The RequestHelper **Class**

```
 1: <?
 2: // controller/RequestHelper.php
 3: // qframe license: http://resources.corrosive.co.uk/pkg/qframe/license.txt
 4:
 5: require 'command/DataStore.php';
 6:
 7: class RequestHelper {
 8:    private $params      = array();
 9:    private $commandArray = array();
10:    private $datastore;
11:
12:    function RequestHelper( ) {
13:       $this->datastore = DataStore::getInstance();
14:       $this->params = $_REQUEST;
15:    }
16:
17:    function getCommand() {
18:       return $this->params['cmd'];
19:    }
20:
21:    function overrideParams( $params ) {
22:       $this->params = $params;
23:    }
24:
25:    function getOrigParams() {
26:       return $_REQUEST;
27:    }
28:
29:    function getParams() {
30:       return $this->params;
31:    }
32:
33:    function saveVar( $name, $value ) {
34:       $this->datastore->setVar( $name, $value );
35:    }
36:
37:    function getVar( $name ) {
38:       return $this->datastore->getVar( $name );
39:    }
40:
41:    function getVars() {
42:       return $this->datastore->getVars();
43:    }
44:
45:    function setMessage( $message ) {
46:       $this->datastore->setMessage( $message );
47:    }
48:
49:    function registerCommand( $name, $status ) {
50:      $this->commandArray[] = array( $name, $status );
51:    }
```

LISTING 24.2   Continued

```
52:
53:    function getCommandArray() {
54:      return $this->commandArray;
55:    }
56: }
57: ?>
```

As you can see, RequestHelper is really a housekeeper; it does not do anything at all flashy. On line 14 it sets a $params property using the $_REQUEST array and allows user access to this array using the getParams() accessor method on line 29. Why have we put a wrapper around a perfectly good superglobal array? The reason is that we could override $_REQUEST using the overrideParams() method on line 21 if we were testing the framework or running it from the command line.

RequestHelper provides convenient methods that provide access to a DataStore object. The DataStore class enables us to store keys and values and make them available across the entire application. It is the main means by which commands communicate data to the presentation layer. The RequestHelper acquires the application's DataStore object on line 13 and provides the saveVar(), getVar(), and getVars() methods (lines 33–43) to register data with it and get data from it. The setMessage() method on line 45 also works with the DataStore class. It really only calls the DataStore method of the same name and sets a simple message that is made available to the presentation layer.

The RequestHelper class has one more role to play. Every Command object uses the registerCommand() method on line 49 to save its name and return value. The RequestHelper object saves this information to an array, which it makes available on line 53 via the getCommandArray() method. You will later see how the Dispatcher object uses this information to select a view to present to the client.

We have mentioned the DataStore object several times in this section. Listing 24.3 demonstrates it.

LISTING 24.3   The DataStore Class

```
1: <?php
2: // command/DataStore.php
3: // qframe license: http://resources.corrosive.co.uk/pkg/qframe/license.txt
4:
5: class DataStore {
6:    private static $instance;
7:    private $vars=array();
8:
9:    private function __construct() {
10:      // no access
```

LISTING 24.3 Continued

```
11:   }
12:
13:   public static function getInstance() {
14:     if ( empty( DataStore::$instance ) ) {
15:       DataStore::$instance = new DataStore();
16:     }
17:     return DataStore::$instance;
18:   }
19:
20:   function setMessage( $msg ) {
21:     $this->vars['message'] = $msg;
22:   }
23:
24:   function getMessage() {
25:     return $this->vars['message'];
26:   }
27:
28:   function setVar( $name, $value ) {
29:     $this->vars[$name] = $value;
30:   }
31:
32:   function getVar( $name ) {
33:     return $this->vars[$name];
34:   }
35:
36:   function getVars() {
37:     return $this->vars;
38:   }
39: }
40:
41: ?>
```

As you can see, the DataStore class does little more than provide an interface for storing and retrieving keys and values. For good or ill, we take full advantage of PHP's loose typing and allow client coders to store data of any type in the class.

The real reason we need this class as well as the RequestHelper class lies on line 9. Notice that we have declared our constructor private, meaning that no one can directly instantiate a DataStore object. We provide a private static property called $instance that stores a DataStore instance for us. We also provide a class-level mechanism by which client code can gain access to a single instance of the DataStore class in the static getInstance() method on line 13. Because it is a static method, getInstance() is called using the class, not via a DataStore object. If the $instance property is empty, as it is the first time DataStore::getInstance() is called, the method instantiates a new DataStore object and stores it in the property. Then the property is returned. A DataStore object is therefore always accessible anywhere in the framework by calling DataStore::getInstance(). Most importantly, it also means that only one

`DataStore` object exists and that all code works with the same one. So, a command can save some data at one point during execution and a view can later access the same data by acquiring the single `DataStore` instance that the system allows. This is known as the **Singleton pattern**.

We have now covered the two principle conduits for messages in our system. Refer to Listing 24.1 to remind yourself of the `RequestHelper` class's first appearance on line 18; then let's move on to the `CommandFactory` class.

The `CommandFactory` **Class**

An instance of the `CommandFactory` class is provided for the `Controller` class by the `ApplicationResources` object in Listing 24.1 on line 19. The `Controller` could instantiate its own `CommandFactory`, but by delegating object creation to the `ApplicationResources` object, we provide it the opportunity to configure the `CommandFactory` for us.

You can see the `CommandFactory` class in Listing 24.4.

LISTING 24.4   The `CommandFactory` **Class**

```
 1: <?
 2: // command/CommandFactory.php
 3: // qframe license: http://resources.corrosive.co.uk/pkg/qframe/license.txt
 4:
 5: require_once 'controller/ApplicationResources.php';
 6:
 7:
 8: abstract class CommandFactory {
 9:    abstract function setDefaultCommand( $str );
10:    abstract function getDefaultCommand();
11:    abstract funotion getCommand( RequestHelper $helper );
12: }
```

The `CommandFactory` class is abstract; it defines the interface that `CommandFactory` implementations must follow. Most importantly, we ensure that all `CommandFactory` classes implement a `getCommand()` method. Why did we define an abstract class instead of simply providing an implementation? You will see the concrete class that we use in a moment, but we also want to ensure that future applications could provide alternative or improved implementations within our framework. By defining an abstract base class, we are building flexibility into our system.

In Listing 24.5, you can see `SimpleCommandFactory`, our `CommandFactory` implementation.

LISTING 24.5   The SimpleCommandFactory **Class**

```php
1: <?
2: // command/SimpleCommandFactory.php
3: // qframe license: http://resources.corrosive.co.uk/pkg/qframe/license.txt
4:
5: require_once 'command/CommandFactory.php';
6: require_once 'controller/ApplicationResources.php';
7:
8: class SimpleCommandFactory extends CommandFactory {
9:   private $packages = array();
10:   private $defaultCmd = "DefaultCommand";
11:
12:   function __construct() {
13:     array_push( $this->packages, "command" );
14:   }
15:
16:   function addPackage( $package_str ) {
17:     array_push( $this->packages, $package_str );
18:   }
19:
20:   function setDefaultCommand( $str ) {
21:     $this->defaultCommand = $str;
22:   }
23:
24:   function getDefaultCommand() {
25:     return $this->defaultCommand;
26:   }
27:
28:   function getCommand( RequestHelper $helper ) {
29:     $cmd = $helper->getCommand();
30:     if ( empty( $cmd ) ) {
31:       $cmd = $this->getDefaultCommand();
32:     }
33:     return $this->getCommandByName( $cmd );
34:   }
35:
36:   private function getCommandByName( $cmd ) {
37:     foreach ( $this->packages as $package ) {
38:       $cmdpath = "$package/$cmd.php";
39:       if ( file_exists( $cmdpath ) ) {
40:         require_once $cmdpath;
41:         $cmd_obj = new $cmd();
42:         if ( $cmd_obj instanceof command ) {
43:           return $cmd_obj;
44:         }
45:       }
46:     }
47:     throw new CommandNotFoundException( "Command: $cmd not found" );
48:   }
49: }
```

The SimpleCommandFactory class maintains a private array called $packages, which contains a list of directories that can be searched for Command classes. We populate it with a single default in the constructor on line 13, but we allow the client coder to add new packages to search with the addPackage() method on line 16. We also manage a $defaultCommand string property, which is settable and get-table using the setDefaultCommand() method on line 20 and the getDefaultCommand() method on line 24.

The heart of the class is the getCommand() method on line 28. On line 29 we call a RequestHelper method—getCommand()—which extracts a cmd request parameter. So, if the GET request to our framework included the name/value pair cmd=AddTask, we would end up with a $cmd value containing the string AddTask here. If no command was provided, we use the default command instead, storing it in the temporary $cmd variable.

We pass our $cmd variable to the private getCommandByName() method, which is on line 36. This loops through the SimpleCommandFactory::$packages array, searching in each directory for a file with the same name as the $cmd string. If such a file is located, we use require_once() on line 40 to access it and then instantiate an object of the command's name. We check that the object is of the type Command before returning it on line 43.

So, for a command to be run, it must exist in one of the packages known by the SimpleCommandFactory object. The filename and the Command object must share exactly the same name. If we were given an "AddTask" command, the SimpleCommandFactory object would look in the command directory for a file called AddTask.php. It would then use require_once() to include the file and attempt to instantiate a class called AddTask.

If no AddTask.php file were found, or if such a file were found but it did not con-tain an AddTask class derived from Command, we would eventually return a CommandNotFoundException on line 47. This an empty class derived from the built-in Exception class, and it serves as a flag for the Controller class.

At heart, the SimpleCommandFactory class is very simple—it translates strings into Command objects.

Now that you know how to find acquire Command objects, we should spend some time discussing the Command class.

The Command **Class**

Command objects enable your framework to grow flexibly. You can simply drop a class that derives from the Command parent class into a command directory and it automatically becomes available to the system. Listing 24.6 demonstrates the Command class.

LISTING 24.6   The Command **Class**

```
1: <?
2: // command/Command.php
3: // qframe license: http://resources.corrosive.co.uk/pkg/qframe/license.txt
4:
5: abstract class Command {
6:   const CMD_SUCCESS = 200;
7:   const CMD_UNPROCESSED = 400;
8:   const CMD_ERROR = 500;
9:
10:   final function execute( RequestHelper $requestHelper ) {
11:     $status = $this->doExecute( $requestHelper );
12:     $requestHelper->registerCommand( get_class( $this ), $status );
13:     return $status;
14:   }
15:
16:   abstract protected function doExecute( RequestHelper $requestHelper );
17: }
```

The Command class is abstract, and a system will likely define many concrete classes that implement it. On lines 6–8 we define three constants. CMD_SUCCESS, CMD_UNPROCESSED, and CMD_ERROR are flags that can be used to signify the execution status of a command.

The execute() method on line 10 is declared final. It contains functionality that all Command classes should have, so we do not want child classes overriding this and providing their own implementation.

execute() requires a RequestHelper object, which we pass on in a call to the abstract doExecute() method. This practice of calling an abstract method from a concrete one is known as the **template method pattern**. We force all Command child classes to implement a doExecute() method (by declaring doExecute() abstract). We then call the method from execute() and work with the return value, even though doExecute() exists only as a declaration. We expect doExecute() to return an integer (usually one of the constant flags we declared at the start of the class), and we pass this return value and the name of the class to RequestHelper::registerCommand() on line 12.

So, when the execute() method of a Command child class is called, its doExecute() method is invoked and RequestHelper is automatically updated. The child class need only implement doExecute() and return a sensible value for all this to happen.

We want to ensure that the only route to doExecute() is via the execute() method, so we declare doExecute() protected. This means that only other commands can invoke doExecute().

Let's return to our Controller class in Listing 24.1 for a recap. The controller instantiates a RequestHelper object and passes it to a CommandFactory object's getCommand() method. The CommandFactory object uses the RequestHelper object to return a Command object, and the Controller object calls the Command object's execute() method, passing it the RequestHelper object. The Command object then invokes its doExecute() method and registers its own name and the doExecute() method's value with RequestHelper.

At this stage, we have processed the user's request, decided which command should take on the job, and invoked the command. The command should have completed its work and registered a status. Incidentally, it probably has used the DataStore object to save data the presentation layer might use later.

So, how are we going to translate all this processing into an interface for our user?

The Dispatcher **Class**

The Dispatcher class is provided to the Controller by the ApplicationResources object. We cover a particular implementation in this section, but we have used an abstract base class again to allow for more sophisticated solutions. The abstract Dispatcher class is shown in Listing 24.7.

LISTING 24.7 The Dispatcher **Class**

```
 1: <?php
 2: // controller/Dispatcher.php
 3: // qframe license: http://resources.corrosive.co.uk/pkg/qframe/license.txt
 4:
 5: require_once 'controller/RequestHelper.php';
 6:
 7:
 8: abstract class Dispatcher {
 9:     private $views;
10:
11:     function __construct( $view_dir ) {
12:         $this->views = $view_dir;
13:     }
14:
```

LISTING 24.7   Continued

```
15:    abstract function getNext( RequestHelper $helper );
16:
17:    function dispatch( RequestHelper $requestHelper ) {
18:       $next = $this->getNext( $requestHelper );
19:       $view = "{$this->views}/$next";
20:
21:       if ( ! is_file( $view ) ) {
22:          throw new DispatchException( "cannot open $view" );
23:       }
24:
25:       include( $view );
26:       exit;
27:    }
28: }
```

In the constructor on line 11, we demand a string argument that we store in the
$views property. This represents the directory where presentation files should be
stored. The Dispatcher class defines two methods besides the constructor. The
first, getNext() (line 15), is abstract and left to client classes to implement. The
second method is dispatch() (line 17), which demands a RequestHelper object
and handles the mechanics of delegating to the view tier. We call getNext() to
get access to a string reference to the view we want to present. We then test that
the view exists on the file system and that it is a file. If the view cannot be found,
or if it is a directory, we throw a DispatchException on line 22.
DispatchException is simply an empty class that extends the built-in Exception
class. If no problems are encountered, we simply include the file, handing responsibility over to the presentation layer. Our work here is done!

Of course, we have yet to implement the getNext() method. What is the logic by
which we choose which view to present to the user? Well, our Dispatcher object
has access to a primed RequestHelper object. We know that this maintains an
array of command names, each one paired with an execution status. This provides enough information to build a logic for dispatch.

In formulating this logic, we have two options. First, we could provide a mechanism for mapping a single command and status combination with a page.
Second, we could provide a mechanism for mapping any or all commands and
status flags in the array to pages.

Remember that Command objects register themselves and their execution statuses
whenever they are called, by calling RequestHelper::registerCommand(). If one
Command object invokes another, which in turn invokes a third Command object, we
could end up with an extensive list in the RequestHelper object's $commandArray

property. We are going to map a view of only the combination of the first `Command` called and its status flag in this example. We will, however, discuss a more flexible mechanism a bit later.

Listing 24.8 shows the `SimpleDispatcher` class, which provides a workable solution for mapping command execution to presentations.

LISTING 24.8   The `SimpleDispatcher` Class

```
 1: <?
 2: // controller/SimpleDispatcher.php
 3: // qframe license: http://resources.corrosive.co.uk/pkg/qframe/license.txt
 4:
 5: require 'controller/Dispatcher.php';
 6:
 7: class SimpleDispatcher extends Dispatcher {
 8:    private $dispatchHash = array();
 9:
10:    function addCondition( $cmd, $target, $status=-1 ) {
11:       $cmd = strtolower( $cmd );
12:       if ( $status > 0 ) {
13:          $this->dispatchHash[ "$cmd.$status" ] = $target;
14:       } else {
15:          $this->dispatchHash[ "$cmd" ] = $target;
16:       }
17:    }
18:
19:    function getNext( RequestHelper $helper ) {
20:       list( $cmd, $status ) = array_pop( $helper->getCommandStack() );
21:       $key = "$cmd.$status";
22:       $view = $this->dispatchHash[$key];
23:       if ( empty( $view ) ) {
24:          $view = $this->dispatchHash[$cmd];
25:       }
26:       return $view;
27:    }
28: }
29: ?>
```

The `SimpleDispatcher` class handles two things: It implements `getNext()` and a method called `addCondition()`, which enables client code to establish the mapping between commands, command status flags, and pages on the system.

`addCondition()` requires the name of a command (that is, the name of a class that extends `Command` class), the path to the view to which the command should be mapped, and optionally an execution flag. Let's work through a quick example. Imagine a `Command` class called `AddTask`. A single command can have a number of views according to the way it executes. First, the `AddTask` command can be called with no data at all. The command might decide that it should do nothing in this case and return Command::CMD_UNPROCESSED. Given a SimpleDispatcher object stored in the variable $simpleDispatcher, we might set up the scenario like this:

```
$simpleDispatcher->addCondition( "AddTask",
                "addtaskform.php",
                Command:CMD_UNPROCESSED );
```

We are saying that we would like the addtaskform.php view presented when AddTask returns CMD_UNPROCESSED. This would typically be when the user arrives at the AddTask context for the first time.

When AddTask successfully completes a mission, it might return Command::CMD_SUCCESS. We would no longer want to present a form in this context, so we would set up a new mapping for this:

```
$simpleDispatcher->addCondition( "AddTask",
                "thankyou.php",
                Command:CMD_SUCCESS );
```

If we don't want to define specific pages for all combinations, we can also set a backstop condition. We do this by omitting the status flag argument:

```
$simpleDispatcher->addCondition( "AddTask", "error.php" );
```

This means that the error.php page is included for all combinations for which no provision has been made. This mechanism is crude but surprisingly flexible.

Let's look again at our addCondition() method. How do we store the conditions provided? In fact, we populate a private associative array property called $dispatchHash. If we are provided with a status flag, we use it and the command name separated by a period as an element key with the target path as the value. So

```
$simpleDispatcher->addCondition( "AddTask",
                "thankyou.php",
                Command:CMD_SUCCESS );
```

is equivalent to the following:

```
$dispatchHash["addtask.200"]="thankyou.php";
```

If we are not provided with a status flag, we change our $dispatchHash element accordingly. So

```
$simpleDispatcher->addCondition( "AddTask", "error.php" );
```

is equivalent to this:

```
$dispatchHash["addtask"]="error.php";
```

In this way, client code can use addCondition() to build up a complete map linking command execution and page presentation.

The getNext() method is declared on line 19 and uses the $dispatchHash array to return the correct page for the current circumstance. On line 20 we call RequestHelper::getCommandArray() to get the record of all commands executed. We acquire the details of the first command called, the primary command, using the array_pop function. First, we attempt to reproduce a specific condition on line 21 by combining the recorded command name with the status flag. If the $dispatchHash property is empty for this combination, we attempt to find a backstop target on line 24 by using the command name alone.

With these few classes we have laid the groundwork for a framework we could use and reuse in building applications. In the next section, we add some classes so you can see the framework in action.

Working with the Framework

The work we have done so far deals with central control, command selection, and view dispatch. Although we have examined the source code in detail, getting a sense of the code's functionality is difficult without trying it first.

We are going to build a very basic example. We'll create code for extracting task data from, and adding task data to, a database, concentrating on two views and two commands.

We will use a MySQL database and a task table that can be created with the following statement:

```
CREATE TABLE tasks (
 id int(11) NOT NULL auto_increment,
 summary varchar(255) default NULL,
 description text,
 person varchar(255) default NULL,
 PRIMARY KEY (id)
);
```

You might want to refer to Listing 24.1 to remind yourself of the way the program flow works. Notice that initialization is handled by an ApplicationResources object.

Implementing ApplicationResources

In Listing 24.9 we create an application-specific ApplicationResources class
called ApplicationResourcesImpl.

LISTING 24.9   The ApplicationResourcesImpl **Class**

```
 1: <?php
 2: // controller/ApplicationResourcesImpl.php
 3: // qframe license: http://resources.corrosive.co.uk/pkg/qframe/license.txt
 4:
 5: require_once 'controller/ApplicationResources.php';
 6: require_once 'controller/SimpleDispatcher.php';
 7: require_once 'command/DataStore.php';
 8: require_once 'command/Command.php';
 9: require_once 'command/SimpleCommandFactory.php';
10:
11: class ApplicationResourcesImpl extends ApplicationResources {
12:     private $dispatcher;
13:     private $commandfactory;
14:
15:     function __construct() {
16:         $this->dispatcher = new SimpleDispatcher( "views" );
17:         $this->commandfactory = new SimpleCommandFactory();
18:     }
19:
20:     function init() {
21:         $this->commandfactory->addPackage("my_commands");
22:         $this->commandfactory->setDefaultCommand( "MyDefault" );
23:         $this->setupDispatcher();
24:         $this->primeDatabase();
25:     }
26:
27:     function primeDatabase() {
28:         $user = "p24_user";
29:         $pass = "cwaffie";
30:         $host = "localhost";
31:         $database = "p24";
32:
33:         $dsn = "mysql://$user:$pass@$host/$database";
34:         $store = DataStore::getInstance();
35:         $store->setVar( "dsn", $dsn );
36:     }
37:
38:     function setupDispatcher() {
39:         $success = Command::CMD_SUCCESS;
40:         $unproc = Command::CMD_UNPROCESSED;
41:         $error  = Command::CMD_ERROR;
42:
43:         $this->dispatcher->addCondition( "MyDefault", "main.php" );
44:         $this->dispatcher->addCondition( "MyDefault", "error.php", $error );
45:         $this->dispatcher->addCondition( "AddTask", "add.php" );
46:         $this->dispatcher->addCondition( "AddTask", "main.php", $success );
47:         return true;
48:     }
49:
```

LISTING 24.9   Continued

```
50:     function getDispatcher() {
51:        return $this->dispatcher;
52:     }
53:     function getCommandFactory() {
54:        return $this->commandfactory;
55:     }
56: }
57: ?>
```

The `ApplicationResourcesImpl` class sets up our application for us. We know that the `Controller` needs objects of type `CommandFactory` and `Dispatcher`, and it is here that we can choose which implementations to provide. In our constructor on line 15, we instantiate a `SimpleDispatcher` object and a `SimpleCommandFactory` object—both of which we store as properties.

The real work of the class takes place in the `init()` method on line 20. This is called by the `Controller` at the start of application flow. We call the `CommandFactory::addPackage()` method to register our own commands directory, `my_commands`, with the system on line 21. We also set a default command string by calling the `setDefaultCommand()` method, completing the configuration of our `CommandFactory` object. From here, it will be smart enough to find any command objects we drop into the `my_commands` directory.

To configure our `SimpleDispatcher` object, we call a utility function called `setupDispatcher()`, which is declared on line 38. We set up a number of conditions between lines 43 and 47. As you can see, we are working with two commands: `MyDefault`, which provides the default action of listing all tasks in the database, and `AddTask`, which handles the adding of task data to the database. In both cases, we set up default views. The `MyDefault` command is associated with a file called `main.php` by default. Only if an error occurs (that is, if `MyDefault::doExecute()` returns `Command::CMD_ERROR`) is another document— `error.ph`—served. The `AddTask` command is associated with a document called `add.php` by default. If the command reports a success, however, this command uses the `main.php` template, too.

After calling `setUpDispatcher()` on line 23, we call another convenience method: `primeDatabase()`. `primeDatabase()` is declared on line 27 and creates a DSN as used by the `PEAR::DB` package. This is then registered with the system's `DataStore` object on line 35. This will be used later to connect to our database.

Finally, we implement the `getDispatcher()` and `getCommandFactory()` methods on lines 50 and 53.

When our `Controller` object runs, it at least has some real objects to work with. We have yet to define our commands and views. Before we get into that, though, let's think briefly about our application's model.

The TaskFacade Object

In this example we are not implementing an entire MVC pattern. We are concentrating on the view and controller tiers (especially the controller tier). In a full MVC pattern example, we would create business objects to represent the data and relationships within our system. We would need to implement a strategy for making these objects persist, and probably a facade object or a series of facade objects to simplify communication with them from the control/command tier. The various structures and techniques for this are beyond the scope of this chapter. We can, however, build a simple `TaskFacade` class whose job it is to work with the database to get and set task data. The `TaskFacade` class is demonstrated in Listing 24.10.

LISTING 24.10   The TaskFacade Class

```
 1: <?php
 2: // facade/TaskFacade.php
 3: // qframe license: http://resources.corrosive.co.uk/pkg/qframe/license.txt
 4:
 5: require_once 'DB.php';
 6:
 7: class TaskFacade {
 8:   private $db_common;
 9:
10:   function __construct() {
11:     // throws Exception from getConnection()
12:     $this->db_common = $this->getConnection();
13:   }
14:
15:   private function getConnection() {
16:     $data = DataStore::getInstance();
17:     $dsn = $data->getVar("dsn");
18:     if ( empty( $dsn ) ) {
19:       throw new TaskFacadeException( "There should be a 'dsn'" );
20:     }
21:     $connection = DB::connect( $dsn );
22:     if ( DB::isError( $connection ) ) {
23:       throw new TaskFacadeException( $connection->getMessage() );
24:     }
25:     return $connection;
26:   }
27:
28:   private function selectQuery( $query ) {
29:     $result = $this->db_common->query( $query );
30:     if ( $result instanceof db_error ) {
```

LISTING 24.10   Continued

```
31:              throw new TaskFacadeException( $result->getMessage() );
32:        }
33:
34:      $ret = array();
35:      while ( $row = $result->fetchRow( DB_FETCHMODE_ASSOC ) ) {
36:        foreach ( $row as $key=>$val ) {
37:          $row[$key] = stripslashes( $val );
38:        }
39:        $ret[] = $row;
40:      }
41:      return $ret;
42:    }
43:
44:    function getTask( $id ) {
45:      $query = "SELECT * FROM tasks WHERE id=$id";
46:      // throws excption from selectQuery
47:      return $this->selectQuery( $query );
48:    }
49:
50:    function getTasks() {
51:      $query = "SELECT * FROM tasks";
52:      // throws excption from selectQuery
53:      $result = $this->selectQuery( $query );
54:      return $result;
55:    }
56:
57:    function setTask( $data_array ) {
58:      if ( ! is_array( $data_array )) {
59:        throw new TaskFacadeException( "setTask() requires an array" );
60:      }
61:
62:      if (  empty( $data_array['summary'] ) ||
63:          empty ( $data_array['person'] ) ) {
64:        throw new TaskFacadeException( "setTask(): missing data" );
65:      }
66:      $fields = array( "person", "summary", "description" );
67:      foreach ( $fields as $key ) {
68:       $add_array[$key] = $data_array[$key];
69:      }
70:
71:      $data_array['id'] = $this->db_common->nextId("tasks");
72:      $result = $this->db_common->autoExecute( "tasks", $add_array,
73:          DB_AUTOQUERY_INSERT );
74:      if ( $result instanceof db_error ) {
75:          throw new TaskFacadeException( $result->getMessage() );
76:      }
77:      return true;
78:    }
79: }
80:
81: class TaskFacadeException extends Exception { }
82:
83: ?>
```

The TaskFacade class should be easy to read by now. In essence, we do no more than use the PEAR::DB package to work with the tasks database. The constructor is declared on line 10 and calls the private getConnection() method to acquire a PEAR::DB_Common object. getConnection() calls DB::connect() in the usual way. Notice how we acquire our DSN from the system's DataStore object, using the getVar() method. If the DSN is not found, we throw a TaskFacadeException object. Because the constructor does not catch any Exception objects, the TaskFacadeException thrown by getConnection() is rethrown to the calling code. All operations in this class that might fail protect themselves with Exception objects in this way.

The public methods used by Command objects are getTask() (line 44), getTasks() (line 50), and setTask() (line 57). These do exactly what you would expect. The getter methods construct SQL statements for extracting data, and the setter method uses the DB_Common::autoExecute() method to automate the data insert.

Now that we have some code to talk to our database, we can implement some Command objects.

The Command **Classes**

All the hard work has already been done, so we will find the Command classes quite simple. Listing 24.11 shows the MyDefault class.

LISTING 24.11   The MyDefault **Class**

```
 1: <?php
 2: // my_commands/MyDefault.php
 3: // qframe license: http://resources.corrosive.co.uk/pkg/qframe/license.txt
 4:
 5: require_once "command/Command.php";
 6: require_once "facade/TaskFacade.php";
 7:
 8: class MyDefault extends Command {
 9:
10:   function doExecute( RequestHelper $requestHelper ) {
11:     $requestHelper->setMessage( "welcome" );
12:     $taskfacade = new TaskFacade();
13:     $tasks = $taskfacade->getTasks();
14:     $requestHelper->saveVar( "tasks", $tasks );
15:
16:     return CMD_SUCCESS;
17:   }
18: }
19: ?>
```

The `MyDefault` class only implements the `doExecute()` class. We call `RequestHelper::setMessage()` on line 11 to welcome the user. We then instantiate a `TaskFacade` object on line 12 and call `getTasks()` on line 13 to get an array containing all the task information in the database. We pass this on to the system's `DataStore` object via the `RequestHelper` object's convenience method, `saveVar()`. Finally, we return `CMD_SUCCESS`.

The `AddTask` class is only slightly more involved than `MyDefault` (see Listing 24.12).

LISTING 24.12   The `AddTask` Class

```php
 1: <?php
 2: // my_commands/AddTask.php
 3: // qframe license: http://resources.corrosive.co.uk/pkg/qframe/license.txt
 4:
 5: require_once "command/Command.php";
 6: require_once "my_commands/MyDefault.php";
 7: require_once "facade/TaskFacade.php";
 8:
 9: class AddTask extends Command {
10:
11:   function doExecute( RequestHelper $requestHelper ) {
12:
13:     $params = $requestHelper->getParams();
14:
15:     if ( empty( $params['addtask_submit'] ) ) {
16:       $params = $requestHelper->setMessage("enter task details");
17:       return CMD_UNPROCESSED;
18:     }
19:
20:     if (  empty( $params['summary'] ) ||
21:         empty( $params['person'] ) ) {
22:       $requestHelper->setMessage("All fields mandatory");
23:       return CMD_ERROR;
24:     }
25:     $taskfacade = new TaskFacade();
26:     $taskfacade->setTask( $params );
27:     $cmd = new MyDefault();
28:     return $cmd->execute( $requestHelper );
29:   }
30: }
31: ?>
```

The `AddTask::doExecute()` method behaves differently according to the client's submission. Remember that we can get an array of request elements from `RequestHelper::getParams()`. We test for a flag argument called `"addtask_submit"`. If this is not present, we assume that we are not being called to act and return `CMD_UNPROCESSED` on line 17.

If the `"addtask_submit"` flag is present, we must assume that we are being asked to handle data. We test the incoming data for the essential "summary" and "person" fields on line 20. If one of them is not present, we use `Request::setMessage()` to report the error to the user and return `CMD_ERROR`.

If all our checks have worked, we instantiate a `TaskFacade()` object on line 25 and call `setTask()`, passing it the user input array.

Finally, we instantiate a `MyDefault` object and call its `execute()` method. This ensures that the user can see an updated list of tasks.

Now all we need to do is create the views for the application.

The Views

All the underlying work is now done. In this section we give the application a face. If all has gone well, the views in our system should be programmatically simple. They will have a few loops and variables to be sure, but all the logic should be tucked away neatly. In our system, our views have an implicit contract with the system. They won't interfere with the intricacies of program logic, and in return they have a right to expect that the `DataStore` object will be primed with the data they need to do their job of presenting information.

Listing 24.13 contains `main.php`, the default view for our system.

LISTING 24.13 The Main View

```
 1: <?php
 2: // views/main.php
 3: // qframe license: http://resources.corrosive.co.uk/pkg/qframe/license.txt
 4:
 5:   $data = DataStore::getInstance();
 6:   $tasks = $data->getVar( "tasks" );
 7: ?>
 8: <!DOCTYPE html PUBLIC
 9:   "-//W3C//DTD XHTML 1.0 Strict//EN"
10:   "http://www.w3.org/TR/xhtml1/DTD/xhtml1-strict.dtd">
11: <html>
12: <head>
13: <title>The Task List</title>
14: </head>
15: <body>
16: <div>
17:
18: <h3> <?php print $data->getMessage(); ?> </h3>
19:
```

LISTING 24.13   Continued

```
20: <p>
21: <b>The tasks</b><br />
22: <a href="?cmd=AddTask">add a task</a>
23: </p>
24: <table border="1">
25: <tr><td><b>owner</b></td><td><b>summary</b></td></tr>
26: <?php
27: foreach ( $tasks as $task ) {
28: print <<<TASK
29:    <tr>
30:    <td>{$task['person']}</td><td>{$task['summary']}</td>
31:    </tr>
32: TASK;
33: }
34: ?>
35: </table>
36: </div>
37: </body>
38: </html>
```

The DataStore object is the main means by which views gain access to data generated by the system, and we acquire the object on line 5 using the static getInstance() method. DataStore is an example of a Singleton object, and only one of them exists in a process at the same time. We acquire an array of task data on line 6 using the getVar() method.

We print any message that has been left with DataStore on line 18. In a real-world application, we would probably use a helper function to test that a message exists before including any formatting. We would also use an include statement to output the message data because it is likely to be something that will be needed on most view pages.

Notice our navigation on line 22. By passing a cmd parameter of 'AddTask' to the Controller, a click on the hyperlink causes the AddTask command to be run and the Dispatcher to switch the view.

On line 27 we loop through the $task array, outputting each row to the browser.

You can see the view presented by main.php in Figure 24.1.

Finally, let's take a quick look at the add.php view. This simply presents a form so the user can add task information (see Listing 24.14).

FIGURE 24.1
The main view.

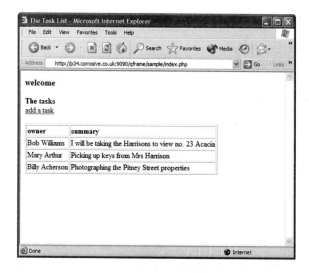

LISTING 24.14   The Add View

```
 1: <?php
 2: // views/add.php
 3: // qframe license: http://resources.corrosive.co.uk/pkg/qframe/license.txt
 4:
 5:   $data = DataStore::getInstance();
 6: ?>
 7: <!DOCTYPE html PUBLIC
 8:   "-//W3C//DTD XHTML 1.0 Strict//EN"
 9:   "http://www.w3.org/TR/xhtml1/DTD/xhtml1-strict.dtd">
10: <html>
11: <head>
12: <title>Add a task</title>
13: </head>
14: <body>
15: <div>
16:
17: <h3> <?php print $data->getMessage(); ?> </h3>
18:
19: <form method="post" action="index.php" />
20: <input type="hidden" name="cmd" value="AddTask" />
21: <input type="hidden" name="addtask_submit" value="true" />
22: <p>Your name<br />
23: <input type="text" name="person" value="<?php print $_REQUEST['name'] ?>" />
24: </p><p>Task summary<br />
25: <input type="text" name="summary" ➥
value="<?php print $_REQUEST['summary'] ?>" />
26: </p>
27: <p> <input type="submit" value="add task" /> </p>
28: </form>
29: <p>
30: </div>
31: </body>
32: </html>
```

There is little new to see in `view.php`. Notice again that we acquire a `DataStore` object and output any user message to the browser. The only other features of interest are our hidden form inputs on lines 20 and 21. By sending a `cmd` parameter with an `"AddTask"` value on line 20, we ensure that our form submission is sent back to the `AddTask` command. It is the `'cmd'` argument that the `CommandFactory` uses to select a command for execution. Also of note is the `"addtask_submit"` field, which is used by the `AddTask` command to confirm that we want our data to be processed.

You can see the `add.php` view in action in Figure 24.2.

FIGURE 24.2
The Add Task view.

Where Now, and Was It Worth It?

The code presented in this chapter is not intended as a framework that can be downloaded and used as is. Much more complete and flexible projects are available that you might consider if you are looking for a framework to use from a client coder's perspective.

If you are interested in using a downloaded framework for your PHP code, several projects are available that might be worth evaluating, including Phrame (`http://sourceforge.net/projects/phrame`) and php.MVC (`http://www.phpmvc.net/`).

The main objective of this chapter has been to demonstrate some of the issues involved in building larger applications and to point to a few possible solutions, taking in some object-oriented techniques along the way. In particular, we have examined a mechanism for adding new commands to an application flexibly. You have learned some techniques for displaying views as a result of command execution, without embedding the responsibility for presentation in the commands themselves.

The ideas presented in this hour are by no means new. If you are interested in pursuing these topics further, there are some places you can visit to get more ideas.

Unsurprisingly, Java programmers are very much concerned with object-oriented design. Now that PHP has moved toward greater support for object-orientation, PHP coders can benefit greatly from the experiences of their colleagues in the world of Java. The J2EE patterns site at http://java.sun.com/blueprints/corej2eepatterns/index.html has more information on all the techniques described in this chapter.

After the framework is written, applications can be developed relatively smoothly using a framework of this sort, but it has to be admitted that our code expends a lot of resources before we even implement an application. This chapter has implemented a design pattern known as a Front Controller—that is, we have routed all requests through a central switchboard object. A strong body of opinion argues that the Front Controller pattern is wrong for PHP applications. It is argued that this approach is resource hungry and relatively inflexible. This position is eloquently summed up by Harry Fuecks at http://www.phppatterns.com/index.php/article/articleview/81/1/1/.

Whatever conclusion you draw, I hope that you have found the techniques examined in this chapter useful and interesting.

Summary

In this chapter, we moved away from language features and delved into the world of object-oriented design. You learned how to create a `Controller` class to process requests from a client. You also learned how to select `Command` objects using a `CommandFactory` class and how to implement `Command` classes. Finally, you learned how to create a `Dispatcher` class to manage the deployment of views.

I very much hope that you have enjoyed reading this book as much as I have enjoyed writing it.

Q&A

Q *You mentioned that there were more sophisticated models for managing dispatch. Did you have anything in mind?*

A One of the problems with the dispatch logic presented in this hour is that it works only with the first command called by the `Controller`. This is not as flexible as it might be. A better solution would be to take into account every command called together with its return value. This would enable you to map templates to complex combinations of commands. One way of managing something like this would be to represent the commands and return values in XML as a DOM object and to implement code in XSLT to match different command/status combinations.

Q *Well, that's it. What next?*

A Now it's up to you. This book contains enough information for you to build your own sophisticated scripts and environments. Armed with this and the wealth of information available online, there should be no stopping you! If this book has been a good starting point for you, you might want to consider some books that take up where we must leave off. In particular, you might like to take a look at *The PHP Developer's Cookbook* by Sterling Hughes and *PHP and MySQL Web Development* by Luke Welling and Laura Thomson.

Workshop

Quiz

1. We did not want our `Command::execute()` method to be overridden by code in child classes. How did we enforce this?

2. Briefly, how did we ensure that there was only one `DataStore` object in our system at any one time?

3. We said that the practice of a method calling and using abstract methods defined in the same class was an example of a design pattern. What was its name?

4. Which keyword did we use to check that an object we had instantiated belonged to the `Command` family?

5. How did we ensure that our `Command` class status flags were unchangeable and available via the class rather than particular object instances?

Answers

1. You can prevent a child class from overriding a method by declaring it final.

2. We made the DataStore object a Singleton. That is, we made its constructor private so a DataStore object could be instantiated only by a static method in the DataStore class itself. The static method can ensure that it returns only the same single instance of a DataStore object when it is called.

3. A method calling and using abstract methods defined in the same class is an example of the template method pattern.

4. We can use instanceof to test the type of an object.

5. You can declare constant properties with the const keyword. A constant property is unchangeable at runtime and is available via the class rather than object instances.

Exercises

1. Review the code presented in this hour. Are there any techniques or issues that might have relevance for your own projects?

2. Get a version of the code in this chapter running on your server. Add Command classes to allow the user to edit tasks. Don't forget to update the ApplicationResourcesImp class and add new views.

3. Flip back through the book and through your notes if you have been making them. If you have followed the book as a course, remember that you should revisit your notes a few times to get the full benefit from the work you have done.

Glossary

`.htaccess` **file**   A document read by the Apache server that can contain certain server directives. The server administrator can control which available directives (if any) are allowed to be set in a `.htaccess` file on a directory-by-directory basis. If allowed, directives can affect the current directory and those below it. `.htaccess` files can contain PHP directives prefixed by `php_flag` or `php_value`. The `.htaccess` file can also be used to set an `AddType` directive that can change the extension associated by the server with PHP documents.

abstract class   A class that is partially implemented and explicitly declared as such. Unimplemented methods are declared abstract and consist of method signatures only. Classes that extend abstract classes must implement all abstract methods or be declared abstract themselves.

anonymous function   A function that is created on-the-fly during script execution and stored in a variable or passed to other functions.

argument   A value passed to a function or method. Arguments are included within the parentheses of a function call. User-defined functions include comma-separated argument names within the parentheses of the function definition. These arguments then become available to the function as local variables.

array   A list variable. That is, a variable that contains multiple elements indexed by numbers or strings. It enables you to store, order, and access many values under one name. An array is a data type.

associative array   An array indexed by strings.

atom With reference to regular expressions an atom is a pattern enclosed in parentheses (often referred to as a *subpattern*). After you have defined an atom, you can treat it as if it were itself a character or character class.

Boolean A data type. Booleans can contain one of the special values true or false.

bounds The number of times a character or range of characters should be matched in a regular expression.

break **statement** Consists of the keyword break. It forces the immediate end of a for or while loop iteration, and no further iterations of the loop take place.

cast The process by which one data type is converted to another.

class A collection of special functions called *methods* and special variables called *properties*. You can declare a class with the class keyword. Classes are the templates from which objects are created.

color resource A special value of the data type resource. It is returned by the imagecolorallocate() function and passed to other image manipulation functions, which can then work with the specified color.

comment Text in a script that is ignored by the interpreter. Comments can be used to make code more readable or to annotate a script.

comparison operator In the form ==, this operator compares two operands and tests for equivalence. It resolves to the Boolean true value if the two operands are equivalent and false otherwise. In the form ===, the operator tests two object variables, returning true only if both variables are references to the same object.

constant Outside of a class, a constant is a value that is set with the define() function and does not change throughout the execution of a script. A constant is global in scope and can be only a number or string. In the context of a class, a constant is a special property declared with the const keyword. A constant property cannot be changed at runtime and is available via the class rather than a class instance.

constructor A special method that is automatically called when an object is instantiated.

continue **statement** Consists of the keyword continue. It forces the immediate end of the current for or while loop iteration. Execution begins again from the test expression (in for loops the modification expression is executed first) and the next loop iteration is begun if the expression resolves to true.

conversion specification Contained within a format control string, a conversion specification begins with a percent (%) symbol and defines how to treat the corresponding argument to `printf()` or `sprintf()`. You can include as many conversion specifications as you want within the format control string, as long as you send an equivalent number of arguments to `printf()`.

cookie A small amount of data stored by the user's browser in compliance with a request from a server or script.

data type Different types of data take up different amounts of memory and behave in different ways when operated on. A data type is the named means by which these different kinds of data are distinguished. PHP has eight data types: integer, double, string, Boolean, object, array, resource, and NULL.

DBA Database abstraction layer. These functions are designed to provide a common interface to a range of file-based database systems.

DBA resource A special value of the data type `resource`. It is returned by the `dba_open()` function and passed to other DBA functions, which can then work with the open database.

DBM Database manager. DBM and DBM-like systems enable you to store and manipulate name/value pairs on your system.

destructor A special method automatically invoked just before an object is removed from memory.

document object model (DOM) A means of accessing an XML document that involves the generation of a tree of nodes organized as parents, children, and siblings.

document type definition (DTD) A set of rules that determines which XML elements can be used in which order for an XML document. A validating XML parser reads a DTD and enforces the rules it describes.

double A data type. Also known as a float, a floating-point number, or a real number, a double is defined by *The Free On-line Dictionary of Computing* as "a number representation consisting of a mantissa [the part after the decimal point], ... an exponent, ... and an (assumed) radix (or "base")." For the purposes of this book, you can think of a double as a number that can contain a fraction of a whole number—that is, a number with a decimal point.

else statement It can be used only in the context of an `if` statement. The `else` statement consists of the keyword `else` and a statement (or series of statements). These statements are executed only if the test expression of the associated `if` statement evaluates to `false`.

entity body   The substance of a document returned by a server to a client. An entity body can also be sent by a client to a server as part of a POST request.

escape   The practice of removing special significance from characters within strings or regular expressions by preceding them with a backslash character (\).

exception   A special object that can be thrown by a method with the throw keyword. An exception object must be of type Exception and includes a message and other error information. Throwing an exception causes a method's execution to end. The calling code is then responsible for handling the exception using the catch keyword.

expression   Any combination of functions, values, and operators that resolves to a value. As a rule of thumb, if you can use it as if it were a value, it is an expression.

field width specifier   Contained within a conversion specification, a field width specifier determines the space within which output should be formatted.

file resource   A special value of the data type resource. It is returned by the fopen() function and passed to other file functions, which can then work with the open file.

float   A data type. It is a synonym for double.

for **statement**   A loop that can initialize a counter variable (initialization expression), test a counter variable (test expression), and modify a counter variable (modification expression) on a single line. As long as the test expression evaluates to true, the loop statement continues to be executed.

foreach **statement**   A loop used to iterate through every element in an array. The loop automatically populates temporary variables with the next array key and values for each iteration.

format control string   The first argument to printf() or sprintf(). It contains conversion specifications that determine the way in which additional arguments to these functions are formatted.

Freetype   An open-source library providing functionality for working with TrueType fonts. The two versions are FreeType 1 and FreeType 2. Both libraries can be used by PHP's image functions to render text in images.

function   A block of code that is not immediately executed but can be called by your scripts when needed. Functions can be built-in or user-defined. They can require information to be passed to them and usually return a value.

GET **request** A request made to a server by a client in which additional information can be sent appended to the URL.

global Consists of the keyword global followed by a variable(s). It causes the associated variables to be accessed in global rather than local scope.

header section Part of an HTTP request or response (it follows the request line or response line). It consists of name/value pairs on separate lines. Names are separated from values by colons.

hint The name of an object type used to qualify an argument in a method declaration. When the method is invoked, it must be passed an object of the defined type for that argument; otherwise, the script fails.

Hypertext Transfer Protocol (HTTP) A set of rules that defines the process by which a client sends a request and a server returns a response.

if **statement** Consists of a test expression and a statement or series of statements. The statement is executed only if the test expression evaluates to true.

image resource A special value of the data type resource. It is returned by the imagecreate() function and passed to other image manipulation functions, which can then work with the dynamic image.

inheritance A term used in the context of object-oriented programming. It is used to describe the process by which one class is set up to include the member variables and methods of another. This is achieved using the extends keyword when the child class is declared.

integer A data type. Integers include all whole negative and positive numbers and zero.

iteration A single execution of a statement (or series of statements) associated with a loop. A loop that executes five times has five iterations.

interface A special class that contains only method signatures. An interface must contain no implementation at all. Classes that implement an interface must implement every method it defines. A class can implement any number of interfaces and takes on the type of any interface it implements.

link resource A special value of the data type resource. It is returned by the mysql_connect() function and passed to other MySQL functions, which can then work with the open database.

method A special function, available only in the context of a class or object.

multidimensional array An array that contains another array as one of its elements.

NULL A special data type. It consists of the value NULL and represents an uninitialized variable—that is, a variable that holds no value.

object Existing in memory rather than as code, an object is an instance of a class, meaning it's the working embodiment of the functionality laid down in a class. An object is instantiated with the new statement in conjunction with the name of the class of which it is to be a member. When an object is instantiated, you can access all its properties and all its methods. An object is a data type.

operand A value used in conjunction with an operator. There are usually two operands to one operator.

operator A symbol or series of symbols that, when used in conjunction with values, performs an action and usually produces a new value.

padding specifier Contained within a conversion specification, a padding specifier determines the number of characters that output should occupy and the characters to add otherwise.

pattern modifier A letter placed after the final delimiter in Perl-compatible regular expressions to refine their behavior.

PEAR The PHP Extension and Application Repository. A quality-controlled library of PHP packages designed to extend the usefulness of PHP.

PEAR::Auth A PEAR package that provides methods for authenticating visitors using usernames and passwords.

PEAR::Config A PEAR package for writing to and reading from configuration files.

PEAR::DB A PEAR package that provides a common interface for talking to many databases.

php.ini The configuration file that determines the way in which PHP runs. The file contains directives that specify a wide range of rules and behaviors.

phpDocumentor A package for producing documentation using comments embedded in source code. It's part of PEAR.

POST request A request made to a server by a client in which additional information can be sent within the request entity body.

precision specifier Contained within a conversion specification, a precision specifier determines the number of decimal places to which a double should be rounded.

private This keyword limits the availability of a method or property to the enclosing class only.

property A special variable, available only in the context of an object or a class.

`protected`   This keyword limits the availability of a method or property to the enclosing class and to any child classes.

`public`   This keyword makes a property or method available to any client code.

query string   A set of name/value pairs appended to a URL as part of a GET request. Names are separated from values by equal signs, and pairs are separated from each other by ampersand (&) characters. The query string is separated from the rest of the URL by a question mark (?). Both names and values are encoded so characters with significance to the server are not present.

reference   The means by which multiple variables can point to the same value. By default, nonobject arguments are passed and assignments are made by value in PHP. This means that copies of values are passed around. As of PHP 5, objects are assigned and passed by reference. Therefore, when you pass an object variable to a method, you pass a handle to a single object, as opposed to a copy of the object.

regular expression   A powerful way of examining and modifying text.

request headers   Key value pairs sent to the server by a client providing information about the client itself and the nature of the request.

request line   The first line of a client request to a server. It consists of a request method, typically GET, HEAD, or POST; the address of the document required; and the HTTP version to be used (HTTP/1.0 or HTTP/1.1).

resource   A special data type. Resources represent handles used to work with external entities (databases and files are good examples of this).

response headers   Key value pairs sent to the client in response to a request. They provide information about the server environment and the data that is being served.

scope   The range of code for which a variable holds a particular value. For example, the value of a variable declared inside a function is unavailable outside that function. The variable is said to be local to the scope of the function.

server variables   Predefined elements that PHP makes available for you in conjunction with your server. You can access these elements via the superglobal `$_SERVER` array. Which elements are made available is server dependent, but they are likely to include common variables such as `$_SERVER['HTTP_USER_AGENT']` and `$_SERVER['REMOTE_ADDR']`.

statement   Represents an instruction to the interpreter. Broadly, it is to PHP what a sentence is to written or spoken English. A sentence should end with a period; a statement should usually end with a semicolon. Exceptions to this include statements that enclose other statements and statements that end a block of code. In most cases, however, failure to end a statement with a semicolon confuses the interpreter and results in an error.

`static`   Used within the context of a function, the `static` keyword ensures that an associated variable maintains the same value across function calls. In the context of a class, a `static` property is available via a class rather than through individual class instances (objects).

status line   The first server response to a client request. The status line consists of the HTTP version the server is using (HTTP/1.0 or HTTP/1.1), a response code, and a text message that clarifies the meaning of the response code.

stream   A flow of data that can be read from and written to. Streams are a new mechanism in PHP that provide a common interface for working with data across a range of contexts.

string   A data type. It is a series of characters.

Structured Query Language (SQL)   A standardized syntax by which different types of database can be queried.

subclass   A class that inherits member variables and methods from another (parent) class.

`superclass`   A parent class.

`superglobal`   A variable available in any scope. Superglobals are always built-in and include $_REQUEST, $_GET, $_POST, and $_SERVER, among others.

`switch`   A statement that compares the result of an operation against any number of different values in turn, executing a particular block of code if a match is found for the test value.

ternary operator   Returns a value derived from one of two expressions separated by a colon. Which expression is used to generate the value returned depends on the result of an initial test expression that precedes the return expressions and is separated from them by a question mark (?).

timestamp   The number of seconds that have elapsed since midnight GMT on January 1, 1970. This number is used in date arithmetic.

type specifier   Contained within a conversion specification, a type specifier determines the data type that should be output.

variable   A holder for a type of data. It can hold numbers, strings of characters, objects, arrays, or booleans. The contents of a variable can be changed at any time.

`while` **statement** A loop that consists of a test expression and a statement (or series of statements). The statements are repeatedly executed as long as the test expression evaluates to `true`.

XML (Extensible Markup Language) A set of rules for defining and parsing markup languages. Such languages are often constructed to structure data for sharing, format data for display, or send instructions to an interpreter.

XSLT (Extensible Stylesheet Language Transformations) A template system for XML documents that makes converting from XML to other formats, such as HTML or WML, easy.

Zend The scripting engine that lies at the heart of the PHP interpreter. Zend was released with the advent of PHP 4, and Zend 2 was released with the advent of PHP 5.

Index

drawing
arcs, 302-303
bar charts, 314
circles, 302
lines, 299-300
polygons, 304-305
rectangles, 303-304
DSN (data source name), 264
DTDs (document type declarations), 434
dynamic functions, 88-89
dynamic images, 319

E

E \ modifier, 382-384
elements
arrays, 108
accessing, 118-119
deleting, 121
DSN, 264
$_FILES array, 196
root, 444
$_SERVER array, 183
sessions, 412
users array, 108
XML, 434, 438
else clause, 65-66
else/if clause, 66-67
email, sending, 286-287
encoding session variables, 413-414
end tags, 30-31
ending sessions, 412
$_ENV array, 182
errors
codes, 197
databases, 249

handling, 354-357
programming, 427
reporting directives, 21
XML documents, 439-441
escape characters, 45, 374-375
escapeshellcmd() function, 426-428
events (XML handlers), 437-438
@example tag, 472
Exception class, 354
exceptions, error handling, 354-357
exec() function, 424
execute() function, 496
existence (classes/functions), 101-103, 172
explode() function, 147
expressions. *See regular expressions*
Extensible Hypertext Markup Language (XHTML), 33, 455
Extensible Markup Language. *See XML*
Extensible Stylesheet Language (XSL), 451-453
external applications, 429
external CGI scripts, 430
external commands, 425-426
external processes, 431

F

f type specifiers, 130
families (objects), 171
fclose() function, 214, 281
feof() function, 215
fgets() function, 214-215

fields
incremented values, 253
widths (strings), 133-134
file() function, 218
fileatime() function, 210
filectime() function, 211
filemtime() function, 211
FileNotFoundException, 357
FileOpenException, 357
files
appending, 218-219
configuration, 475-480
creating, 213
date information, 210-211
deleting, 213
documents, including, 203-205
control structures, 206
for loop, 206-207
include_once statement, 207-208
include_path statement, 208-209
return values, 205
set_include_path function, 209
htaccess, 20
.html extension, 20
include, 172-173
locking, 220
opening, 213-214
php.ini, 20-22
reading from, 214
feof() function, 215
fgetc() function, 217-218
fgets() function, 214-215
file() function, 218

resultsets, 255-257

retrieving
documents from remote
addresses, 278-279
objects, 173-174
serialized data from databases, 236-237
Web pages, 278-281

return statements, 87-88, 205

return values
included documents, 205
PEAR DB package, 265

rmdir() function, 221

root elements, 444

rows
adding, 250
databases, 258-259
number returned by data-
base queries, 254-255
tables, 255-256
unique IDs, 266

running
commands, 424-426
external applications, 429

S

s \ modifier, 382-383

S \escape character, 374

s type specifiers, 130

saving
functions, 93-95
state, 191-192

scope (function variables),
89-90

script tags, 30

scripting engines (Zend), 9

scripts, 27-28
configuration problems, 30
configure, 17-19
file uploads, 197-198
HTML, adding, 33-34
limiting runs, 59
output, 28
printing to browsers, 32
source code, 29
testing, 29-30
uploading, 28

security
cookies. See cookies
gaps, plugging, 426-428
programming errors/omis-
sions, 427
Web, 431

@see tag, 472

semicolon (;), 42

sending mail, 286-287

Serializable interface, 363

serialize() function, 173, 235

$_SERVER array, 182-183

servers
database connections,
247-248
headers, 277
NNTP connections,
284-286
PHP supported, 13
variables, 271, 274
HTTP_REFERER, 183,
272-273
HTTP_USER_AGENT,
183, 272-273
listing of, 272
PATH_INFO, 272-273
QUERY_STRING, 183,
272-273

REMOTE_ADDR, 183,
272-274
REMOTE_HOST, 272-274
Web, 282

sessions
array variables, 410
cookies, 393
elements, deleting, 412
ending, 412
functions, 405-406
IDs, 413
starting, 406-407
variables
accessing, 408-412
encoding/decoding,
413-414
registering, 407

session_decode() function, 414

session_destroy() function, 412

session_encode() function, 413

session_start() function,
406-407

_set() function, 351

setcookie() function, 391-393

setDate_array() function, 336

setDate_request() function, 336

setDate_timestamp() function,
336

setName() method, 163

settype() function, 47-48

setUpdater() function, 353

setYearStart() function, 337

set_include_path() function, 209

shapes, drawing
circles, 302
lines, 300
polygons, 304-305
rectangles, 303-304

short tags, 30

short_open_tag directive, 21

breaking into arrays, 147

case, converting, 145

cleaning up, 142-143

currency, 148-151

format control, 137

format specifier flags, 151

formatting, 129

   arguments, switching, 137

   example, 135-136

   field width specifications, 133-134

   padding specifiers, 132-133

   precision specifications, 134

   printf() function, 129-130

   specifiers, 135-136

   storing, 138

   type specifiers, 130-132

functions Web site, 152

indexing, 138

lengths, 138

numbers, 147-148

pattern matching

   anchoring, 377

   backslash characters, 374-375

   bounds, 372

   character matching, 372-373

   character ranges, matching, 373-374

   combining patterns, 377

   global matches, 377-380

   matching recurring characters, 371-372

   modifiers, 381-384

   preg_match() function, 370-371

   replacing patterns, 380-381, 384-385

   strings, splitting, 385

   subpatterns, 375-377

portions

   extracting, 140

   replacing, 143-144

query, 401-403

splitting, 385

substrings

   finding, 139-140

   replacing, 144-145

text

   adding to images, 308-309

   numbers as, 147-148

   wrapping, 146-147

tokenizing, 140-142

white space, deleting, 143

strip_tags() function, 142-143

strlen() function, 138

strpos() function, 139-140

strstr() function, 139

strtok() function, 140-142

strtolower() function, 145

strtoupper() function, 145

Structured Query Language.
   See SQL

str_replace() function, 144-145

subclasses, 352

subpatterns, 375-377, 516

subscript() function, 103

substr() function, 140

substr_replace() function, 143-144

substrings

   finding, 139-140

   replacing, 144-145

superglobal variables, 182

   $_COOKIE, 182

   elements, 183

   $_ENV, 182

   $_FILES, 182, 196-197

   $_GET, 182

   $_GLOBALS, 182

   looping through, 182-183

   $_POST, 182

   $_REQUEST, 182

   $_SERVER, 182

switch statement, 67-69

system() function, 425-426

T

tables

   data additions, 250-253

   fields, listing all, 255-256

   rows

      adding, 250

      listing all, 255-256

      unique IDs, 266

   SQLite, 260-262

   updating, 267

tags

   ASP, 30

   code blocks, 30-31

   DocBlocks, 471-472

   end, 30-31

   HTML, 133

   <pre>, 133

   script, 30

   short, 30

   standard, 30

   start, 30-31

   XML, 434

Wouldn't it be great

if the world's leading technical publishers joined forces to deliver their best tech books in a common digital reference platform?

They have. Introducing
InformIT Online Books
powered by Safari.

- ## Specific answers to specific questions.
  InformIT Online Books' powerful search engine gives you relevance-ranked results in a matter of seconds.

- ## Immediate results.
  With InformIt Online Books, you can select the book you want and view the chapter or section you need immediately.

- ## Cut, paste, and annotate.
  Paste code to save time and eliminate typographical errors. Make notes on the material you find useful and choose whether or not to share them with your workgroup.

- ## Customized for your enterprise.
  Customize a library for you, your department, or your entire organization. You pay only for what you need.

POWERED BY Safari

InformIT
Online Books

informit.com/onlinebooks

Get your first 14 days **FREE!**
InformIT Online Books is offering its members a 10-book subscription risk free for 14 days. Visit **http://www.informit.com/onlinebooks** for details.

Your Guide
to Computer
Technology

www.informit.com

Sams has partnered with **InformIT.com** to bring technical information to your desktop. Drawing on Sams authors and reviewers to provide additional information on topics you're interested in, **InformIT.com** has free, in-depth information you won't find anywhere else.

ARTICLES

Keep your edge with thousands of free articles, in-depth features, interviews, and information technology reference recommendations—all written by experts you know and trust.

POWERED BY
Safari

ONLINE BOOKS

Answers in an instant from **InformIT Online Books'** 600+ fully searchable online books. Sign up now and get your first 14 days **free**.

CATALOG

Review online sample chapters and author biographies to choose exactly the right book from a selection of more than 5,000 titles.

   www.samspublishing.com